Gender and Psychopathology

PERSONALITY AND PSYCHOPATHOLOGY

A Series of Monographs, Texts, and Treatises

David T. Lykken, Editor

1. The Anatomy of Achievement Motivation, *Heinz Heckhausen.**
2. Cues, Decisions, and Diagnoses: A Systems-Analytic Approach to the Diagnosis of Psychopathology, *Peter E. Nathan.**
3. Human Adaptation and Its Failures, *Leslie Phillips.**
4. Schizophrenia: Research and Theory, *William E. Broen, Jr.**
5. Fears and Phobias, *I. M. Marks.*
6. Language of Emotion, *Joel R. Davitz.*
7. Feelings and Emotions, *Magda Arnold.*
8. Rhythms of Dialogue, *Joseph Jaffe* and *Stanley Feldstein.*
9. Character Structure and Impulsiveness, *David Kipnis.*
10. The Control of Aggression and Violence: Cognitive and Physiological Factors, *Jerome L. Singer* (Ed.).
11. The Attraction Paradigm, *Donn Byrne.*
12. Objective Personality Assessment: Changing Perspectives, *James N. Butcher* (Ed.).
13. Schizophrenia and Genetics. *Irving I. Gottesman* and *James Shields.**
14. Imagery and Daydream Methods in Psychotherapy and Behavior Modification, *Jerome L. Singer.*
15. Experimental Approaches to Psychopathology, *Mitchell L. Kietzman, Samuel Sutton,* and *Joseph Zubin* (Eds.).
16. Coping and Defending: Processes of Self-Environment Organization, *Norma Haan.*
17. The Scientific Analysis of Personality and Motivation, *R. B. Cattell* and *P. Kline.*
18. The Determinants of Free Will: A Psychological Analysis of Responsible, Adjustive Behavior, *James A. Easterbrook.*
19. The Psychopath in Society, *Robert J. Smith.*
20. The Fears of Adolescents, *J. H. Bamber.*
21. Cognitive–Behavioral Interventions: Theory, Research, and Procedures, *Philip C. Kendall* and *Steven D. Hollon* (Eds.).
22. The Psychobiology of the Depressive Disorders: Implications for the Effects of Stress, *Richard A. Depue* (Ed.).
23. The Mental Health of Women, *Marcia Guttenberg, Susan Salasin,* and *Deborah Belle* (Eds.).
24. Assessment Strategies for Cognitive–Behavioral Interventions, *Philip C. Kendall* and *Steven D. Hollon* (Eds.).

*Titles initiated during the series editorship of Brendan Maher.

The list of titles in this series continues on the last page of this volume.

Gender and Psychopathology

Edited by

IHSAN AL-ISSA

Department of Psychology
University of Calgary
Calgary, Alberta, Canada

ACADEMIC PRESS 1982

A Subsidiary of Harcourt Brace Jovanovich, Publishers

NEW YORK LONDON
PARIS SAN DIEGO SAN FRANCISCO SÃO PAULO SYDNEY TOKYO TORONTO

ACADEMIC PRESS, INC.
111 Fifth Avenue, New York, New York 10003

United Kingdom Edition published by
ACADEMIC PRESS, INC. (LONDON) LTD.
24/28 Oval Road, London NW1 7DX

Library of Congress Cataloging in Publication Data
Main entry under title:

Gender and psychopathology.

(Personality and psychopathology)
Includes bibliographical references.
Includes index.
1. Psychology, Pathological. 2. Sex differences (Psychology) 3. Sex differences. I. Al-Issa, Ihsan. II. Series. [DNLM: 1. Identification (Psychology) 2. Sex factors. W1 PE861 BF 692.2 G325]
RC455.4.S45G47 1982 616.89 82-8869
ISBN 0-12-050350-6 AACR2

PRINTED IN THE UNITED STATES OF AMERICA

82 83 84 85 9 8 7 6 5 4 3 2 1

Contents

II

Developmental Perspective

III

Gender and Major Psychopathology

V
Gender and Mind–Body Problems

Contributors

Numbers in parentheses indicate the pages on which the authors' contributions begin.

IHSAN AL-ISSA (3, 53, 83, 153, 279), *Department of Psychology, University of Calgary, Calgary, Alberta T2N 1N4, Canada*

ANNE CAMPBELL[1] (237), *School of Criminal Justice, Rutgers University, Newark, New Jersey 07102*

HANS J. EYSENCK (257), *Department of Psychology, Institute of Psychiatry, De Crespigny Park, Denmark Hill, London SE5 8AF, England*

LINDA S. FIDELL (221), *Department of Psychology, California State University at Northridge, Northridge, California 91330*

IRIS GOLDSTEIN FODOR (179), *Department of Educational Psychology, New York University, New York, New York 10003*

JOHN P. FOREYT (337), *Department of Medicine, Baylor College of Medicine, Houston, Texas 77030*

G. KEN GOODRICK (337), *Department of Medicine, Baylor College of Medicine, Houston, Texas 77030*

CONSTANCE L. HAMMEN (133), *Department of Psychology, University of California, Los Angeles, Los Angeles, California 90024*

ELIZABETH HECHT (103), *Department of Psychiatry and Biobehavioral*

[1] Present address: Department of Criminal Justice, Temple University, Philadelphia, Pennsylvania 19122.

Sciences, Neuropsychiatric Institute, The Center for the Health Sciences, University of California, Los Angeles, Los Angeles, California 90024

JULIA R. HEIMAN (305), *University of Washington, School of Medicine, Harborview Community Mental Health Center, Seattle, Washington 98104*

JOY LELAND (201), *Social Sciences Center, Desert Research Institute, University of Nevada System, Reno, Nevada 89506*

PATRICIA A. MAFFEO[2] (31), *Student Health Service, University of Kentucky, Lexington, Kentucky 40536*

IVAN N. MENSH (103), *Division of Medical Psychology, Department of Psychiatry and Biobehavioral Sciences, University of California, Los Angeles, School of Medicine, Los Angeles, California 90024*

JOHAN VERHULST (305), *Harborview Community Mental Health Center, University of Washington, Seattle, Washington 98104*

INGRID WALDRON (321), *Department of Biology, University of Pennsylvania, Philadelphia, Pennsylvania 19104*

[2] Present address: Psychological Services Section, Tennessee Valley Authority, Chattanooga, Tennessee 37401.

Preface

This book attempts a comprehensive review of the relationship between gender and psychopathology. Part I is an introduction to some of the major themes and issues that are treated in greater detail later in the volume. In particular, the reader is introduced to models of mental health that link deviation from gender role expectations with the definition of psychopathology and its treatment. Thus, the reader is provided with a background to theory and research that relates masculinity, femininity, and androgyny to different types of psychopathology.

Part II considers the interactions among gender, psychopathology, and age. Fluctuation in gender differences in psychopathology from one life-stage to another gives the reader a detailed illustration of how biological and social factors interact throughout the life cycle and influence the relationship between gender and psychopathology. Parts III–V include almost the whole spectrum of psychopathology: Functional disorders (depression, schizophrenia, phobia), personality disorders (crime, alcoholism, drug use and abuse), psychophysiological disorders, and sexual function and dysfunction. In addition to gender differences in symptoms and etiology of psychopathology, much attention is given to methodological problems that are responsible for some false conclusions and mythical beliefs. The intention of these chapters is to change old biases, provide new insights, and generate more research on gender differences.

Although the relationship between gender and psychopathology has long been recognized by researchers and clinicians, it is only since the mid-1960s and the emergence of women's studies as an independent discipline that this research area has been systematically investigated. Thus, the past decade has witnessed an increase in the number of articles and texts devoted entirely to the mental health of women and to gender differences in psychopathology. However, these recent publications have put much emphasis on the sociocultural approach, to the relative neglect of other perspectives. This may be in part a reaction to psychiatric research, which has taken the opposite biological perspective. The present volume, particularly the last five chapters, attempts to consider psychopathology both from a genetic-biological and from a sociocultural perspective. Neither perspective provides a complete understanding of psychopathology, but they should complement each other.

This volume will serve as a basic text for both graduate and advanced undergraduate students who are taking courses in women's studies, abnormal psychology, or counseling. It can also serve as a reference book for behavioral and social scientists (clinicians and researchers) in psychology, psychiatry, counseling, sociology, anthropology, and social work.

I am grateful to David Lykken, editor of the Academic Press series *Personality and Psychopathology* for his encouragement and comments on the whole volume. Thanks to James Inglis, Jeanette McGlone, Louise G. Richards, Otfried Spreen, and Kathleen Wells for their comments on individual chapters of this volume.

I

Introduction

1

IHSAN AL-ISSA

Gender and Psychopathology in Perspective[1]

This chapter aims at introducing the reader to major research findings and theoretical issues discussed in the remaining parts of the book. First, the meaning and use of concepts such as *psychopathology, sex,* and *gender* are clarified. Since psychiatry assumes an organic basis for psychopathology, and applies specific syndromes to patients regardless of their gender, it is necessary to explain next how sexual status is integrated into different models of mental health. This is followed by a discussion of the interaction between gender, age, and psychopathology from childhood to adulthood to old age. The next two sections of the chapter cover specific types of major psychopathology, including depression, schizophrenia, and phobia as well as personality disorders (alcoholism, drug abuse, and crime). The last section of this chapter deals with the interaction between genetic and environmental factors in the development of gender identity and gender roles and with sexuality, psychophysiological disorders, and obesity.

Concepts

The term *psychopathology* is usually used as a substitute for mental illness or psychiatric disturbance. In contrast to *sex,* which refers to the biological expression of maleness and femaleness, *gender* indicates the social aspects of

[1] This work was completed during a Killam Resident Fellowship at the University of Calgary.

ISBN: 0-12-050350-6

being a male or a female (the concept *sex* is more ambiguous than *gender* because it also refers to sexual behavior). In their usage, however, the two concepts are interchanged without any implications for their original biological or social meaning.

The concepts *gender* and *sex* are often used in combination with other terms. Gender (sex) role represents social expectations about how males and females should behave, whereas gender (sex) identity reflects a conviction about, and acceptance of, being biologically a male or a female. Thus, gender role may be considered as the overt behavioral expression of gender identity. Sex-typing is used to indicate the process by which society transforms male and female into masculine and feminine, respectively.

Gender role and gender identity are inferred from measures that cover a wide area consisting of personality traits, recreational and vocational interests, and behavioral samples indicating preferences. These heterogeneous measures have been selected empirically because they can distinguish between the sexes. One assumption underlying these measures is that all sex differences are related to gender roles. However, many items included in these measures have nothing to do with gender role expectations. For example, Spence (1979) found that one masculinity-femininity test differentiates between men and women on the basis of their preference for types of ablution (men tend to take showers, whereas women are inclined to take baths). Type of ablution is obviously not part of gender roles (i.e., part of the societal belief system about appropriate behavior of men versus women) and should not be included in the measurement of gender roles.

Another measurement problem that makes the interpretation of data in the area of gender and psychopathology rather difficult is the tendency of researchers to confuse masculine and feminine traits with overt role behavior. Masculine and feminine traits describe general predispositions that may influence behavior but could not always be inferred from it. An individual may manifest behavior that is consistent with conventional roles and social expectations but incompatible with his or her predisposition and self-image in order to avoid aversive social consequences. Gender role preference, which involves activities one would prefer to engage in, also differs from gender role adoption, which refers to behavior one actually manifests. Whereas gender role preference of a woman, for example, may tend to be masculine, her gender role adoption may be feminine in order to conform with social demands. More often than not, studies of gender differences are predominantly based on self-reports that do not distinguish between social expectations and personal experience (Unger, 1981). Thus, these methodological problems may account for the low reliability of measures of masculinity and femininity (Constantinople, 1973; Spence, 1979). These problems may also explain many inconsistent findings in the relationship between gender and psychopathology.

The distinction between gender identity (a belief) and gender role (a behavior) is not made clear in studies of gender and psychopathology. There is usually overlap between the sexes in almost all gender role behavior, but this is not true for gender identity. With the exception of transsexuals, the belief of belonging to the gender that is compatible with one's own anatomy and the lack of any wish to change one's biological sex appear to be almost universal among normals and mental patients (there is the rare delusion of belonging to the opposite sex in schizophrenics, but in contrast to transsexuals who *feel like* members of the opposite sex, schizophrenics have a true belief that they *are* members of the other sex). Gender identity is intact even among those whose sexual orientation is inverted. Efforts expended on the study of disturbance in gender identity such as its "reversal" in patients (i.e., adopting the identity of the opposite sex) may not yield significant information about the nature of psychopathology because individuals—both normals and patients—generally show no hesitation in designating themselves to the gender that is compatible with their anatomy.

Gender and Mental Health

In considering the ideological basis of gender and psychopathology, Maffeo (Chapter 2, this volume) introduces the reader to three major models of mental health. First, she discusses the traditional model, which accepts different standards of mental health for males and females. This model also assumes that deviation from gender role is pathological. Second, there is the masculinity model, which is based on the idea that masculine traits and behavior are more desirable and more highly valued than feminine ones and they should indicate better mental health. Finally, the androgyny model implies that a combination of masculinity and femininity rather than either one is conducive to better psychological adjustment.

Acceptance of any of the three mental health models seems to change from one historical period to the other. In recent years, the traditional model has been subjected to criticism because of its biological approach to mental health and its sexist orientation (e.g., labels such as *penis envy* and *masculine protest* are attached to females who deviate from gender role expectations). In contrast, the androgyny model has become popular in both research and clinical practice. Maffeo, however, suggests that the imposition of any model in society may create conflicts between individual predisposition and societal demands. She believes that some individuals, because of temperament, past history, and goals or values, may not be suited to a specific model. For example, a female who is inclined to masculine behavior and a male who is predisposed to feminine behavior may suffer from conflicts and psychopathology if their inclinations and predispositions are repressed (see also Eysenck, Chapter 12, this volume, for further exposition of this view).

Research has now thrown strong doubts on the basic assumption of the traditional mental health model that deviation from gender role behavior is related to psychological maladjustment (Spence, 1979). Evidence suggests that instrumental behavior (or masculine traits) and expressive behavior (feminine traits) per se rather than their appropriateness or inappropriateness for the individual's gender are related to positive mental health. Also, some degree of masculine aggressiveness and dominance combined with relative lack of feminine emotional vulnerability is positively associated with psychological adjustment in *both* men and women. Thus, these data appear to give little support to the traditional view that deviation from gender role is pathological. However, it should be noted that research on gender and mental health, regardless of its orientation, tends to focus attention on individual deficits (study of traits and behavior) and may neglect the external circumstances that interact with personal problems.

Gender and Patterns of Psychopathology

The research reported by Maffeo deals mainly with data based on measures that consist primarily of desirable characteristics (e.g., the Bem Scale, the Personal Attributes Questionnaire, and so on). Psychopathology may, however, involve undesirable gender-related characteristics and behavior. It has been suggested that individuals may react to stress by either exaggerating the negative characteristics of their own sex or by adopting the undesirable aspects of the opposite sex (Al-Issa, 1980; Chesler, 1972). It is assumed that there is a male pattern of psychopathology associated with masculine characteristics and a female pattern associated with feminine characteristics (i.e., certain types of psychopathology reflect high masculinity and high femininity, respectively). Research on the relationship between femininity and depression (Chapter 6, this volume) or phobia (Chapter 8, this volume) as well as data on gender role in schizophrenia (Chapter 7, this volume) are consistent with this approach.

It is also believed that individuals are more vulnerable to patterns of psychopathology that are compatible with their own sex than to those of the opposite sex. The prevalence of neurosis in females and personality disorders in males supports this belief (see, e.g., data in Chapter 4, this volume). Another type of evidence is derived from studies of gender-related symptoms of hospitalized patients (Eaton, Sletten, Kitchen, & Smith, 1971; Zigler & Phillips, 1960). Zigler and Phillips found more men than women in the categories of self-indulgence and turning against others (drinking, rape, robbery, assaultive behavior), but more women than men in the categories of self-deprivation, turning against the self (depression, suicidal attempts, bodily complaints, tension) and avoidance of others (perplexed, apathetic, withdrawn). Eaton *et al.* (1971) also found that females cried easily, attempted suicide, and talked about suicide more than males. Male patients, on the other hand, felt like killing someone, carried weapons, were arrested, fought with others often, and drank too much.

Studies of gender and patterns of psychopathology raise the question whether stereotypic gender characteristics or behavior in patients are symptoms of the illness or the cause of it. However, these characteristics and behavior, particularly in childhood, are found to be predictive of the development of later psychopathology. For example, follow-up studies reveal that, for both males and females, antisocial behavior in childhood (male pattern) is more predictive of schizophrenia and other psychiatric disturbances than is withdrawal or shyness (female pattern) (Al-Issa, Chapter 7, this volume; Robins, 1966). Personality disorders and antisocial behavior also seem to be related to the dimension of psychoticism for both sexes (Eysenck, Chapter 12, this volume).

Gender and Psychopathology during the Life Cycle

Child Psychopathology

The overall rates of child psychopathology are higher among boys than among girls, but they tend to become almost equal during adolescence. Changes in sex differences from childhood to adolescence reflect complex interactions between biological and environmental factors. Although the stresses and strains of childhood and adolescence may be implicated in these changes, some disorders such as infantile autism and psychosis, which are more prevalent among boys, appear so early and in such a severe form that they suggest biological factors. In support of the biological hypothesis is the observation that psychosis continues to be higher among boys from childhood to adolescence regardless of changes in the amount of stress experienced by, or gender role demands made on, boys and girls. In contrast, increase of emotional disorders around menarche in girls could reflect the influence of biological changes or social reaction to these changes. In both childhood and adolescence, sex differences in psychopathology may be influenced by such artifacts as referral to clinics by adults, defensiveness and unwillingness in the admission of symptoms, and sex bias in the contents of measures used (e.g., fear schedules tend to emphasize situations related to females more than males). For example, aggression, which is involved in most male disturbance, may explain the excess of referral of boys to clinics because it creates problems for adults. Thus, aggressive behavior, which may be biologically determined, may influence sex difference in overall rates of child psychopathology. Also, the superiority of girls in verbal abilities (which may be due to biological predisposition or environmental factors) may account for their relative low rate of learning disabilities which, in turn, may reduce their referral to clinics. Furthermore, an excess in mental retardation among boys may contribute to higher rates of learning disabilities, which inflate their rates of mental illness.

The interaction between gender, family disturbance, and child psychopathology reported by Al-Issa in Chapter 3 (this volume) raises many questions. Why is family discord and disruption related to the development of antisocial behavior only in boys but not to neurosis or emotional disturbance in either boys or girls? Why is family discord less harmful for girls than is long-term institutionalization away from home? Why is severe punishment associated with aggression in boys and passivity or low assertiveness in girls? In recent years, attention has been given to the excessive rate of disturbance among children of single-parent families. The importance of this research is emphasized by the estimate that as many as 4 of every 10 American children born in the 1970s will spend part of their childhood in a single-parent family, usually with their mother as head of the household. These children of divorced parents in turn are more likely than others to experience divorce themselves (Bane, 1976). Studies discussed by Al-Issa (Chapter 3, this volume) also suggest that a shift may be taking place from traditional research that emphasizes the effect of father absence on child identity to the consideration of the life situation of female heads of families who have to cope with multiple sources of stress.

Adult Psychopathology

It is believed by some professionals and researchers that women are more vulnerable to mental illness than men. In the early 1970s, Phyllis Chesler (1972), a psychologist, and Walter Gove (Gove & Tudor, 1973), a sociologist, claimed that the rate of mental illness is higher among women than among men. Although Chesler's conclusions about the predominance of mental illness among women became popular, her data were based on raw numbers and percentages and did not take into account the sex ratio in the American population at large. For example, she concluded that state and county mental hospitals are custodial old-age homes for women because of the larger number of institutionalized females, but she did not consider the excess of women 65 and older in the general population. Gove based his conclusions on a narrow definition of mental illness that included only neuroses and functional psychosis but excluded organic and toxic conditions, mental retardation, alcohol disorders, drug disorders, organic brain syndromes, and personality disorders. A high rate of alcohol disorders, for example, seems to account for higher overall admission of males in state and county hospitals. Thus, conclusions about the relative prevalence of psychopathology among men and women should be limited to specific types of mental illness. Furthermore, sex differences also vary with the kind of institution or mental health facility (Al-Issa, Chapter 4, this volume).

In explaining sex differences in adult psychopathology, Al-Issa (Chapter 4) considers the stress hypothesis. Gender role may determine the amount and type of stress as well as the context in which it occurs and the resources available to the individual to deal with it. Al-Issa also examines the relationship between marital status and mental illness. He drew attention to many factors that might mediate the impact of marital status (number of children, lack of intimate relationship, employment, and socioeconomic status to be discussed in detail in a later section on depression). There is a need for the investigation of stressful life events associated with excessive rates of mental illness in both children in and mothers heading single-parent families (Bane, 1976). In addition to the stress hypothesis, Al-Issa discusses the alternative view that sex differences may not be real but may be artifacts of social factors such as willingness to report symptoms, role obligations, contact with mental health facilities, and bias in diagnosis, hospitalization and treatment. The relationship between marital status and mental illness, which varies between the sexes, is explained in terms of selective factors; that is, psychiatric disturbance may prevent marriage or may result in the disruption of marriage, thus increasing the number of mentally ill singles or formerly marrieds, respectively. Finally, societal evaluation of females in terms of their degree of physical attractiveness is related to mental illness not only as a source of stress, but as a factor in diagnosis and the perception of illness.

Psychopathology among the Aged

The complexity of factors involved in explaining sex differences in mental illness is further illustrated by the interaction between gender, age, and psychopathology presented by Mensh and Hecht in Chapter 5, this volume. In their review of cross-national data from Australia, Canada, Israel, Scandinavia, the United Kingdom, and the United States, they observe certain general trends. They found that an increase in the overall prevalence rate of psychopathology with age exists for both sexes, but that the increase tends to be higher for females than males. The overall rates also tend to be higher among women than men at age 65 and older. However, there are some cross-national variations. For example, the tendency for an increase in psychopathology with age is reversed in Canadian hospital admissions. Similarly, an Australian study of first admissions among the elderly is favorable to women (i.e., they have lower rates than men). Mensh and Hecht indicate that the evidence for more psychopathology among elderly women may be the result of their advantage over men in mortality, which leaves more of them who are at risk. They also observe that hospital dynamics (policies for hospitalization, discharge, rehospitalization, differences in samples and in methods used in community studies) may influence the direction of sex differences among the elderly.

In their discussion of the rates of specific subtypes of psychopathology (depression, schizophrenia, alcoholism) among men and women over 65, Mensh and Hecht raise the question whether these represent separate disorders from those experienced at earlier years or whether they are simply a recurrence or a continuation of disorders that have existed earlier in life and are first identified in old age because of changed life situations. In contrast to other life stages, the increase of organic disorders among those 65 or older complicates the study of the rates of psychopathology. Sex differences in the causes of death among psychiatric patients aged 65 years and older reported by Mensh and Hecht may reflect biological predisposition by sex in the general population (e.g., men dying from respiratory disorder, women dying from diabetes mellitis) or may be due to gender-linked behavior observed in other life stages (high rate of suicide and alcoholism among men; cf. Waldron, Chapter 15, this volume for sex differences in the causes of mortality). Data reported on suicide also raise many issues related to the interaction among gender, age, and psychopathology. Why does suicide increase steadily with age for males but reach a peak between 45-54 for females and decrease over the next four decades? What are the causes of the recent decrease in the ratio of male-female suicide in childhood, middle, and old age? Is this change related to gender role or is it the artifact of more sophisticated methods of recording suicides? Why is suicide more common among men in the lower social class and among women in the upper social class? Why is marital status protective against suicide for both sexes and at all ages except among married men over the age of 80?

The advantage women have over men in longevity does not only result in more women at risk, but it may also leave many of them without partners and deprive them of intimate relationships and social support. As in other life stages, socioeconomic status and marital status are expected to affect the life satisfaction and mental health of the elderly widow and widower.

Gender and Major Psychopathology

Depression

One firmly held view among professionals and researchers is that the rates of depression are higher among women than among men. This has been more recently popularized by a review of Western and cross-cultural studies by

Weissman and Klerman (1977). Hammen (Chapter 6, this volume) challenges the reliability and validity of conclusions about sex differences in depression by examining the substance and meaning of the evidence from both institutions and community studies. She exposes the inadequacy of data based on treatment settings for reaching a conclusion about higher rates of depression among women, for example, methodological problems in sampling, control of demographic and referral variables, and misdiagnosis of depression. She notes that although overall rates of depression may be found to be higher for women, no sex differences are observed when age, marital status, education, income level, and other demographic factors are partialled out. Community studies using diagnostic interviews indicate that there are sex differences in *lifetime prevalence*, which is based on retrospective reports, but no sex differences in *current* major or minor depression. On symptom scales, only poor, uneducated, formerly married young adult women report more symptoms of depression than men. Both clinical diagnosis and rating scales in community studies are biased against women because they emphasize the presence of affective symptoms, which are more characteristic of depression in women, than cognitive and somatic symptoms, which are more often reported by men.

Hammen's evaluation of studies on sex differences in depression is timely. Although Weissman and Klerman (1977) do not subscribe to biological theories, their conclusions about the universality of higher rates in women would suggest that they are more biologically predisposed to depression. North American evidence reported by Hammen as well as other surveys in developing countries that reveal no sex differences (Leighton, Lambo, Hughes, Leighton, Murphy, & Macklin, 1963; Orley & Wing, 1979) or higher rates among males (Ananth, 1978) argue against biological factors as a major cause of depression in women. It is also possible that the higher rate of depression among women is an artifact of social factors. Hammen points out that evidence revealing the unwillingness of males to report depressive symptoms and to seek treatment is compatible with the view that these symptoms may represent a violation of gender role standards for men. Consistent with studies reported in Chapter 4, Hammen also reports no sex differences in the overall amount of stress. However, she raises the question of whether women experience more stressful life events that are specific to depression or simply perceive and react to stress differently from men. Theories of depression are discussed by Hammen within the context of gender role. For example, contrary to psychoanalytical prediction, dependency as a feminine characteristic is not significantly associated with depressive scores. She also reviews some of the most recent evidence on helplessness and its implications for depression in men and women.

Overall, Chapter 6 represents a shift now taking place in theory and research from an emphasis on the dynamics of the person to the study of the conditions under which people become depressed, for example, employment status, socioeconomic status, marital status, and number of children. However, current findings in this area are inconsistent, and future research is needed to explain these inconsistencies. For example, Brown and Harris (1978) found that there are fewer cases of depression among employed women. Others also found that employed women show less impairment and better response to treatment than nonemployed women (Mostow & Newberry, 1975; Weissman & Paykel, 1974). More recently, Bebbington, Hurry, Tennant, Sturt, and Wing (1981) confirmed the strong relationship between present employment status and the prevalence of affective disorder for both men and women. They found that even part-time employment, which is higher among women, is as strongly associated with the prevalence of affective disorders as is full time employment. In contrast, others failed to find an association between employment and affective symptoms (Newberry, Weissman, & Myers, 1979; Pearlin, 1975; Radloff, 1975). Similarly contradictory results are reported on the relationships between socioeconomic status or presence of children in the home and depression. Although the relationship between socioeconomic status and depression in women is well established (see review by Brown & Harris, 1978, 1982), this finding is not replicated in another study using the same methodology and population pool (Bebbington *et al.*, 1981). Similarly, the presence of children of under 15 years in the home, when studied as a vulnerability factor in depression (Brown & Harris, 1978), was found to have no direct relationship with affective disorders; its effect is mediated through employment because it makes it less likely for women to be at work and it is the latter factor that increases the risk for depression (Bebbington *et al.*, 1981). Thus, the direction of the relationship between depression and many demographic variables is still far from being firmly established.

Schizophrenia

One difference between depressed and schizophrenic patients is that whereas a large number of depressed patients remain untreated and in the community, the majority of schizophrenic patients tend to turn up for psychiatric care. The research on gender and schizophrenia reported by Al-Issa (Chapter 7, this volume) therefore deals primarily with treated cases. Using raw data and percentages, Chesler (1972) popularized the view that there are more schizophrenic females than males. In contrast, the overall evidence reveals no sex differences in schizophrenia except that males tend to have the illness at an earlier age than females. There is also interaction among gender, marital status, and schizophrenia with more single male and married female patients.

Other research reviewed by Al-Issa indicates that there exist sex differences in symptomatology, premorbid adjustment, prognosis, and etiology. These data raise the question of whether one is dealing with entirely different "diseases" with an altogether different underlying process or whether one is dealing with the same "disease" manifesting itself in different forms, by sex.

Although evidence for a definite etiological process is far from being established in schizophrenia, available data reveal sex differences in factors associated with schizophrenia. For example, physiological and biological factors (autonomic responsivity and recovery, low level of monoamine oxidase) and pregnancy or birth complications are more associated with male (early and severe form) than female (late and relatively mild form) schizophrenia. In contrast, environmental factors seem to be more involved in the development and cause of schizophrenia in women (early parental loss, age of daughter at onset of mother's illness, broken homes, lack of intimate relationships, presence of disturbed persons in the home). Evidence on the etiology of male schizophrenia in adults is consistent with data from child psychopathology (Chapter 3, this volume) revealing that boys are more prone to severe disorders with organic involvement. That males are overrepresented in process schizophrenia and females in reactive schizophrenia also suggests sex differences in etiology, since biological factors are believed to be involved in the process type and environmental factors are related to the reactive type. However, because of unreliability of the diagnosis of schizophrenia and the tendency of psychiatrists to confuse it with depression (Cooper, Kendell, Gurland, Sharpe, Copeland, & Simon, 1972; Fleiss, Gurland, Simon, & Sharpe, 1973), research on sex differences in the etiology of schizophrenia should be considered with caution. Furthermore, family and twin studies reported by Al-Issa (Chapter 7, this volume) do not reveal more genetic involvement in the development of schizophrenia in males than in females, a finding that is incompatible with the physiological and biochemical data.

Studies on gender role and gender identity reviewed by Al-Issa are based on stereotypic notions as to the interests, preferences, body image, and general characteristics of males and females. Many tests used are inadequate (unreliable, invalid) for the measurement of the concepts they claim to measure. Researchers are not clear about whether gender disturbance is part of the schizophrenic process or merely a result of institutionalization. Al-Issa points out that a concept such as reversal of gender role, which is used in research in schizophrenia, is only useful to the extent that it may reveal a relationship between nonconformity to social role expectations and the diagnosis, hospitalization, discharge, and rehospitalization of male and female patients. Studies of age patterns and subtypes of schizophrenia in men and women may provide more useful information for understanding the nature of sex differences than studies of disturbance in gender role and gender identity in schizophrenia (Lewine, 1981; Zigler & Levine, 1981).

Phobia

Since there is no reason to believe that the excess of phobia in adult females is due to sex differences in genetic or biological vulnerability, Fodor (Chapter 8, this volume) emphasizes social learning and gender role expectations. Many simple phobias that are reported more often by women seem to represent a retention or an exaggeration of childhood fears. Fodor raises the question whether the early training of boys for mastery and girls for helplessness could account for the persistence of childhood fears in adult women. The excess of agoraphobia in young, newly married women rather than in other life stages suggests a relationship between certain social conditions during this life stage and the development of the disorder. This is, for example, evident in the finding reported by Fodor that discontented housewives (those who wanted to work outside the home but could not) tend to be more symptomatic, more severely agoraphobic, and to need more help with their phobia than do contented housewives. Factors investigated in depression such as marital status, number of children, employment, and intimate relationships may also be relevant to the development of agoraphobia in females. Sex differences in agoraphobia symptoms seem to be related to gender role expectations; agoraphobic males report less disability (helplessness, dependency), which may be a result of social pressure on them to work efficiently.

Research data and theory presented by Hammen on depression (Chapter 6, this volume) may be compared with those on phobia. In both instances, for example, male patients tend to report physical, rather than the typical affective, symptoms. Helplessness seems to be relevant to the development of both depression and agoraphobia. Not unlike depression, the high rate of agoraphobia among women is not a universal phenomenon but is associated with specific demographic factors (age, marital status, occupational status). Finally, the last two decades have seen a move away from the psychoanalytical approach and toward the cognitive and behavioral approaches to the treatment of both depression and phobia.

Gender and Personality Disorders

Personality disorders tend to be consistently more prevalent among males than females. However, these disorders have not always been seriously considered as subtypes of psychopathology. Gove and Tudor (1973), for example, did not include them in their definition of mental illness. Mechanic (1978) reported that services for neurosis, which is higher in females, are more available than are services for personality disorders. Personality disorders have only recently been considered a psychiatric illness (Robbins, 1966). Murphy

(1976) also reported that in other cultures (e.g., the Eskimos in the Arctic and the Yoruba tribe in Nigeria) personality disorders are not considered an illness to be treated by shamans, or healers. The tendency to exclude these disorders from the domain of psychiatry may be due, in part, to the fact that antisocial behavior is more visible and has a more immediate impact on others and thus is more often controlled by formal norms or established laws than by the psychiatric establishment.

Alcoholism

Based on the stereotype that drinking is a masculine activity, it has often been suggested that because rigid gender roles are breaking down, the rates of drinking and drinking problems are becoming equalized between the sexes. Leland (Chapter 9, this volume) finds no evidence in support of this view in the United States and Canada: Drinking, heavy drinking, and problem drinking have been higher among males in these countries. However, Leland presents data revealing that the sex ratio for drinkers or heavy drinkers varies with age, marital status, income, education, ethnicity, religion, and geographical location. For example, the percentage of drinkers is equal among the sexes in the separated or divorced group. Relevant to data on the high rate of institutionalization of female heads of single-parent families discussed earlier, Leland reports that the incidence of heavy drinking is over twice as high among this group as among wives. In contrast to findings on the protective role of employment against psychiatric disorders, heavy drinking is 68% higher among employed women than among housewives. Leland argues that the finding that employed married women have higher rates of heavy and problem drinking than single women or housewives not in the labor force is against the stereotype of the female alcoholic as a housewife with a hidden problem.

Consistent with evidence on other types of psychopathology, studies indicate the existence of sex differences in the etiology of problem drinking (cf. Chapter 7, this volume). Genetic evidence for problem drinking is more consistent in studies of males than females. In contrast, female drinking is more associated with environmental factors (psychiatric disturbance or alcoholism in the family, peer models, spouse, etc.). The early data also suggested that life-change events are associated with onset of alcohol abuse in women, although some recent research reveals just the opposite. Leland shows how physiological factors may influence sex differences in drinking. She suggests that the higher rate of alcohol absorption in women, which has aversive consequences, may result in avoidance of drinking among women (cf. Barry, 1982).

Most studies on gender and motivation for drinking hypothesize a relationship between gender role conflicts (masculine characteristics such as power as opposed to feminine characteristics such as dependency and warmth) and alcoholism. Leland points out that many methodological and conceptual problems cast doubts on the validity of data derived from this approach. In addition, the focus of these studies on internal motives and predispositions may overlook the influence of environmental factors on the drinking habits of men and women. Sex differences in the social context and pattern of drinking reported by Leland illustrate how social roles (marital, occupational) may influence the frequency and the amount of drinking.

Research on the consequences and effects of alcohol pose many questions concerning the interaction between biological and environmental factors. Women report more health problems than men, but it is not clear whether this tendency is the result of sex differences in willingness to admit symptoms, mentioned earlier in this chapter, or true physical vulnerability. Sex differences in the causes of death among alcoholics may, however, reflect a tendency in the general population rather than gender-related effects specific to alcohol (i.e., death of alcoholic males from lung cancer, heart disease, suicide is similar to causes of male death in the general population described by Waldron, Chapter 15). Many sex differences in alcohol-related diseases (Korsakoff psychosis, cirrhosis of the liver) and in the behavioral effects of alcohol (aggression, sexuality, anxiety) reported by Leland could be either the result of biological differences or may simply reflect the life experiences of the two sexes. Many traditional beliefs of biological effects of alcohol on male aggression and sexual response have been demonstrated to be the result of beliefs and expectancy regarding the effects of alcohol.

Problems related to the social consequences of drinking (problems with the law, police, job, etc.) are investigated in males rather than females. Women, however, suffer more adverse consequences from heavy drinking than men, which may reflect negative societal response to female drinking. Also, the problems of women are more often related to the drinking of others. As a result of the high rate of heavy drinking among males, wives more often have to cope with the stress of living with an alcoholic husband (Al-Issa, 1980). Since alcohol poses different problems for men and women, research on treatment and outcome should give particular attention to gender; but as Leland points out, current research in this area is complicated by many methodological problems.

Drug Use and Abuse

Data reported by Fidell (Chapter 10, this volume) demonstrate how sex differences in drug use and abuse vary with the legality and strength of the drug. However, if alcohol is added to other drugs, there is an overall heavier involvement of males than females. She points out that inconsistent findings in the study of gender and substance use and abuse often result from biased sampling, techniques used, and other research problems.

Many sex differences in the demographic characteristics of heroin addicts discussed by Fidell may reflect those in the general population (female addicts are less likely to be employed and more likely to be economically dependent than are men). Female addicts are more likely to be married than are their male counterparts, a finding similar to that in other types of psychopathology (e.g., schizophrenia). The interaction between gender and heroin addiction is quite similar to that reported on alcoholism (Chapter 9, this volume): The female addict tends to report more psychiatric symptoms and physical illnesses and is believed to be sicker than her male counterpart; treatment centers are more suitable for handling male than female problems; both males and females who are undifferentiated (low on masculinity and femininity) tend to be addicts; and family environment is more strongly associated with drug abuse in females.

Factors in the excessive prescription of psychotropic drugs to females outlined by Fidell include physician bias, sex differences in patient behavior and report of symptoms, contact with physicians, and so on (see Chapters 4 and 6 for further discussion of these factors). Many correlates of heavy use of psychotropic drugs (being neurotic, retired, unemployed, divorced, separated, widowed) do not clearly indicate the direction of causality; for example, it is unclear whether sick people who take drugs work less or whether those who work less become sick and start using drugs. There are sex differences in the motivation for the use of psychotropic drugs (centering around employment for men and around the home for women). Fidell suggests that excessive use of these drugs by women may reinforce the sick role and increase dependency, apathy, and lack of initiative to change a stressful environment. She also draws attention to tranquilizers as a major method of female suicide. Evidence presented here supports the feminist view that women should seek therapies that deal with their life situation and the social context rather than those that put the responsibility on the patient.

Crime

Is crime a subtype of psychopathology, a cause of psychopathology, or does it have nothing to do with it at all? In Chapter 11, Campbell reveals that theorists and researchers have often used a psychopathology model of crime, but they tend to apply it to female criminality more than male criminality. This model assumes that crime is an irrational and illogical action without meaning to the criminal. She traces this model to Lambroso and Freud at the end of the nineteenth century: Crime is equated with masculinity, and female criminals are considered as pseudo-males. Biological evidence in support of this model (extra Y chromosome, body type, hormones) is negative. The psychoanalytical approach equates female criminality with sexuality, promiscuity, and lack of love. Campbell notes that the emphasis on sexuality reflects society's attitude toward women rather than the cause or expression of female crime. She critically evaluates current research that attempts to relate female criminality to gender roles in general and to masculinity in particular. Unfortunately, research on gender roles and crime, not unlike its psychoanalytical counterpart, is based on the psychopathology model of crime.

In contrast, the sociological model of criminality, which has been mainly applied to males, turns its attention from gender role deviance to social and economic variables to explain crime. If applied to female criminality, this model would suggest that female criminal behavior, similar to its male counterpart, is a rational response to the socioeconomic structure of society. Campbell points out that class differences are more important than sex differences in understanding criminality. Thus, recent increases in crime rates among women is not because they have become more masculine or liberated but because their active part in society has opened up new opportunities for crime. Similarly, prostitution involves material motives rather than pathology. Campbell's approach to shoplifting as well as to sex differences in rates of homicide and the means of achieving it is a contextual one (e.g., shoplifting is related to the involvement of women in shopping) that rejects the psychopathology model.

Campbell observes that many methodological problems make it difficult to arrive at a definite conclusion from studies about the role of psychopathology in female criminality (representativeness of samples taken from prison population, low reliability of diagnosis, treatment of crime as a homogenous phenomenon, and absence of control groups or lack of control of demographic variables such as social class). Also, the direction of causality is unclear because the relationship between crime and psychopathology may indicate that mental illness is a response to imprisonment rather than a cause of it. Alternatively, criminality and psychopathology may have the same underlying causation. However, patterns of psychopathology among the sexes in prison is almost the same as in the general population. Campbell notes that a reversal of the national trend, with higher rates of alcoholism among female criminals, may only reflect the tendency of the justice system to punish women more severely than men for public offenses associated with drinking. The discrimination of the justice system against females in certain situations but against males in others (e.g., homosexuality) may, in part, indicate firmly held stereotypes about the behavior of the sexes (Al-Issa, 1980).

Gender, Psyche, and Soma: A Case for Interaction

The last section of this book reflects the view accepted by most contemporary researchers that role behavior is determined by an interaction among biological, social, and psychological factors. It also reflects the present uncertainty about the extent to which each of these factors contributes to behavior. Biological factors are only considered as a predisposition toward behavior, which unfolds within a certain social and cultural context.

Gender and Genes

One way of determining whether certain behavior is due to inherent biological factors is to observe its consistency across space and time. One finding reported by Eysenck (Chapter 12, this volume) is that gender differences in sexual attitudes are universal across nations, with men revealing more interest in impersonal sex, promiscuity, voyeuristic activities, and other paraphilias. The universality of sexual attitudes is also illustrated in the predominance of polygyny rather than polyandry (women having more than one husband) across cultures. These gender differences in sexual attitudes seem to persist among persons in the Western world despite the recent impact of the sexual revolution on both males and females. Some differences in sexual attitudes are found even among sexually inverted individuals; that is, both male homosexuals and transsexuals are more promiscuous and less inclined to settle into stable and enduring sexual relationships than are their female counterparts (Green, 1975; Hoffman, 1968). Another type of evidence presented by Eysenck in support of the biological hypothesis in gender role development is the universality of patriarchy across cultures and throughout history.

The universality of sexual attitudes and patriarchy seems to support sociobiological theory. Eysenck notes, however, that this theory is completely biological and genetic and should be supplemented by sociological, social learning, and other theories. Since sociobiological theory accepts the inevitability of double standards, it is considered sexist (Lowe & Hubbard, 1979; Maccoby, 1979). Maccoby (1979), for example, argued that social characteristics need not be considered genetically based simply because they survive for centuries and characterize many or most societies. She suggested that the universality of social behavior may be the product of cultural transmission because it proved to be adaptive for human modes of life. Such behavior can change rapidly in accord with changes in the social conditions that made them adaptive.

Additional evidence for the influence of biological factors discussed by Eysenck is related to the observation that some gender differences tend to persist even under conditions of social pressure to eradicate them. Eysenck considers data reported by Spiro (1979) to demonstrate how attempts to minimize sexual dimorphism in a kibbutz have failed. However, both the design of the kibbutz experiment and the conclusion of biological predetermination from it have been criticized. One criticism discussed by Eysenck is that outside influences from nearby urban areas were not controlled during the kibbutz experiment. Mednick (1981) also questioned the assumption that the social utopia introduced in the kibbutz is a complete revolution of gender roles. She maintains that the Marxist analysis that dictated the institutional arrangements in the kibbutz did not deal with the patriarchal social system in which gender roles are embedded. For example, she notes that women in the kibbutz were given masculine work but men did not seriously try to take up traditional feminine work.

Evidence reveals that personality, particularly psychoticism, may mediate between genetic and biological factors on the one hand and sexually dimorphic behavior on the other. For both males and females, high scores on psychoticism are associated with male sexual attitudes as well as with masculine pathological behavior such as psychopathy, criminality, and addiction. Theory and research (genetic, behavioral) on psychoticism could be extrapolated to the understanding of sexual dimorphism.

In conclusion, Eysenck proposes a theory that postulates that a conflict between social norms and biological predisposition toward sex-specific types of behavior may lead to an increase in psychopathology. In contrast, matching the two is more likely to result in less psychopathology. Although this theory is biologically oriented, unlike the traditional model of mental health (see Chapter 2, this volume), which dichotomizes gender role behavior, it postulates an overlap between gender roles: Some women may have more masculine inclinations than most men, and some men may have more feminine predispositions than most women. Eysenck also puts forward the hypothesis that, in a society that prescribes rigid sex-typing for the majority, men and women who are predisposed to cross-sex behavior would suffer from conflicts, agony, unhappiness, and psychopathology. Research on the relationship between mental health on the one hand and masculinity, femininity, and androgyny on the other is discussed by Maffeo in Chapter 2 and is relevant to this hypothesis.

Gender and Hormones

Studies indicating the influence of prenatal and postnatal hormones on sexually dimorphic behavior and gender identity provide additional support to the genetic hypothesis presented by Eysenck. Animal work reviewed by Al-Issa (Chapter 13, this volume) reveals that prenatal and neonatal injection of testosterone (male hormone) has morphological (e.g., the genitalia) as well as behavioral (mating and nonmating) effects on various species. These early influences of male hormone also sensitize the brain structures that mediate sexually dimorphic behavior to the action of hormones in adulthood. On the human level, similar evidence is provided from research on cases of sex hormone abnormalities (androgenital syndrome, progestin-induced hermaphroditism, androgenital insensitivity syndrome, Turner's syndrome). These clinical cases strongly support the view that an excess of androgen during the prenatal period in a genetic female is associated with the development of masculine behavior and interest even when the children are reared as girls. In contrast, genetic males who are not exposed prenatally to androgen develop feminine behavior and interests even when they are reared as boys. However, regardless of prenatal hormonal influences, being reared consistently as a male or a female, particularly during the first 3 or 4 years of life, is crucial in the development of gender identity. Furthermore, data reveal that differentiation into a postnatal feminine gender role or gender identity is neither dependent on prenatal gonadal hormones nor on the presence of a second X chromosome. It has been suggested that, because the developing female fetus is less dependent on the presence of hormones, females are less vulnerable to abnormalities in childhood and adulthood (gender disorders and paraphilias). However, conclusions from work on hormonal abnormalities should be accepted with caution because the studies are carried out on a small number of selected clinical cases by only one group of researchers (i.e., John Money and his associates). The orientation of the researchers also reflects the traditional view that sexually dimorphic behavior is polar and the individual may show either masculine or feminine behavior but not both. Such orientation may also have led to the conclusion that the human brain is differentiated as either male or female. More recent research on androgyny suggests that the brain contains mechanisms for both male and female behavior (Beach, 1977). Thus, there is a need for the replication of studies on hormonal abnormalities with larger numbers of cases by researchers who do not subscribe to the traditional view of masculinity and femininity.

Research on the relationship between hormonal levels in adults and gender role behavior is inconsistent. Although androgen seems to control libido in both sexes, there is no consistent relationship between the degree of sexual drive and function and hormone levels circulating in the blood. Animal work indicates that prenatal and neonatal levels of androgen are related to sexual orientation and sexual inversion. However, studies on the effect of hormones on human homosexuality are inconsistent. Since body build is determined by hormones, research on the relationship between body build and sexually dimorphic behavior or homosexuality reviewed by Al-Issa may provide useful data on the effect of biological factors on gender role.

Extensive research has been carried out on the relationship between hormonal fluctuations and psychopathology in adult females, but the results are confounded by methodological problems (subject selection, techniques used). Emotional disturbance during the menstrual cycle, pregnancy, childbirth, ingestion of contraceptive pills, and menopause are found to be more relevant to cognitive factors (expectation and beliefs), general personality predisposition, and stressful life events than to hormonal changes. A growing body of research deals with male hormonal cyclicity and physiological synchrony among couples, but its implication for the understanding of gender role behavior is not yet clear.

Gender and Sexuality

The interface between biological and environmental factors is further pursued by Heiman and Verhulst (Chapter 14, this volume), who discuss gender and sexuality. Although women exceed men in the number of sexual response cycles, their sexual response tends to be more variable than men's (e.g., presence of orgasm or time to reach it during intercourse). The physiological hypothesis that women need more stimulation than men in order to achieve orgasm is rejected by Heiman and Verhulst. For example, they argue strongly that the relative variability in female sexual interest and arousability during menstruation, pregnancy, and after childbirth is less likely to be the result of actual physiological changes than of awareness of these changes.

Clinical theory and research data discussed by Heiman and Verhulst support the notion that rigid adherence to gender roles is characteristic of dysfunctional couples. Treatment of sexual dysfunction seems to result in more flexible gender role behavior. Laboratory research on the relationship between physiological measures of genital vasocongestion, self-reports of sexual arousal, and affective reaction to erotic stimuli (positive or negative evaluation of these stimuli) reveals significant interaction with gender. Lower subjective-physiological correlation in women than in men is associated with the female negative affective response to erotic stimuli.

Cross-cultural studies indicate that sexual repression affects women more often than men (Eysenck in Chapter 12 also presents research indicating that female sexual attitudes are more influenced by environmental factors). Heiman and Verhulst consider the hypothesis that male sexuality is less restricted than female sexuality because excessive repression of the male may interfere with procreation. They also point out that since most cultures are male dominated, men tend to legislate repressive rules against female sexuality (this explanation does not, however, apply to homosexuality, which is punished in males rather than in females, in most cultures). Demographic factors such as socioeconomic status and religious background are shown to interact with gender and sexuality.

Psychopathology (depression, mania, schizophrenia, anxiety, drug use and abuse) also interacts with gender and sexual behavior and sexual functioning. Symptoms of psychopathology often influence social relationships and thus may have an indirect effect on sexuality (e.g., in schizophrenia). Alternatively, symptoms such as those in depression and anxiety may inhibit sexual interest and functioning (textbooks of abnormal psychology and psychiatry often list changes in sexual functioning as symptoms of psychopathology). Finally, the classification system of sexual dysfunction, which is medical, biological, and individual-centered in orientation is evaluated. As an alternative to the traditional system, Heiman and Verhulst suggest an interactional approach that emphasizes the interpersonal nature of human sexuality in the study of gender-related issues.

Gender and Psychophysiological Disorders

Research presented by Waldron (Chapter 15, this volume) revealing that sex differences in psychophysiological disorders are uniform in direction across cultures and throughout historical periods provides strong evidence for genetic factors. However, since these differences are variable in magnitude, they also demonstrate environmental influences. For example, death rates from coronary heart disease are about twice as high for men as for women in the United States. This trend was the same in the United States in the past (as well as in other countries at the present), except that the magnitude of the difference is much larger now. Thus, sex differences in coronary heart disease in the contemporary United States reflect both factors that vary cross-culturally and historically (smoking, type-A or coronary-prone behavior pattern) and factors that are consistent cross-culturally (protective effects of female hormones, female susceptibility to nicotine overdose reactions, which affects rate of smoking).

Changes in the sex ratio of psychophysiological disorders during the life cycle may also reveal the interaction between biological and environmental influences. Hypertension, for example, is more common among men than women for adults under age 50, but it is higher among women of older ages. Although selective factors may account for this age pattern (i.e., high mortality of men with high blood pressure so that men with hypertension are less likely to survive to older age), Waldron observes that since female blood pressure tends to increase more rapidly with age in many cultures, inherent biological factors may contribute to sex differences at older age. In contrast, for ages 20-30, an excess of male high blood pressure relative to that of the female is found in societies with economic competition or with more contact of people of different cultures; these stresses may affect men more than women and may contribute to sex differences at a younger age in these societies. Changes in sex ratio of other psychophysiological disorders such as asthma and headache during the life cycle may also reflect biological and environmental influences.

Although the majority of psychophysiological disorders are higher in males than females, the rates of rheumatoid arthritis indicate the opposite trend. Waldron considers psychological and biological factors to explain higher rates of rheumatoid arthritis in women, but unfortunately these factors are not so widely explored as they are in other types of psychophysiological disorders. There is, for example, a substantial amount of research on the relationship between high rates of physiological disorders and the male life style (see Waldron, Chapter 15), but we know very little about whether some aspects of the female life style make her more vulnerable to certain disorders such as rheumatoid arthritis or diabetes mellitis. Behavior that is more expected or accepted for men is a major contributor to their higher death rates. Yet studies reported by Waldron suggest that some cultural and social settings might bring about a reversal in the mortality sex ratio.

Gender and Obesity

Overweight and obesity are purely physical phenomena. However, they tend to have more psychological and social repercussions for females than for males. Foreyt and Goodrick (Chapter 16, this volume) observe that demographic factors (age, race, social class, recent migration, social mobility) are more important in predicting overweight in females than in males. The female role is also associated with more factors conducive to obesity than the male role (food habits, dieting, and exercise). For example, the female role as a homemaker is conducive to overweight because it involves food preparation, lack of exercise, and the accumulation of fat through childbearing. Low levels of activity and exercise are also compatible with the traditional stereotype of ladylike behavior.

Since obesity is considered a deviation from acceptable standards of physical attractiveness, it is more often related to psychological adjustment in women than in men. Like physical unattractiveness, it may become a source of stress or a factor in the perception, diagnosis, and treatment of psychopathology. Also, hospitalization, through a fattening diet (starchy food) and lack of exercise, may increase obesity and may, in turn, contribute to the unattractiveness of mental patients (cf. Chapter 4).

Foreyt and Goodrick point out that psychological and physiological problems reported by obese persons may not result from obesity itself but from dietary restrictions to reduce it. There is more concern about dieting among females than males, but this is due to sex differences in weight consciousness rather than to actual sex differences in overweight and obesity. In considering the futility of weight reduction programs and the physiological and psychological damage to women resulting from them, Foreyt and Goodrick conclude that such programs should be avoided by females. Consistent with the feminist approach, he suggests that dealing with the attitudes of society toward obese women may be far more beneficial than attempts to treat the women's obesity. Weight reduction programs and plastic surgery (cf. Al-Issa, 1980) that attempt to improve the self-image of women may reinforce stereotypes of the female as a sexual object and may perpetuate her treatment by society as a beauty symbol rather than as a real person.

Summary and Conclusion

In addition to methodological problems in the measurement of gender role and gender identity, most data reported on gender and psychopathology are mainly correlational, providing no clear indication whether gender identity and gender role disturbance are manifestations of psychopathology or whether they are the cause of it. Research in gender and psychopathology is mostly based on the traditional model of mental health, which assumes that deviation from gender roles is pathological. In contrast, the androgyny model suggests that flexibility rather than rigidity of gender roles is conducive to better mental health.

The belief that women are more vulnerable to mental illness than men has received no empirical support; sex differences in mental illness are not consistent but vary with the type of institution and the definition of mental illness. There is, however, a gender-related pattern of psychopathology. In explaining sex differences, a major question is whether they are biologically determined or the result of gender-related stresses and other social artifacts such as willingness to report symptoms, contact with physicians, and use of psychiatric facilities. Similarly, many sex differences in symptoms tend to reflect gender role behavior in the normal population (aggression, dependency), but their relationship with psychopathological processes underlying mental illness still remains ambiguous. One early influence on the development of psychopathology and referral to psychiatric facilities originates within the family. Demographic variables such as socioeconomic status, marital status, and employment may have different impacts on psychopathology in males and females, but the evidence in this area is inconsistent. The effect of these variables may be mediated by other factors, for example, the impact of marital status on psychopathology may be expressed through number of children and degree of intimacy in the relationship. The excess of psychopathology among members of single-parent families has attracted the attention of researchers in recent years. Consistencies and variations in sex differences in psychopathology, suicide, and mortality throughout the life cycle (from infancy to old age) illustrate the interplay between complex biological and environmental factors.

Research on depression and phobia challenges the validity of the popular view that women are more vulnerable to affective disorders than men. A high rate of affective disorders in women is not a general phenomenon but is related to factors such as age, marital status, socioeconomic status, and so on. There has been a shift in both research and treatment of affective disorders from emphasis on the dynamics of the person (e.g., in psychoanalysis) to the study of environmental factors. Sex differences in symptoms, premorbid adjustment, and prognosis of schizophrenia could involve both biological and environmental factors. However, data suggest that environmental factors are more related to the development of schizophrenia in females. Studies of other types of psychopathology in women demonstrate the same tendency.

Sex differences in drug use and abuse vary with the legality and strength of the drugs. However, problem drinking and heavy drinking are consistently higher in males than in females. Research on sex differences in drug use and abuse has traditionally emphasized gender-related psychological conflicts and internal motives and given no consideration to the external environment and social context. More recent data indicate that sex differences are associated with demographic factors (marital status, occupational status, education, ethnicity, and religion). The effects and consequences of drinking seem partly to be due to biological predisposition and partly to reflect social expectations and sex stereotypes. The causes and effects of excessive use of prescribed psychotropic drugs by women raise both research and social issues. A basic problem that complicates the study of gender and crime is the relative uncertainty about whether crime is the manifestation of psychopathology, the cause of it, or completely independent of it. There is sex bias in the interpretation of crime; in contrast to male criminality, which is attributed to external conditions such as the socioeconomic structure of society, female criminality is considered to be by traditional theorists a sign of mental illness. An inspection of the data reveals that poor design and methodological problems make it difficult to arrive at a definite conclusion about the role of psychopathology in female criminality.

Sociobiological theory suggests that the universality of patriarchy and sex differences (e.g., in sexual attitudes) support genetic predisposition in the development of gender roles, but this theory completely excludes environmental factors. The evidence supports the view that gender role and gender identity are the products of interaction among genetic, psychological, and social factors. Both personality dimensions such as psychoticism and bodybuild may mediate between genes and sexually dimorphic behavior. Since there is overlap in gender role behavior between males and females, it is suggested that the imposition of rigid sex-typing in society may result in unhappiness, conflicts, and psychopathology. Animal work as well as clinical cases of hormonal abnormalities demonstrate that a predisposition toward sexually dimorphic behavior is determined prenatally and neonatally. The role of female hormones in psychopathology has not been well established. The female sexual response (sexual interests and arousability) appears to be more influenced by environmental factors than that of the male. Different types of psychopathology such as schizophrenia, depression, and anxiety interact with gender and sexual behavior. A system of classification of sexual dysfunction that is based on interpersonal relationship has been suggested to replace the present individualistic medical system. Sex differences in physiological disorders across cultures and throughout history reveal a consistency in direction but a variability in magnitude giving support to the genetic and environmental hypotheses, respectively. Also, shifts in these sex differences from one life stage to the other could also provide useful information about the effects of biological and environmental factors. The major causes of higher rates of mortality among men seem to be linked to behavior that is accepted for males. Overweight and obesity have more psychological and social repercussions for females than for males. Like physical unattractiveness, they may become a source of stress or a factor in the perception and diagnosis of psychopathology. Furthermore, stress of dieting in weight reduction programs for women is associated with many psychological and physiological problems.

References

Al-Issa, I. *The psychopathology of women.* Englewood Cliffs, New Jersey: Prentice Hall, 1980.

Ananth, J. Psychopathology in Indian females. *Social Science and Medicine,* 1978, 12(B), 177-178.

Bane, M. J. *Here to stay: American families in the twentieth century.* New York: Basic Books, 1976.

Barry, H., III. Cultural variations in alcohol abuse. In I. Al-Issa (Ed.), *Culture and psychopathology.* Baltimore, Maryland: University Park Press, 1982.

Beach, F. Cross-species comparisons and the human heritage. In F. Beach (Ed.), *Human sexuality in four perspectives.* Baltimore, Maryland: Johns Hopkins Univ. Press, 1977.

Bebbington, P., Hurry, J., Tennant, C., Sturt, E., & Wing, J. K. Epidemiology of mental disorders in Camberwell. *Psychological Medicine,* 1981, *11,* 561-579.

Brown, G. W., & Harris, T. *Social origins of depression: A study of psychiatric disorders in women.* London, England: Tavistock Publications, 1978.

Brown, G. W., & Harris, T. Social class and affective disorders. In I. Al-Issa (Ed.), *Culture and psychopathology.* Baltimore, Maryland: University Park Press, 1982.

Chesler, P. *Women and madness.* Garden City, New York: Doubleday, 1972.

Constantinople, A. Masculinity-femininity: An exception to the famous dictum? *Psychological Bulletin*, 1973, *80*, 389-407.

Cooper, J. E., Kendell, R. E., Gurland, B. J., Sharpe, L., Copeland, J. R. M., & Simon, R. *Psychiatric diagnosis in New York and London*. London and New York: Oxford Univ. Press, 1972.

Eaton, M. E., Sletten, I. W., Kitchen, A. D., & Smith, R. J. The Missouri automated psychiatric history: Symptom frequencies, sex differences, use of weapons and other findings. *Comprehensive Psychiatry*, 1971, *12*, 264-267.

Fleiss, J. L., Gurland, B. J., Simon, R., & Sharpe, L. Cross-national study of diagnosis of mental disorders: Some demographic correlates of hospital diagnosis in New York and London. *International Journal of Social Psychiatry*, 1973, *19*, 180-186.

Gove, W. R., & Tudor, J. F. Adult sex roles and mental illness. *American Journal of Sociology*, 1973, *78*, 812-835.

Green, R. Adults who want to change sex; adolescents who crossdress; and children called "Sissy" and "Tomboy." In R. Green (Ed.), *Human sexuality: A health practitioner's text*. Baltimore, Maryland: Williams and Wilkins, 1975.

Hoffman, M. *The gay world: Male homosexuality and the social creation of evil*. New York: Basic Books, 1968.

Leighton, A. H., Lambo, T. A., Hughes, C. C., Leighton, D. C., Murphy, J. M., & Macklin, D. B. *Psychiatric disorder among the Yoruba*. Ithaca, New York: Cornell Univ. Press, 1963.

Lewine, R. R. J. Sex differences in schizophrenia: Timing or subtypes? *Psychological Bulletin*, 1981, *90*, 423-444.

Lowe, M., & Hubbard, R. Sociobiology and biosociology: Can science prove the basis of sex differences in behavior? In R. H. Hubbard & M. Lowe (Eds.), *Genes and gender* (Vol. 2):*Pitfalls in research on sex and gender*. New York: Gordian Press, 1979.

Maccoby, E. E. Woman's sociobiological heritage: Destiny or free choice? In J. E. Gullahorn (Ed.), *Psychology and women: In transition*. New York: Wiley, 1979.

Mechanic, D. Sex, illness behavior and the use of health services. *Social Science and Medicine*, 1978, *12*, 207-214.

Mednick, M. T. S. The revolution that never was. *Contemporary Psychology*, 1981, *26*, 101-102.

Mostow, E., & Newberry P. Work role and depression in women: A comparison of workers and housewives in treatment. *American Journal of Orthopsychiatry*, 1975, *45*, 538-548.

Murphy, J. M. Psychiatric labeling in cross-cultural perspective. *Science*, 1976, *191*, 1019-1028.

Newberry, P., Weissman, M. M., & Myers, J. K. Working wives and housewives: Do they differ in mental status and social adjustment? *American Journal of Orthopsychiatry*, 1979, *49*, 282-291.

Orley, J., & Wing, J. K. Psychiatric disorders in two African villages. *Archives of General Psychiatry*, 1979, *36*, 513-520.

Pearlin, L. I. Sex roles and depression. In N. Datan & L. Ginsberg (Eds.), Normative life crises. *Proceedings of the Fourth Life-span Development Psychology Conference*. New York: Academic Press, 1975.

Radloff, L. S. Sex differences in depression. *Sex Roles*, 1975, *1*, 249-265.

Robins, L. N. *Deviant children grown up*. Baltimore: Williams and Wilkins, 1966.

Robbins, L. L. An historical review of the classification of behavior disorders and one current perspective. In L. Eron (Ed.), *The classification of behavior disorders*. Chicago, Illinois: Aldine, 1966.

Spence, J. T. Traits, roles and the concept of androgyny. In J. E. Gullahorn (Ed.), *Psychology and women: In transition*. New York: Wiley, 1979.

Spiro, M. *Gender and culture: Kibbutz women revisited*. Durham, North Carolina: Duke Univ. Press, 1979.

Unger, R. K. Through the looking glass: No wonderland yet! *Presidential address to Division 35 (Psychology of Women), American Psychological Association 89th Annual Convention*. Los Angeles, California, August 24-28, 1981.

Weissman, M. M., & Klerman, G. L. Sex differences and the epidemiology of depression. *Archives of General Psychiatry*, 1977, *34*, 98-111.

Weissman, M. M., & Paykel, E. S. *The depressed woman*. Chicago, Illinois: Univ. of Chicago Press, 1974.

Zigler, E., & Levine, J. Age on first hospitalization of schizophrenics: A developmental approach. *Journal of Abnormal Psychology*, 1981, *90*, 458-467.

Zigler, E., & Phillips, L. Social effectiveness and symptomatic behaviors. *Journal of Abnormal and Social Psychology*, 1960, *61*, 231-238.

2

PATRICIA A. MAFFEO

Gender as a Model for Mental Health

This chapter will define gender-related concepts, describe conceptions of mental health, and identify how these two sets of conceptions are related. The main purpose of the chapter is to present the theoretical rationale for, review the empirical evidence surrounding, and critique each of the gender-based models of mental health. It will also discuss the limitations of our knowledge base in relation to evaluation of the models, as well as limitations of mental health models in general.

Gender and Concepts of Mental Health

Gender is a social category scheme that is based on differentiation by biological sex and establishes differentiation in terms of psychological variables. Unger (1979) refers to gender as the nonphysiological components of sex that are culturally regarded as appropriate to males or females. Symbolism associated with the ascription of maleness or femaleness has been widespread, in some societies extending to inanimate objects; it perhaps gains its salience from its core reference to one's body type. Gender differentiations established by society have tended to assume the force of prescriptions for mental health, another area of symbolism with which our culture has been preoccupied.

Gender has served as a model of mental health primarily in terms of its stereotyped psychological correlates in the forms of personality characteristics

ISBN: 0-12-050350-6

and social roles. Gender ascriptions differentiating males and females have been taken directly to specify mental health, as in the traditional model; ascriptions to only one of the gender categories have been taken as healthier, as in the masculinity model; or ascriptions to both categories have been required for maximum health in all persons, as in the androgyny model. The latter two models would seem to have the long-term effect of removing gender symbolism from models of mental health, as the same standard is proposed for both male and female categories.

The models refer to those personality characteristics and social roles that are components of gender identity. These contents have often been subsumed under the term *sex roles*, a usage that Sherif (1980) argues should be reserved for normative patterns of interactions between males and females. As used here, *personality characteristics* refer to relatively stable predispositions of individuals that lead to consistencies across categories of socially significant behavior. The personality characteristics that this chapter will consider have been labeled *masculine* or *feminine*, according to their stereotypic associations with the gender categories. Masculinity and femininity have been conceptualized by Bakan (1966) in terms of *agency* and *communion*, which refer to self-assertion, self-expansion, and the establishment of separations versus cooperation, contact, and union, respectively. Parsons and Bales (1955) have conceptualized masculinity and femininity in terms of *instrumentality* versus *expressiveness*. *Social roles* refer to behavioral enactments associated with the occupation of particular positions within social groups. Widely held assumptions regarding the nature of the personality characteristics of an individual or social roles occupied on the basis of gender category membership are regarded as *stereotypes*.

It is well to remember that *gender identity*, conceptualized by Sherif (1980) as the set of an individual's psychological relationships to gender in society, is formed in the context of the individual's lifelong affiliations with family, school, ethnic group, or other relevant social groupings. It is in relation to such reference persons, groups, and categories that particular gender-related beliefs, motivations, and values are formed. Behaviors can be understood only in terms of the norms and support systems of the particular groups to which the individual is psychologically related. Gender-based beliefs related to the contents of mental health standards would, of course, also be related to such reference groupings, and such beliefs may, in part, influence an individual's standing on typical mental health indexes, such as self-esteem.

The idea that a person who fulfills a particular cultural or subcultural standard may experience a sense of well-being and pride, as in the self-esteem index, contains a certain amount of face validity. However, Jahoda (1958), in her extensive review of mental health conceptualizations then available in the literature, rejected as inadequate "states of well-being" as unitary criteria of mental health. This judgment was based on considerations regarding the inappropriateness of happiness to certain life situations and the frequent conflict between personal desires and social norms. Indeed, an important agenda for the women's movement and its offshoot in psychology has been the attempt to free individuals from the constraints of personally unsatisfactory gender-related norms.

Jahoda (1958) proposed six criteria culled from the literature for mentally healthy functioning: attitudes toward the self; growth, development, or self-actualization; integration; autonomy; perception of reality; and environmental mastery. Certain of these criteria would seem to be more closely associated with either masculine or feminine personality characteristics or social roles. Autonomy appears, for example, to be more closely related to masculinity; perception of social reality, insofar as an empathic understanding of other individuals is involved, would appear to relate more closely to femininity. Environmental mastery, under which are subsumed adequacy in both love and work, appears to involve both femininity and masculinity, respectively, whereas integration would seem to involve some working combination of both masculinity and femininity. These considerations point up a problem for the evaluation of gender-based models, namely, that the evaluative outcome is dependent on the particular criterion of mental health adopted. Influential thinkers in the field, however, have defined mental health in ways that encompass both masculinity and femininity, and some have specified a multiple criterion approach—simultaneous attainment with respect to a number of the criteria—for the determination of mental health. The multiple criterion approach is clearly more compatible with the androgyny gender-based model of health.

Smith (1950), proposing adjustment, integration, and cognitive adequacy as criteria for mental health, suggests that maximal attainment on all three criteria would be possible only in an ideal society and, furthermore, that the three criteria may not be fully compatible with one another. A society may, for example, press for adjustment at the expense of integration. Smith mentions in particular the conflict between values of Christian altruism and competitive individualism in present American culture, but does not note that the pressure to conform to these values varies considerably by gender. Prior to the present decade, gender linkages with mental health concepts have often been invisible in general theories of mental health, but at times come to light indirectly when gender rather than mental health becomes the focus of study. This chapter will elaborate and evaluate these linkages, which have only recently become articulated as models.

Smith's formulation makes clear that reference group standards can set limits on overall mental health in his multiple criterion approach. With respect to gender linkages, if either the traditional or the masculinity models to be discussed were adopted on a wide scale by society, individuals adapting to societal norms would maximize adjustment at the expense of integration of conflicting personal tendencies. However, a society that adopted the androgyny model would appear to provide a social context in which normative demands were consistent with the demands of personal integration. If integration is specified in the mental health model, an androgyny conception with respect to gender would seem to always be favored.

It has been suggested that mental health is a qualitatively different state from that of mental illness. Observations in support of this distinction are that similar pathogenic events lead to mental illness in one case but not in another, that organic processes are implicated in some forms of mental illness, and that there are similarities in experiences and defense mechanisms among persons who feel in need of treatment and those who do not (Jahoda, 1958). Bradburn (1969) reports independence between his survey respondents' reports of positive and negative affects, although questioning was not in terms of amount. Logan and Kaschak (1980) found sex differences on mental illness but not on mental health indicators, indicating that health is something other than simple absence of illness. This chapter will consider both mental health and illness indicators as they relate to gender identity, leaving the discussion of specific types of psychopathology to other contributors to this volume.

Some of the findings to be reviewed in this chapter relate to self-assessed mental health or illness, which has been criticized on the grounds that people will be unable to respond validly because of the operation of defenses or will be unwilling to do so because of a desire to cast themselves in a good light (Bradburn, 1969). Many of the measures employed, however, have been found to be minimally correlated with social desirability or have demonstrated the necessary construct validity to challenge the criticisms (Berzins, Welling, & Wetter, 1978; Bradburn, 1969; Spence & Helmreich, 1978). Evidence yet to be reported does suggest the concerns to be more valid for one gender grouping than another. However, mental health or illness indexes in this review are not limited to self-reports, but include data from treatment records and behavioral data from experimental situations.

The Traditional Model

Theoretical Rationale

The traditional model of mental health based on gender postulates that gender identity should be consonant with biological sex for optimal functioning. The model is often based on the idea that biological sex differences are widespread and that it is desirable and healthy for an individual to emphasize characteristics that are consistent with such biological predispositions (Eysenck, Chapter 12, this volume). Another justification assumes that society will benefit by division of social roles along sex-typed lines (Parsons & Bales, 1953). The model proposes differential standards for males and females, based on stereotypes. Males are considered healthy when they exhibit personality characteristics such as independence, assertiveness, competitiveness, and rationality. Females are considered healthy when they exhibit personality characteristics such as warmth, emotional expressiveness, a concern for relationships, and dependency. It is also assumed that healthy individuals adopt social roles considered appropriate for their sex, for example, a breadwinner role in the case of the male, and a nurturant homemaker role in the case of the female.

It is difficult to find explicit articulated statements of the traditional model of mental health. The traditional model is implicit when the psychoanalytic concept of penis envy is used to imply that women who compete with men in the world of work are engaged in a neurotic denial of femininity (Thomas, 1962). It is similarly implicit in Deutsch's (1944/1973) conception of the female as naturally passive, masochistic, and narcissistic, with the implication that deviations from these qualities represent defensive failures of adjustment. Lerner (1978) has narrowed the connection somewhat, suggesting that norms for traditional traits and roles may have adaptive consequences for individuals who are insecure with respect to core gender identity and have a borderline level of adjustment.

Social learning theorists (Kagan, 1964; Mussen & Rutherford, 1963) have assumed that it was the function of socialization agents to foster the development of appropriate masculine or feminine orientations in children. Deviations have generally been considered to be undesirable in this approach, and to result from inadequate socialization.

LaTorre (1979) encouraged sex-typing on the grounds that since society expects some degree of gender differentiation, an individual with an androgynous identity will most likely be rejected. He further argued that attempts to foster the development of both masculine and feminine qualities in children would not only be a much more difficult task in terms of content to be learned, but also in terms of the discriminations required concerning the appropriate situations for the expression of each domain. He suggested that this discrimination would be difficult for the young child and that the resulting confusion and conflict would likely lead to psychopathological symptoms.

Empirical Evidence

Research conducted from within the traditional perspective, assessing masculinity and femininity as mutally exclusive bipolar traits, has not yielded consistent support for the association of high levels of sex-typing with adjustment. High femininity in females has been correlated with high anxiety, low self-esteem, and low social acceptance (Consentino & Heilbrun, 1964; Emmerich, 1959; Gall, 1969; Gray, 1959; Sears, 1970; Sopchak, 1952). Although high masculinity has been correlated with superior adjustment during adolescence (Mussen, 1961), it has been correlated with high neuroticism and low self-acceptance during adulthood (Harford, Willis, & Deabler, 1967; Mussen, 1962). The traditional model, especially in the case of females, has been further weakened by evidence to be presented under the topics of the androgyny model and the masculinity model.

Despite the lack of empirical validation, there is evidence that clinicians and counselors have held differential standards of mental health for males and females, based on gender stereotypes. The first line of evidence consists of therapist or counselor attitudes about mental health standards. Broverman, Broverman, Clarkson, Rosenkrantz, and Vogel (1970), for example, found that there was high agreement among clinicians as to which pole of a set of bipolar adjectives represented more healthy behavior for an adult. Clinician standards for men did not differ from those for an adult, sex unspecified. However, clinicians considered healthy women ideally to be less independent, less logical, and less competent than the healthy man or adult. Further evidence revealing differential therapist attitudes is reported by Neulinger (1968), Aslin (1977), and Delk and Ryan (1977).

The second line of evidence consists of clinical or counseling analogue studies. Miller (1974), for example, found that a patient described as passive was rated by clinicians as better adjusted when labeled female as opposed to male. Passivity was also found to be targeted more often for intervention when attributed to a male. Abramowitz, Weitz, Schwartz, Amira, Gomes, and Abramowitz (1975); Bowman (1976); Feinblatt and Gold (1976); Schlossberg and Pietrofesa (1973); and Thomas and Stewart (1971) also reported analogue studies revealing differential clinician standards for males and females.

A third line of evidence comes from a study of actual therapists and patients. Fabrikant (1974) found that therapists and patients differed in their perception of their therapists' beliefs. Whereas therapists stated they felt that marriage should be a partnership and that there should be a single standard of sexual behavior for marital partners, patients believed their therapists' attitudes were that the male should dominate the marriage and that they held a sexual double standard.

A fourth line of evidence indicating acceptance by clinicians of the traditional model comes from the "Report of the Task Force on Sex Bias and Sex-Role Stereotyping in Psychotherapeutic Practice" (1975). Female members of APA divisions 12, 17, 29, and 35 were surveyed, asking for instances of sexism encountered as either consumers or practitioners of psychotherapy. "Fostering of traditional sex roles" was articulated as one of the four principal categories into which instances of sexism fell.

Failures to find differential mental health standards for males and females have been reported by Billingsley (1977), B. J. Goldberg (1976), L. H. Goldberg (1974), Harris and Lucas (1976), Kahn (1977), Maslin and Davis (1975), Maxfield (1976), and Stearns, Penner, and Kimmel (1978). However, the intent of attitude or analogue studies, particularly those conducted subsequent to the well-publicized Broverman study (Broverman *et al.*, 1970), may well have been transparent to subjects, leading to the elicitation of socially desirable responses from subjects and masking differential standards for males and females that may have existed.

In any event, therapist responses in an analogue situation may not relate directly to actual therapeutic behavior. The study by Fabrikant (1974), for example, indicated that therapists' reports of their attitudes differed from their actual patients' perceptions of them. No studies have been conducted, either of process or outcome, which compare sexist (traditional) with nonsexist therapy (Sherman, 1980).

Criticism

LaTorre's (1979) conviction that sex-typing of children would relieve them of the necessity to make behavioral discriminations seems to ignore the fact that behavioral discriminations are continually required in any ongoing social interchange, whatever one's gender identification. Bem (1978) has criticized the traditional model of mental health for preventing many individuals from developing and utilizing both masculine and feminine characteristics, which will arise spontaneously in both sexes if not inhibited by the imposition of contradictory social control processes. Gender-related socialization, therefore, involves the additional discrimination that a whole class of possible behaviors are not to be engaged in because of one's gender. Lerner (1978) has further discussed ways in which gender-related stereotypes have an inhibiting effect on development. Stereotypes create pressure to conform to ideal generalizations of males and females, rather than allowing development of unique potentials or skills. Negative effects of stereotypes have also been described by Farrell (1974). The traditional model can be further criticized for its lack of empirical validation, which has been discussed earlier in this section.

The Androgyny Model

Theories of Sex Role Integration

The androgyny model of mental health has been implicit in the writings of Jung, Bakan, Block, and Rebecca, Hefner, and Oleshansky, although these authors did not use the term *androgyny*. The model was explicit and labeled *androgyny* by Sandra Bem. The model suggests that the healthy personality can and should include both sets of characteristics conceived of as masculine and feminine. Jung (1951/1959) introduced the concepts of *animus* and *anima* to refer to unconscious archetypal modalities that are projected onto persons of the opposite sex. In Jung's terms, a man's anima refers to drives for relatedness, concreteness, emotionality, and instinct. A woman's animus represents drives for aggressive assertiveness, rationality, discrimination, separation, and judgment. Jung thought animus and anima were integrated into conscious thought and behavior in certain high-functioning individuals during the adult developmental phase of individuation, in which psychological tendencies not previously acknowledged are admitted into awareness (Jung, 1939/1959).

Bakan (1966) similarly postulated that males and females differentially embody two fundamental modalities of all living forms—*agency* and *communion*. Agency, the male principle, represents the organism as an individual, concerned with self-assertion, mastery, and the establishment of separations. Communion, the female principle, represents the individual in relation to others, concerned with cooperation, contact, and union. Bakan felt that a developmental task for the individual was to integrate agency and communion, both necessary human qualities.

Block (1973) discussed sex role integration as a developmental phenomenon in the context of Loevinger's (1966) theory of ego development. Loevinger's theory postulates a series of milestones that represent ways of organizing experience that are characterized by impulsiveness, conformity, conscientiousness, and autonomy. At the autonomous level of ego development, individuals are described as integrating opposing tendencies of the personality, including masculine and feminine tendencies.

Rebecca, Hefner, and Oleshansky (1976) postulated a model of sex role development consisting of three stages. In Stage I, sex role conceptions are undifferentiated. During Stage II, the child develops polarized sex role concepts as a result of cognitive and socialization processes. In Stage III, stereotypic sex roles are transcended through flexible choice of behavioral and emotional expression in accordance with situational demands and personal integrity.

Bem (1976) has been a major proponent of the idea that psychological androgyny, as opposed to sex-typing, is associated with mental health. Bem took no position regarding the development of an androgynous personality, but reasoned that human beings need both instrumental and expressive characteristics to be personally effective. She developed the first measure of psychological androgyny, which has since been widely used.

Empirical Evidence

The idea that psychological androgyny is associated with superior mental health has received a moderate amount of empirical support. Traditional approaches assumed that masculine and feminine personality characteristics were mutually exclusive, and measures reflected the proximity of an individual's score to one end of a bipolar masculinity-femininity continuum. However, several measures are now available that allow assessment of masculinity and femininity conceptualized as orthogonal unipolar personality characteristics. Bem's Sex Role Inventory (Bem, 1974), Spence and Helmreich's Personality Attributes Questionnaire (Spence & Helmreich, 1978), and Berzins, Welling, and Wetter's PRF-Andro Scale (Berzins *et al.*, 1978) yield assignment to masculine, feminine, androgynous, and undifferentiated sex role categories based on joint classification of the masculinity and femininity subscales of these measures. Investigators using the three instruments have generally found persons classified as androgynous to have the highest self-esteem, followed by masculine, feminine, and undifferentiated persons (Bem, 1977; Evanoski & Maher, 1979; O'Connor, Mann, & Bardwick, 1978; Spence & Helmreich, 1978; Wetter, 1975). High scores on the masculinity scale generally have the highest association with self-esteem. Evanoski and Maher (1979), for example, investigated the relationship of masculinity, femininity, and their combination to self-esteem. For self-esteem, masculinity accounted for the greatest proportion of variance for each group, although femininity added a significant proportion of variance in each group except males. The combination of masculinity and femininity added a significant proportion above that contributed by its individual components only for the high socioeconomic status group, indicating the particular advantage of androgyny for this group.

Wells (1979) examined the relationship between sex role category and several indexes of psychological adjustment, namely, mastery, social relations, superior adjustment (coping), and self-esteem. Masculine adolescents were found to have superior mastery; androgyny was related to superior social relations among girls, whereas only femininity contributed to superior social relations among boys. With respect to adjustment (or coping), high masculinity alone was predictive of superior adjustment in girls, whereas both femininity and masculinity were predictive in boys; masculine girls were found to have highest self-esteem, whereas for boys the perplexing finding of highest self-esteem among undifferentiated subjects was obtained. A general trend in this study seems to indicate the particular importance of cross-gender characteristics on certain criterion measures.

Waterman and Whitbourne (1979) found androgynous individuals to have highest scores on the Inventory of Psychosocial Development, measuring adaptive traits developed during Eriksonian life stages. The androgynous group was followed in order by masculine, feminine, and undifferentiated groups, each of which differed significantly from each other. Orlofsky (1977) found that a significantly larger proportion of female undergraduates who fell into the highest category of Eriksonian ego identity were androgynous; the largest proportion of males in this category were sex-typed, but this difference was not significant.

Several studies suggest that androgynous persons may be advantaged in terms of marital satisfaction or adjustment. Goldstein (1979) found wives' satisfaction to be greater in androgynous dyads, a relationship that was stronger the greater the degree of the wife's job involvement. This suggests that the advantages of particular sex role categories may be dependent on the status of social role adoptions. Nettles (1978) found persons in problem marriages to be less androgynous, but could not rule out self-esteem as a more general factor accounting for this result.

Bem and Lenney (1976) found androgynous subjects to be more situationally adaptive and flexible with respect to exhibiting masculine and feminine stereotyped behavior, and to report more comfort when engaging in counterstereotypic behavior. Helmreich, Spence, and Holahan's (1979) conceptual replication found androgynous males to show significantly greater flexibility (lower sex-typed preference scores) than did masculine males. Among both sexes, androgynous subjects showed greater comfort with all types of tasks, although they were not significantly different from masculine subjects on this variable. However, relationships were low in magnitude, either because associations between personality dimensions and behaviors are generally low or because the behaviors themselves were inherently trivial.

Baucom and Danker-Brown (1979) showed that whereas sex-typed subjects showed both cognitive and motivational deficits in response to a helplessness manipulation, androgynous subjects showed only dysphoric mood. Results are consistent with the association of androgyny with flexibility.

The idea of androgyny can be extended to social role adoptions as well as personality traits, suggesting that a person could be healthier having adopted a combination of instrumental and expressive roles, for example, an occupational as well as a family role. Gove and Tudor (1973) and Gove (1972) provide evidence that the married of both sexes have lower mental illness rates than the unmarried, due in part to the benefits of emotional support. This suggests that the expressive roles that marriage facilitates have a positive effect on mental health for both sexes. However, mental illness rates are higher for married women than for married men, whereas rates are equal or slightly higher for men among the never married, widowed, or divorced. Gove and Tudor (1973) thought that married men were advantaged in these studies because they occupied both family and work roles and thus had two sources of gratification, whereas the women studied often did not have instrumental work roles or work roles commensurate with their levels of education. Gove and Geerken (1977), examining the presence of psychiatric symptomatology among employed husbands, employed wives, and unemployed wives, found that employed wives reported fewer symptoms than unemployed wives, providing support for a social role explanation of the differential illness rates for men and women.

Ilfeld (1977) also documented benefits of employment for women, finding that women's psychiatric symptoms fell to the overall level of men's only for those with upper-, upper-middle-, or lower-middle-class occupational statuses. Birnbaum (1975) similarly found that employed professional women, whether single or married, possessed higher self-esteem in their middle adult years than did equally gifted unemployed homemakers.

Gove and Tudor (1973) suggested that women's greater adoption of the service role, that is, a readiness to adjust or subordinate one's needs to those of others, may contribute to the higher symptom rate among married women. There is some evidence that the presence of children may decrease satisfaction and conflict with occupational demands for both sexes (Campbell, Converse, & Rodgers, 1976; Hicks & Platt, 1970; Pleck, Staines, & Lang, 1980). Birnbaum (1975) reported, however, that her sample of single professional women regretted having missed out on motherhood. Later in the life span, parents with empty nests were found to be less depressed than nonparents or parents with children still at home (Radloff, 1975).

Livson (1976) studied two groups of healthy women, one group whose level of adjustment improved between ages 40 and 50, the other whose level of adjustment remained stable between these ages. The stable group was labeled *traditional* on the basis of Q-sorts indicating gregariousness and nurturance; the improvers were labeled *independent* on the basis of Q-sorts indicating ambition, skepticism, and unconventionality. Livson suggested that the fit between a woman's life style and personality may be responsible for the interruption of the development of independents during those middle adult years focused on child rearing, although neither group resented their parenting role. Hoffman and Fidell (1979) also provide evidence that women who have made life choices consistent with gender identity appear to be well-adjusted.

Criticism

The androgyny model of mental health has been criticized on theoretical grounds by Sandra Bem, one of its original proponents. Bem (1980) stated that although the model was initially proposed with the partial intent of freeing women and men from the constraints of sex role stereotypes, the effect was to substitute a dual for a single standard of behavior. Individuals according to the androgyny model must strive toward two ideals—both masculinity and femininity—rather than toward only one or the other.

Another criticism of the androgyny models rests on empirical findings that contradict the relationship of androgyny with adjustment or suggest that the apparent advantages of androgyny are due predominantly to the contribution of its masculinity component. These findings are suggestive of a third model of mental health based on gender—a masculinity model.

The Masculinity Model

Empirical Evidence

In a number of investigations there is no clear advantage for androgynous over masculine subjects for one or both sexes. In some instances the androgynous, and in others, the masculine, groups obtained higher scores; these groups often did not differ significantly from each other but differed significantly from one or both of the other two groups. Wetter (1975), for example, found that androgynous individuals were significantly higher on self-esteem than indeterminate or feminine-typed persons; they scored slightly but not significantly higher than masculine-typed persons of both sexes. Self-esteem was directly related to masculinity scores in this study and was generally orthogonal to femininity scores. Bem (1977), alternatively, found self-esteem scores to be significantly higher in androgynous females than in masculine females, whereas masculine males possessed highest self-esteem scores, although not significantly higher than the scores of androgynous males. Self-esteem in this study was found to be significantly related to masculinity only in males, but to both masculinity and femininity in females. Evanoski and Maher (1979) similarly found that masculinity alone accounted for significant proportions of the variances for the variables self-esteem and inner-directedness in males. Deutsch and Gilbert (1976) found that traditionally sex-typed men rated themselves as significantly better adjusted than androgynous men. Colten (1978) found that masculine and androgynous women possessed the lowest levels of anxiety and depression but that the groups did not differ significantly from each other. Jones, Chernovetz, and Hansson (1978) found that androgynous males showed significantly greater externality of control and problem drinking than did masculine males, and that masculine females reported more sexual maturity than androgynous females.

Theoretical Rationale

A number of explanations have been advanced to account for "masculine supremacy" effects. Bem's (1975) finding that androgynous and masculine women were more interactive with a kitten than were feminine women may be explained by suggesting that masculine (assertive) characteristics are necessary precursors to the expression of feminine (nurturant) qualities.

A second explanation advanced is based on the observation that masculine characteristics are more valued by our society (Broverman *et al.*, 1970; McKee & Sherriffs, 1959; Sherriffs & McKee, 1957). Persons high in masculine characteristics should receive more social reinforcements and resultantly feel more self-confident (Jones *et al.*, 1978; Kelly & Worell, 1977; Yager & Baker, 1979).

Yager and Baker (1979) suggest a third explanation, one related to the learning principle that small, immediate rewards are more powerfully reinforcing than are larger, delayed rewards. They suggest that although there may be long-term rewards associated with femininity, such as longer life, lower incidence of health problems, and interpersonal closeness, these tend to be overshadowed by the more immediate gratifications of powerful jobs, greater influence, and economic self-sufficiency. The rewards of the masculine role may be not only more immediate but less subtle in their impact.

Kelly and Worell (1977) have further suggested that androgynous persons may be troubled by the presence of greater behavioral conflict due to the simultaneous activation of masculine and feminine response tendencies. This problem, it would seem, results from a lack of construct validity in our presently available measures of androgyny. Whereas Bem (1978) conceptually defined androgyny as a functional blend of masculine and feminine characteristics into a single act, our measures of androgyny reflect simply the high presence of both kinds of characteristics in a single individual (Kaplan, 1979). If the androgynous person is skilled in functionally blending masculinity and femininity, the possibility of conflict should be alleviated or greatly reduced.

Criticism

Although a number of studies have shown either no clear advantages or, in the case of the Jones *et al.* (1978) study, disadvantages for the androgynous over the masculine group, there have been many instances in which femininity also contributed a significant proportion of variance toward a positive outcome, for example, in studies by Bem (1977); Bem, Martyna, and Watson (1976); Evanoski and Maher (1979); Spence, Helmreich, and Stapp (1975); Waterman and Whitbourne (1979); and Wells (1979). This lends credence to the view that androgyny is more desirable than masculinity in many instances.

Bem (1976) postulated an association between androgyny and adaptability, which suggests that androgynous individuals should have an overall advantage rather than an advantage on any or every particular variable. An examination of the performance of the sex types across a number of criterion variables is required to test this hypothesis. Jones *et al.* (1978) followed this procedure and concluded that masculinity was more strongly related to positive outcomes across eight studies that they conducted. Although these authors reported on an impressive program of research, their data were limited to one age group in one geographical locale and described criterion variables singly rather than in combination. These comments are not intended to single out this study for particular criticism, since in many ways it is more adequate than most reported on. They are intended to suggest that conclusions must be suspended until a more complete analysis is undertaken, that is, one that gives attention to statistical power, methodological adequacy of designs, reliability and validity of measures, and conceptual relevance of dependent variables to the problem, including the range of variables requiring investigation.

Finally, advantages for masculine over androgynous groupings have been found more often for male subjects (Bem, 1977; Deutsch & Gilbert, 1976; Evanoski & Maher, 1979; Jones *et al.*, 1978; Silvern & Ryan, 1979). Watson (1979) has suggested that the self-esteem of masculine males is defensively inflated, a process that he did not find to be present in androgynous males or in females. Babl (1979) also reported that masculine males increase their masculinity and antisocial behavior scores as a form of compensatory responding under conditions of threat. Because of the possibility that scores on self-report measures may reflect defensively motivated distortions, associations between indexes of well-being and masculinity in males must be viewed with caution. Yager and Baker (1979) further suggest that the masculine supremacy effect is most evident with self-report as opposed to behavioral measures and may represent a form of method variance.

Limitations of Our Knowledge Base

There are, at present, a number of considerations that limit our ability to draw conclusions and to endorse a particular gender-based model of mental health. First, many of our findings are correlational in nature, making it difficult to know what leads to what. Does self-esteem, for example, result from high levels of masculinity and femininity, or is self-esteem a precursory quality associated with the development of these positively valued clusters of traits? Some writers have suggested that the sex role inventories are measuring nothing other than self-esteem, since only socially desirable items are included in the scales (Jones *et al.*, 1978; Myers & Sugar, 1978). Use of the *t*-ratio or combination *t*-ratio and median-split approach would seem to circumvent this problem somewhat, as would the use of self-esteem scales that do not mirror the social competency items of the androgyny scales.

Second, many of our findings are gender specific. In some cases, different sex role categories for males and females appear to have an advantage on some variables, and in other cases, data for one sex or the other is simply missing.

It is well to remember, also, that findings expressed in terms of a comparison of the various sex role categories may be limited to the particular scale employed (Kelly, Furman, & Young, 1978; Lenney, 1979). The scales have been developed from somewhat differing theoretical perspectives and use differing items, presentation formats, etc. (Worell, 1978). It is perhaps not surprising that Kelly *et al.* (1978) found a large proportion of subjects classified into different sex role categories by the several measures of androgyny.

Another problem with research in this area is the failure to consider the salience to the individual of the variables studied. Markus (1977) has pointed out that traditional self-description inventories such as those considered here do not assess whether or not the trait being measured forms a well-articulated schema that is important to the respondent. It is unclear whether salience should be assessed with respect to the personality scale labels of masculinity and femininity or with respect to the component factors of these scales. Salience with respect to social roles would seem to refer to whether or not particular roles are specifically desired. In a similar vein, Garnets and Pleck (1979) suggested that sex role strain leading to low self-esteem will occur when there is a discrepancy between real self-concept and same-sex ideal, but only when the sex role variable is highly salient to the individual. Their analysis predicts that a sex-typed person will have self-esteem equivalent to an androgynous person as long as sex-typing corresponds to the same-sex ideal. Such cognitive variables have been inadequately investigated, although the studies cited by Livson (1976) and Hoffman and Fidell (1979), which investigated the fit between personality and social roles, are steps in this direction.

Finally, the database needs to be completed with respect to the simultaneous evaluation of an individual on several criteria for mental health, as extensive development on one dimension may lead to the neglect of others also necessary for health (Block, 1973; Jung, 1939/1959; Smith, 1950). The relationships between gender-associated traits and roles and mental health criteria also require fuller assessment across the life span. We know, for example, that masculinity in males is correlated with superior adjustment in adolescence but not in adulthood (Mussen, 1961, 1962), that bright women choosing the homemaker role had higher self-esteem after making this choice but lower self-esteem than their professional counterparts 15–20 years later (Birnbaum, 1975; Rossi, 1965), and that males and females with empty nests showed less depression than counterparts with no children or with children still at home (Radloff, 1975). Longitudinal studies would be helpful in sorting out cohort effects.

Limitations of Mental Health Models

In conclusion, it is important to bear in mind general problems associated with the postulation of models. The first has to do with the interface between the model and a particular individual. A general standard of behavior cannot take into account individual differences due to temperament, past history, goals, or values. These, however, must be considered in, at the very least, tailoring a general standard to a particular individual. It is this consideration that led Bem to retract her emphasis on androgyny as a model for mental health.

A second problem has to do with the interface between the model and a particular historical period, with its associated cultural and subcultural norms. For example, the traditional model of mental health may have been more viable during the Victorian era or in the 1950s, post-World War II; the masculinity model may have been more viable during the war years; and the androgyny model may have been more viable during the 1970s, particularly among liberals, intellectuals, or those with high socioeconomic status.

Despite these considerations, it is still appropriate to expand our knowledge base and to make considered judgments regarding advantages and disadvantages of particular gender-related traits or social roles based on normative data. Since gender has served as an organizing principle in society, it is well to bring the mental health implications of gender-associated characteristics into the realm of scientific investigation.

References

Abramowitz, S. I., Weitz, L. J., Schwartz, J. M., Amira, S., Gomes, B., & Abramowitz, C. V. Comparative counselor inferences toward women with medical school aspirations. *Journal of College Student Personnel,* 1975, *16,* 128-130.

Aslin, A. L. Feminist and community mental health center psychotherapists' expectations of mental health for women. *Sex Roles,* 1977, *3,* 537-544.

Babl, J. D. Compensatory masculine responding as a function of sex role. *Journal of Consulting and Clinical Psychology,* 1979, *47,* 252-257.

Bakan, D. *The duality of human existence.* Chicago, Illinois: Rand-McNally, 1966.

Baucom, D. H., & Danker-Brown, P. Influence of sex roles on the development of learned helplessness. *Journal of Consulting and Clinical Psychology,* 1979, *47,* 928-936.

Bem, S. L. The measurement of psychological androgyny. *Journal of Consulting and Clinical Psychology,* 1974, *47,* 155-162.

Bem, S. L. Sex role adaptability: One consequence of psychological androgyny. *Journal of Personality and Social Psychology,* 1975, *31,* 634-643.

Bem, S. L. Probing the promise of androgyny. In A. Kaplan & J. Bean (Eds.), *Beyond sex role stereotypes: Readings toward a psychology of androgyny.* Boston, Massachusetts: Little, Brown, 1976.

Bem, S. L. On the utility of alternative procedures for assessing psychological androgyny. *Journal of Consulting and Clinical Psychology,* 1977, *45,* 196-205.

Bem, S. L. Beyond androgyny: Some presumptuous prescriptions for a liberated sexual identity. In J. Sherman & F. Denmark (Eds.), *Psychology of women: Future directions of research.* New York: Psychological Dimensions, 1978.

Bem, S. L. *Gender schema theory: A cognitive account of sex typing.* Address presented at the meeting of the American Psychological Association, Montreal, Canada, September 1980.

Bem, S. L., & Lenney, E. Sex-typing and the avoidance of cross-sex behavior. *Journal of Personality and Social Psychology,* 1976, *33,* 48-54.

Bem, S. L., Martyna, W., & Watson, C. Sex typing and androgyny: Further explorations of the expressive domain. *Journal of Personality and Social Psychology,* 1976, *34,* 183-190.

Berzins, J. I., Welling, M. A., & Wetter, R. E. A new measure of psychological androgyny based on the Personality Research Form. *Journal of Consulting and Clinical Psychology,* 1978, *46,* 126-138.

Billingsley, D. Sex bias in psychotherapy: An examination of client sex, client pathology, and therapist sex on treatment planning. *Journal of Consulting and Clinical Psychology,* 1977, *45,* 250-256.

Birnbaum, J. A. Life patterns and self esteem in gifted family oriented and career-committed women. In M. T. S. Mednick, S. S. Tangri, & L. W. Hoffman (Eds.), *Women and achievement: Social and motivational analyses.* New York: Halsted Press, 1975.

Block, J. H. Conceptions of sex role: some cross-cultural and longitudinal perspectives. *American Psychologist,* 1973, *28,* 512-526.

Bowman, P. R. The relationship between attitudes toward women and the treatment of activity and passivity (Doctoral dissertation, Boston University School of Education, 1976). *Dissertation Abstracts International,* 1976, *36,* 5779B. (University Microfilms No. 76-11, 644)

Bradburn, N. M. *The structure of psychological well-being.* Chicago, Illinois: Aldine, 1969.

Broverman, I. K., Broverman, D. M., Clarkson, F. E., Rosenkrantz, P., & Vogel, S. R. Sex-role stereotypes and clinical judgments of mental health. *Journal of Consulting Psychology,* 1970, *34,* 1-7.

Campbell, A., Converse, P. A., & Rodgers, W. L. *The quality of American life: Perceptions, evaluations, and satisfaction.* New York: Russell Sage Foundation, 1976.

Colten, M. E. *Sex role identity, self esteem and social skills.* Paper presented at the meeting of the American Psychological Association, Toronto, Canada, August 1978.

Cosentino, F., & Heilbrun, A. B. Anxiety correlates of sex-role identity in college students. *Psychological Reports,* 1964, *14,* 729-730.

Delk, J. L., & Ryan, T. T. A-B status and sex stereotyping among psychotherapists and patients. *The Journal of Nervous and Mental Disease,* 1977, *164,* 253-262.

Deutsch, C. J., & Gilbert, L. A. Sex role stereotypes: Effect on perceptions of self and others and on personal adjustment. *Journal of Counseling Psychology,* 1976, *23,* 373-379.

Deutsch, H. *The psychology of women* (Vol. 1)—*Girlhood.* New York: Bantam, 1973. (Originally published, 1944.)

Emmerich, W. Parental identification in young children. *Genetic Psychology Monographs,* 1959, *60,* 257-308.

Evanoski, P. J., & Maher, T. J. *Masculinity, femininity, and psychological well-being.* Paper presented at the meeting of the American Psychological Association, New York, September 1979.

Fabrikant, B. The psychotherapist and the female patient: Perceptions and change. In V. Franks & V. Burtle (Eds.), *Women in therapy.* New York: Brunner/Mazel, 1974.

Farrell, W. *The liberated man.* New York: Random House, 1974.

Feinblatt, J. A., & Gold, A. R. Sex roles and the psychiatric referral process. *Sex Roles,* 1976, *2,* 109-122.

Gall, M. D. The relationship between masculinity-femininity and manifest anxiety. *Journal of Clinical Psychology,* 1969, *25,* 294-295.

Garnets, L., & Pleck, J. H. Sex role identity, androgyny, and sex role transcendence: A sex role strain analysis. *Psychology of Women Quarterly*, 1979, *3*, 270-283.

Goldberg, B. J. Mental health practice as social control: Practitioners' choices of therapy goals as a function of sex of client, situations, and other practitioners' opinions (Doctoral dissertation, State University of New York at Stony Brook, 1975). *Dissertation Abstracts International*, 1976, *36*, 5256B. (University Microfilms No. 76-7570)

Goldberg, L. H. Attitudes of clinical psychologists toward women (Doctoral dissertation, Illinois Institute of Technology, 1973). *Dissertation Abstracts International*, 1974, *35*, 1017B-1018B. (University Microfilms No. 74-16, 997)

Goldstein, E. *Androgyny in dual-career couples: Its relation to wives' marital satisfaction*. Paper presented at the meeting of the American Psychological Association, New York, September 1979.

Gove, W. R. The relationship between sex roles, marital status and mental illness, *Social Forces*, 1972, *51*, 282-292.

Gove, W. R., & Geerken, M. R. The effect of children and employment on the mental health of married men and women. *Social Forces*, 1977, *56*, 66-76.

Gove, W. R., & Tudor, J. F. Adult sex roles and mental illness. *American Journal of Sociology*, 1973, *78*, 812-835.

Gray, S. W. Perceived similarity to parents and adjustment. *Child Development*, 1959, *30*, 91-107.

Harford, T. C., Willis, C. H., & Deabler, H. L. Personality correlates of masculinity-femininity. *Psychological Reports*, 1967, *21*, 390-395.

Harris, L. H., & Lucas, M. E. Sex-role stereotyping. *Social Work*, 1976, *21*, 390-395.

Helmreich, R. L., Spence, J. T., & Holahan, C. K. Psychological androgyny and sex role flexibility: A test of two hypotheses. *Journal of Personality and Social Psychology*, 1979, *37*, 1631-1644.

Hicks, M., & Platt, M. Marital happiness and stability: A review of research in the 60's. *Journal of Marriage and the Family*, 1970, *32*, 553-574.

Hoffman, D. M., & Fidell, L. S. Characteristics of androgynous, undifferentiated, masculine, and feminine middle-class women. *Sex Roles*, 1979, *5*, 765-782.

Ilfeld, F. W. *Sex differences in psychiatric symptomatology*. Paper presented at the meeting of the American Psychological Association, San Francisco, California, August 1977.

Jahoda, M. *Current concepts of positive mental health*. New York: Basic Books, 1958.

Jones, W. H., Chernovetz, M. E. O'C., & Hansson, R. O. The enigma of androgyny: Differential implications for males and females? *Journal of Consulting and Clinical Psychology*, 1978, *46*, 298-313.

Jung, C. G. Aion: Researches into the phenomenology of the self. In *Collected works* (Vol. 9). New York: Pantheon, 1959. (Originally published, 1951.)

Jung, C. G. Conscious, unconscious, and individuation. In *Collected works* (Vol. 9): *The archetypes and the collective unconscious*. New York: Pantheon, 1959. (Originally published, 1939.)

Kagan, J. Acquisition and significance of sex-typing and sex role identity. In M. L. Hoffman & L. W. Hoffman (Eds.), *Review of child development research*. New York: Russell Sage Foundation, 1964.

Kahn, L. G. Effects of sex and feminist orientation of therapists on clinical judgments (Doctoral dissertation, Columbia University, 1976). *Dissertation Abstracts International*, 1977, *37*, 3613B. (University Microfilms No. 76-29, 598)

Kaplan, A. G. Clarifying the concept of androgyny: Implications for therapy. *Psychology of Women Quarterly*, 1979, *3*, 223-230.

Kelly, J. A., Furman, W., & Young, V. Problems associated with the typological measurement of sex roles and androgyny. *Journal of Consulting and Clinical Psychology*, 1978, *46*, 1574-1576.

Kelly, J. A., & Worell, J. New formulations of sex roles and androgyny: A critical review. *Journal of Consulting and Clinical Psychology*, 1977, *45*, 1101-1115.

LaTorre, R. A. *Sexual identity*. Chicago, Illinois: Nelson-Hall, 1979.

Lenney, E. Androgyny: Some audacious assertions toward its coming of age. *Sex Roles*, 1979, *5*, 703-719.

Lerner, H. E. Adaptive and pathogenic aspects of sex-role stereotypes: Implications for parenting and psychotherapy. *American Journal of Psychiatry*, 1978, *135*, 48-52.

Livson, F. B. Patterns of personality development in middle-aged women: A longitudinal study. *International Journal of Aging and Human Development*, 1976, *7*, 107-115.

Loevinger, J. The meaning and measurement of ego development. *American Psychologist*, 1966, *21*, 195-206.

Logan, D. D., & Kaschak, E. The relationship of sex, sex role, and mental health. *Psychology of Women Quarterly*, 1980, *4*, 573-580.

McKee, J. P. & Sherriffs, A. C. Men's and women's beliefs, ideas, and self-concepts. *American Journal of Sociology*, 1959, *64*, 356-363.

Markus, H. Self-schemata and processing information about the self. *Journal of Personality and Social Psychology*, 1977, *35*, 63-78.

Maslin, A., & Davis, J. L. Sex-role stereotyping as a factor in mental health standards among counselors-in-training. *Journal of Counseling Psychology*, 1975, *22*, 87-91.

Maxfield, R. B. Sex-role stereotypes of psychotherapists (Doctoral dissertation, Adelphi University, 1976). *Dissertations Abstracts International*, 1976, *37*, 1914B. (University Microfilms No. 76-22, 816)

Miller, D. The influence of the patient's sex on clinical judgment. *Smith College Studies in Social Work*, 1974, *44*, 89-100.

Mussen, P. H. Some antecedents and consequents of masculine sex typing in adolescent boys. *Psychological Monographs*, 1961, *75* (No. 2, Whole No. 506).

Mussen, P. H. Long-term consequents of masculinity on interests in adolescence. *Journal of Consulting Psychology*, 1962, *26*, 435-440.

Mussen, P., & Rutherford, E. Parent-child relations and parental personality in relation to young children's sex-role preferences. *Child Development*, 1963, *34*, 589-607.

Myers, A. M., & Sugar, J. *A critical analysis of scoring the BSRI: Implications for conceptualization*. Paper presented at the meeting of the American Psychological Association, Toronto, Canada, August 1978.

Nettles, E. J. *The relationship of ego development and sex role conception*. Paper presented at the meeting of the American Psychological Association, Toronto, Canada, August 1978.

Neulinger, J. Perceptions of the optimally integrated person: A redefinition of mental health. *Proceedings of the 76th Annual Convention of the American Psychological Association*, 1968, *3*, 553-554.

O'Connor, K., Mann, D. W., & Bardwick, J. M. Androgyny and self esteem in the upper-middle class: A replication of Spence. *Journal of Consulting and Clinical Psychology*, 1978, *46*, 1168-1169.

Orlofsky, J. L. Sex-role orientation, identity formation, and self-esteem in college men and women. *Sex Roles*, 1977, *3*, 561-575.

Parsons, T., & Bales, R. F. *Family, socialization and interaction process*. Glencoe, Illinois: Free Press, 1955.

Pleck, J. H., Staines, G. L., & Lang, L. Conflict between work and family life. *Monthly Labor Review*, March 1980, pp. 29-32.

Radloff, L. Sex differences in depression: The effects of occupation and marital status. *Sex Roles*, 1975, *1*, 249-265.

Rebecca, M., Hefner, R., & Oleshansky, B. A model of sex-role transcendence. In A. Kaplan & J. Bean (Eds.), *Beyond sex role stereotypes: Readings toward a psychology of androgyny*. Boston, Massachusetts: Little, Brown, 1976.

Report of the task force on sex bias and sex-role stereotyping in psychotherapeutic practice. *American Psychologist,* 1975, *30,* 1169-1175.

Rossi, A. S. Barriers to the career choice of engineering, medicine or science among American women. In J. A. Mattfeld & C. G. Van Aken (Eds.), *Women and the Scientific Professions.* Cambridge, Massachusetts: MIT Press, 1965, 51-127.

Schlossberg, N. K., Pietrofesa, J. J. Perspectives on counseling bias: Implications for counselor education. *Counseling Psychologist,* 1973, *4,* 44-54.

Sears, R. R. Relation of early socialization experiences to self-concepts and gender role in middle childhood. *Child Development,* 1970, *41,* 267-289.

Sherif, C. W. *Needed concepts in the study of gender identity.* Presidential address, American Psychological Association, Montreal, Canada, September 1980.

Sherman, J. A. Therapist attitudes and sex-role stereotyping. In A. M. Brodsky & R. T. Hare-Mustin (Eds.), *Women and psychotherapy.* New York: Guilford, 1980.

Sherriffs, A. C., & McKee, J. P. Qualitative aspects of beliefs about men and women. *Journal of Personality,* 1957, *25,* 451-464.

Silvern, L. E., & Ryan, V. L. Self-rated adjustment and sex-typing on the Bem Sex-Role Inventory: Is masculinity the primary predictor of adjustment? *Sex Roles,* 1979, *5,* 739-764.

Smith, M. B. Optima of mental health. *Psychiatry,* 1950, *13,* 503-510.

Sopchak, A. L. Parental "identification" and "tendency toward disorders" as measured by the MMPI. *Journal of Abnormal and Social Psychology,* 1952, *47,* 159-165.

Spence, J. T., & Helmreich, R. *Masculinity and femininity: Their psychological dimensions, correlates, and antecedents.* Austin: Univ. of Texas Press, 1978.

Spence, J. T., Helmreich, R., & Stapp, J. Ratings of self and peers on sex role attributes and their relation to self esteem and conceptions of masculinity and femininity. *Journal of Personality and Social Psychology,* 1975, *32,* 29-39.

Stearns, B. C., Penner, L. A., & Kimmel, E. *Sexism among psychotherapists: A case not yet proven.* Paper presented at the meeting of the American Psychological Association, Toronto, Canada, August 1978.

Thomas, A. Pseudo-transference reactions due to cultural stereotyping. *American Journal of Orthopsychiatry,* 1962, *32,* 894-900.

Thomas, A. H., & Stewart, N. R. Counselor responses to female clients with deviate and conforming career goals. *Journal of Counseling Psychology,* 1971, *18,* 352-357.

Unger, R. K. Toward a redefinition of sex and gender. *American Psychologist,* 1979, *34,* 1085-1094.

Waterman, A. S., & Whitbourne, S. K. *Androgyny and psychosocial development among college students and adults.* Paper presented at the meeting of the American Psychological Association, New York, September 1979.

Watson, W. *Sex role identity and defensively high self-esteem.* Paper presented at the meeting of the American Psychological Association, New York, September 1979.

Wells, K. *Gender-role identity and psychological adjustment in adolescence.* Paper presented at the meeting of the American Psychological Association, New York, September 1979.

Wetter, R. E. *Levels of self-esteem associated with four sex role categories.* Paper presented at the meeting of the American Psychological Association, Chicago, August 1975.

Worell, J. Sex roles and psychological well-being: Perspectives on methodology. *Journal of Consulting and Clinical Psychology,* 1978, *46,* 777-791.

Yager, G. G., & Baker, S. *Thoughts on androgyny for the counseling psychologist.* Paper presented at the annual meeting of the American Psychological Association, New York, September 1979.

II

Developmental Perspective

3

IHSAN AL-ISSA

Gender and Child Psychopathology

Many problems in child psychopathology tend to confound the study of its relationship with gender. Since children undergo a relatively fast intellectual, motor, and social development, it is difficult to apply the same criterion for abnormality from one stage of development to the other. The application of a stable criterion for abnormality in child psychopathology is made more complex by the fact that boys and girls experience different rates in some areas of development. In contrast to adult psychopathology, many behavior problems associated with certain stages of development in childhood may be transitory or they may occur so early and in such a severe form that they may reflect biological rather than environmental factors.

Childhood abnormalities are also completely dependent on the value judgment of adults, particularly parents and teachers who play the double role of designating certain behavior as abnormal as well as influencing the development and course of such behavior. Thus, the rates of referral of boys and girls to psychiatric treatment may depend not on whether the behavior is problematic for the child, but rather on its impact on adults. For example, aggression, which is problematic to adults, is more likely to precipitate adult intervention than are anxiety or depression, which are less visible but more problematic for the child. Similarly, the same behavior—such as sexual promiscuity—may be considered by adults as more acceptable for one sex (boys) than for the other (girls). Changes in family structure and the sudden increase of the number of working mothers and children living in single-parent homes as a

ISBN: 0-12-050350-6

result of separation or divorce have brought about various problems that might impact differently on the adjustment of boys and girls.

This chapter first deals with sex differences in the type of child psychopathology that might be considered as similar to severe disturbances in adulthood, such as psychosis, depression, neurosis, conversion, and so on. This is followed by sex differences as revealed in studies using a multivariate statistical approach to child psychopathology. These studies have used checklists, rating scales, and questionnaires with teachers and parents in order to investigate behavior problems that may not be considered as part of traditional psychiatric syndromes. Related to this approach are surveys of fear and anxiety in children. The third section discusses developmental disorders and learning disabilities. The last section reviews research dealing with the effects of family interaction, particularly in single-headed families, on the psychological adjustment of boys and girls.

Sex Differences in Child Psychopathology

A survey of treatment facilities by Gove and Herb (1974) reveals that child psychopathology is more prevalent in boys than in girls, but by age 15-19, female rates tend to catch up with or even slightly exceed male rates. Similarly, Graham and Rutter (1977), in a review of community studies and psychiatric clinics, concluded that childhood disorders are much more common in boys than in girls, with the sex ratio becoming more nearly equal in adolescence. However, they reported that depression and conversion disorders are equally common among boys and girls, in contrast to their predominance among females in adult life. Another exception to the advantage of girls over boys is epidemic hysteria, which is more frequent among adolescent girls who live in a closed community such as a boarding school or hospital and who may respond to group anxiety related to pregnancies, sexual activities, work stress, or death of a compatriot (Al-Issa, 1980; Graham & Rutter, 1977). Similarly, anorexia nervosa afflicts mainly females in late adolescence and early adulthood. Also, the protection against psychiatric disturbance among girls in childhood is not evident among brain damaged children, where there are equal rates among boys and girls (Rutter, Graham, & Yule, 1970; Shaffer, Chadwick, & Rutter, 1975).

Changes in the sex ratio of psychiatric disorders from childhood to adolescence are the result of an increase in emotional disorders among females as they pass from childhood to adulthood. For example, Gove and Herb (1974) found that there are more males than females between 5 and 9 in treatment facilities for neurosis, but this tendency is reversed between 10 and 19. A study of first referral to psychiatric services in Scotland by Baldwin

(1968) reveals that males are higher on neuroses up to 14, but between 15 and 19 the rates of females are almost double those of males. Similarly, Rutter, Tizard, and Whitmore (1970), in the Isle of Wight study, found more neurotic disorders among girls than boys in early adolescence. S. B. G. Eysenck (1963) reported that neuroticism (emotional instability) scores of boys and girls are quite similar at ages 7 and 8, but from 9 on there is a clear increase for girls but no change for boys, resulting in a wide gap between the sexes at 16. The rates of admission for depression are also higher for females than for males between the ages of 10 and 20, a tendency that continues in adulthood (Rosenthal, 1970). Graham (1979) pointed out that although in childhood boys and girls tend to be equally affected by anxiety-withdrawal disorders, in middle and late adolescence the sex ratio changes so that there is an increase in the number of girls suffering from severe anxiety and depression.

All studies report an excess of boys in the various types of psychoses. The excess of males in psychosis is greater than that found in most other psychiatric and physical disorders except conduct disorder and minimal brain function (Werry, 1979a). Similarly, there is an excess of schizophrenia among boys in childhood and adolescence (Al-Issa, Chapter 7, this volume). Other disorders that are higher in boys than in girls are infantile autism (M to F ratio, 3:1), attention deficit disorder with hyperactivity (M to F ratio, 10:1), conduct disorders (M to F ratio, 4:1 to 12:1), and chronic motor tic disorder (M to F ratio, 3:1) (American Psychiatric Association, 1980).

Explaining Sex Differences in Child Psychopathology

Gove and Herb (1974) suggested the stress hypothesis to explain high rates of admission to psychiatric services in boys during childhood and the reversal of such a trend in adolescence. They noted that life tends to be more stressful for young boys than for young girls, but with advancing age sex differences in the experience of stress tends to disappear and by late adolescence life becomes more stressful for girls than boys. They suggested that boys are more vulnerable to stress because their physical and intellectual development is slower than that of girls, making them less able to meet adult expectations. Boys also get into more conflicts with parents and teachers because of their aggressiveness. Another stress factor noted by Gove and Herb is that more stringent gender role expectations are imposed on boys than girls. Whereas girls are allowed to carry out masculine activities, feminine behavior in boys is considered a serious matter. It is not only that the range of appropriate behavior is limited for boys, but that their opportunity to acquire masculine behavior is minimal because, both at home and in school, they live in a predominantly feminine environment. In mid-adolescence, however, boys start to find school more rewarding than girls because they tend to catch up with and even surpass girls in some academic areas. A change in the character of school work also takes place in adolescence, with increasing emphasis on subjects (science, mathematics) in which boys are able to outperform girls. Furthermore, school becomes less stressful to boys than girls in adolescence because it becomes more compatible with the career goals of males than females. Although girls are allowed to take part in masculine activities in childhood, there is much pressure on them to adopt traditional feminine roles in adolescence. This pressure to conform to specific gender role stereotypes tends to induce conflicts and anxiety in girls.

The stress hypothesis suggested by Gove and Herb does not explain sex differences in the subtypes of child psychopathology. For example, conduct disorders and psychosis are not only higher among males in childhood but they are also higher in adolescence, regardless of changes in gender role expectations and stress levels postulated by Gove and Herb. Also, late adolescence may be more stressful for boys than for girls because of higher pressure on boys to achieve (Hoffman, 1977). Indeed, the peak in schizophrenic breakdown among males in late adolescence and early adulthood may be partly due to stresses and conflicts in occupational choice (Al-Issa, Chapter 7, this volume; Rosenthal, 1970). It has also been suggested that severe childhood disorders such as autism and childhood schizophrenia, which are predominant in males, are more likely to be related to certain types of brain abnormality rather than to gender roles (Hingtgen & Bryson, 1972; Ornitz, 1973; Rutter, 1968). Rosenthal (1970), for example, has pointed out that congenital factors that are not genetic in nature could account for the greater vulnerability to schizophrenia in the young male; a view that is supported by the finding that, among psychotic children, there is an excess of organic and neurological cases among boys (Goldfarb, 1970).

Sex differences in treated cases that are reported by Gove and Herb (1974) may simply reflect the rate of referral of boys and girls, which in turn may be influenced by the nature of the psychopathology. Rosenthal (1970) discussed the possibility that higher rates of childhood schizophrenia in males may in part reflect a greater parental anxiety about behavior disorders in male children because males diagnosed as schizophrenic tend to be more aggressive, destructive, and less easy to manage, so that mothers are more inclined to bring boys than girls for professional help. Similarly, although there is a tendency for explaining the excess of hyperactivity in boys in terms of the greater vulnerability of males to neonatal damage, it is quite possible that since most of the symptoms of hyperactivity are of the aggressive or conduct disorder type, higher rates of hyperactivity in boys may reflect the general aggressiveness of males, which tends to result in excessive referral rates (Werry, 1979b).

In contrast to gender role theory postulated by Gove and Herb (1974), the aggressiveness of the male, which is associated not only with hyperactivity but with other psychiatric disturbances in boys, may be attributed to biological factors (Al-Issa, Chapter, 13, this volume). Similarly, the increase in neuroticism and anxiety levels in girls about the time of puberty and adolescence may also result from physical and biological changes. Macfarlane, Allen, and Honzik (1954) found an increase in the frequency of problems such as emotional dependence, shyness, fears, and irritability a year before menarche. They suggested that an increase in tension a year or so before menarche may be due either to physiological changes or to social aspects of maturation, or probably to both factors. Another study of girls treated at a psychiatric hospital also indicates an increase in anxiety states in the year before menarche (Howarth, cited in Graham & Rutter, 1977).

In summary, there are higher rates of psychiatric disturbance in boys than in girls in childhood, but these rates become equalized in adolescence. The hypothesis that stress is associated with gender role does not entirely account for these sex differences. For example, psychosis and conduct disorders are higher in boys than in girls in both childhood and adolescence, regardless of changes in gender role demands during these two stages of development. In addition to the stress hypothesis, biological factors may be involved in sex differences in child psychopathology.

Multivariate Approach to Sex Differences in Child Psychopathology

In addition to the clinical approach, researchers have used a quantitative approach to child psychopathology by examining the distribution of behavior disorders among treated and untreated children in the general population. By using rating scales and checklists, it was possible to find patterns of behavior that cluster into factors or dimensions.

In an early study by Peterson (1961), teachers were asked to rate a sample of 831 students in kindergarten through sixth grade on a problem checklist. Peterson found the responses to form two clusters, called *conduct problem* and *personality problem*. These two dimensions reflect aggression in the conduct problem cluster and withdrawal or inhibition in the personality problem cluster. Items with the highest loadings on conduct problem were disobedience, disruptiveness, boisterousness, fighting, attention-seeking, and restlessness, whereas items with the highest loadings on personality problem were those describing feelings of inferiority, lack of self-confidence, social withdrawal, tendency to become flustered, self-consciousness, shyness, and anxiety. Among four age groups (kindergarten, Grades 1 and 2, Grades 3 and

4, and Grades 5 and 6), it was found that boys consistently revealed more conduct problems than girls. Younger boys also had more personality problems, but this trend is reversed around the third and fourth grades, after which the scores for girls exceeded those for boys. The conduct problem shows an age-related trend in which boys and girls scored lower for the third and fourth grade age groups than for the other three age groups. The same age trend was true for personality problem scores of boys, but girls revealed a general rise from kindergarten to grades five and six. Other studies do not show a decrease in children's behavior problems in the third and fourth grades (Ross, 1980). Ross suggested that systematic differences in teachers may be correlated with the grade level at which they teach. He noted that "since the environment's tolerance is part of the definition of a behavior problem, it may be that this tolerance finds expression in the way a teacher rates the behaviors found in the classroom [Ross, 1980, p. 24]."

Werry and Quay (1971), in a study of the prevalence of behavior problems in kindergarten and Grade 1 and 2 children, used a 55-item checklist containing problems usually found among children referred to child guidance clinics. Items in the checklist included problems such as restlessness, self-consciousness, boisterousness, shyness, jealousy, inattentiveness, disobedience, and destructiveness. Teachers' rating resulted in a mean number of 11.4 problems for the 926 boys and 7.6 for the 827 girls in the sample. Thirty-six of the problems occurred with significantly higher frequency among boys, with only five problems more common among girls. Boys were higher on conduct problems (restlessness, boisterousness, disobedience, profane language and swearing, irritability), whereas girls were higher on personality problems (shyness, seriousness, jealousy, sensitivity, and physical complaints).

Rather than using teachers, Miller, Hampe, Barrett, and Noble (1971) asked parents to rate children on the Louisville Behavior Checklist. The checklist scales yield rating scores in the areas of aggression, inhibition, and learning disabilities as well as general ability. They found that the mean scores of boys and girls were not significantly different except in the area of learning disorders (boys also manifested more extreme behavior than girls on the aggressiveness and learning disability dimensions). This finding is surprising considering clinic referrals with a high male to female ratio, usually about 3:1. Similarly, data from parents seem to be in sharp contrast to the teachers' rating of school behavior, which indicates a predominance of problems in boys. Other studies of parents' rating support the Miller *et al.* finding. For example, Macfarlane *et al.* (1954) and Mensh, Kantor, Domke, Gildea, and Glidewell (1959) found no sex difference in total deviant behavior. However, Macfarlane *et al.* found more aggression in the male and more inhibition in the female. Beller and Newbauer (1963) and Lapouse and Monk (1964) also found impulsive aggression in males and inhibition and anxiety in females.

Thus, parents tend to find an equal amount of deviant behavior in their male and female children, but tend to see males as more aggressive and females as more anxious and inhibited. Similarly, although teachers observe a larger amount of overall disturbance in, and have more trouble with, boys than girls (Peterson, 1961; Werry & Quay, 1971), their rating of children is consistent with that of parents in revealing an excess of males with conduct problems and an excess of females with personality problems.

A more recent study by Achenbach and Edelbrock (1981) used the Child Behavior Checklist with parents of normal and disturbed children (referred to an outpatient mental health setting) aged between 4 and 16. Of 51 behavior problems that revealed a significant difference between boys and girls, 26 reflected higher scores for girls; 25, higher scores for boys. Nineteen of the 25 items on which boys scored higher were associated with externalizing for boys, whereas the remaining 5 were not consistently associated with either externalizing or internalizing. By contrast, only one of the items (screams a lot) on which girls scored higher was associated with externalizing for girls. Of the remaining 25 items on which girls scored higher, 10 were associated with internalizing and 15 were not associated with either internalizing or externalizing. Thus, there was a significant tendency of boys to score higher on externalizing items and girls on internalizing items. Since externalizing is similar to the conduct problem dimension and internalizing is similar to the personality problem dimension, the Achenbach and Edelbrock (1981) finding is consistent with the data discussed earlier.

The finding by Achenbach and Edelbrock (1981) that the mean total behavior problem scores for nonreferred boys and girls were almost identical at all ages and that those for the referred children reveal no consistent gender effects supports previous research in revealing that parents do not perceive boys as presenting more problems than girls. Achenbach and Edelbrock observed that the excessive rate of referral of boys to mental health and special educational services (Baldwin, Robertson, & Satin, 1971; Rosen, 1979; Wing, Baldwin, & Rosen, 1972) may result more from the conflicts between their behavior and official norms than from quantitative differences in problems. Miller *et al.* (1971), in the study described earlier, also observed that it is the tolerance of significant adults in the child's environment rather than an absolute standard of normality that provides the basis for the definition of behavior disorders. They suggested that the basic problem is difficulty with formal learning. When failure to learn occurs in boys, they react with aggression. When it occurs in girls, they are more likely to react with social withdrawal. Since children are often referred when they become problems to adults, and since aggression is more likely to become a problem to adults, boys are more likely to be referred for treatment. The strong interaction between learning disorders and behavior problems may explain the discrepancy between the teachers' rating and the parents' rating of boys and girls. When teachers are used as respondents, there is a higher incidence of problems among boys, whereas when parents are the respondents, there is no sex difference. It is possible that boys who have more difficulty with learning find school a more aversive situation and respond to it with behavior seen by teachers as aggressive, hyperactive, and antisocial. Boys may also behave differently at home, where they are rated as no more problematic than girls by parents.

Sex Differences in Fear and Anxiety

Studies in the previous section, which revealed a tendency of girls to respond to stress with avoidance, withdrawal, and inhibition, would suggest that they may also exhibit more fear and anxiety than boys. Fodor (Chapter 8, this volume) reported that there is a general tendency of adult females to have more phobias than adult males. This section deals with studies of childhood fears that are based on observations, rating scales, fear surveys, and questionnaires.

Kagan (1971, 1977) reported that, in infancy, females express more fears and become upset by novel stimuli at an earlier age than males. A female infant under 6 months is more likely than the male to cry in a strange laboratory or in an unusual situation. When a mother and infant are first situated behind a wire barrier and the mother is then signaled to put the infant on the opposite side, many 1-year-old girls tend to cry as well as to remain close to the mother. Boys, on the other hand, are more likely to start some activity or to attend to some event in the surroundings. Kagan observed that even though the action of boys in situations of uncertainty may be task-irrelevant, their activity may be protective against fear. In contrast, girls' earlier display of fear, motor inhibition, and tendency to stay close to the mother may be due to the fact that they are biologically precocious as compared with boys, and this may result in earlier cognitive development and awareness of their surroundings. Thus, their fear reaction is only an attempt to assimilate unfamiliar events or to resolve the uncertainty they generate. Kagan (1977) gives the example of a 4-month-old baby who has formed a cognitive picture of the crib and room at home and is brought to a new situation in the laboratory with a different crib. Although girls in this situation may be immature in their coping methods and have no effective way to deal with the realization that they are not in a familiar place and hence start crying, they are mature enough to recognize the change in their physical environment. The boy who has not yet developed a distinct cognitive picture of his environment may not recognize the change or discrepancy in his environment. As an alternative to the hypothesis of differential precocity in cognitive development, Kagan (1977) suggested that the early withdrawal and fearfulness of girls might indicate innate reflexive tendencies. However, no evidence is presented to support either of the two hypotheses.

Studies of sex differences in fear of strangers and novel situations in infancy appear to be inconsistent (Maccoby & Jacklin, 1974). Tennes and Lampl (1964) found that female infants display a more intense fear of strangers than male infants. Other studies, however, did not find sex differences (Bronson, 1970, 1972; Lewis & Brooks, 1974), except that girls become fearful at an earlier age than boys (Robson, Pederson, & Moss, 1969). Goldberg and Lewis (1969) found that 13-month-old girls appear more helpless and cry more than their male counterparts when separated from the mother. A replication of this study by Jacklin, Maccoby, and Dick (1973) indicates that the difference between the sexes in fear after separation from the mother is not a general phenomenon, but it is influenced by the experimental situation.

The initial settling into a group, a potentially fear-arousing situation preschool children have to face, reveals sex differences. For example, girls seem to cope better and cry less than boys in this situation (Blurton-Jones & Leach, 1972). Whereas boys are fearful and inhibited, girls walk more, talk more, and laugh more during the first day of nursery school (McGrew, 1972). Boys also settle less well and express more distress than girls during the first week at a play group (Smith, 1974). Smith suggested many possible explanations for these sex differences among preschool children. First, children arriving at play groups may be a select sample. Since mothers are more protective of girls, they tend to send less fearful girls to play groups. Second, girls tend more quickly than boys to attach themselves to a member of the staff (usually a female). Third, older girls may be more friendly to a new girl than older boys to a new boy. Finally, since boys as a group tend to show greater variability than girls, the results might have been affected by a larger number of boys experiencing extreme levels of fear. As in the hypotheses put forward by Kagan (1977) to explain fear in infancy, there is little evidence in favor of any one of the four hypotheses over the others.

When the overall frequency of fears in childhood is investigated, there are no clear-cut sex differences. In a study that asked mothers to keep a diary for 3 weeks of their children's fears, Jersild and Holmes (1935) found no sex differences from infancy to 6 years of age. Similarly, in a group of 2- to 6-year-old children, Jersild and Holmes found no sex differences in the frequency of fears displayed in situations actually presented to them, except that girls revealed more intense fears than boys in these situations. A study of the frequency of specific fears from age 1.5 to 14 by Macfarlane *et al.* (1954) revealed that girls have only a slight advantage over boys in the frequency of fears (an average of 25.4 for girls and 33.7 for boys).

However, girls undergo a dramatic increase in fears during adolescence. For example, Macfarlane *et al.* (1954) found that girls have five times more fears than boys at 13. Scherer and Nakamura (1968) also reported that among children just over 10, girls checked significantly larger number of fears and indicated a greater intensity of these fears than boys. Rutter, Tizard, and Whitmore (1970) noted that although animal phobia is initially found in both sexes, it becomes rare in boys as early as age 10 or 11, suggesting a decrease in the fears of boys in early adolescence.

In self-reports during adolescence and adulthood, females consistently show higher number of fears than males. A study of young persons (average ages: males = 19.5 years; females = 18.7 years) indicates that, with the exception of fear of noise, which is about equal in both sexes, females exceed males in fears related to tissue damage (prospect of surgical operation, dead animals, dead people), social and interpersonal (feeling rejected, looking foolish), animals (dogs), classical (enclosed places), and miscellaneous fears (Grossberg & Wilson, 1965).

Studies of anxiety using self-report questionnaires with children aged 6 and over frequently find no sex differences, but in those studies that find sex differences, girls usually score higher than boys. After age 18, however, most studies show higher anxiety among women (Maccoby & Jacklin, 1974).

One important issue is whether there are sex differences in the continuity of emotional behavior between infancy and later childhood. Bronson (1970) studied changes in fear during the first 8.5 years of life. The level of fear seems to remain stable for boys during this period. However, girls reveal little consistency in their fears from infancy to early childhood. Also, the relative precocity of fear onset among boys was a reliable predictor of later fear, and those boys who exhibited an early fear of novel situations tended to remain more fearful than those boys who showed their first fear reaction at a later stage of infancy. In contrast, the relationship between the age of onset of fears in girls and later rating of shyness was not significant. In support of data discussed earlier, boys and girls obtained similar average fears during the four age periods investigated (10-15 months; 2-3.5 years; 4-6 years; 6.5-8.5 years).

It has been suggested that results from self-report measures of fear and anxiety during adolescence may not reflect true sex differences but be an artifact of two factors. As in the case of adult psychopathology discussed in Chapter 4 (this volume), it was assumed that because of social expectations, girls are less defensive and more willing to report fears than boys (Hersen, 1973; Maccoby & Jacklin, 1974). A second factor discussed by Maccoby and Jacklin is the tendency of fear schedules used to investigate sex differences to emphasize fears that are specific to females rather than males, which may bias results against women and young girls. The social expectation hypothesis has received inconsistent support. For example, responses of males and females are not differentially affected by social desirability, which is a tendency to endorse socially acceptable items (Farley & Mealiea, 1971; Geer, 1965). Similarly, most studies do not show a greater tendency among boys and men to lie and be defensive or a tendency among girls and women to be more candid in reporting anxiety (Block, 1976). Nevertheless, in approaching fear objects, there is more discrepancy between the self-report and the behavior of men than of women. High-fear females showed agreement between verbal and motor responses and did not approach a small German shepherd dog; high-fear males, on the other hand, approached the dog (Geer, 1965). This raises the possibility that high-fear males are affected by social expectations in a real life situation rather than during verbal report. In examining data indicating that self-report, behavioral and physiological (heart rate) indexes for fear in 9-11-year-old girls are well integrated, Hetherington and Parke (1975) suggested that the same degree of integration may not be present for boys because norms dictating less fearfulness for them may weaken the link between self-report measures and other indexes of fear.

Maccoby and Jacklin (1974) suggested that the content of anxiety scales deal with fear-provoking situations that affect females more than males (for example, items from the General Anxiety Scale for Children such as "Do you get scared when you have to walk home alone at night?", "When you are home alone and someone knocks on the door, do you get a worried feeling?"). Thus, an affirmative response to these questions may reflect the training of girls to avoid certain dangers. There are, however, very few items in the scales dealing with boys' specific fears (fear of public humiliation or failure, fear of appearing cowardly). Studies of fear and anxiety show a relationship between the content of the scales and the direction of sex differences (Rothstein & Boblitt, 1970). Although girls tend to exceed boys on total anxiety scores, the greatest differences between the sexes are on items such as "alone in the woods at night"; "alone at home hearing someone try to get in"; "alone in the woods and surprised by a violent thunderstorm." Manosevitz and Lanyon (1965) found that although, on average, women experience more intense fear than men, these fears involve social and interpersonal fears. On the other hand, men experience more intense fear in situations involving failure. On the two items in the test whose content appears to be neutral for both sexes, the average rating for males exceeded that for females (noise of vacuum cleaner; being an adopted child). In support of the view that the quality of fear may affect the direction of sex differences is the general finding that so-called overanxious disorder, which is characterized by worry about the future and overconcern about academic, athletic, and social competence, is more common in boys than in girls (American Psychiatric Association, 1980). Also, in an epidemiological study of adults by Warheit, Holzer, and Arey (1975), it was found that there are three times as many females as males with severe fears and phobias, but an inspection of the items included in the scale revealed that the affirmative responses of women seem to be an accurate assessment of the actual dangers and harm to which women are exposed. Thus, in the study of sex differences, it is necessary to examine the qualitative nature of fears and the situations related to these fears.

Developmental Disorders and Learning Disabilities

Boys are more vulnerable to harm in utero and during birth and childhood than are girls. Statistics reveal higher rates of fetal mortality, stillbirth, and mortality in the first year of life among boys (Gadpaille, 1972; Waldron, 1976). Even though the period of gestation is slightly shorter for girls than for boys, the skeletal maturation of girls as measured by the shape and degree of ossification or hardening of the bones is 4 to 6 weeks advanced compared to boys. In an analysis of sex differences in physical and neurological development of 15,000 children, Singer, Westphal, and Niswander (1968) found that of 248 possible abnormalities, 65% had higher incidence among males whereas only 26.6% had higher incidence among females. In a study of neurological and physical disorders among disabled children by Bradshaw and Lawton (1978), it was found that cerebral palsy, epilepsy, blindness, deafness, and congenital abnormalities were higher in boys than in girls. Many sex-linked physical problems and diseases such as color blindness and hemophilia (a disease in which the blood does not clot) afflict males more often than females. The male is also more susceptible to infectious diseases such as bacterial meningitis than is the female (Parkman, 1977).

Sex-linked disorders are carried by genes on the X-chromosomes and will affect the individual unless they are offset by normal genes on a second X. Thus, girls, who have two Xs, have a better chance of escaping sex-linked disorders, whereas boys have no protection against many sex-linked defects because they lack a second X. Reinisch, Gandelman, and Spiegel (1979) pointed out that the male Y chromosome carries much less genetic information than the second X carried by the female, increasing the probability of more sex-linked characteristics in males. They also pointed out that since the male fetus needs androgen in sufficient amount at a critical time in order to develop morphologically, physiologically, and neurologically, he is more liable to errors than is the female fetus. This vulnerability of the male is also demonstrated among children of psychotic women. M. A. Taylor (1969), for instance, found stillbirth, birth defects (deafness, muteness, cerebral palsy, blindness, and mental retardation) and death within the first 4 days after birth, to be more prevalent among male infants than among female infants when conception coincided with maternal psychotic breakdown. Because of the high risk of spontaneous abortion of the male fetus, fewer males are born to these women.

It was suggested that in schizophrenia, a serum factor specifically toxic to the Y chromosome either in sperm or in the fertilized ova in the early stages of gestation is responsible for these deleterious effects on the male.

Boys are much more likely than girls to be referred to clinics for learning disabilities and other developmental problems, including speech defects such as stuttering and language disorders, reading disabilities, limited vision, impaired learning, deafness, and mental retardation (Barfield, 1976). However, Rutter (1977) pointed out that although there is strong male predominance (4:1) in childhood in nearly all disorders that involve a specific delay in development such as speech or language delay, specific reading retardation, and the clumsy child syndrome, this is less obvious in the case of nocturnal enuresis. Girls are initially quicker to acquire urinary continence at night than are boys. By age 2-3, 45% of all girls but only 23% of all boys are dry at night. This difference decreases until bedwetting becomes as uncommon in boys as in girls between 4 and 6. After age 7, the ratio of boys to girls starts to increase until, by the mid-teens, boys are twice as likely to wet as girls (Douglas, 1973; Miller, 1973; Rutter, Yule, & Graham, 1973). The greater number of boys is the result of both an increase in their susceptibility to relapse and their slower rate of spontaneous recovery. Girls tend to have a better prognosis than boys. For example, of girls wet at age 11, 60% have become dry by 13 as compared to only 36% of boys. However, sex differences in prognosis are not significant at an earlier age or among older teenagers (Shaffer, 1977). The rate of fecal soiling (encopresis) is 18% for boys and 8% for girls at the age of 3 (Richman, Stevenson, & Graham, 1975) and 1.3% for boys and .3% for girls between 10 and 12 years old (Rutter, Tizard, & Whitmore, 1970).

Explaining Sex Differences in Learning Disabilities

One of the early sex differences is in the acquisition and mastery of language. Girls acquire vocabulary faster (Nelson, 1973) and obtain higher scores on word fluency tests than boys (Herzberg & Lapkin, 1954). Since language is essential for early school achievement and success, sex differences in linguistic abilities are considered to account for the larger number of boys with articulation problems, more severe and less correctable speech disorders (Bentzen, 1963; Schnell, 1946, 1947), reading disabilities (Bentzen, 1963; Eisenberg, 1966; Maccoby & Jacklin, 1974), and other learning disabilities.

One hypothesis put forward to explain the superiority of girls over boys in linguistic abilities is that mothers tend to talk to and vocally reinforce girls more than boys (Harris, 1977). However, the mothers' greater interaction with girls may be the result of the girls' precocious verbal development rather than the cause of it; that is, since girls are more responsive than boys to verbal stimulation from mothers, they may shape the behavior of their mothers and increase their communication with them. A longitudinal study by Pawlby and Hall (1980) indicates that a mother's level of interaction with her baby is related to the child's later linguistic competence, though this was only true for girls. Thus, the frequency with which mothers spoke to them, touched them, looked at them, presented them with objects, and smiled at them at 20 weeks of age is related to the girls' language and speech performance at 27 months.

Gullahorn (1979) suggested that although female infants might initially be only slightly more predisposed than male infants toward responsiveness to verbal stimulation, mutual reinforcement between parent and infant may result in large vocabulary gain for girls. She pointed out that both girls' developing verbal abilities and gender role expectations may then increase girls' dependence on verbal information processing. In contrast, pressure from parents and others may exacerbate the relative verbal disadvantage of boys. Furthermore, the lower average facility of boys with words may encourage their reliance on spatial abilities, a tendency that may further enhance the development of their spatial predispositions. Learning experience and the expectation of adults may also play a part in sex difference in certain abilities. A cross-cultural study by Johnson (1973-1974) reveals that among elementary school children, girls tend to score higher in reading skills than boys in Canada and the United States, but lower in England and in Nigeria, where teachers expected boys to be better readers than girls. Similarly, the advantage of males in spatial abilities was not found among the Eskimos (Berry, 1966).

Gove and Herb (1974) suggested that the male child faces the problem of interacting with teachers of the opposite sex, which may contribute to his learning difficulties. It appears, however, that male teachers do not have a significantly favorable effect on the achievement of male students. Furthermore, the sex of the teacher may not be a disadvantage for boys, since male teachers seem to interact with boys and girls substantially as female teachers do (Good & Brophy, 1977).

Maturational differences in brain asymmetry is another hypothesis put forward to explain females' superiority in language acquisition and development. Since sex differences in language appear early in life and since language is associated with lateralized left-hemisphere information processing, it has been suggested that girls may experience earlier onset of left-hemisphere specialization. A clinical index of language lateralization is derived from the relationship between chronological age and the incidence of epileptic lesions in the right or left hemispheres of boys and girls. D. C. Taylor (1969) suggested that before age 2, the left hemisphere appears to be more at risk than the right; but after that age, when the left hemisphere becomes dominant, the differential risk is reversed. It was found that the time period after birth during which there is a greater incidence of left than of right-sided epilepsy is shorter for girls than for boys. Thus, the female left hemisphere remains vulnerable for a shorter period because it matures earlier than the male left hemisphere. The tendency for associated movements (movements that accompany an intended motor function but are not necessary for its performance, e.g., as when the middle finger of the right hand is voluntarily raised and the left involuntarily rises, the movement of the right side is called *associated movement*) is also considered to be an index of the degree of central nervous system maturation. It was found that girls are consistently more mature, showing fewer associated movements than boys (Connolly & Stratton, 1968). This type of evidence indicating that girls are developmentally ahead of boys in attaining left-hemisphere dominance and, consequently, show greater brain laterality, is used to explain greater facility of girls for language at a younger age. In contrast, it is suggested that because males mature less rapidly, they may never become as lateralized for speech as females (Buffery & Gray, 1972).

However, the evidence is not unequivocally in support of sex differences in the onset of hemispheric specialization. A review of the literature indicates that hemispheric specialization in both sexes exists at as early an age in development as researchers have been able to study (Witelson, 1977). A study by McGlone (1976) suggests more asymmetrical left-hemispheric control of verbal abilities in men than in women. She found no greater verbal deficit among women with left temporal lesions as compared to right temporal lesions. Men with left-hemisphere lesions did, however, show impaired verbal functioning in comparison to men with right-hemispheric lesions and to women with lesions on either the left or the right side of the brain. However, females seem to show a bias in using left-hemisphere linguistic strategies for processing spatial as well as verbal information (Inglis & Lawson, 1981). For example, among brain-damaged subjects, the degree of language impairment from left-hemisphere lesions is related to visuospatial disability in females but not in males (McGlone & Kertesz, 1973). In contrast, among cases of right-hemisphere brain-damage, women exhibit less of a performance deficit than men on various spatial measures (e.g., the Wechsler Block Design Test) (Inglis & Lawson, 1981; Lansdell, 1962, 1968; Lansdell & Urbach, 1965). However, it is not clear how far female dependence on verbal mediation for both verbal and spatial tasks is also related to advanced verbal abilities in women.

The female advanced physical maturation is postulated to explain early superior mental abilities (Sherman, 1978). Physical maturation seems to be related to mental abilities, and the more physically mature individual tends to score higher on mental ability tests at all ages tested, as far back as 6.5 years of age (Tanner, 1978). Because she believed that physical maturity reflects central nervous system maturity, Waber (1979) compared early with late physically maturing females as well as early with late physically maturing males on verbal and spatial tasks in order to find out whether the effect of maturation rate was stronger than the effect of sex. If maturation is in fact the dominant factor, early maturers are expected to reveal more of a female pattern (verbal abilities better than spatial abilities) independent of sex. In contrast, late maturers are expected to show more of a male pattern (spatial abilities better than verbal abilities) regardless of sex. Her results reveal that, within each sex, late maturers scored better than early maturers for spatial abilities, but the prediction on verbal abilities was not confirmed.

Another attempt to explain sex differences in verbal abilities, made by Broverman, Klaiber, Kobayashi, and Vogel (1968), is based on the different effect of sex hormones. They argue that since estrogen is more excitant than androgen, females tend to be more activated, or less inhibited, than males. Activation facilitates the neural transmission involved in verbal tasks that are dependent on simple, overlearned perceptual skills. Parlee (1972) noted that female superiority is not restricted to simple tasks that do not require mediation by higher cognitive processes, but women seem to excel on almost all measures of language, such as reading comprehension and verbal creativity. Furthermore, she pointed out that the relationship between cognitive functions and the activity of the autonomic nervous system in humans has not yet been demonstrated. Studies of individuals with hormonal abnormalities give some support to the relationship between androgen on the one hand and verbal or performance IQ scores on the other (Reinisch *et al.*, 1979). For example, male subjects with androgen insensitivity syndrome (i.e., cannot utilize androgen) exhibit significant superiority for verbal in comparison to performance IQ, a finding quite similar to the pattern obtained in normal female samples. However, females with the androgenital syndrome (i.e., with excessive amount of adrenal androgen) do not reveal significant differences between verbal and performance IQ, giving no support to the hormonal hypothesis.

Mental retardation, which is twice as high in males as in females (American Psychiatric Association, 1980), may also inflate the rates of learning disabilities in boys. The variability hypothesis has been suggested to explain the predominance of mental retardation in males (Lehrke, 1972, 1978). The hypothesis predicts that a greater number of males than females would be represented on the extreme levels of intelligence, even though the mean intelligence scores of the sexes are the same. Thus, there would be more geniuses and mentally retarded males than females in the general population. The greater male variability is explained by Lehrke (1972) in terms of sex-linked (X chromosome) inheritance. Lehrke cited statistics from institutions and the community that reveal higher rates of retardation among males than females. However, Nance and Engel (1972) suggest that the excess of retardation among boys in the 1970s may be due to selective factors. They found that during the 1950s and 1960s, there was an increase in the differential between the number of retarded males and females in public institutions. In contrast to these relatively recent trends, they reported that females prevailed in institutions at the beginning of the twentieth century. Changes in the number of boys and girls admitted to institutions may reflect parental attitudes, community pressure, and resources rather than the actual incidence of retardation. How selective institutionalization may effect sex ratio in mental retardation may also be illustrated by the rates of Down's syndrome. Oster (1953) found that 54.79% of individuals with Down's syndrome were boys, as compared to 51.15%, the percentage of male children born in the general population. However, when the sex ratio is compared across types of care regimes, Oster found that males exceed females in institutions, whereas females exceed males among those residing at home. Also, Fabia and Drolette (1970) reported that there are more females than males with Down's syndrome who die early, particularly from congenital heart disease. These studies suggest that there may not only be a bias in institutionalizing retarded males, but also that retarded females may be more susceptible to early death (losing their advantage of longer survival in the general population), which may, in turn, influence the sex ratio in retardation.

The sex-linked hypothesis suggested by Lehrke (1972) predicts certain family similarities in IQ. Since intelligence is transmitted through major genes on the X chromosome, it is predicted that the test scores of mother and daughter, father and daughter, and mother and son are highly correlated, because in each case the parent and child have one X chromosome in common. However, the correlation between father and son should be lower, since they have no X chromosome in common (fathers transmit a Y, rather than an X, chromosome to their sons). In the same vein, it is predicted that retarded women run a greater risk of having retarded children than do retarded men. Reed and Reed (1965), for example, found twice as many retarded children in families with a retarded mother and a father of normal or unknown intelligence as in families with a retarded father and a mother of normal or unknown intelligence. This is expected from the sex-linked (X chromosome) hypothesis since the mother passes an X chromosome to all her children, whereas the father does so only to his daughters. Anastasi (1972) has, however, pointed out that environmental factors may explain the excess of retarded children of retarded mothers. She indicated that mothers traditionally play the major role in childrearing and thus have more influence than fathers on the development of the intellectual abilities of their children. A more recent examination of the data by Kamin (1978) found no evidence that the IQ of one sex is more influenced by environmental factors than the IQ of the other sex.

Family Relations and Child Psychopathology

Parents form a major part of the environment on which children are entirely dependent. One problem in the study of gender and child psychopathology is whether the family has an equal impact on the development of psychopathology in boys and girls. It is found that family discord and disruption, such as by mental illness of a parent, is more related to antisocial behavior in boys than in girls (Hetherington, Cox, & Cox, 1977a; Rutter, 1970). However, family characteristics (for example, antagonistic relations between parents) are not associated with neurosis and emotional disturbances in either boys or girls (Bennett, 1960; Rutter, 1970).

Family disturbance may result in the institutionalization of children away from home. Wolkind and Rutter (1973) reported that most children who develop antisocial behavior while "in care" for short periods tend to be boys. With long-term care, however, girls seem to be at least as susceptible to ill effects as are boys. Thus, for girls, family discord seems less harmful, whereas long-term institutionalization appears to have damaging effects. It may be that institutionalized girls have been deprived of an essential experience within the family or have suffered from certain harmful experiences within the institution.

R. Sears, Whiting, Nowlis, and P. Sears (1953) related maternal reports of punishment to the child's aggressive behavior in nursery school. Severe punishment for aggression was positively correlated with aggression in school for boys, but there was a curvilinear relationship for girls. That is, severe punishment was related to passivity and low assertiveness rather than to aggression in daughters. In a study of 5-year-old children with behavior problems, Becker, Peterson, Luria, Shoemaker, and Hellmer (1962) also found different relationships between parental punishment and aggression for boys and girls. Linear relationship with child aggression in the home was found for boys and girls; but in school, this relationship was found only for boys. For girls, moderate rather than high levels of parental hostility and punishment were related to aggression in school.

In recent years, attention has been given to psychiatric disturbance, in general, and antisocial behavior, in particular, in single-parent families. There is more psychiatric disorder among children with divorced, separated, and remarried parents than in those whose biological parents are still living together (Lavik, 1977). However, the excess of psychiatric disorder in mother-headed families attracted more attention than in father-headed families because only about 8.4% of children in single-parent homes live with their fathers (Hetherington & Martin, 1979).

High rates of utilization of psychiatric services by women heading families without spouses (Al-Issa, Chapter 4, this volume) are reflected in the rates of utilization among children in female-headed families. Children in such families are admitted to outpatient psychiatric services at a rate approaching 1 admission per 160 population, or more than double the admission rate of children in two-parent families. Similar excess admission to state and county mental hospitals is found among children in female-headed families. The youngest children in single-parent families show the most adverse effects. Children aged 6-17 in female-headed families have an admission rate at outpatient psychiatric services more than double that of 6-17-year-old children in two-parent families. In contrast, children under 6 have an admission rate that is four times that of children under 6 in two-parent families (Belle, 1980).

Boys in mother-headed families are more antisocial, more impulsive and more rebellious against authority figures than boys in intact families (Hetherington, Cox, & Cox, 1977b; Santrock, 1975). Children from these families seem to be overrepresented among delinquents (Biller, 1976; Finer, 1974; Lynn, 1974). However, differences in acting out and antisocial behavior between children in nuclear and single-parent families are not evident among girls (Gurin, Veroff, & Feld, 1960; Hetherington *et al.*, 1977a; Hoffman, 1970; Langner & Michael, 1963; Nye, 1957; Rosenberg, 1965; Santrock, 1975). Also, excess in psychiatric disturbance, especially conduct disorders, is more likely to be found in children whose parents have been divorced than in those in which the father has died. Indeed, whereas children of divorced parents are more likely to manifest their disturbance in conduct disorders, children whose fathers have died are more likely to show depression, anxiety, and habit disturbance (Felner, Stolberg, & Cowen, 1975; Hetherington, 1972; Santrock, 1975; Tuckman & Regan, 1966).

In contrast to more recent research that indicates that separation and divorce have a greater influence in the development of conduct disorders in boys than in girls, older studies of delinquency suggest that broken homes are more frequent among female than male delinquents (Hetherington & Martin, 1979). Female delinquents are usually referred to courts for incorrigible or acting-out sexual behavior. Hetherington and Martin suggested that the effect of living in a mother-headed family or a single-parent home on girls may manifest itself in acting-out sexually rather than aggressively during adolescence.

It appears that particularly among younger children, sons experience more problems of adjustment than do daughters of divorced parents (Wallerstein & Kelly, 1980). One factor suggested by Kurdek (1981) to explain the effect of divorce on younger sons is that younger boys are exposed to more stress and less support from both adults and peers. Furthermore, since mothers are usually the family heads, the boy's adjustment problems may be due to stresses involved in living with an opposite-sex parent. It has also been suggested that girls are more psychologically resilient than boys (Wallerstein & Kelly, 1980).

In an attempt to explain the finding that boys in mother-headed families respond with more antisocial aggressive behavior than girls, Hetherington and Martin (1979) suggested that because of the greater assertiveness and aggressiveness of boys, they may need firmer discipline and more control by the father. Boys are also less compliant to authority than girls, as well as less compliant to mothers than to fathers. Furthermore, Hetherington and Martin noted that it is more necessary for boys than girls to have a male model who exhibits self-controlled and nonaggressive behavior at home.

Bacon, Child, and Barry (1963) investigated the theory that crime is a compulsive masculine behavior and a defense against initial feminine identification as a result of father absence. They found that both theft and personal crimes, such as assault, rape, and murder are more common in those societies whose households provide the least contact with the father. Thus, the high rate of antisocial behavior among boys in mother-headed families in the West has received cross-cultural support. However, consistent with social learning theory and modeling, children in mother-headed families would show feminine behavior as well. One extreme example is the practice of couvade by adult males in societies with exclusive contact with the mother in childhood; husbands go to bed and follow the procedure for childbearing during the time the wife is in labor (Burton & Whiting, 1967). Indeed, studies reveal that in father-absent families, adolescent boys tend to exhibit both masculine (toughness and aggression) and feminine (dependency) behavioral patterns (Hetherington & Parke, 1975). It appears that children reared in female-headed families show negative characteristics associated with both masculinity and femininity.

In general, parents and children in single-parent families suffer from more psychiatric disturbance because they are exposed to many stresses. For example, parents suffer from the overburden of tasks and financial problems, with one parent as an agent for socialization without other adults to serve as a buffer between child and unstable parent. However, it is the mother's ability to cope with these stresses and her emotional stability that may determine the adjustment of the children. In fact, research consistently reveals that children from conflictual and disturbed nuclear families are more poorly adjusted than those from well-functioning single-parent homes (McCord, McCord, & Thurber, 1962; Nye, 1957).

Finally, with recent increase in the number of working couples, research in the relationship between maternal employment and the psychopathology of children is of particular interest; but data on the negative effects of maternal employment are inconsistent (Etaugh, 1974; Hetherington & Martin, 1979; Hoffman, 1974). Hetherington and Martin (1979) pointed out that as long as employment brings satisfaction to the mother and increases the involvement of the father in childrearing, it tends to have a positive effect on children.

However, if it is associated with less contact with children and poor adult supervision, it may have aversive effects. In general, lack of adequate supervision appears to have a particularly damaging effect on the social and cognitive development of girls (Woods, 1972). Furthermore, maternal employment tends to be more closely associated with delinquency in girls than in boys (Nye, 1958).

Summary

Both community studies and psychiatric facilities reveal that the overall rates of psychopathology are higher in boys than in girls during childhood, but the sex ratio becomes nearly equal during adolescence. A change in the sex ratio is the result of an increase in emotional disorders among females during adolescence. The hypothesis regarding stress associated with gender roles cannot explain the high rates of male conduct disorders and psychosis in childhood and adolescence as well as in early adult life. Early severe childhood disorders such as infantile autism and psychosis, which are predominant in males, seem to be associated with organic, rather than environmental, factors. The increase in fear, anxiety, and tension just before menarche and during adolescence could also arise from both biological and social factors.

The quantitative statistical approach to behavior problems in childhood reveals two dimensions: the *conduct problem,* which reflects aggressive behavior, and the *personality problem,* which involves inhibited and withdrawn behavior. Whereas boys tend to score higher on conduct problems, girls exceed boys on personality problems. Teachers tend to perceive significantly higher behavioral problems in boys than in girls. In contrast, there is no sex difference in the total deviant behavior as rated by parents. However, both teachers and parents tend to see boys as more aggressive and girls as more anxious and inhibited. The excessive rate of referral of boys to mental health and special educational services by teachers may result more from conflicts between their behavior and official norms than from quantitative differences in problems. Difficulties in the formal learning situation may also contribute to boys' higher rate or referral.

Some data suggest that fear in infancy appears earlier in girls than in boys. Sex differences in fear of strangers and fear of separation in infancy are inconsistent. Boys reveal more fear in play groups and nursery school. However, overall rates of fears appear to be quite similar in childhood. Girls undergo a dramatic increase in fears during adolescence. Self-report measures consistently reveal higher rates of fear and anxiety among females. Social desirability and willingness to report symptoms do not explain these large sex differences. The contents of questionnaires and rating scales may be biased against females by containing fear-provoking situations that affect females more than males.

Boys are more vulnerable to fetal mortality, stillbirth, and mortality in the first year of life. There are also more physical and neurological abnormalities in boys than in girls. Many of these abnormalities are sex-linked and are carried by genes on the X chromosome (e.g., color blindness, hemophilia). Mental retardation, learning disabilities, enuresis, and encopresis are also higher in boys. One general hypothesis to explain the predominance of learning disabilities in boys is that, as compared to girls, they tend to have a disadvantage in linguistic abilities. The superiority of girls over boys in language and verbal abilities is attributed to the tendency of mothers to vocally reinforce girls more than boys. However, biological factors may be involved in determining higher verbal skills in girls. Although teachers' expectations seem to influence the performance of boys and girls in certain subjects (reading), the sex of the teacher by itself may not be a significant factor. Maturational differences in brain asymmetry have been also suggested to explain females' superiority in language acquisition and development, but the evidence in this area is not unequivocal. Early physical maturation and, perhaps, early brain maturation are related to advanced mental abilities in both sexes. The relationship between female hormones and linguistic abilities has also been suggested. Finally, the excess of mental retardation among boys may contribute to their disadvantage in school performance; the sex-linked theory of intelligence, sex bias in institutionalization, and environmental factors are suggested to explain sex differences in mental retardation.

Family discord and disruption is more related to antisocial behavior in boys than in girls. However, family characteristics are not associated with emotional disturbance in either boys or girls. Long-term institutionalization has ill effects on both boys and girls. Severe punishment by parents is positively associated with aggression in school for boys but not for girls. There are no sex differences in the relationship between parental punishment and aggression in the home. There is more psychiatric disorder among children with divorced, separated, or remarried parents than among those whose biological parents live together. Among children in the general population, those in female-headed families have the highest rates of admission to psychiatric facilities. The youngest children, below the age of 6, show the most ill effects. Antisocial behavior and delinquency are more evident in boys than in girls in mother-headed families. Also, excess in conduct disorders is more likely to be found in children whose parents have been divorced rather than in those in which the father has died. For girls, living in a mother-headed family or a single-parent home tends to manifest itself in acting-out sexually rather than aggressively during adolescence. It appears that sons experience more problems of adjustment than daughters of divorced families. In general, single-parent families are faced with more stress than are nuclear families. It is the mothers' emotional stability and ability to cope with stress that is the decisive factor in the adjustment of children. The evidence on the relationship between maternal employment and the development of psychopathology in children is not consistent. However, maternal employment that results in less contact with children and in poor adult supervision may have an adverse effect on children.

References

Achenbach, T. M., & Edelbrock, C. S. Behavioral problems and competencies reported by parents of normal and disturbed children aged four through sixteen. *Monographs of the Society for Research in Child Development,* 1981, *46* (1, Serial No. 188).

Al-Issa, I. *The psychopathology of women.* Englewood Cliffs, New Jersey: Prentice-Hall, 1980.

American Psychiatric Association. *Diagnostic and statistical manual of mental disorders* (3rd ed.). (DSM-III). Washington, D.C.: Author, 1980.

Anastasi, A., Four hypotheses with a dearth of data: Response to Lehrke's "A theory of X-linkage of major intellectual traits." *American Journal of Mental Deficiency,* 1972, *76,* 620-622.

Bacon, M. K., Child, I. L., & Barry, H., III. A cross-cultural study of correlates of crime. *Journal of Abnormal and Social Psychology,* 1963, *66,* 291-300.

Baldwin, J. A. Psychiatric illness from birth to maturity: an epidemiological study. *Acta Psychiatrica Scandinavica,* 1968, *44,* 313-333.

Baldwin, J. A., Robertson, N. C., & Satin, D. G. The incidence of reported deviant behavior in children. *International Psychiatry Clinics,* 1971, *8,* 161-175.

Barfield, A. Biological influences on sex differences in behavior. In M. Teitelbaum (Ed.), *Sex differences: Social and biological perspectives.* Garden City, New York: Anchor Books, 1976.

Becker, W. C., Peterson, D. R., Luria, Z., Shoemaker, D. J., & Hellmer, L. A. Relations of factors derived from parent-interview ratings to behavior problems of five-year-olds. *Child Development,* 1962, *33,* 509-535.

Belle, D. Who uses mental health facilities? In M. Guttentag, S. Salasin, & D. Belle (Eds.), *The mental health of women.* New York: Academic Press, 1980.

Beller, E. K., & Newbauer, P. B. Sex differences and symptom patterns in early childhood. *Journal of the American Academy of Child Psychiatry,* 1963, *2,* 417-433.

Bennett, I. *Delinquent and neurotic children: A comparative study.* New York: Basic Books, 1960.

Bentzen, F. Sex ratios in learning and behavior disorders. *American Journal of Orthopsychiatry,* 1963, *33,* 92-98.

Berry, J. W. Temne and Eskimo perceptual skills. *International Journal of Psychology,* 1966, *1,* 207-229.

Biller, H. B. The father and personality development: Paternal deprivation and sex-role development. In M. E. Lamb (Ed.), *The role of the father in child development.* New York: Wiley, 1976.

Block, H. Issues, problems and pitfalls in assessing sex differences: A critical review of the psychology of sex differences. *Merrill-Palmer Quarterly,* 1976, *22,* 283-308.

Blurton-Jones, N. G., & Leach, G. M. Behavior of children and their mothers at separation and greeting. In N. G. Blurton-Jones (Ed.), *Ethological studies of child behavior,* London and New York: Cambridge Univ. Press, 1972.

Bradshaw, J., & Lawton, D. Some characteristics of children with severe disabilities. *Journal of Biosocial Sciences*, 1978, *10*, 107-120.

Bronson, G. W. Fear of visual novelty: Developmental patterns in males and females. *Developmental Psychology*, 1970, *2*, 33-40.

Bronson, G. W. Infants' reactions to unfamiliar persons and novel objects. *Monographs of the Society for Research in Child Development*, Serial No. 146, Vol. 37, No. 1, March 1972.

Broverman, D. M., Klaiber, E. L., Kobayashi, Y. P., & Vogel, W. Roles of activation and inhibition in sex differences in cognitive abilities. *Psychological Review*, 1968, *75*, 23-56.

Buffery, A. W. H., & Gray, J. A. Sex differences in the development of spatial and linguistic skills. In C. Ounsted & D. C. Taylor (Eds.), *Gender differences: Their ontogeny and significance*. London, England: Churchill Livingstone, 1972.

Burton, R. V., & Whiting, J. W. M. The absent father and cross-sex identity. *Merrill-Palmer Quarterly*, 1967, *7*, 85-95.

Connolly, K., & Stratton, P. Developmental changes in associated movements. *Developmental Medicine and Child Neurology*, 1968, *10*, 49-56.

Douglas, J. W. B. Early disturbing events and later enuresis. In I. Kolvin, R. MacKeith, & S. R. Meadow (Eds.), *Bladder control and enuresis. Clinics in Developmental Medicine* (Nos. 48-49). London, England: SIMP/Heinemann, 1973.

Eisenberg, L. The epidemiology of reading retardation and a program for preventative intervention. In J. Money (Ed.), *The disabled reader: Education of the dyslexic child*. Baltimore, Maryland: Johns Hopkins Univ. Press, 1966.

Etaugh, C. Effects of maternal employment on children: A review of recent research. *Merrill-Palmer Quarterly of Behavior and Development*, 1974, *20*, 71-98.

Eysenck, S. B. G. *Manual of the Junior Eysenck Personality Inventory*. San Diego, California: Educational and Industrial Testing Service, 1963.

Fabia, J., & Drolette, M. Malformation and leukemia in children with Down's syndrome. *Pediatrics*, 1970, *45*, 60.

Farley, F. H., & Mealiea, W. L. Dissimulation and social desirability in the assessment of fears. *Behavioral Therapy*, 1971, *2*, 101-102.

Felner, R. D., Stolberg, A., & Cowen, E. L. Crisis events and school mental health referral patterns of young children. *Journal of Consulting and Clinical Psychology*, 1975, *43*, 305-310.

Finer, M. *Report of the committee on one-parent families* (2 vols.). London, England: Her Majesty's Stationery Office, 1974.

Gadpaille, W. J. Research into the physiology of maleness and femaleness. *Archives of General Psychiatry*, 1972, *26*, 193-206.

Geer, J. H. The development of a scale to measure fear. *Behavior Research and Therapy*, 1965, *3*, 45-53.

Goldberg, S., & Lewis, M. Play behavior in the year-old infant: Early sex differences. *Child Development*, 1969, *40*, 21-31.

Goldfarb, W. Childhood psychosis. In P. H. Mussen (Ed.), *Carmichael's manual of child psychology* (3rd ed.). New York: Wiley, 1970.

Good, T., & Brophy, J. *Educational psychology: A realistic approach*. New York: Holt, 1977.

Gove, W., & Herb, W. Stress and mental illness among the young: A comparison of the sexes. *Social Forces*, 1974, *53*, 256-265.

Graham, P. Epidemiological studies. In H. C. Quay & J. S. Werry (Eds.), *Psychopathological disorders of childhood*. New York: Wiley, 1979.

Graham, P., & Rutter, M. Adolescent disorders. In M. Rutter & L. Hersov (Eds.), *Child psychiatry*. Oxford, England: Blackwell, 1977.

Grossberg, J. M., & Wilson, H. K. A correlational comparison of the Wolpe-Lang fear survey schedule and the Taylor Manifest Anxiety Scale. *Behavior Research and Therapy*, 1965, *3*, 125-128.

Gullahorn, J. E. Sex-related factors in cognition and in brain lateralization. In J. E. Gullahorn (Ed.), *Psychology and women: In transition*. New York: Wiley, 1979.

Gurin, G., Veroff, J., & Feld, S. *Americans view their mental health*. New York: Basic Books, 1960.

Harris, L. J. Sex differences in the growth and use of language. In E. Donelson & J. E. Gullahorn (Eds.), *Women: A psychological perspective*. New York: Wiley, 1977.

Hersen, M. Self-assessment of fear. *Behavior Therapy*, 1973, *4*, 241-257.

Herzberg, F., & Lapkin, M. A. A study of sex differences on the Primary Mental Abilities Test. *Educational and Psychological Measurement*, 1954, *14*, 687-689.

Hetherington, E. M. Effects of paternal absence on personality development in adolescent daughters. *Developmental Psychology*, 1972, *7*, 313-326.

Hetherington, E. M., Cox, M., & Cox, R. The aftermath of divorce. In J. H. Stevens, Jr., & M. Mathews (Eds.), *Mother-child, father-child behaviors*. Washington, D.C.: National Association for the Education of Young Children, 1977. (a)

Hetherington, E. M., Cox, M., & Cox, R. *The development of children in mother-headed families*. Paper presented at Conference on Families in Contemporary America at George Washington University, Washington, D.C. June 1977. (b)

Hetherington, E. M., & Martin, B. Family interaction. In H. C. Quay & J. S. Werry (Eds.), *Psychopathological disorders of childhood* (2nd ed.). New York: Wiley, 1979.

Hetherington, E. M., & Parke, R. D. *Child psychology*. New York: McGraw-Hill, 1975.

Hingtgen, J. N., & Bryson, C. Q. Recent developments in the study of early childhood psychoses: Infantile autism, childhood schizophrenia, and related disorders. *Schizophrenia Bulletin*, Spring 1972, *1* (Experimental issue No. 5), 8-54.

Hoffman, L. W. Moral development. In P. Mussen (Ed.), *Handbook of child psychology*. New York: Wiley, 1970.

Hoffman, L. W. Effects of maternal employment on the child—A review of the research. *Developmental Psychology*, 1974, *10*, 204-228.

Hoffman, L. W. Changes in family roles, socialization, and sex differences. *American Psychologist*, 1977, *32*, 644-657.

Inglis, J., & Lawson, J. S. Sex differences in the effects of unilateral brain damage on intelligence. *Science*, 1981, *212*, 693-695.

Jacklin, C. N., Maccoby, E. E., & Dick, A. E. Barrier behavior and toy preference: Sex differences (and their absence) in the year-old child. *Child Development*, 1973, *44*, 196-200.

Jersild, A. T., & Holmes, F. B. Children's fears. *Child Development Monographs*, No. 20. New York: Teachers' College, Columbia University Press, 1935.

Johnson, D. D. Sex differences in reading across cultures. *Reading Research Quarterly*, 1973-1974, *9*, 67-86.

Kagan, J. *Change and continuity in infancy*. New York: Wiley, 1971.

Kagan, J. Psychology of sex differences. In F. A. Beach (Ed.), *Human sexuality in four perspectives*. Baltimore, Maryland: Johns Hopkins Univ. Press, 1977.

Kamin, L. Sex differences in susceptibility of IQ to environmental influence. *Child Development*, 1978, *49*, 517-518.

Kurdek, L. A. An integrative perspective on children's divorce adjustment. *American Psychologist*, 1981, *36*, 856-866.

Langner, G. S., & Michael, S. T. *Life stresses and mental health*. New York: Free Press, 1963.

Lansdell, H. A sex difference in effect of temporal lobe neurosurgery on design preference. *Nature*, 1962, *194*, 852-854.

Lansdell, H. Effect of extent of temporal lobe ablations on two lateralized deficits. *Physiology and Behavior*, 1968, *3*, 271-273.

Lansdell, H., & Urbach, N. Sex differences in personality measures related to size and side of temporal lobe ablations. *Proceedings of the American Psychological Association*, 1965, *73*, 113-114.

Lapouse, R., & Monk, M. A. Behavior deviations in a representative sample of children: Variation by sex, age, race, social class and family size. *American Journal of Orthopsychiatry*, 1964, *34*, 436-446.

Lavik, N. Urban-rural differences in rates of disorder: A comparative psychiatric population study of Norwegian adolescents. In P. J. Graham (Ed.), *Epidemiological approaches in child psychiatry*. New York: Academic Press, 1977.

Lehrke, R. A theory of X-linkage of major intellectual traits. *American Journal of Mental Deficiency*, 1972, *76*, 611-619.

Lehrke, R. Sex linkage: A biological basis for greater male variability in intelligence. In R. T. Osborne, C. E. Noble, & N. Weyl (Eds.), *Human variation: The biopsychology of age, race, and sex*. New York: Academic Press, 1978.

Lewis, M., & Brooks, J. Self, other, and fear: Infants' reactions to people. In M. Lewis & L. A. Rosenblum (Eds.), *The origins of fear*. New York: Wiley, 1974.

Lynn, D. B. *The father: His role in child development*. Belmont, California: Brooks/Cole, 1974.

Maccoby, E. E., & Jacklin, N. J. *The psychology of sex differences*. Stanford, California: Stanford Univ. Press, 1974.

McCord, W., McCord, J., & Thurber, E. Some effects of paternal absence on male children. *Journal of Abnormal and Social Psychology*, 1962, *64*, 361-369.

Macfarlane, J. W., Allen, L., & Honzik, M. P. *A developmental study of the behavior problems of normal children between twenty-one months and fourteen years*. Berkeley: Univ. of California Press, 1954.

McGlone, J. Sex differences in functional brain asymmetry. In M. A. Wittig (Chair), *Determinants of gender differences in cognitive functioning*. Symposium presented at the meeting of the American Psychological Association, Washington, D.C., September 1976.

McGlone, J., & Kertesz, A. Sex differences in cerebral processing of visuospatial tasks. *Cortex*, 1973, *9*, 313-320,

McGrew, W. C. *An ethological study of childrens' behavior*. New York: Academic Press, 1972.

Manosevitz, M., & Lanyon, R. E. Fear survey schedule: A normative study. *Psychological Reports*, 1965, *17*, 699-703.

Mensh, I. N., Kantor, M. B., Domke, H. R., Gildea, M. C-L., & Glidewell, J. C. Children's behavior symptoms and their relationship to school adjustment, sex, and social class. *Journal of Social Issues*, 1959, *15*, 8-15.

Miller, L. C., Hampe, R., Barrett, C. L., & Noble, H. Children's deviant behavior within the general population. *Journal of Consulting and Clinical Psychology*, 1971, *37*, 16-22.

Miller, P. M. An experimental analysis of retention control training in the treatment of nocturnal enuresis in two institutionalized adolescents. *Behavior Therapy*, 1973, *4*, 288-294.

Nance, W. E., & Engel, E. One X and four hypotheses: Response to Lehrke's "A theory of X-linkage of major intellectual traits," *American Journal of Mental Deficiency*, 1972, *76*, 623-625.

Nelson, K. Structure and strategy in learning to talk. *Monographs of the Society for Research in Child Development*, 1973, *38* (1-2, Serial No. 149).

Nye, F. I. Child adjustment in broken and in unhappily unbroken homes. *Marriage and Family Living*, 1957, *19*, 356-360.

Nye, F. I. *Family relationships and delinquent behavior.* New York: Wiley, 1958.

Ornitz, E. M. Childhood autism: A review of the clinical and experimental literature. *California Medicine,* 1973, *118,* 29-47.

Oster, J. *Mongolism.* Copenhagen: Danish Science Press, 1953.

Parkman, R. *Immunology.* In A. J. Schaffer & M. E. Avery (Eds.), *Diseases of the newborn* (4th ed.). Philadelphia, Pennsylvania: Saunders, 1977.

Parlee, M. B. Comments on "Roles of activation and inhibition in sex differences in cognitive abilities." *Psychological Reports,* 1972, *79,* 180-184.

Pawlby, S. J., & Hall, F. Early interactions and later language development of children whose mothers came from disrupted families of origin. In T. M. Field (Ed.), *High-risk infants and children: Adult and peer interactions.* New York: Academic Press, 1980.

Peterson, D. R. Behavior problems of middle childhood. *Journal of Consulting Psychology,* 1961, *25,* 205-209.

Reed, E. W., & Reed, S. C. *Mental retardation: A family study.* Philadelphia, Pennsylvania: Saunders, 1965.

Reinisch, J. M., Gandelman, R., & Spiegel, F. S. Prenatal influences on cognitive abilities: Data from experimental animals and human genetic and endocrine syndromes. In M. A. Wittig & A. C. Petersen (Eds.), *Sex-related differences in cognitive functioning.* New York: Academic Press, 1979.

Richman, N., Stevenson, J., & Graham, P. Prevalence of behaviour problems in 3-year-old children: An epidemiological study in a London borough. *Journal of Child Psychology and Psychiatry,* 1975, *16,* 272-287.

Robson, K. S., Pederson, F. A., & Moss, H. A. Developmental observations of dyadic gazing in relation to the fear of strangers and social approach behavior. *Child Development,* 1969, *40,* 619-627.

Rosen, B. M. An overview of the mental health delivery system in the United States and services to children. In I. H. Berlin & I. A. Stone (Eds.), *Basic handbook of child psychiatry* (Vol. 4). New York: Basic Books, 1979.

Rosenberg, M. *Society and the adolescent self-image.* Princeton, New Jersey: Princeton Univ. Press, 1965.

Rosenthal, D. *Genetic theory and abnormal behavior.* New York: McGraw-Hill, 1970.

Ross, A. O. *Psychological disorders of children. A behavioral approach to theory, research and therapy* (2nd ed.). New York: McGraw-Hill, 1980.

Rothstein, W., & Boblitt, W. E. Expressed fears of psychiatric inpatients. *Journal of Clinical Psychology,* 1970, *26,* 277-279.

Rutter, M. Concepts of autism: A review of research. *Journal of Child Psychology and Psychiatry,* 1968, *9,* 1-25.

Rutter, M. Sex differences in children's responses to family stress. In E. J. Anthony & C. M. Koupernik (Eds.), *The child and his family.* New York: Wiley, 1970.

Rutter, M. Classification. In M. Rutter & L. Hersov (Eds.), *Child psychiatry: Modern approaches.* Oxford, England: Blackwell, 1977.

Rutter, M., Graham, P., & Yule, W. A neuropsychiatric study in childhood. *Clinics in Developmental Medicine* (Nos. 35-36). London, England: SIMP/Heinemann, 1970.

Rutter, M., Tizard, J., & Whitmore, K. *Education, health and behaviour: Psychological and medical study of childhood development.* New York: Wiley, 1970.

Rutter, M., Yule, W., & Graham, P. Enuresis and behaviour deviance: Some epidemiological considerations. In I. Kolvin, R. MacKeith, & S. R. Meadow (Eds.), *Bladder control and enuresis. Clinics in Developmental Medicine. (Nos. 48-49).* London: SIMP/Heinemann, 1973.

Santrock, J. W. Father absence, perceived maternal behavior, and moral development in boys. *Child Development,* 1975, *46,* 753-757.

Scherer, M. W., & Nakamura, C. Y. A fear survey schedule for children (FFS-FC): A factor analytic comparison with manifest anxiety (CMAS). *Behavior Research and Therapy,* 1968, *6,* 173-182.

Schnell, H. Sex differences in relation to stuttering: Part I. *Journal of Speech Disorders,* 1946, *11,* 277-298.

Schnell, H. Sex differences in relation to stuttering: Part II. *Journal of Speech Disorders,* 1947, *12,* 23-38.

Sears, R. R., Whiting, J. W. M., Nowlis, V., & Sears, P. S. Some childrearing antecedents of aggression and dependency in young children. *Genetic Psychology Monographs,* 1953, *47,* 135-234.

Shaffer, D. Enuresis. In M. Rutter & L. Hersov (Eds.), *Child psychiatry.* Oxford, England: Blackwell, 1977.

Shaffer, D., Chadwick, O., & Rutter, M. Psychiatric outcome of localized head injury in children. In R. Porter & D. W. Fitzsimons (Eds.), *Outcome of severe damage to the central nervous system.* (CIBA foundation symposium No. 34.) Amsterdam: Elsevier-Excerpta Medica-North-Holland, 1975.

Sherman, J. *Sex-related cognitive differences: An essay on theory and evidence.* Springfield, Illinois: Thomas, 1978.

Singer, J. E., Westphal, M., & Niswander, K. R. Sex differences in the incidence of neonatal abnormalities and abnormal performance in early childhood. *Child Development,* 1968, *39,* 103-122.

Smith, K. P. Social and situational determinants of fear in the play group. In M. Lewis & L. A. Rosenblum (Eds.), *The origins of fear.* New York: Wiley, 1974.

Tanner, J. *Fetus into man: Physical growth from conception to maturity.* Cambridge, Massachusetts: Harvard Univ. Press, 1978.

Taylor, D. C. Differential rates of cerebral maturation between sexes and between hemispheres. *Lancet,* 1969, *2,* 140-142.

Taylor, M. A. Sex ratio's of newborns: Associated with pre-partum and post-partum schizophrenia. *Science,* 1969, *164,* 723-724.

Tennes, K. H., & Lampl, E. E. Stranger and separation anxiety in infancy. *Journal of Nervous and Mental Disease,* 1964, *139,* 247-254.

Tuckman, J., & Regan, R. A. Intactness of the home and behavioral problems in children. *Journal of Child Psychology and Psychiatry,* 1966, *7,* 225-233.

Waber, D. P. The meaning of sex-related variations in maturation rate. In J. E. Gullahorn (Ed.), *Psychology and women: In transition.* New York: Wiley, 1979.

Waldron, I. Why do women live longer than men? *Social Science and Medicine,* 1976, *10,* 349-362.

Wallerstein, J. S., & Kelly, J. B. *Surviving the breakup: How children and parents cope with divorce.* New York: Basic Books, 1980.

Warheit, G. J., Holzer, C. E., III, & Arey, S. A. Race and mental illness: An epidemiological update. *Journal of Health and Social Behavior,* 1975, *16,* 243-256.

Werry, J. S. The childhood psychoses. In H. C. Quay & J. S. Werry, *Psychopathological disorders of childhood.* New York: Wiley, 1979. (a)

Werry, J. S. Organic factors. In H. C. Quay & J. S. Werry, *Psychopathological disorders of childhood.* New York: Wiley, 1979. (b)

Werry, J. S., & Quay, H. C. The prevalence of behavior symptoms in younger elementary school children. *American Journal of Orthopsychiatry,* 1971, *41,* 136-143.

Wing, L., Baldwin, J. A., & Rosen, B. M. The use of child psychiatric services in three urban areas: an international case-register study. In J. K. Wing & A. M. Hailey (Eds.), *Evaluating a community psychiatric service: The Camberwell Register 1964-71*. London and New York: Oxford Univ. Press, 1972.

Witelson, S. F. Early hemisphere specialization and interhemisphere plasticity: An empirical and theoretical review. In S. Segalowitz & F. Gruber (Eds.), *Language development and neurological theory*. New York: Academic Press, 1977.

Wolkind, S., & Rutter, M. Children who have been "in care"—an epidemiological study. *Journal of Child Psychology and Psychiatry*, 1973, *14*, 97-105.

Woods, M. B. The unsupervised child of the working mother. *Developmental Psychology*, 1972, *6*, 14-25.

4

IHSAN AL-ISSA

Gender and Adult Psychopathology

Two influential studies by Chesler (1972) and by Gove and Tudor (1973) have concluded that the rates of mental illness are higher for women than for men. They have also suggested that because the female role is more stressful than that of the male, women tend more often to be mentally ill. Since genetic research does not suggest that inheritance might favor one sex over the other (Rosenthal, 1970), role theory could provide a promising alternative explanation of sex differences in mental illness.

However, studies claiming higher rates of mental illness among females as well as the explanation of their data in terms of role theory have been subjected to many criticisms (Dohrenwend & Dohrenwend, 1976). For example, these studies have not distinguished between different psychiatric entities and have ignored sex differences in certain types of psychopathology that tend to be higher among males. Furthermore, trends over time for different types of mental illness have not been analyzed. Factors other than gender role stress have been suggested to explain sex differences in mental illness. Thus, the conclusion that women are more often mentally ill than men needs further examination. Since other chapters in this volume report on research on various specific subtypes of mental illness, this chapter will deal with the evidence on overall rates of mental illness and the general categories of psychopathology, which include psychosis, neurosis, and personality disorders. Gender role theory as well as other theories put forward to explain sex differences in mental illness will also be discussed.

ISBN: 0-12-050350-6

Sex Differences in the Rates of Mental Illness

Gove and Tudor (1973) found that in 1967 women had higher rates than men in first admission for functional psychosis and neurosis in both public and private hospitals. Similar data from general hospitals, psychiatric outpatient care, and private practice led the authors to the conclusion that the frequency of mental illness is higher for females than for males. However, this general conclusion is not supported by later studies of admission rates in the 1970s. Statistics for mental health facilities in 1972 reported by Belle (1980) indicate that men utilize state and county mental hospitals at higher rates than women. It is only women's use of private mental hospitals that is higher than that of men's. Men and women are about equally represented at community mental health centers and at outpatient psychiatric services. Belle also found that when all facilities are considered, men and women utilize them at equal rates. Kramer (1977) reported that when Veterans Administration (VA) hospitals are added to all other facilities, males have an excessive rate of mental illness.

Rates of admission that are inconsistent with those reported by Gove and Tudor (1973) may be the result of differences in the definition of mental illness. The narrow Gove and Tudor definition of mental illness has excluded personality disorders and thus has underestimated the rates of mental illness for men. Indeed, when all patients admitted to state and county hospitals are considered, the rates of males are higher than those of females even prior to the 1970s (M to F 1.14:1 in 1946; 1.32:1 in 1955; and 2.27:1 in 1972) (Kramer, 1977). The decrease in the female rates for admission in the 1950s and 1960s to all mental institutions reported by Kramer may have increased the gap in the rates of admission between the sexes.

In contrast to data from mental health facilities, community studies are more representative of psychiatric disturbance in the population because they include both treated and untreated cases. Gove and Tudor (1973) reported that studies published after World War II reveal that the overall rates of mental illness are consistently higher for women than for men. In contrast, the pre-World War II community studies show consistently higher rates for men. This trend applies, however, only to the overall rates of mental illness. The major subtypes of functional psychiatric disorders do not indicate a reversal between the earlier and later studies. For instance, Dohrenwend and Dohrenwend (1976) found that the rates of personality disorders are consistently higher for men in both the earlier and later studies. The Dohrenwends also found no consistent evidence of higher male rates of either psychosis or neurosis in the pre-1950 studies. In the post-1950 studies, Dohrenwend, Dohrenwend, Link, Neugebauer, and Wunsch-Hitzig (1980) reported that the rates of neurosis among women appear on the average to be greater than twice the rate of males. The ratio of female to male for personality disorders in these studies is

.66:1, but Dohrenwend *et al.* (1980) pointed out that this ratio is expected to be higher because many people given this diagnosis spend part of their lives in prison or other institutions and the figures thus tend to underestimate sex differences.

Many community studies reviewed by Gove and Tudor (1972) used objective self-report measures of mild signs and symptoms (psychological, physical) that are only indirectly associated with mental illness. In contrast to studies on treated and untreated cases that are inconsistent in showing higher rates of mental illness among women, self-report studies are consistent in indicating that women are more likely to obtain higher scores than men (Gove and Tudor, 1973). A more recent review of both local community studies and nationwide studies confirms the consistent trend found by Gove and Tudor (Dohrenwend *et al.*, 1980). Dohrenwend *et al.* observed that high scores similar to those obtained by psychiatric patients are obtained more often by women than by men. They also found that the screening scales used in community studies are highly correlated with measures of self-esteem, helplessness-hopelessness, sadness and anxiety. These characteristics are similar to those constituting demoralization, which is described by Frank (1961/1973) as a major factor in help-seeking and relief, particularly through psychotherapy. Dohrenwend *et al.* (1980) suggested that high scores on the screening scales and demoralization are more likely to be experienced by minority groups and persons such as housewives and the poor.

Marital Status and Mental Illness

Gove (1972) found that community surveys and studies of utilization of mental institutions (published after World War II until 1968) reveal that married women have higher rates of mental illness than married men. However, more recent utilization rates of different mental health facilities reported by Belle (1980) for 1969, 1970-1971 and by Milazzo-Sayre (1977) for 1975 reveal that in state and county mental hospitals, men have higher rates than women among the married, giving no support to the Gove finding.

In contrast to married people, Gove reported that most data indicate that single men have higher rates than single women. Gove's findings on the formerly married are less consistent, but again most studies show that men have higher rates for both the divorced and widowed categories. Belle's (1980) more recent data indicate that sex differences among the formerly married vary with the type of institution. In state and county mental hospitals, men have higher rates than women among the separated or divorced, the widowed, and the never married. Similarly, in all other facilities (general hospital inpatient psychiatric units, outpatient psychiatric services, private mental hospitals), widowed and divorced or separated men have higher rates than women. However, among the never married, men have higher rates in general hospital inpatient psychiatric units, whereas women have higher rates in outpatient psychiatric services and private mental hospitals. For both sexes, however, the highest rates of utilization, regardless of the type of facility, are among the divorced or separated.

Belle (1980) found that the highest rate for utilization of mental health facilities is by women who head families without spouses. In 1970, women heads of families were admitted to outpatient psychiatric services at a rate that exceeded one admission for every 100 female family heads in the population (over 1.5 for every 100 black female family heads in the population). The admission rate of divorced and single female family heads was similarly high. Women who were separated from their husbands and headed families had an admission rate of over 3 per 100 of the population. Widowed family heads, however, appear far less vulnerable; their utilization rate was less than .3 per 100 of these women in the population.

Explaining Sex Differences in Mental Illness

There are two major approaches to explaining sex differences in mental illness. One approach suggests that sex differences are caused by stresses related to gender role. It is assumed that because the female role is more stressful than the male role, women tend to have more mental illness than men. The second approach postulates that female rates of mental illness are comparable to those of males, but because of their gender role, they become more involved with the psychiatric profession. According to this approach, the high rate of mental illness among females is an artifact of three factors: (*a*) women may report more illness than men because it is culturally more acceptable for them to be ill; (*b*) the sick role is more compatible with female than male role responsibilities and therefore they may have more contact with psychiatric facilities; and (*c*) social roles are imputed with differential power, and since the female role involves less power than the male role, women are more vulnerable to the accusation of madness and to confinement in mental institutions.

The Stress Hypothesis

Mental illness may be related to stresses involved in the biological or social roles of men and women. The biological hypothesis has mainly concentrated on the relationship between disturbances in the female reproductive functions, particularly hormonal imbalance and depression, anxiety, and tension. In this section, I discuss the social role aspect of the stress hypothesis and defer the biological hypothesis to Chapter 13. I deal here with marriage, stress, and mental illness; stressful life events and mental illness; and physical attractiveness, stress, and mental illness.

MARRIAGE, STRESS, AND MENTAL ILLNESS

A general version of the stress hypothesis put forward by Gove (Gove, 1972; Gove & Tudor, 1973) has emphasized the disadvantages of marriage for women. He considered the position of the housewife as frustrating and unsatisfactory as compared with the position of the male jobholder. Housework, according to Gove, tends to be unstructured, which may allow females to brood on their problems as compared with the constant demands put on males in their jobs outside the home. Even when she works, the wife's position tends to be stressful because her job is not only below her educational level but is also considered secondary to her main role as a housewife.

Marriage as a source of stress may, however, depend on the particular position of the person and may not be applicable to all married females, as postulated by Gove. For example, G. Brown and Harris (1978) have shown that vulnerability to mental illness in marriage among females is associated with (*a*) lack of intimate relations with a husband; (*b*) loss of mother by death or separation before age 11; (*c*) having three or more children aged 14 or under at home; (*d*) lack of full or part-time employment; and (*e*) working-class background.

Contrary to the stress hypothesis put forward by Gove, it has been suggested that divorce may contribute relatively more to decreased life satisfaction and increased depression for women than for men (Radloff, 1975; Spreitzer, Snyder, & Larson, 1975). Other studies reviewed by P. Brown and Fox (1979) also indicate that divorced women experience more situational stress and report more distress than divorced men. For example, whereas the disadvantaged economic situation of divorced women is a source of tension, worry, and anxiety, the financial position of divorced men is more likely to be less deprived and their work role remains largely unchanged. Also, mothers usually assume the additional childrearing responsibilities of a single parent, which relieve fathers from the stresses of the parental role. Why, then, are divorced men generally more vulnerable to mental illness than divorced women? P. Brown and Fox (1979) suggested that a higher rate of mental illness among divorced men may be due to their feelings of being cut off from vital social roles and the resulting loss of their sense of social meaning and purpose. Although divorce increases male opportunities and resources for socializing, divorced men tend to report an increase in feeling of restlessness and emotional isolation (Hetherington, Cox, & Cox, 1976). It appears that gender role socialization is more important than is the availability of social opportunities in determining the behavior of divorced men and women. Women are trained to cope through seeking the help and support of others (e.g., to seek professional help, to join informal groups or social organizations to meet their social and emotional needs during divorce). They are also better prepared to establish intimate relations with other persons. On the other hand, male early socialization may discourage the development of skills for intimacy and could add to feelings of alienation and loss of meaning in life.

The selection hypothesis should also be considered to explain the relationship between marital status and mental health. This hypothesis suggests that sex differences in mental illness among the married or divorced may reflect premorbid personality rather than any differential reaction to stressors involved in marital status. That is, unstable men are less likely than unstable women to get married, which may result in higher rates of mental illness among married women than married men. Similarly, the higher rate of mental illness among the divorced than the married may not be due to a higher level of stress in divorce, but to the fact that psychiatric illness tends to contribute significantly to marital breakdown (Briscoe, Smith, Robins, Marten, & Gaskin, 1973). It may, however, be noted that, when only depression was investigated by Briscoe and Smith (1973), they found evidence in support of the stress hypothesis. They found that depressed divorced women were more likely than depressed divorced men to have been depressed during the marriage, whereas depressed divorced men were more likely to have become depressed during the marital separation. Furthermore, the higher rate of mental illness among divorced men in particular may be influenced by the tendency of men to remarry more often and more quickly than women. This tendency among men increases the probability that those who remain unmarried have poorer mental health, thus inflating the rates among divorced males. Combined with the stress hypothesis, data on the selection hypothesis would lead to the conclusion that mental illness could be the result of marital status as well as the cause of it.

STRESSFUL LIFE EVENTS AND MENTAL ILLNESS

It is commonly believed that there are more stressors in the lives of women than of men (Chesler, 1972; Gove & Tudor, 1973). However, there is no evidence that women report more life stressors than men. For example, women do not score higher than men on life-change units or on stressful life events (Markush & Favero, 1974; Uhlenhuth, Lipman, Balter, & Stern, 1974). Yet, they tend to report more symptoms than men. It appears that although the sexes may have the same levels of life stressors, women may subjectively experience more distress than men. Horowitz, Schaefer, and Cooney (1974) reported that, when subjects were asked to imagine how much stress they would be under if certain stressful events were to occur, women tended to rate events as more stressful than men. Some events appear to be more traumatic for women than for men, such as changing residence, especially moving to another city or state. (Maternal loss also seems to make women more vulnerable to depression and schizophrenia than men [Seidenberg, 1975; see also Chapter 7, this volume]). Malzberg (1969) has observed that immigration introduces a more difficult process of adjustment and a higher rate of admission among foreign-born females than males. Cochrane and Stopes-Roe (1977) found that among Indian immigrants in Britain, the extent of crowded living is associated with psychiatric symptoms of women rather than of men. In contrast, other stressful life events may be more traumatic to men than to women. Stressors related to socioeconomic status and educational level are negatively associated with mental illness in the two sexes, but this association is less intense among females than males (Hollingshead & Redlich, 1958; Milazzo-Sayre, 1979). Cochrane and Stopes-Roe (1977) found that among Indian males, the longer the residency in Britain, the fewer symptoms they report. However, the length of residency is not significantly related to female symptoms. There is also some evidence that indicates that stresses such as those associated with social disintegration are related to a high rate of mental illness either in women (in the Yoruba villages, Nigeria) or in men (in Stirling County, Nova Scotia) depending on cultural background (Leighton, Lambo, Hughes, Leighton, Murphy, & Macklin, 1963). Bebbington, Hurry, Tennant, Sturt, and Wing (1981) found that employment status of the spouse is related to affective disorders in men and women in opposite directions. In men, those with a wife at home are less at risk than those whose wife goes to work. In women, there is a nonsignificant trend for those whose husbands are at home to be more at risk than their counterparts with working husbands. These sex differences in the effects of stress strongly suggest that contrary to current practice in stress research, different stress values should be assigned to events for males and females.

The selection of items included in most lists of life events tends to represent events in men's, rather than women's, lives (Makosky, 1980). For example, life events related to work tend to apply to a larger number of men than women. On the other hand, events that apply to women such as rape, physical assault, abortion, and child care are not included in the lists of events. Women also tend to report more events in which they are not the central figure, but in which there were people important to them, such as family members and friends (B. S. Dohrenwend, 1976). A potential research area is the study of sex differences in the nature of stressful events such as intensity, duration, and controllability and the relationship of gender to symptoms (Brown & Harris, 1978; Makosky, 1980). For example, B. S. Dohrenwend (1973) found that women's symptoms are mainly affected by events they could not control, whereas men's symptoms are related to all events. Conclusions about the relationship between stress and mental illness in men and women should consider the kind and nature of events impinging on them.

More recently, a study by Kanner, Coyne, Schaefer, and Lazarus (1981) of the relationship between minor events and symptoms raised some questions about the different impact of these events on the sexes. These minor events are represented in the hassles and uplifts of everyday life (*hassles* are irritating, frustrating, distressing events such as losing things, traffic jams, arguments, financial and family concerns; *uplifts* are positive experiences such as joy derived from the manifestation of love, relief from hearing good news, feeling healthy, eating out, etc.). Kanner *et al.* (1981) found that although hassles are positively related to psychological symptoms and negative affect in both sexes, uplifts are positively related to symptoms in women but not in men. Thus, uplifts may have different significance for men and women, based on gender-related values. Kanner *et al.* also suggested that there may be gender differences in coping, with women emphasizing the positive aspects of situations. Since uplifts may be part of the coping response of females to hassles, it is possible that they may occur in the same situational context as hassles. As in studies of major life events, gender differences in the impact of uplifts may be due to different situational contexts faced by the two sexes.

Finally, many sex differences such as those that are noticed in rural and urban areas cannot be explained on the basis of stresses related to gender role (Dohrenwend & Dohrenwend, 1974). For example, the stress hypothesis would predict lower rates of mental illness for women in rural than in urban areas because the female role is less stressful in rural areas. However, studies published after 1950 show higher rates of neurosis for women than men in both rural and urban areas. For psychosis, contrary to the role theory, women tend to have higher rates in rural areas, whereas men tend to show higher rates in urban areas. Data on sex differences in mental illness, particularly those revealing a consistently high rate of neurosis among women and personality disorders among men, would suggest that the two sexes are different in their style of reaction to, rather than in the amount of, stress.

PHYSICAL ATTRACTIVENESS, STRESS, AND MENTAL ILLNESS

Since physical attractiveness is more related to the happiness, self-esteem, and emotional stability of women than men (Kirkpatrick & Cotton, 1951; Lerner, Orlos, & Knapp, 1976; Mathes & Kahn, 1975), research in this area is more relevant to female than male mental health. It is assumed that physically unattractive females are subjected to a stressful and harsh environment and therefore are more vulnerable to mental illness than are attractive females (Al-Issa, 1980). In support of this hypothesis, Farina, Fischer, Sherman, Smith,

Groh, and Mermin (1977) reported that hospitalized women were rated less attractive than a group of women living in the community. They also found that the less attractive a female patient, the more disturbed she is perceived to be by the ward staff. Indeed, female patients themselves tend to perceive the severity of their psychopathology relative to their physical attractiveness. Thus, the less attractive patients were, the more they regarded themselves as sick and the longer they estimated they would remain in the hospital. The relationship between patients' mental status and attractiveness was confirmed by Farina *et al.*, who found that the less attractive a patient is, the longer she remains in the hospital. More recently, Napoleon, Chassin, and Young (1980) found that less attractive persons have more severe diagnoses and longer stays in the hospital, supporting the general findings of Farina *et al.*

However, the relationship between physical attractiveness and mental illness is replicated when only an undifferentiated socioeconomic group is compared with patients (Napoleon *et al.*, 1980). When socioeconomic status was controlled by Napoleon *et al.*, they found that patients tended to be less attractive than upper- and middle-class women, but were not different from lower-class women in the community. This would suggest that unattractiveness may be a nonspecific source of stress that could result in many bad outcomes such as mental illness and low socioeconomic status. Indeed, physical unattractiveness tends to be associated with many negative social consequences, including lower social mobility (Al-Issa, 1980; Elder, 1969). Furthermore, physical attractiveness may not be related to the rates of mental illness as such, but rather to the social consequences of displaying symptoms of mental illness; that is, persons who are poor and unattractive may be sent to state hospitals whereas those who are affluent and/or attractive and display the same symptoms are referred to other facilities. Thus, physical attractiveness may not only be related to the onset of mental illness but also to the social consequences of being mentally ill (Napoleon *et al.*, 1980).

Finally, hospitalization could affect attractiveness; hospitalized patients may not be allowed to groom themselves adequately or they may simply stop paying attention to their appearance. Hence hospitalization may cause bad looks rather than vice versa. Farina *et al.* formulated this hypothesis, but they have rejected it on the grounds that unattractiveness was associated with the social maladjustment of these women before they were given psychiatric diagnosis and hospitalization.

Studies relating attractiveness to psychological adjustment are usually carried out with young females. Bersheid and Walster (1974) suggested that women who are attractive when young have more to lose than those who are not, and they predicted that they will show more psychological problems later in life. In support of this hypothesis, they found that women who were highly attractive when young, as judged from their college photographs, tended to be less happy and poorly adjusted to life in their forties. No such relationship between physical attractiveness and happiness in later life was observed for men. The tendency of women to remain as residents of mental institutions at an older age (Howard & Howard, 1974; Mensh, 1969) would suggest a relationship between physical attractiveness, aging, and the duration of hospitalization.

Sex Differences in the Report of Symptoms

Women tend to report more physical and psychiatric symptoms than men (Cooperstock, 1978; Nathanson, 1975; Phillips & Segal, 1969). Mechanic (1974) found that this tendency becomes quite noticeable as early as the eighth grade.

Phillips and Segal (1969) suggested that women may not actually have more symptoms than men, but they tend to report more symptoms because the expression of malaise and distress by women is more acceptable by society. Men, on the other hand, are expected to grin and bear it and to avoid the public display of emotional behavior. They argued that, particularly among men, illness is considered a feminine characteristic that should be avoided. Men are, therefore, more willing to ignore or conceal their psychological disturbance and underreport psychiatric symptoms.

One hypothesis that arises from the Phillips and Segal approach is that men are rejected more than women for manifesting the same symptoms. Phillips (1964) investigated this hypothesis by presenting married white women with five vignettes that described a man or a woman as a paranoid schizophrenic, a simple schizophrenic, a depressive neurotic, a phobic-compulsive, and a normal individual. Using a social distance scale indicating how close a relation the respondent was willing to tolerate with individuals in the case abstracts, he found that males are rejected more strongly than females exhibiting identical behavior and consulting the same help source such as a clergyman, physician, psychiatrist, or mental hospital. Eisenthal (1971) also found that the male version of clinical cases was rated by undergraduates of both sexes as more mentally ill than the female version of the same behavior. A replication of the Phillips study by Yamamoto and Dizney (1967) revealed that male and female cases were rejected at about the same rate, giving no support to the Phillips and Segal (1969) hypothesis. However, a larger number of help sources was suggested for men than women, implying that mental illness in men is taken more seriously than it is in women. Rather than using vignettes, Farina, Felner, and Boudreau (1973) investigated attitudes toward male and female expatients as job applicants in real life situations. They found that when faced with a female former patient, female subjects accepted her to work with them like a normal female. On the other hand, male subjects objected to working with a male expatient. Either the sex of the normal subjects or of the patients (or both) appears to be crucial in the acceptance of former mental patients.

Studies carried out by Gove (1980) indicate that the reporting of more psychiatric symptoms by women than men in community surveys is not influenced by social desirability or need for approval. However, Al-Issa (1980) suggested that the rejection of patients and the social desirability of symptoms may depend on whether these symptoms are compatible with gender role expectations; that is, the more these symptoms deviate from gender role expectations, the less they are desirable and the more they are rejected by others (antisocial behavior in the female and submissive emotional behavior in the male; see Hammen, Chapter 6, this volume).

The reporting of certain symptoms may also be influenced by research techniques that may favor the detection of male or female disturbance (personality disorders or neurosis, respectively) (Dohrenwend & Dohrenwend, 1974). Since male disturbance (personality disorders) is visible and has an aversive impact on others, it is likely that it receives the immediate reaction and control of the police, courts, and other social agencies. Female disturbance (neurosis), on the other hand, is less visible and depends mainly on self-report. Dohrenwend and Dohrenwend (1974) have observed that community studies published before 1950, which show an excess of mental illness among males, have used key informants and official records that tend to identify personality disorders more than neurosis. In contrast, studies after 1950, which indicate higher rates of mental illness among females, have used direct interviews and inventories that focus more on neurosis (anxiety, depression, physiological disturbances) than on personality disorders.

Studies of sex differences in the reporting of psychiatric symptoms do not clearly demonstrate that the tendency of women to report more symptoms is an artifact of gender role rather than the actual experience of these symptoms. In investigating this problem, it is necessary to use a criterion for the presence of symptoms that is independent of self-report. This can be achieved more easily with physical, than with psychiatric, symptoms. Pflanz (1978), for instance, found that household interviews indicate that women report more dyspeptic stomach complaints of the ulcer type than men, in the ratio of 1:.8. However, when the frequency of ulcers is assessed by other methods (ulcers clinically confirmed by x-ray), the number of men is greater than that of women (W to M, 1:4). Phillips and Segal (1969) also found that women report significantly more psychological distress than men even when the two groups are matched for physical symptoms. From these studies, which are based on physical symptoms, it is difficult to reach a conclusion about the extent to which the tendency to report symptoms rather than the actual experience of them can account for sex differences in mental illness.

Sex Differences in Contact with Physicians

It is found that women are more involved with health service than are men (Hinkle, Redmont, & Plummer, 1960; Nathanson, 1975). A major hypothesis to explain this tendency is that the role obligations of women give them more time and to incur less loss when attending health clinics (Nathanson, 1975). It is predicted that women with more role obligations would have less contact with health services. Studies reviewed by Nathanson (1975) indicate that the report of sickness is lower among married women than among the single, widowed, or divorced, supporting the hypothesis that the more demanding situation of married women makes it difficult for them to contact clinics and adopt the sick role. Similarly, G. W. Brown, Bhrolchain, and Harris (1975) found that women with young children at home tend to have a much lower rate of contact with physicians for psychiatric treatment as compared to women in another life stage. Similarly, wives with a job outside the home also report significantly fewer physical symptoms than do housewives (Feld, 1963).

Related to sex differences in the contact with health facilities is the tendency of clinicians to prescribe more drugs and to attribute poor mental health to women. Sex bias in the prescription of psychotropic drugs is discussed by Fidell in Chapter 10, this volume. Most research on sex bias in mental health is based on the finding by Broverman, Broverman, Clarkson, Rosenkrantz, and Vogel (1970) that both male and female professionals tend to see a healthy, mature male as almost the same as a healthy mature adult, whereas a healthy mature female was perceived as being significantly different from a healthy adult person. Healthy adult persons and healthy adult men were ascribed characteristics indicating competency such as being dominant, active, and independent, whereas women were rated lower on these characteristics. Broverman *et al.* concluded that general standards of health for an adult person are applied to men only, whereas healthy women are seen as significantly less healthy by adult standards. Analog studies on clinical judgment do not consistently show that, for a comparable level of psychiatric disorder, clinicians are more likely to perceive mental illness in women than men. For example, Gomes and Abramowitz (1976) found that sex bias tends to favor the female-identified, rather than the male-identified, stimulus-person. They found that the deviant female was perceived as especially mature, even by those clinicians whose personal reaction to her was negative. In another study, Abramowitz, Roback, Schwartz, Yasuna, Abramowitz, and Gomes (1976) concluded that the impact on clinical judgment of varying the patient's gender was slight. In fact, the patient received better prognosis and elicited slightly more empathy when identified as a woman. An overall examination of the data by Maffeo (1979) reveals that whereas later studies show bias in favor of women, early studies are consistent in indicating bias against women. She raised the question whether in later studies professionals may have become more sensitized to the potential for sex-related bias. It is not clear from the present studies how far changes in the attitudes of professionals are related to shifts in sex differences in the rates of mental illness referred to earlier in this chapter (i.e., recent decrease in the number of hospital admissions for women). Studies of clinical judgment are also based on abstract description of cases and their results may be difficult to generalize to an actual clinical situation. In addition to gender, factors that appear to influence clinical judgment are the political belief of the professional or the client (Abramowitz, Abramowitz, Jackson, & Gomes, 1973) and the context in which the behavior of the client takes place (Coie, Pennington, & Buckley, 1974). Furthermore, consideration should be given to clinician sex bias when differential diagnoses are given to the profiles of men and women with identical clinical features, such as giving a diagnosis of hysterical personality to the female and that of antisocial personality to the male (Warner, 1979). Fink, Shapiro, Goldensohn, and Daily (1969) found that general practitioners tend to give psychiatric diagnoses to women more than twice as often as to men. A general implication of studies on sex bias in diagnosis is that the clinician may influence the tendency of one sex over the other to maintain contact with mental health facilities.

Studies of the hypothesis that help-seeking behavior is an artifact of social factors rather than actual sex differences in mental illness should control for the level of psychiatric disturbance of, and the perceived need for help by, the subject. Gove (1980) reported two studies (Gove, 1978; Gurin, Veroff, & Feld, 1960) demonstrating that when controlling for self-report of impairment, women are no more likely than men to seek professional help. A third study reported by Blumenthal (1967) reveals that men are in fact more likely to seek help than are women. However, more recent studies of depression reveal that men are less willing to seek help (Hammen, Chapter 6, this volume).

Statistics on the rates of mental illness are more often based on prevalence (number of new and old cases) than on incidence (number of new cases only), and thus sex differences may be confounded by length of treatment and hospitalization. Cooper, Fry, and Kalt (1969), in a follow-up of patients in general practice in Britain, found that the F to M ratio of rates of onset of illness (based on incidence) is less than that based on prevalence. After a follow-up 1 year later, 26% of male patients and 43% of female patients were still in treatment. Eaton, Sletten, Kitchen, and Smith (1971) found 56% of the males and 72% of the females had been hospitalized before (see also sex differences in rehospitalization in schizophrenia, Chapter 7, this volume). Although a more recent study (Mann, Jenkins, & Belsey, 1981) did not find sex differences in the length of contact with general practitioners, factors related to continuation of treatment are still not sufficiently explored. Females continue treatment with their general practitioners for longer periods either because psychiatric illness lasts longer in women than men or because of other factors unrelated to the illness (report of symptoms, attitude of physicians). For example, a study of hospitalized patients by Doherty (1976) indicates that for both males and females, patients who accepted formal and informal hospital rules (conform to normative hospital expectations) were released earlier. However, type of diagnosis (neurosis versus personality disorder) is associated with the length of hospitalization for males only. In contrast, actual behavioral pattern and social relationship were more important in the length of hospitalization of females.

The explanation of sex differences in mental illness in terms of help-seeking behavior applies only to treated cases in health services, not to untreated cases in the community. Many patients in the community have had no contact with psychiatric services. Thus, sex differences in community studies can hardly be explained by the tendency of one sex to use psychiatric facilities more than the other.

Gender Roles, Power, and Mental Illness

In an analysis of social roles, Sarbin (1969) and Sarbin and Allen (1968) differentiated between ascribed and achieved roles on the basis of the degree of choice the person exercises in entering them. At one extreme, ascribed roles are granted to persons simply by virtue of their inherent characteristics or by virtue of their membership in society; for example, sex roles (male, female), kinship (mother, father, son), and roles related to age (juvenile, adult). At the other extreme, an achieved role is characterized by attainment or option by the person him- or herself, through training and personal achievement (physician, student, waiter, football player). More recently, Sarbin and Juhasz (1978) suggested that ascribed roles are more related to mental illness than are achieved roles because they are the minimal position a person may hold in a group; unlike achieved roles, the loss of ascribed roles, such as a family role, reduces the person to the status of a nonperson or mental patient. The relationship between ascribed roles such as those of family roles and mental illness is evident in the finding that referral for psychiatric treatment tends to originate predominantly within the family (Hollingshead & Redlich, 1958; Linn, 1961).

In an attempt to explain the high rate of mental illness among women, Sarbin and Juhasz (1978) have observed that since the performance of man is heavily weighted with occupational roles (achieved roles) and woman's behavior is biased toward the performance of family roles (ascribed roles), woman is more vulnerable to the label *mad*. As there is more power associated with achieved roles, in a strained relationship between a male and a female over role enactment, it is more likely that the female will be degraded to the status of a mental patient. This view is supported in a study by Linn (1961) that demonstrates that there is a greater likelihood for female patients living with their spouses or parents to be hospitalized by these persons than for male patients in the same living situations. Clausen and Yarrow (1955) also found that, even after recognizing a serious problem, wives are usually at a loss at what might be done if the husbands do not themselves accept that there is something wrong with them. In their achieved roles, husbands may be committed to a hospital when they get in trouble with the police (Linn, 1961), but the police are usually reluctant to initiate hospitalization because they do not regard commitment as a proper law reinforcement (Bittner, 1967). Another avenue for the hospitalization of men is when they have strained relationships with their employers, but again Linn (1961) found that men are more likely to be dismissed from their jobs than to be sent to a mental hospital. Thus, power within and outside the family may give the male an "idiosyncrasy credit" that enables him to avoid psychiatric treatment and hospitalization (Scheff, 1966). It does not, however, explain the high rate of psychiatric disturbance among untreated females in the community (Brown *et al.*, 1975; Dohrenwend *et al.*, 1980).

Summary and Conclusion

Mental health statistics indicate that sex differences vary depending on the definition of mental illness and the type of facility. Using a narrow definition of mental illness that includes, for example, only psychosis and neurosis, yields higher rates among women than men. However, when all patients admitted to state and county hospitals are considered, men tend to have higher rates than women. By using a similarly broad definition of mental illness, it was found that more women utilize private mental hospitals than men. Moreover, the sexes are about equally represented at community mental health centers and outpatient psychiatric services.

Early studies in which mental illness is narrowly defined indicate that married women have higher rates of mental illness than married men. In contrast, single status seems to favor women. When all admissions are considered in later studies, married women have lower rates than married men in some facilities such as county and state hospitals. Furthermore, among the formerly married, males tend to have higher rates in inpatient services, whereas females tend to have higher rates in outpatient clinics. The highest rate of utilization of mental health facilities is among women who head families without spouses.

Community studies that deal with both treated and untreated cases indicate that the rates of personality disorders are consistently higher for men than for women. On the other hand, women tend to have higher rates of neurosis than men. Community studies based on self-report measures of psychological and physical distress consistently reveal higher scores for women than men. These screening scales, which seem to measure demoralization, are significantly related to self-esteem, helplessness-hopelessness, sadness, and anxiety. Women seem to share this tendency with marginal persons and minority-group members.

It has been suggested that sex differences in mental illness may be influenced by the tendency of women to report more symptoms and to have more contact with physicians. Similarly, the rates of hospitalization are explained by the differential powers of the sexes. Thus, sex differences in mental illness are not true differences, but the artifact of social factors. These factors may, however, apply to statistics from mental health facilities rather than to community studies. Also, the hypothesis that women's lives are more stressful, which may result in higher rates of mental illness, has received little support. A consistently higher rate of neurosis among women and higher rates of personality disorders among men would suggest that sex differences are in the style of reaction to, rather than the amount of, stress.

Stresses associated with mental health may also be different for women and for men. For example, physical attractiveness is related to the emotional stability of women, but not of men. Marriage and single status may expose the sexes to different kinds of stress.

References

Abramowitz, S. I., Roback, H., Schwartz, J., Yasuna, A., Abramowitz, C. V., & Gomes, B. Sex bias in psychotherapy: A failure to confirm. *American Journal of Psychiatry*, 1976, *133*, 706-709.

Abramowitz, S. I., Abramowitz, C. V., Jackson, C., & Gomes, B. The politics of clinical judgment: What nonliberal examiners infer about women who do not stifle themselves. *Journal of Consulting and Clinical Psychology*, 1973, *41*, 385-391.

Al-Issa, I. *The psychopathology of women*. Englewood Cliffs, New Jersey: Prentice-Hall, 1980.

Bebbington, P., Hurry, J., Tennant, C., Sturt, E., & Wing, J. K. Epidemiology of mental disorders in Camberwell. *Psychological Medicine*, 1981, *11*, 561-579.

Belle, E. Who uses mental health facilities? In M. Guttentag, S. Salasin, & D. Belle (Eds.), *The mental health of women*. New York: Academic Press, 1980.

Berscheid, E., & Walster, E. H. Physical attractiveness. In L. Berkowitz (Ed.), *Advances in Experimental Social Psychology* (Vol. 7). New York: Academic Press, 1974.

Bittner, E. Police discretion in emergency apprehension of mentally ill persons. *Social Problems*, 1967, *14*, 278-292.

Blumenthal, M. Sex as a source of heterogeneity in mental health survey. *Journal of Psychiatric Research*, 1967, *5*, 75-87.

Briscoe, C. W., & Smith, M. D. Depression and marital turmoil. *Archives of General Psychiatry*, 1973, *29*, 812-917.

Briscoe, C. W., Smith, J., Robins, E., Marten, S., & Gaskin, F. Divorce and psychiatric disease. *Archives of General Psychiatry*, 1973, *29*, 119-125.

Broverman, I. K., Broverman, D. M., Clarkson, F. E., Rosenkrantz, P., & Vogel, S. R. Sex role stereotypes and clinical judgments of mental health. *Journal of Consulting and Clinical Psychology*, 1970, *34*, 1-7.

Brown, G. W., Bhrolchain, M. N., & Harris, T. Social class and psychiatric disturbance among women in an urban population. *Sociology*, 1975, *9*, 225-254.

Brown, G. W., & Harris, T. *Social origins of depression. A study of psychiatric disorders in women*. London: Tavistock, 1978.

Brown, P., & Fox, H. Sex differences in divorce. In E. S. Gomberg & V. Franks (Eds.), *Gender and disordered behavior*. New York: Brunner/Mazel, 1979.

Chesler, P. *Women and madness*. Garden City, New York: Doubleday, 1972.

Clausen, J. A., & Yarrow, M. R. Paths to the mental hospital. *Journal of Social Issues*, 1955, *11*, 25-32.

Cochrane, R., & Stopes-Roe, M. Psychological and social adjustment of Asian immigrants to Britain: A community survey. *Social Psychiatry*, 1977, *12*, 195-206.

Coie, J. D., Pennington, D. F., & Buckley, H. H. Effects of situational stress and sex roles on attributions of psychological disorders. *Journal of Consulting and Clinical Psychology*, 1974, *42*, 559-568.

Cooper, B., Fry, J., & Kalt, G. W. A longitudinal study of psychiatric morbidity in a general practice population. *British Journal of Preventive and Social Medicine*, 1969, *23*, 210-217.

Cooperstock, R. Sex differences in psychotropic drug use. *Social Science and Medicine*, 1978, *12*, 179-186.

Doherty, E. G. Length of hospitalization in a short-term therapeutic community: A multivariate study of sex across time. *Archives of General Psychiatry*, 1976, *33*, 87-93.

Dohrenwend, B. P., & Dohrenwend, B. S. Social and cultural influences on psychopathology. *Annual Review of Psychology*, 1974, *25*, 417-452.

Dohrenwend, B. P., & Dohrenwend, B. S. Sex differences in psychiatric disorders. *American Journal of Sociology*, 1976, *81*, 1447-1471.

Dohrenwend, B. P., Dohrenwend, B. S., Link, B., Neugebauer, R., & Wunsch-Hitzig, R. *Mental illness in the United States: Epidemiological estimates*. New York: Praeger, 1980.

Dohrenwend, B. S. Social status and stressful life events. *Journal of Personality and Social Psychology*, 1973, *28*, 225-235.

Dohrenwend, B. S. *Anticipation and control of stressful life events: An exploratory analysis*. Paper presented at the Eastern Psychological Association Convention, New York, April 22-24, 1976.

Eaton, M. E., Sletten, I. W., Kitchen, A. D., & Smith, R. J. The Missouri automated psychiatric history: Symptom frequencies, sex differences, use of weapons and other findings. *Comprehensive Psychiatry*, 1971, *12*, 264-267.

Eisenthal, S. Attribution of mental illness in relation to sex of respondent and sex of rated stimulus person. *Psychological Reports*, 1971, *28*, 471-474.

Elder, G. Appearance and education in marriage mobility. *American Sociological Review*, 1969, *34*, 519-533.

Farina, A., Felner, R., & Boudreau, L. Reactions of workers to male and female mental patient job applicants. *Journal of Consulting and Clinical Psychology*, 1973, *41*, 363-372.

Farina, A., Fischer, E. H., Sherman, S., Smith, W. T., Groh, T., & Mermin, P. Physical attractiveness and mental illness. *Journal of Abnormal Psychology*, 1977, *8*, 510-517.

Feld, S. Feelings of adjustment. In F. I. Nye & L. W. Hoffman (Eds.), *The employed mother*. Chicago, Illinois: Rand McNally, 1963.

Fink, R., Shapiro, S., Goldensohn, S., & Daily, E. The "filter down" process in psychotherapy in a group medical care program. *Journal of Public Health*, 1969, *59*, 245-257.

Frank, J. D. *Persuasion and healing*. Baltimore, Maryland: Johns Hopkins Univ. Press, 1973. (Originally published, 1961).

Gomes, B., & Abramowitz, S. I. Sex-related patient therapist effects on clinical judgment. *Sex Roles,* 1976, *2,* 1-13.

Gove, W. R. The relationship between sex roles, marital status, and mental illness. *Social Forces,* 1972, *51,* 34-44.

Gove, W. R. Sex differences in mental illness among adult men and women: An evaluation of four questions raised regarding the evidence of the higher rates of women. *Social Science and Medicine,* 1978, *12,* 179-186.

Gove, W. R. Mental illness and psychiatric treatment among women. *Psychology of Women Quarterly,* 1980, *4,* 345-362.

Gove, W. R., & Tudor, J. F. Adult sex roles and mental illness. *American Journal of Sociology,* 1973, *78,* 812-835.

Gurin, G., Veroff, J., & Feld, S. *Americans view their mental health.* New York: Basic Books, 1960.

Hetherington, E. M., Cox, M., & Cox, R. Divorced fathers. *The Family Coordinator,* 1976, *25,* 417-428.

Hinkle, L. E., Redmont, R., & Plummer, N. An explanation of the relation between symptoms disability and serious illness in two homogeneous groups of men and women. *Women in Industry,* 1960, *50,* 1327-1336.

Hollingshead, A. B., & Redlich, F. C. *Social class and mental illness.* New York: Wiley, 1958.

Horowitz, M. J., Schaefer, C., & Cooney, P. Life event scaling for recency of experience. In E. K. E. Gunderson & R. H. Rahe (Eds.), *Life stress and illness.* Springfield, Illinois: Thomas, 1974.

Howard, E. M., & Howard, J. L. Women in institutions: Treatment in prisons and mental hospitals. In V. Franks & V. Burtle (Eds.), *Women in therapy.* New York: Brunner/Mazel, 1974.

Kanner, A. D., Coyne, J. C., Schaefer, C., & Lazarus, R. S. Comparison of two modes of stress measurement: Daily hassles and uplifts versus major life events. *Journal of Behavioral Medicine,* 1981, *4,* 1-39.

Kirkpatrick, C., & Cotton, J. Physical attractiveness, age, and marital adjustment. *American Sociological Review,* 1951, *16,* 81-86.

Kramer, M. *Psychiatric services and the changing institutional scene, 1950-1985.* (DHEW Publication No. [ADM] 77-433.) Washington, D.C.: National Institute of Mental Health, 1977.

Leighton, A. H., Lambo, T. A., Hughes, C. C., Leighton, D. C., Murphy, J. M., & Macklin, D. B. *Psychiatric disorder among the Yoruba.* Ithaca, New York: Cornell Univ. Press, 1963.

Lerner, R. M., Orlos, J. B., & Knapp, J. R. Physical attractiveness, physical effectiveness and self-concept in late adolescence. *Adolescence,* 1976, *11,* 313-326.

Linn, E. L. Agents, timing and events leading to mental hospitalization. *Human Organization,* 1961, *20,* 90-98.

Maffeo, P. A. Thoughts on Stricker's "Implications of research for psychotherapeutic treatment of women." *American Psychologist,* 1979, *34,* 690-695.

Makosky, V. P. Stress and the mental health of women: A discussion of research and issues. In M. Guttentag, S. Salasin, & D. Belle (Eds.), *The mental health of women.* New York: Academic Press, 1980.

Malzberg, B. Are immigrants psychologically disturbed? In S. C. Plog & R. B. Edgerton (Eds.), *Changing perspectives in mental illness.* New York: Holt, 1969.

Mann, A. H., Jenkins, R., & Belsey, E. The twelve-month outcome of patients with neurotic illness in general practice. *Psychological Medicine,* 1981, *11,* 535-550.

Markush, R., & Favero, R. Epidemiologic assessment of stressful life events, depressed mood, and psychophysiological symptoms—A preliminary report. In B. P. Dohrenwend & B. S. Dohrenwend (Eds.), *Stressful life-events: Their nature and effects.* New York: Wiley, 1974.

Mathes, E. W., & Kahn, A. Physical attractiveness, happiness, neuroticism and self-esteem. *Journal of Psychology*, 1975, *90*, 27-30.

Mechanic, D. *Politics, medicine and social science*. New York: Wiley, 1974.

Mensh, I. N. The aging population and mental health. In S. C. Plog & R. B. Edgerton (Eds.), *Changing perspectives in mental illness*. New York: Holt, 1969.

Milazzo-Sayre, L. Admission rates to state and county psychiatric hospitals by age, sex, and marital status, United States 1975. (Statistical note No. 142, U.S. Department of Health, Education and Welfare.) Washington, D.C.: National Institute of Mental Health, 1977.

Milazzo-Sayre, L. Admission rates by the highest level of education attained—State and county mental hospitals, United States 1975. (Statistical note No. 151. U.S. Department of Health, Education and Welfare.) Washington, D.C.: National Institute of Mental Health, 1979.

Napoleon, T., Chassin, L., & Young, R. D. A replication and extension of "physical attractiveness and mental illness." *Journal of Abnormal Psychology*, 1980, *89*, 250-253.

Nathanson, C. Illness and the feminine role: A theoretical review. *Social Science and Medicine*, 1975, *9*, 57-62.

Pflanz, M. Sex differences in abnormal illness. *Social Science and Medicine*, 1978, *12B*, 171-176.

Phillips, D. L. Rejection of the mentally ill: The influence of behavior and sex. *American Sociological Review*, 1964, *29*, 679-687.

Phillips, D. L., & Segal, B. E. Sexual status and psychiatric symptoms. *American Sociological Review*, 1969, *34*, 58-72.

Radloff, L. S. Sex differences in depression. *Sex Roles*, 1975, *1*, 249-265.

Rosenthal, D. *Genetic theory and abnormal behavior*. New York: McGraw-Hill, 1970.

Sarbin, T. R. The scientific status of the mental illness metaphor. In S. C. Plog & R. B. Edgerton (Eds.), *Changing perspectives of mental illness*. New York: Holt, 1969.

Sarbin, T. R., & Allen, V. L. Role theory. In G. Lindzey & E. Aronson (Eds.), *The handbook of social psychology* (Vol. 1). Reading, Massachusetts: Addison-Wesley, 1968.

Sarbin, T. R., & Juhasz, J. B. The social psychology of hallucinations. *Journal of Mental Imagery*, 1978, *2*, 117-144.

Scheff, T. J. *Being mentally ill: A sociological theory*. Chicago, Illinois: Aldine, 1966.

Seidenberg, R. *Corporate wives—corporate casualties?* Garden City, New York: Doubleday, 1975.

Spreitzer, E., Snyder, E., & Larson, D. Age, marital status and labor force participation as related to life satisfaction. *Sex Roles*, 1975, *1*, 235-247.

Uhlenhuth, E. H., Lipman, R. S., Balter, M. B., & Stern, M. Symptom intensity and life stress in the city. *Archives of General Psychiatry*, 1974, *31*, 759-764.

Warner, R. Racial and sexual bias in psychiatric diagnosis: Psychiatrists and other mental health professionals compared by race, sex, and discipline. *The Journal of Nervous and Mental Disease*, 1979, *167*, 303-310.

Yamamoto, K., & Dizney, H. Rejection of the mentally ill: A study of attitudes of student teachers. *Journal of Counseling Psychology*, 1967, *14*, 264-268.

5

IVAN N. MENSH
ELIZABETH HECHT

Psychopathology and Sex Differences in the Aged

With few exceptions, colleagues in the study of psychopathology among older individuals have reported data on one or two of the three variables of psychopathology, gender, and age, but *only rarely* have the three been analyzed for their interactions. Thus, many studies have examined mental disorders in men and women in the decades of life past age 60. However, seldom have the three variables been evaluated together.

We have limited our search and reporting primarily to the literature published since 1975. We did not venture into neurophysiology, biochemistry, or genetics and the association of these complex phenomena with the variables of psychopathology, gender, and age, although our earlier intent was to include studies in these fields. Limitations of space precluded our carrying out this earlier design.

Because a chapter on depression is included in this volume (Hammen, Chapter 6), we do not survey this range of psychopathology except for the depressed phase of manic-depressive disorder. Also, readers who desire information on the several areas of psychopathology of aging, where there is not the interaction studies of our three focused variables, are referred to Kaplan's *Psychopathology of Aging* (1979).

We respond to the need to study mental illness and gender as these may vary as a function of age in the elderly. Field (1972) noted that there are "more people over 65 in North America now than at any other time in recorded history [p. 33]." Siegel (1980) has analyzed recent and anticipated demo-

ISBN: 0-12-050350-6

graphic trends for the elderly as these interact in health care planning. Sex ratios in the population by broad age groups for the decades from 1950 to 2020 spell out a conclusion of significance to our topic: "Male mortality has been higher than female mortality at each age of life for many decades in the United States. . . . The death rates for the sexes at the various age groups have been steadily diverging, to the greater advantage of women [Siegel, 1980, p. 296]." The sex ratio at birth is 100 males to 105 females, ranges in the 15-29 year age group from 98 to 101, drops to 88-100 in the middle years, 30-64, and then drops to 68 to 90 for those 65 and over, and from 56 to 83 for individuals past 75. And as Gruenberg (1980) has summarized, "In each age group one sex differs a little bit from the other (for senile dementia, 'the most common dementia . . . one-fourth of the people . . . can expect to develop it if they live to 80.'), and from the total population, but none of these differences is statistically significant within a given decade of observation [p. 98]." We shall see.

Epidemiological Studies

Community and Institutional Studies

One of the limitations of the three-variable analyses is the recent shift from use of the older Diagnostic and Statistical Manual (DSM-II) to DSM-III (American Psychiatric Association, 1980). The reader will have to translate from the older terminology of 146 diagnoses and codes in DSM-II to the 176 in DMS-III. The multiaxial evaluation in DSM-III would be useful because of its definitions along the several axes, all important to our understanding of psychopathology, gender, and age, but this is too recent for our purpose. Investigators would profit from the evaluation encompassing not only clinical diagnosis but also those conditions not attributable to a mental disorder that are a focus of attention or treatment . . . personality disorders . . . physical disorders and conditions . . . severity of psychosocial stressors . . . and highest level of adaptive functioning in the past year.

Gomberg and Franks (1979) conclude from their summary of the data on mental illness that, at least in Western industrial societies, more women than men are mentally ill. This balance holds whether the data are from mental hospital admissions, general practice data, or community surveys. However, this broad conclusion is tempered by the controversy between Dohrenwend and Dohrenwend (1976) and Gove and Tudor (1977), with the former finding higher rates for women in 3 studies and for men in 8 studies, and the latter identifying 34 of 35 studies with higher rates for women. But neither relates age *and* sex to mental illness in a three-way analysis.

Epidemiological data reflect not only international variations but also national and state variations (see, for example, McCabe, 1975; Rinder Bollerup, 1975; Weeke, Bille, Videbech, Dupont, & Juel-Nielsen, 1975; Weeke, Kastrup, & Dupont, 1979; Weissman & Myers, 1978, 1980). Milazzo-Sayre (1978) assessed the "many factors that affect the population dynamics of mental hospitals [p. 2]." These include the availability and utilization of alternate care facilities for the aged, outpatient and aftercare resources, reduction in the length of stay in hospital, community mental health centers and their affiliation and interaction with state mental hospitals, the effectiveness of screening procedures against inappropriate admissions, and administrative changes, for example, introduction of a geographic unit system or a deliberate attempt to reduce the hospital resident population. "These factors are highly interrelated and affect the rates of admission, readmission, and duration of stay, which in turn generate changes in the resident patient population [Milazzo-Sayre, 1978, p. 2]." Out of this complex interaction come the most recent data, for the 1971-1975 period—both the number and rate of resident patients aged 65 and over decreased in all states but Alaska, Florida, Iowa, and New Hampshire (Alaska had the greatest increase, 350% in number of patients and 27% in rate per 100,000 population). The three-way interaction of mental illness, sex, and age appears in a subsequent Milazzo-Sayre report (1979b) on admission rates. Summarizing her Tables 1b and 2, we have the following rates of admission per 100,000 population:

	Age	Admission rate	Age	Admission rate	Age	Admission rate
Men	14-17	125	18-64	212-408 (median 362)	65 and over	144
Women	14-17	75	18-64	145-219 (median 202)	65 and over	65

Admissions to mental hospitals for the second quarter of 1975 thus show that, in the early teenage years, women are admitted at a rate only 60% that for men; in the broad age range of 18-64, the proportion drops to 56% (a 15% decrease in numbers). In the later years, 65 and over, the rate is 45%, a 25% decrease from the teenage years. For all ages, white women were admitted at a rate 56% of that for white men and, for all other races, the women's rate was 53% that for men. There are, of course, in addition to the variables reviewed by Milazzo-Sayre, other complex issues in these differential rates of admission to mental hospitals, varying from the significantly larger proportion of women in the later years—a men-women ratio of 68 to 100 (Siegel, 1980, p. 297), and therefore a much larger number of individuals at risk for mental illness among the women—to the range of resources available to the sexes as a function of their socioeconomic state, marital status, and other personal and demographic factors.

Baribeau-Braun, Goldstein, and Braun (1979) reviewed the work of numerous other investigators before undertaking their own study of readmissions of older patients to psychiatric facilities and pointed out that: (*a*) the elderly are the fastest growing segment (numerically) of the population, thus there are large numbers at high risk for psychiatric care; (*b*) the incidence of psychopathology rises with age, with those over 65 most susceptible; (*c*) psychosocial and economic factors have a greater impact on hospitalization and readmission of the elderly than in younger age groups (see also Butler & Lewis, 1977); and (*d*) there has been, since 1950, an increasing rate of admission of older patients to psychiatric hospitals and also an increasing number of readmissions.

On the positive side, Baribeau-Braun *et al.* note that, in a number of studies of Canadian mental hospitals, 75% of patients over the age of 65 (in a total hospital population of 6400) returned to their own homes within 2 months, and there was a discharge rate of over 70% for the elderly suffering from functional illness. However, 55% of the patients had to be readmitted to mental hospitals and 44% to psychiatric units in general hospitals. In the Baribeau-Braun *et al.* (1979) study of a sample ($N = 83$) of patients from a psychogeriatric ward, a multivariate analysis of age, sex, marital status, family-community relationships, and life stresses indicated that readmissions of older men could be predicted much better than of older women, that is, 100% of the men and 88.5% of the women behaved as predicted (but 86% of the men were correctly identified by the multivariate analysis as single admissions, versus only 46% of the women).

Persson (1980) examined the prevalence of mental disorders among 70-year-olds in the urban population of Gothenburg, Sweden, identified and evaluated 85% of the 460 subjects in this age range, in 1971-1972, and reported a "total morbidity" of 17% for men and 26% for women, excluding "mild neuroses" (13% and 16%, respectively). The morbidity pattern of other mental disorders for these older, community-living individuals was

Disease category	Men	Women
Psychoses	3%	3.5%
Neuroses	7	12
Alcoholism	3	0
Oligophrenia	0	.4
Dementias	7	3

Though relatively few in number, the morbidity of one out of four women in this age range in the community, and one in six for men, is a high rate with significant sex differences, as portrayed above.

Srole and Fischer (1980) report another community study, this in the United States and with a history of two decades, sampling a midtown Manhattan community with interviews of 1660 adults in 1954 for a random, area-type probability sample aged 20-59. In 1974, 68% were located, now 40-79 years old. The General Mental Health Impaired rate was the index. After studying four cohorts (born in 1900, 1910, 1920, and 1930) in 1954 and in 1974, the investigators conclude, "Life-cycle progression across those decades has not been discriminatory in its effects on the genders [Srole & Fischer, 1980, p. 215]." However, they also report that the cohorts of women born in 1920 and 1930 have mental impairment rates below the levels (by 50% to 60%) of the women born in 1900 and 1910, "and a roughly corresponding increase in their wellness frequencies [Srole & Fischer, 1980]." Srole and Fischer (1980) accept the "strong circumstantial evidence that parallel long-term trends of liberation from the demeaning deprivations of poverty have had similar eugenic mental health effects [p. 220]." It is important to note that Weissman and Klerman (1980) ask, "How much does the decline in . . . specific disorders account for the decrease? [Furthermore, their] follow-up data test, and challenge, two widely accepted beliefs . . . that overall rates of mental illness increase with increasing urbanization and . . . that aging, per se, is associated with increasing mental distress and impairment [p. 230]."

Pitt (1980) has estimated the probability for Canadians throughout the life span of first admission to a mental illness hospital or unit, for men and women. For men, the probability rises from less than .1% at age 1 to over .7% at ages 20-25, decreases to .4% in the sixties, rises to nearly .5% in the seventies, then drops to .3% in the eighties. The probabilities for women are nearly 1.0% at ages 25-30, just under .6% in the sixties, about .8% in the late seventies, and still over .75% in the eighties.

Kastrup's (1980) nationwide census of psychiatric outpatients in Denmark provides, of course, a database that, unfortunately, is not modeled in most studies other than Scandinavian. Since 1957, there has been a census every 5 years, enumerating both inpatients and day care patients. Of the 5 million Danish population in 1977, there were .89 men per 1000 population who were in outpatient psychiatric treatment, and .80 women per 1000 population. In 1976, there were 2.26 men per 1000 and 2.95 women per 1000 who were psychiatric inpatients, and .43 men per 1000 and .37 women per 1000 in day treatment programs. What is important for the present review is the increase with age in overall prevalence rate for both sexes. Rates per 1000 population for 1976 are reported (it is significant also that between 1959 and 1974 there was a 71% increase in the number of admissions to psychiatric hospitals).

	Age group							
	15-24		25-44		45-64		65+	
	M	F	M	F	M	F	M	F
Service								
Outpatient	.40	.32	1.02	1.09	.76	1.27	.25	.51
Inpatient	.93	.54	1.32	1.24	2.41	2.67	5.95	8.49
Day care	.30	.23	.62	.48	.49	.44	.17	.22
Total	1.63	1.09	2.96	2.81	3.66	4.38	6.37	9.22

These data for Denmark demonstrate the steady, overall increase in psychiatric care with increasing age. Using the early years as a baseline, the increases in later years for men are 80%, 240%, and over 290%; and, for women, over 160%, more than 300%, and nearly 750%, respectively, with the male-female ratio shifting over the four age groups from 1.50:1.05 to .84:.69. The concentration of patients in inpatient facilities also is reflected in the shifts from 45% to 66% for men in the three younger age groups, to 93% for those 65 and older; and, for women, from 44% to 61% to 92%. Although the proportion of both men and women in the over-65 age range in inpatient treatment is the same, 93% and 92%, the women are hospitalized at a rate 143% above that for men.

Similar trends have been reported in Türkü, Finland by Salokangas (1979) in an analysis of data on first admissions for psychosis for three time periods—1949-1950, 1959-1960, and 1969-1970. As in Denmark, the Finnish data show an increase in incidence over the age span for the most recent period of 1969-1970, from 91 per 100,000 for women aged 15-29 to 30-50 to 60 and older, by 130% and 450%; and, for men in these age groups from 108 per 100,000 a slight decrease of 2% and then an increase by over 300% in the over-60 age group. The increase in rate with age again is significantly higher in the elderly, and especially among elderly women patients.

Tardiff and Sweillam (1980) surveyed all patients admitted during 1974-1975 to the public psychiatric hospitals in two Long Island, New York counties, a total of 9365 individuals. The age and sex distributions were

Age	Men (N = 5233)	Women (N = 4132)
Under 18	6%	5%
18-34	38	29
35-64	45	47
65-	10	18

These data from a localized and geographically small area do not correspond with those from Scandinavia cited previously on the increase in admissions with age. However, with fewer women than men admitted, the over-65 group of women is 80% greater than for men, a differential greater than that at other age levels.

In still another culture, in 1972, Levav and Arnon (1976) surveyed a sample of 451 men and 445 women in six Israeli villages with a population of 2269. Clinic and welfare office records were reviewed and then a door-to-door screening was conducted. The data were summarized on a 4-point scale of emotional ill health and four "degrees of caseness" (almost certainly psychiatric, probably, possible, and no evidence). Five previous prevalence studies in Israel, from 1956 to 1968, also were reviewed. "Good health and adjustment" prevalence rates were distributed by age group and sex as follows:

	Age group			
	20-29	30-39	40-64	65+
Men	72.5%	58.6%	36.1%	61.3%
Women	42.6	25.2	26.0	19.0

Individuals who "almost certainly" or "probably" were psychiatrically ill were found in these proportions:

	Age group			
	20-29	30-39	40-64	65+
Men	16.0%	22.0%	42.0%	26.0%
Women	23.5	47.0	46.5	67.0

The majority of men 65 and over were judged to be in good psychologic health (61%). Only 19% of women in this age range were rated at this level of adjustment, significantly fewer than the 25%-43% of women at younger ages, and the 36%-72.5% of men at all ages.

More surprising are the data from a prevalence study of psychiatric disorders in Canberra (Henderson, Duncan-Jones, Byrne, Scott, & Adcock, 1979). This 1977 community survey of 360 men and 395 women estimated case rates by age group and sex in a population whose age groupings are indicated as follows, together with the case rates:

	Percentage of population		Case rates	
	M	F	M	F
18-64	2-16%	3-17%	6-9.5	6-11
65+	3	4	7	5

The ranges are those in the various age groupings from 18 to 64, totaling 97% of the sample for men and 96% for women. The case rates displayed median values of 8 for men aged 18-64 and 9 for women in this age range. Admittedly, this is a community survey and not data from psychiatric care facilities, but the data are discrepant from the community studies reported earlier (cf. p. 106 ff), especially in its rates of the over-65s, which are less than the median values, and the lower rates among the older women than among their male counterparts. Criteria of psychiatric morbidity, survey methodology, sampling: These variables and others may account for the Canberra data as they are distinctly different from other studies.

Finally, in a report titled in part, "neurological disorders," Broe, Akhtar, Andrews, Caird, Gilmore, and McLennan (1976) summarize the data from three surveys of over 800 individuals living at home—one a random sample of 200 people, all living at home and 65 or older (there was a 20-30% refusal rate in the three surveys, so there is a sampling bias probability), with equal numbers of respondents below and above age 75; another, a sample of 300 patients from the general practice of six general practitioners; and a third sample of 308 people from town registers; the latter two samples were not age-stratified. Medical histories, general practitioner and hospital records, clinical and psychiatric examinations in a clinic or at home for the 308, a neurological examination when a neurological diagnosis was in question—these represented the data sources. There were 318 men and 490 women, 488 aged 65-74 and 320 aged 75 or older among the total number sampled.

Neurological diagnoses, one or two in number for stroke, were reported at a rate of 73 per 1000, without significant sex or age variation, as was true also for the 87 per 1000 with transient ischaemic attacks. For other conditions, the following rates per 1000 were tabulated

	Senile dementia	Dementia of all types
65-74	24	43
75-	109	140
Mild degree	53%	—
Moderate or severe	47%	—

The 4½-fold jump in rate for senile dementia and 3¼ for all dementias for these community-living men and women aged 75 and over, as compared to the rates for the "youngsters" in the age range 65-74, is remarkable. Finally, consistent with Gruenberg's observations (1980), Broe *et al.* (1976) conclude from their study of these 808 older individuals that senile dementia, rather than cardiovascular disease, is the most important cause of dementia in the elderly, especially in women and in subjects over age 75.

Mortality Studies

The mortality of older men and women who are psychologically ill is critical to the patients, to their families, to the communities, and to mental health care planners. A Dutch study of a 2-year mortality period and a Swedish 15-year follow-up study suggest trends, at least for their samples and populations. Giel, Dijk, and van Weerden-Dijkstra (1978) reported the deaths of 1506 patients over a 2-year period from a total of 17,211 age 20 or over long-stay patients (2 years or more in hospital) in all Dutch mental hospitals as of the end of the 1969 calendar year.

	In hospital	Discharged	Died	General population mortality
Men				
20-59	611-1959(1600)[a]	118-163(138)	7-95(38)	1-38(8)
60-80+	392-1881(1109)	13-91(38)	129-202(196)	102-140(121)
Women				
20-59	423-1843(1260)	77-144(128)	10-66(28)	1-18(4)
60-80+	783-2167(1696)	27-135(78)	147-271(252)	55-213(139)

[a] The figures in parentheses are median values for the ranges in the several decades of patients in the 20-59 and 60+ age groups.

The 62% greater mortality for men 60 and older and nearly 110% for women, compared to the rates in the general population (the 3.75- and seven-fold differential for younger patients must be examined in light of the much smaller base rates, i.e., 8 and 4) indicate the predictable fate of these older men and women. Every fifth or sixth male patient 60 years old or older and every sixth or seventh older woman patient will die within 2 years in hospital; this is about five times the probability of discharge for the men and more than three times the probability of discharge for the women (see also Dastoor, Klingner, Müller, & Kachanoff, 1979).

In a Scandinavian follow-up study begun in 1957 by Erik Strömgren and with additional data gathered in 1961 and 1975, a rural population of 6000 on the island of Samsø (only 5000 in 1975) was evaluated in a community psychiatric research and service project. Nielsen, Homma, and Biørn-Henriksen (1977) looked at all causes of death among the 778 men and women 65 or older in the 1957 older population of 994 who had died prior to 1976 (78% of the probands). Twenty-two categories, including psychiatric disorders and an "other disorders" grouping, showed significantly higher deaths from respiratory and urogenital disorders in men and from diabetes mellitus and fractures in women. Only 10 cases (7 women and 3 men) of psychiatric disorders were reported, an unusually small number in a population of 5000-6000. However, although 58% of the total population were judged to be without mental illness and only 1% were in psychiatric hospital, 23% were diagnosed with dementia: "[There was] a high frequency of probands with dementia and cerebrovascular disorders . . . in old people's homes or nursing homes [Nielsen *et al.*, 1977, p. 557]."

Finally, Peck, Wolloch, and Rodstein (1978) surveyed mortality rates in a home for the aged and identified a statistically significant difference in mortality among the women residents, those with chronic brain syndrome (CBS) dying sooner than women not so diagnosed. This differential was demonstrated even though the former were judged, on admission, to be in good physical condition, at a rate exceeding residents without the diagnosis of CBS but judged on admission to be in poor health. For men in the home, presence or absence of CBS was not a significant factor in mortality rates.

The Main Psychopathologies

Manic-Depressive Disease(s)

Jamison (1979) recently summarized the literature on manic-depressive disease in the elderly and noted (*a*) that the lifetime risk for the disease(s?) is approximately 13% for women and 2% for men, but also that (*b*) epidemiologic data for the elderly is much less precise and comprehensive; (*c*) the ratio of women to men with unipolar depression is 3:1, for bipolar illness the ratio is 1.5:1, and (*d*) for patients 65 and older the ratio is 2:1. Jamison hypothesizes that the longer lifespan in women and the higher suicide rate among men may account for these differences in rate. Another significant variable discussed by Jamison is age at onset of manic-depressive illness. It is rare to observe an onset after age 65, she observed, and there is the question whether in such instances this is late-life onset, or another disease entity altogether. Commenting on Kraepelin's observations 60 years ago and more recent studies as well, Jamison (1979) concludes "for any . . . elderly patient experiencing a manic episode, the odds are overwhelming that the attack will represent a recurrence rather than a first event, this is consistent, of course, with the recurrent nature of the illness itself [p. 82]." (See also Dean & James, 1980; Loranger & Levine, 1978.)

The importance of evaluating interaction effects among specific psychological illness, neurological status, and other patient characteristics such as drug abuse where this is not the primary diagnosis has been demonstrated, for example, by Himmelhoch, Neil, May, Fuchs, and Licata (1980) in their study of about 80 consecutive admissions for primary bipolar affective disorder to an Affective Disorders Clinic during 1973-1976, of patients aged 55 or older.

The mean age was 63 among the 39 men and 42 women. Their response to lithium treatment was significantly associated with gender (i.e., 80% of women and 60% of men were judged to have had a good response to the treatment, and 20% of women and 40% of men had a poor response). "However, this finding [significantly greater incidence of poor treatment response among men] disappeared in later analyses that controlled for neurological status and drug abuse . . . probably because of the known higher incidence of both alcohol abuse and cerebral vascular disease among men [Himmelhoch *et al.*, 1980, p. 942]."

Shulman and Post (1980) reviewed studies of bipolar affective disorder since 1955 and, following a computer search of all inpatients aged 60 and older who had been admitted to the Bethlem Royal and Maudsley Hospitals during 1967-1976, evaluated the data. Earlier studies had reported evidence of manic symptoms in 6-18% of older "depressives." A 1973 age-incidence United Kingdom national sample reported that, in males, there is a distinct rise over the age of 60 and, in the seventies, mania surpasses the incidence of neurotic depression and approaches that of psychotic depression at age 75. This may be due to mania as an aspect of dementia in very old age. The Shulman and Post data revealed only 49 women and 18 men admitted for manic-depressive disorder in 10 years to the two hospitals, a ratio of 2.7:1. For these patients, age at time of the first affective episode and the first manic episode ranged from 17 to 85; for men, the mean ages were, respectively, 45 and 53; for women, 50 and 62. These gender variations were not significant for first affective episode but were significant (*p* .05) for first manic episode. Furthermore, 11 of the 18 men and 5 of the 49 women also demonstrated cerebral-organic or other neurological abnormality, a significant (*p* .05) variation between the sexes. Three of the women "went on to develop a dementing illness [Shulman & Post, 1980, p. 28]."

In a Swiss study, Angst (1978) followed patients admitted between 1959 and 1963 to the Bürgholzli Clinic, 95 with bipolar manic-depressive illness and 159 patients with unipolar disease. The follow-up was done at 5-year intervals up to 1975. Mean age of the 37 men and 58 women in the bipolar group (the unipolar sample was not reported in 1978) was 61 years. At the 15-year follow-up, 27% had died, mean age 69, with the survivors averaging age 61. During the study, 1176 affective episodes were recorded for all 95 patients, median of 9. There were no significant sex differences in the data from the 37 men and 58 women, but 60% of the women exhibited "pure depressive syndromes" (men, 35%); 14% with manic syndromes (men 35%); depression-manic sequence, 17% and 15%; and manic-depressive sequence, 9% and 13%, respectively. The investigator concluded that there is "a preponderance of depressive manifestations in bipolar disorder, a preponderance of depression among female patients, and amazingly little change with age [Angst, 1978, p. 69]." For the patients, age of onset was reported in the following pattern (%):

	Age group			
	10-19	20-39	40-59	60-69
Men	6	20	10	1
Women	8	26	21	3

The nearly 5% with onset at age 60 or later is greater than the "rare" instance reported by other investigators, for example, Jamison (1979). Furthermore, 41% of the women but only 29% of the men had the first episode at age 40 or later, with the number of subsequent episodes not gender-related. These data also are at variance with Watts' (1966) study of manic-depressive disease patients who used general practice as the site of investigation, unlike the psychiatric hospital population evaluated by Angst. Watts observed the highest frequency of the disorder at ages 45-55 for women and 55-75 for men, with reactive (neurotic) depression more frequent at younger ages and with more women than men evidencing these episodes.

Schizophrenia(s)

Mensh reviewed (1979) the literature on the older schizophrenic and could locate only an occasional report, for example, the Juel-Nielsen (1975) report of a 10-year study in Denmark, which examined differential rates for men and women. Juel-Nielsen's data were from a 1957-1967 study that concluded, among other findings, that over the decade studied, the rates for schizophrenia in old age (65+) had remained practically unchanged for males, whereas a significant increase was seen for females (M, 297 increased to 301 per 100,000 population; F, 347 increased to 416 per 100,000 population; an increase of more than 1% for men but about 20% for women). As observed previously with reference to manic-depressive disease in the elderly, there is controversy (Mensh, 1979) about the existence of schizophrenia as a disease with onset in the later years (60-65 and later) as a first-time occurrence of the disorder in the patient.

Since that review, Lewine (1980) reported his study of two series of 200 patients in each series, all first-admissions to the Helsinki, Finland psychiatric hospitals, the first series admitted in 1950 and the second in 1960. Of the 200, 36 were deceased at the time of study and their case records provided the database. The surviving 144 patients were personally interviewed, and all 200 patients were classified as typical schizophrenia, schizophreniform psychosis, or paranoid psychosis, with age at onset and age at first hospital admission specified. There were 32 men and 65 women diagnosed as typical, 22 and 36 as schizophreniform, and 10 and 12 as paranoid, respectively. Up to 32% of the men became ill between age 16 and 60, as was true also for the women; but in the age 61-65 range, only 6-10% of the men and none of the women apparently had the initial onset of schizophrenic illness this late in life, and no man or woman among the 200 studied had an onset at age 66 or later. Data for age at first admission to hospital for schizophrenia showed 6-20% of the male admissions were aged 61-70 and 1.5% of the women, with 6% of men and 1.5% of the women aged 66 or older at first admission.

Organic Brain Diseases

In discriminating Alzheimer's type disease from senile dementia, Gruenberg (1980) concludes that "Alzheimer's disease presents a pathological picture identical to that seen in senile brain disease, but it occurs before people reach the age of 65 [p. 92]." However, reflecting the uncertainties, Butler's introduction (1980) to the Second Conference on the Epidemiology of Aging appears not to offer the differentiation suggested by Gruenberg and others: "We are all aware of the considerable impact of Alzheimer's disease/senile dementia [sic], which affects so many older Americans and is a contributing factor in a large number of nursing home admissions in this country [p. 4]."

Jarvik, Ruth, and Matsuyama (1980) reported their 6-year follow-up study of organic brain disease in surviving twins (begun in 1946 by Kallman and Sanders) and several other studies published since 1961. One-half of the studies surveyed, including Jarvik *et al.*, have small and highly selected samples, so that generalization is risky. The two studies that specify gender variations have very unequal men-women ratios and are more than a decade old.

Rosin (1977) studied dementia among patients in an Israeli hospital for chronic diseases for the 3-year period of 1972-1974. Among admissions to a ward designed to diagnose and treat dementia and/or behavior problems, 70% were over 65 years old. The diagnoses and follow-up of 81 of these patients, identified as "patients with global dementia" on the criteria of severe memory deficit and impairment in orientation and cognitive function, indicated nearly one-half with primary dementia (17 men, 21 women, mean ages 75 and 77); about one-third with arteriosclerosis (17, 14, 72, and 70, respectively); and the remaining 12 suffering also from Parkinsonism or dementia with brain tumor. The latter group was the youngest, and fewest in number, ages 45 to 63, unlike the mean ages of 70-77 for the other patients. Age and gender variations are not reported for the follow-up. Of the 81 individuals in the study, 11 had gone home over the 3-year period, 19 still were in hospital, 9 had been discharged but had to be readmitted, 9 had left hospital for nursing homes, and the remaining 33 apparently were deceased.

Comparative Studies

Weeke and Strömgren (1978) provide data from a long-time (15 years) comparison of age and sex distribution for the major psychiatric disorders of patients in all Danish psychiatric hospitals, for the years up to 1972. They order these data by sex, age, and diagnosis as follows:

	Age group 15-29		30-59		60-99	
	M	F	M	F	M	F
Schizophrenia	372	146	1021	685	1022	1327
Manic-depressive	52	49	174	367	167	426
Presenile and senile organic disorders	65	26	246	198	1121	1854
Cerebrovascular disease reactive condition	280	340	906	1060	182	308

Median rates per 100,000 population for these main diagnoses were

	Age group 15-44		45-64		65-	
	M	F	M	F	M	F
Schizophrenia	85	36	154	123	275	297
Manic-depressive	12	14	31	60	38	90
Organic conditions	14	11	60	48	90	347
Reactive conditions	58	80	87	105	38	56

The increasing rates with age for the schizophrenias reflect the need for long-term hospitalization rather than new cases among the older patients, especially for women, whose rates were lower than those of men for the ages up to 65, then go up to nearly 300 per 100,000 population. Among patients with manic-depressive disease, the rates for women in the years up to age 45 are comparable to those for men (12 and 14) but then are nearly double the male rate from 45 to 64 and more than 2½ times as great in the years beyond 65.

The pattern, but not the rates, for the organic diagnoses is similar to that for the schizophrenias. The low rates for both sexes in the years up to age 45 increase more than 400% for men and women in the middle years, 45 to 64, and then, for patients 65 and older there is a 50% increase in rate for men and more than a 600% increase for women. Unlike the other three main diagnoses, reactive conditions show a decrease in rate in the later years after a peak in the 45-64 age range, to rates below any of those of the older patients suffering from other disorders (only reactive conditions and manic-depressive disorders among men show a similar rate, 38 per 100,000 population).

In comparable studies in Canada, Bland (1977) reported rates for the functional psychoses per 100,000 population. Because of the variations over the years, median values for three major age ranges are listed.

	Age group 15-39		Age group 40-59		Age group 60-80+	
	M	F	M	F	M	F
Schizophrenia	46	48	22	36	4	6
Affective psychoses	13	23	31	53	22	28
Paranoid states	4	4	6	9	8	8
Reactive psychoses	9	11	9	13	9	9

The comparability of the two studies just summarized obviously does not extend to the reported rates. In only 1 of the 12 sets of data do they even look alike, that is, manic-depressives in the 30-59-year-old age range (Weeke & Strömgren, 1978) and affective disorders in patients in their forties and fifties (Bland, 1977; see also Dixon & Lovett Doust, 1978). Different countries, different diagnostic criteria, different categorization of the functional psychoses—at least these variations trouble us as we seek to understand the associations among psychopathological conditions, gender, and age.

Krupinski and Stoller (1975) examined a half-century pattern of psychiatric hospitalization in Australia, beginning in 1919. The study included nine cohorts of patients admitted between 1919 and 1962 and followed them until 1971. They noted an increase in first admissions, primarily in the older age groups and especially among men, mainly with senile brain disorders, alcoholism, depressive states, and other psychoneuroses. The 1971 follow-up of the 1957-1959 cohort of men 60 and older showed a rate of 175 per 100,000 population increasing to nearly 500, and the rate for older women increasing from 125 to 275 per 100,000; data which are favorable to women, unlike those from most other reports. There was an increase of first admission rates of patients with diagnoses of schizophrenia and senile brain disorders, and a decrease in the hospitalization incidence of affective psychoses (especially for patients in manic episodes) and organic brain disorders. The latter decrease seemed mainly associated with the fewer numbers of patients with central nervous system syphilis, labeled by Krupinski and Stoller as *general paralysis of the insane* (GPI), a term seldom seen today.

Turner and Sternberg (1978) reported a study of admissions of patients 65 or older to a Bristol, England psychiatric hospital in an 80-bed ward serving a population of 40,000 elderly. Admissions and the resident population 65 or older were included over the 1972-1974 period, for a total of 204 patients, 37% men and 63% women. The data were evaluated in 1976. In the age group 65-69, there were 18 men and 23 women; in 70-79, 29 and 63; in 80-89, 27 and 35; and in 90-95, 1 and 8, respectively. Among the men, only 22% experienced more than one admission, compared to 78% of the women, a significant variation (*p* .05). The diagnostic classification was as follows:

	M	F
Depression	28%	48%
Dementia	49	32
Schizophrenia/paranoid states	3	9
Delirium	5	4
Hypomania	8	1
Other	0	5
No psychiatric disease	7	2

The pattern of discharges also was examined and the following variations were noted—the men were discharged to a general hospital or died in hospital; the women returned to their own homes or to relatives' homes, were discharged to homes for the elderly, or were still in hospital in 1976.

Finally, in the area of the dementias, but equally applicable to other psychopathology among older men and women, we quote Gruenberg (1978):

> The Urgent Next Questions. . . . Does the age-specific incidence [of senile brain disease and senile dementia] stop rising and begin to fall? . . . Do the younger cases [Alzheimer's disease] aggregate in the same families as the older cases [of senile dementia]? . . . Does the age-specific incidence rate rise smoothly from 50 years of age onward? . . . Does the sex ratio remain constant throughout the age span? . . . Is there an association between prior frequency of infections and the probability of developing this condition [dementia]? . . . What are the precursors [pp. 452-454]?

Alcoholism

Schukit and Pastor (1979) have written about alcohol-related psychopathology in the aged, also reviewing studies published during 1965-1975, noting general population rates of 2-10% and special population rates (veterans, nursing home residents, psychiatrically ill, general medical wards and outpatients) ranging from 5% to 50%, and 10%-20% among the elderly. As in schizophrenia and manic-depressive disease, there is the question whether the older alcoholic is the young alcoholic in later years or an advanced age phenomenon in some elderly individuals. Schukit and Pastor believe that both classes of alcoholics exist, quoting the 1974 reports of Pascarelli and Zimberg on a San Francisco study of older alcoholics in which one-third of the sample had begun alcohol use after age 60. Data from the 1975 Washington State Client Oriented Data Acquisition Process tapes indicated almost 10% of the alcoholics were 60 or over and in about one-half of these the drinking problem began after age 40. Comparing younger alcohol abuse patients with older ones, Schukit and Pastor (1979) summarized the Washington state data and concluded that the older alcoholics are more likely to be male, caucasian, and poorly educated. Epidemiology, organic brain disease, skid-row alcoholics, and types and course of drinking patterns were examined by these writers. Interestingly, but not unexpectedly, they conclude with the comment, "Perhaps even more than with younger alcoholics, one must take care to consider alcoholism as a possible explanation for any psychopathology in the aged. If you do not look for alcoholism, you will not find it [Schukit & Pastor, 1979, p. 224]."

Glatt, Rosin, and Janhar (1978) summarized several earlier studies of alcoholism conducted in the 1960s and 1970s. These sampled widely varying populations, for example, geriatric unit residents, patients referred for psychiatric consultations from a domiciliary or hospital alcoholic unit, and community studies. As usual, sampling presents a problem as we evaluate such data. For example, Glatt *et al.* describe samples of 36 patients in a geriatric unit, 67 in a consultation program, and 92 seen over a 10-year period, representing a 2% sample of all age groups among 4500 alcoholics seen in the decade. With these important reservations in mind, we may then note that, among 36 geriatric and 67 psychiatric patients, the latter were mainly aged 65 to 70, more women than men were in their seventies, and they outnumbered the men in both samples, more so among the geriatric patients. The investigators concluded that there were two major groups of alcoholic patients: The first were heavy drinkers with a long-standing history of this behavior; the second group consisted of previously moderate drinkers who apparently were responding to stresses of changing physical, mental and/or social and economic state. There was a slight preponderance of the latter (late-life stress responders) in whom precipitating factors and reactive behaviors could be identified. However, the psychiatric sample was largely middle-class and the geriatric group mainly working class. This variable was not evaluated as a covariant. In these two samples, age, gender, and marital status were distributed thus:

	M (37%)	F (63%)
Aged 60+	5%	10-12%
Widowed [a]	11	31

[a] United States ratio of widows to widowers is 4:1.

Glatt *et al.* (1978) ask whether, in the later years, alcoholics "cut down" or "mature out"? They believe that there are two main groups of older alcoholic individuals: those who have continued their drinking behavior from earlier years and those who have shifted to problem drinking due to stresses especially associated with aging.

Barnes (1979) compared data from 1969 and 1975 on alcohol use among older persons, the latter from two counties of western New York state, in a stratified random sample of 1041 respondents interviewed from a population of 1.36 million. The 1969 report indicated that 47% of the individuals sampled who were 60 or older were abstainers, and that 14% of the men and 1% of the women in this age range were heavy drinkers. Age and sex variables were tabulated in Barnes' study and his review of previous studies.

	Abstain		Heavy drinkers M	Heavy drinkers F	Age
Cahalan, Cisin, & Crossley (1969), national sample	47		14	1	60-
Barnes & Russell (1978), western N.Y.	47		16	1	60-
Johnson & Goodrich (1974), Manhattan	51				65-
Rathbone-McCuan, Lohn, & Levenson (1976), Baltimore	55		27	5	55-
Barnes (1979), western N.Y.					18-96
Age	M	F			
18-49	8	8	46	46	
50-59	9	18	41	5	
60-69	25	28	24	0	
70-96	22	45	6	2	

Keeping in mind Schukit and Pastor's caveat and our concern over sampling bias, we may generalize that the best estimate of alcoholic drinking problems among women 60 years of age or older is 1-5% in community studies, significantly fewer than the estimates of 14-30% among men at these ages by a factor of 6 to 14 (see also Mellinger, Balter, Manheimer, Cisin, & Parry, 1978). Does our sexist society permit better concealment of problem drinking of alcohol by women, especially in the later years, than is possible for men, or are these reliable differences?

Suicide

For all ages, the ratio of death rates per 100,000 population for suicide by sex has changed over the past 30 years. The National Center for Health Statistics (1978) reports rates that indicate a ratio of M:F deaths by suicide of 3.4-3.5:1 from 1950 to 1960, a drop to 2.6-2.7:1 in the 1960s, and a range of 2.6-2.8:1 from 1970 through 1976. For 1976, there were 19,943 male and 7339 female deaths reported, beginning at age 5 and extending to 85 and older. Among the men, 16,001 (82%) were under age 65 and for the women 6278 (86%) were less than 65. Rates per 100,000 population, for men, began (ages 5-14) at .7 and steadily increased to 47.5 over the succeeding eight decades. For the women suicides, the rate began (again at ages 5-14) at .2, increased to 12.7 by ages 45-54, then decreased to 5.4 over the next four decades. Comparing 1964 and 1976 rates, the M:F ratios were distributed as follows:

		Age group	
	5-34	35-64	65-85+
1964	2.4-4.0	2.1-3.5	3.8-14.5
1976	2.8-3.8	2.1-2.7	4.0- 8.8

These rates reflect over the dozen years of the two reports a decrease in the ratio of M:F suicides in the later years, 75 and older, a decrease shown also for ages 5-14, and 45-64, to the disadvantage of the girls and women. Data on white deaths by suicide and deaths of all others show the rates for white males exceeding those for all other males and for both white and all other females. Nonwhite females display the lowest rates among the four populations, less than 5 per 100,000 except for a rate of 7 at ages 20-39, dropping then until ages 60-74, when there again is a peak of 5, then at about a rate of 2 at ages 74-84. Breed and Huffine (1979) have reported similar observations and associate the differential rates with the difference in the process of aging, that is, women in the United States have "experienced major qualitative role changes throughout . . . adult life. . . . Men experience greater sequential role conflict than women [p. 302]." After reviewing the many variables in suicide, Breed and Huffine conclude that the best single predictor of suicide is sex.

An important variable in the study of suicidal behavior is the ratio of attempts to completed acts (*successful* is an unfortunate term). Among others, LaTorre and McLeoad (1978) and Payne (1975) have observed the decreasing ratio of attempts to completed suicides with increasing age. The elderly white male in the United States is particularly vulnerable and attempts and accomplishes suicide at a rate 3-5 times that of the rate at other ages for both sexes.

Farmer, Preston, and O'Brien (1977) followed similar data for Greater London over a quarter-century beginning in 1949. They first note that suicide is a relatively rare event and, second, that death rates from this cause were higher for men than for women at all ages during the 1949-1953, 1959-1963 and 1969-1973 periods (based on the last three decennial censuses). As in the United States, there was a rise in rates with increasing age but, since 1949-1953, a significant decrease was observed in the number of deaths by suicide of men over age 45 (for younger men, rates were up in the two earlier periods, but down in 1969-1973). Among women, the suicide rates increased in all age groups during the two earlier periods but, by 1969-1973, the rates had fallen below the 1949-1953 levels in all age groups over 40. Below age 40, the rates remained higher than in 1949-1953. Greater London rates were higher for both sexes than in surrounding areas, and for all ages, excepting men over 75. Southeast England has the highest suicide rate in the United Kingdom, but in 1949-1953 the Greater London rate did not differ significantly from the rest of the United Kingdom. Suicide in men was more common among those in lower social class, the converse was true for women.

Age and sex data on suicides in Alberta, Canada were examined by Hellon and Solomon (1980) for 1951-1976, using 1951 as the base year and 100 as the base rate in the comparison of age-specific rates. The rates for the six 5-year periods for age and sex were

	M			F		
	15-59	Mdn	60-	15-59	1-14	60-
1951	100	100	100	100	100	100
1956	72-208	107	121	37-424	110	205
1961	78-212	145	110	26-488	50	172
1966	72-347	177	94	60-925	108	179
1971	93-750	245	81	103-725	160	115
1976	91-981	196	97	105-1188	215	231

These data obviously do not demonstrate the usual pattern. The two-decade increase in rates for both men and women at ages from adolescence to age 60, the decrease for older men from 110 to 97 (nearly the rate in 1951), and the great increase for older women, median value at 179 and at a peak of 231 in 1976, are indeed startling statistics.

In contrast, there is the study of eastern Canada by Malla and Hoenig (1979). These investigators related not only sex but also marital status to the rates of suicide per 100,000 population. The median rates were as follows:

	Age group							
	15-59		60-69		70-79		80-	
	Single	Ever married	Single	Ever married	Single	Ever married	Single	Ever married
Men	32	8	38	6.5	18	12	0	4
Women	4	2	10	1	0	0	0	0

As Breed and Huffine (1979) and others have reported, marital status is an important discriminant at all ages (but note the exception among the married 80+ men), and again it is the men who are at greater risk, especially in the sixties (highest also for women in this age range).

Lindelius (1979) in Sweden selected an even longer time span than other investigators when he studied trends in suicide from the mid-eighteenth century until 1975, but we shall note only the data since 1950, the sixth period since 1750. Unfortunately, there are no data separately specifying the rates for the later years.

	M			F		
	15-34	35-49	50-	15-34	35-49	50-
1950	144	247	407	54	78	111
1960	152	309	518	70	86	168
1965	194	305	564	84	118	188

Lindelius noted that rates had risen from 2 per 100,000 population in 1749 to 20 per 100,000 in 1975. And, in comparing rates in 1950 and 1975, he concluded that for individuals 50 years old or more, there was no observed increase in suicide rate among men and only an "inconsiderable" increase among women. He came to this by tabulating suicides by age and sex in 1950 and 1975 as a percentage of all deaths. In 1975, for the decades from 15 to 34 for men, 15-24% were from suicide, dropping to 4-20% in ages 35-64 and to .7% for men 65 and older. The comparable figures for women were 18-32%, 3-12% and .3%.

Marshall (1978) has written about "the claim that there is a downward bias in the reporting of suicide" and disputes it, arguing that "changes in economic status have led to an increase in the well-being of aged males in America [p. 767]." He quotes the relatively stable suicide rate for 65-74-year-old white women over the quarter-century from 1947 to 1972 (10 per 100,000 population) and the decrease for white men in this decade of life from 52 to less than 40, a change in M:F rates from about 5:1 to less than 4:1. In explanation, Marshall (1978) cited the changes in economic conditions for this sample of our population as more relevant than shifts in social and political conditions, drawing this conclusion from "correlational and dynamic multivariate analyses [p. 767]." Marshall does not indicate why the changes in society have not equally affected older white women, perhaps inferring that the latter are more insulated from change than are men (but see Breed & Huffine, 1979). Again, there is the reminder, and caution, about the comparability or lack of comparability of suicide rates (e.g., Atkinson, Kessel, & Dalgaard, 1975).

Frederick (1978) does believe that, although men have had higher suicide rates than women at least since 1955, in ratios ranging from 2:1 to 7:1, "there has been a trend toward narrowing this margin in the older age groups, particularly over 60 years of age [p. 176]." From 1955 to 1975 there was a 200% increase in the suicide rate for men and a 128% increase for women in the 10-24 age range. During these 20 years the greatest decrease was among men 55 years old or older, with the main reduction, 28%, among 60-64-year-olds. Among older women, the greatest decrease was 70%, for 65-69-year-olds. Frederick reports these rates per 100,000 population as follows:

	15-59		30-59		60-84	
	M	F	M	F	M	F
1955	4-12	1-4	13-39	5-10	42-55	8-10
1965	6-16	2-6.5	18-38	8-13	36.5-49	7-10
1975	12-28	3-8	22-30	9-13	30-42.5	7-10

The uncertainty about trends that is produced in the reader is reinforced again by each successive study, for example, Atchley's (1980) observation that "suicide rates for males increase *in a straight line* from age 15 to 85. There is no sudden surge at age 65 or at any other age for that matter [p. 141]." Also creating uncertainty is the report by Kramer, Pollack, and Redick (1972) on 1955-1965 suicide trends by age and sex in 18 countries: "[S]uicide rates were uniformly higher for males than for females. . . .[A] general increase with age . . . for males, but the age pattern . . . for females was inconsistent. . . .[T]he general rise in . . . rates which occurred world-wide from 1955 to 1965 was mainly due to increases in suicide rates at younger ages [pp. 141-142]."

Summary

Understanding and, perhaps at some later time, prediction of the complex interactions of gender, psychopathology, and aging have become more urgent as the decades bring greater and greater proportions of men and women who are living into their sixties, seventies, eighties, and nineties, a span of years in individuals encompassing what once was an entire family generation. The professional and scientific literature has reported studies of gender, psychopathology, and age as these variables have appeared interrelated among two of three of these dimensions, but relatively rarely have interactions among all three been studied. It has been our intent to review the main body of reports where the complex interactional dynamics of these significant life variables have been explored. At this present phase of our knowledge the data are primarily statistical.

The differential death rate for men and women, to the advantage of women, will continue to diverge in the same direction with the continuing greater probability for psychopathology among aging women because there will be so many more and therefore more to be at risk than men in the later years. (Among women, in 1980, 17.6% are 60 and over; for men, 13.6% [Siegel, 1980, p. 292].) Suicide and alcoholism reportedly are the primary areas in which mortality and morbidity are greater for older men. Furthermore, although the proportion of women in the later years who are mentally ill, as identified in community and institutional studies, is greater than has been observed for men, this differential rate is in dispute among a number of investigators. Part of the controversy is associated with different interpretations of the data and, particularly, with failure of a number of observers to examine "the many factors that affect the population dynamics of mental hospitals [Milazzo-Sayre, 1978, p. 2]." In community studies there are the effects of bias introduced by (*a*) sampling variations, (*b*) different instruments and methodologies for determining psychopathology, and (*c*) differing interpretations of the significance of the data.

There also is the question whether, in the main psychopathological conditions, their first appearance after age 60 represents a disease state distinct from the psychopathology of earlier years, or whether the disorder has been in existence earlier in the life of the individual and now is first identified because of changed life situations. Finally, the reader is referred to Gruenberg's six "Urgent Next Questions" (1980, pp. 452-454). The answers will be important to our understanding and prediction of the interrelationships among gender, psychopathology, and age in the later decades of life.

References

American Psychiatric Association. *Diagnostic and statistical manual of mental disorders* (3rd ed.). (DSM-III). Washington, D.C.: Author, 1980.

Angst, J. The course of affective disorders: II. Typology of manic-depressive illness. *Archives of Psychiatry and Neurological Sciences,* 1978, *226,* 65-73.

Atchley, R. C. Aging and suicide: Reflection of the quality of life? In S. G. Haynes & M. Feinleib

(Eds.), *Second conference on the epidemiology of aging.* (National Institutes of Health Publication No. 80-969.) Bethesda, Maryland: National Institutes of Health, 1980.

Atkinson, M. W., Kessel, W. I. N., & Dalgaard, J. B. The comparability of suicide rates. *British Journal of Psychiatry,* 1975, *127,* 247-256.

Baribeau-Braun, J., Goldstein, S., & Braun, C. A multivariate study of psychogeriatric readmissions. *Journal of Gerontology,* 1979, *34,* 351-357.

Barnes, G. M. Alcohol use among older persons: Findings from a western New York state general population survey. *Journal of the American Geriatric Society,* 1979, *27,* 224-250.

Barnes, G. M., & Russell, M. Drinking patterns in western New York state: Comparison with national data. *Journal of Studies of Alcohol,* 1978, *39,* 1148-1157.

Bland, R. C. Demographic aspects of functional psychoses in Canada. *Acta Psychiatrica Scandinavia,* 1977, *55,* 369-380.

Breed, W., & Huffine, C. L. Sex differences in suicide among older white Americans: A role and developmental approach. In O. J. Kaplan (Ed.), *Psychopathology of aging.* New York: Academic Press, 1979.

Broe, G. A., Akhtar, A. J., Andrews, G. R., Caird, F. I., Gilmore, A. J. J., & McLennan, W. J. Neurological disorders in the elderly at home. *Journal of Neurology, Neurosurgery, and Psychiatry,* 1976, *39,* 362-366.

Butler, R. N. Introduction. In S. G. Haynes & M. Feinleib (Eds.), *Second conference on the epidemiology of aging.* (National Institutes of Health Publication No. 80-969.) Bethesda, Maryland: National Institutes of Health, 1980.

Butler, R. N., & Lewis, M. I. *Aging and mental health: Positive psychosocial approaches.* St. Louis, Missouri: Mosby, 1977.

Cahalan, D., Cisin, I., & Crossley, H. American drinking practices. *Monographs of the Rutgers Center of Alcohol Studies* (No. 6). New Brunswick, New Jersey: Journal of Studies on Alcohol, Inc., 1969.

Dastoor, D. P., Klingner, A., Müller, H. F., & Kachanoff, R. A psychogeriatric assessment program. V.: Three-year follow-up. *Journal of the American Geriatric Society,* 1979, *27,* 162-169.

Dean, K. G., & James, H. D. The spatial distribution of depressive illness in Plymouth. *British Journal of Psychiatry,* 1980, *136,* 167-180.

Dixon, L. M., & Lovett Doust, J. W. The diagnostic potential of rheoencephalography in psychiatry. *Psychiatrica Clinica,* 1978, *11,* 219-232.

Dohrenwend, B. P., & Dohrenwend, B. S. Sex differences in psychiatric disorders. *American Journal of Sociology,* 1976, *81,* 1447-1454.

Farmer, R. D. T., Preston, T. O., & O'Brien, S. E. M. Suicide mortality in Greater London: Changes during the past 25 years. *British Journal of Preventive and Social Medicine,* 1977, *31,* 171-177.

Field, M. *The aged, the family, and the community.* New York: Columbia Univ. Press, 1972.

Frederick, C. J. Current trends in suicidal behavior in the United States. *American Journal of Psychotherapy,* 1978, *32,* 172-200.

Giel, R., Dijk, S., & van Weerden-Dijkstra, J. R. Mortality in the long-stay population of all Dutch mental hospitals. *Acta Psychiatrica Scandinavia,* 1978, *57,* 361-368.

Glatt, M. M., Rosin, A. J., & Janhar, P. Alcoholic problems in the elderly. *Age and Ageing,* 1978, *7,* 64-71. (Supplement)

Gomberg, E. S., & Franks, V. (Eds.). *Gender and disordered behavior: Sex differences in psychopathology.* New York: Brunner/Mazel, 1979.

Gove, W. R., & Tudor, J. F. Sex differences in mental illness: A comment on Dohrenwend and Dohrenwend. *American Journal of Sociology,* 1977, *82,* 1327-1336.

Gruenberg, E. M. Epidemiology of senile dementia. In B. S. Schoenberg (Ed.), *Advances in neurology* (Vol. 19). New York: Raven, 1978.

Gruenberg, E. M. Senile dementia: A disease. In S. G. Haynes & M. Feinleib (Eds.), *Second conference on the epidemiology of aging.* (National Institutes of Health Publication No. 80-969.) Bethesda, Maryland: National Institutes of Health, 1980.

Hellon, C. D., & Solomon, M. I. Suicide and age in Alberta, Canada, 1951 to 1977. *Archives of General Psychiatry*, 1980, *37*, 505-510.

Henderson, S., Duncan-Jones, P., Byrne, D. G., Scott, R., & Adcock, S. Psychiatric disorder in Canberra: A standardized study of prevalence. *Acta Psychiatrica Scandinavia*, 1979, *60*, 355-374.

Himmelhoch, J. M., Neil, J. F., May, S. J., Fuchs, C. Z., & Licata, S. M. Age, dementia, dyskinesias, and lithium response. *American Journal of Psychiatry*, 1980, *137*, 941-945.

Jamison, K. R. Manic-depressive illness in the elderly. In O. J. Kaplan (Ed.), *Psychopathology of aging.* New York: Academic Press, 1979.

Jarvik, L. F., Ruth, V., & Matsuyama, S. S. Organic brain syndrome and aging: A six-year follow-up of surviving twins. *Archives of General Psychiatry*, 1980, *37*, 280-286.

Johnson, L., & Goodrich, C. *Use of alcohol by persons 65 years and over: Upper East Side of Manhattan.* (Report to the National Institute on Alcohol Abuse and Alcoholism.) New York: Mt. Sinai School of Medicine, 1974.

Juel-Nielsen, N. Epidemiology. In J. G. Howells (Ed.), *Modern perspectives in the psychiatry of old age.* New York: Brunner/Mazel, 1975.

Kaplan, O. J. *Psychopathology of aging.* New York: Academic Press, 1979.

Kastrup, M. A nation-wide census of psychiatric out-patients in Denmark. *Acta Psychiatrica Scandinavia*, 1980, *61*, 245-255.

Kramer, M., Pollack, E. S., & Redick, R. W. *Mental disorders/suicide.* Cambridge, Massachusetts: Harvard Univ. Press, 1972.

Krupinski, J., & Stoller, A. Changing patterns of psychiatric hospitalization in the past fifty years: A cohort study. *Australian and New Zealand Journal of Psychiatry*, 1975, *9*, 231-239.

LaTorre, R. A., & McLeoad, E. Machiavellianism and clinical depression in a geriatric sample. *Journal of Clinical Psychology*, 1978, *34*, 659-660.

Levav, I., & Arnon, A. Emotional disorders in six Israeli villages. *Acta Psychiatrica Scandinavia*, 1976, *53*, 387-400.

Lewine, R. R. J. Sex differences in age of symptom onset and first hospitalization in schizophrenia. *American Journal of Orthopsychiatry*, 1980, *50*, 316-322.

Lindelius, R. Trends in suicide in Sweden 1749-1975. *Acta Psychiatrica Scandinavia*, 1979, *60*, 295-310.

Loranger, A. W., & Levine, P. M. Age at onset of bipolar affective illness. *Archives of General Psychiatry*, 1978, *35*, 1345-1348.

McCabe, M. S. Demographic differences in functional psychoses. *British Journal of Psychiatry*, 1975, *127*, 320-323.

Malla, A., & Hoenig, J. Suicide in Newfoundland and Labrador. *Canadian Journal of Psychiatry*, 1979, *24*, 139-146.

Marshall, J. R. Changes in aged white male suicide: 1948-1972. *Journal of Gerontology*, 1978, *33*, 763-768.

Mellinger, G. D., Balter, M. B., Manheimer, D. I., Cisin, I. H., & Parry, H. J. Psychic stress, life crises, and use of psychotherapeutic medications: National Household Survey data. *Archives of General Psychiatry*, 1978, *35*, 1045-1052.

Mensh, I. N. The older schizophrenic. In O. J. Kaplan (Ed.), *Psychopathology of aging.* New York: Academic Press, 1979.

Milazzo-Sayre, L. *State trends in resident patients—State and county mental hospital inpatient services 1971-1975.* (Mental Health Statistical Note No. 150, DHEW Publication No. [ADM] 78-158.) Washington, D.C.: US Govt. Printing Office, 1978.

Milazzo-Sayre, L. *Admission rates by the highest level of education attained—State and county mental hospitals, US 1975.* (Mental Health Statistical Note No. 151, DHEW Publication No. [ADM] 79-158.) Washington, D.C.: US Govt. Printing Office, 1979.

National Center for Health Statistics. *Facts of life and death.* Washington, D.C.: Public Health Service, US Department of Health, Education and Welfare, Author, 1978.

Nielsen, J., Homma, A., & Biørn-Henriksen. Follow-up 15 years after a geronto-psychiatric prevalence study: Conditions concerning death, cause of death, and life expectancy in relation to psychiatric diagnosis. *Journal of Gerontology,* 1977, *32,* 554-561.

Payne, E. Depression and suicide. In J. C. Howells (Ed.), *Modern perspectives in psychiatry and old age.* New York: Brunner/Mazel, 1975.

Peck, A., Wolloch, L., & Rodstein, M. Mortality of the aged with chronic brain syndrome: Further observations in a five-year study. *Journal of the American Geriatric Society,* 1978, *26,* 170-176.

Persson, G. Prevalence of mental disorders in a 70-year-old urban population. *Acta Psychiatrica Scandinavia,* 1980, *62,* 119-139.

Pitt, B. Growing points in the psychiatry of old age. Part I: Specialty and body of clinical knowledge. *Canadian Journal of Psychiatry,* 1980, *25,* 1-14.

Rathbone-McCuan, E., Lohn, H., & Levenson, J. *Community survey of aged alcoholics and problem drinkers.* (Report to the National Institute on Alcohol Abuse and Alcoholism.) Baltimore, Maryland: Levindale Geriatric Research Center, 1976.

Rinder Bollerup, T. Prevalence of mental illness among 70-year-olds domiciled in nine Copenhagen suburbs. *Acta Psychiatrica Scandinavia,* 1975, *51,* 327-339.

Rosin, A. J. The physical and behavioral complex of dementia. *Gerontology,* 1977, *23,* 37-46.

Salokangas, R. K. R. First admissions for psychosis in Türkü (Finland): A time trend study. *Acta Psychiatrica Scandinavia,* 1979, *60,* 249-262.

Schukit, M. A., & Pastor, P. A., Jr. Alcohol-related psychopathology in the aged. In O. J. Kaplan (Ed.), *Psychopathology of aging.* New York: Academic Press, 1979.

Shulman, K., & Post, F. Bipolar affective disorder in old age. *British Journal of Psychiatry,* 1980, *136,* 26-32.

Siegel, J. S. Recent and prospective demographic trends for the elderly population and some implications for health care. In S. G. Haynes & M. Feinleib (Eds.), *Second conference on the epidemiology of aging.* (National Institutes of Health Publication No. 80-969.) Bethesda, Maryland: National Institutes of Health, 1980.

Srole, L., with Fischer, A. K. The Midtown Manhattan Longitudinal Study versus "The Mental Paradise Lost" Doctrine. *Archives of General Psychiatry,* 1980, *37,* 209-221.

Tardiff, K., & Deane, K. The psychological and physical status of chronic psychiatric inpatients. *Comprehensive Psychiatry,* 1980, *21,* 91-97.

Tardiff, K., & Sweillam, H. Assault, suicide, and mental illness. *Archives of General Psychiatry,* 1980, *37,* 164-169.

Turner, R. J., & Sternberg, M. P. Psychosocial factors in elderly patients admitted to a psychiatric hospital. *Age and Ageing,* 1978, *7,* 171-177.

Watts, C. A. H. *Depressive disorders in the community.* Bristol, England: John Wright & Sons, 1966.

Weeke, A., Bille, M., Videbech, T., Dupont, A., & Juel-Nielsen, N. Incidence of depressive syndromes in a Danish county. *Acta Psychiatrica Scandinavia,* 1975, *51,* 28-41.

Weeke, A., Kastrup, M., & Dupont, A. Long-stay patients in Danish psychiatric hospitals. *Psychological Medicine,* 1979, *9,* 551-556.

Weeke, A., & Strömgren, E. Fifteen years later. A comparison of patients in Danish psychiatric institutions in 1957, 1962, 1967, and 1972. *Acta Psychiatrica Scandinavia*, 1978, *57*, 129-144.

Weissman, M. M., & Klerman, G. L. Psychiatric nosology and the Midtown Manhattan study (Letter to the Editor). *Archives of General Psychiatry*, 1980, *37*, 229-230.

Weissman, M. M., & Myers, J. K. Affective disorders in a US urban community. *Archives of General Psychiatry*, 1978, *35*, 1304-1311.

III

Gender and Major Psychopathology

6

CONSTANCE L. HAMMEN

Gender and Depression

It is widely accepted that more women than men are depressed. Articles on sex differences in depression commonly conclude with a summary similar to Silverman's (1968) statement following a comprehensive review: "There appear to be no exceptions to the generalization that depression is more common in females than males, whether it is the feeling of depression, neurotic depression or depressive psychosis [p. 74]." A more recent version of the same conclusion appeared in *Newsweek* when Myrna Weissman, a contemporary authority on the matter, stated in a letter to the editor: "I reviewed international data that covered a period of more than 40 years and found virtually no exception to this finding, that women predominate among those who are depressed [Weissman, 1980]."

This chapter challenges these conclusions. The clarity of the assertions belies the complexity of the issues and data involved. Moreover, an unproductive debate has characterized much of the analysis of sex differences issues, pitting the argument that the depression is real against the position that it is an artifact. Such a useless controversy springs from and supports an overly simplistic concept of illness behavior and may have distracted researchers from studying more specifically the conditions under which people do experience depression.

An additional difficulty in this matter has been a tendency in the sex differences literature to give seemingly equal weight to studies of depression based on transitory mood states and on clinically significant syndrome depres-

ISBN: 0-12-050350-6

sion. Reflecting the uncertainty of the field about the continuity of normal mood depression and syndrome depression, such practices nonetheless obscure meaningful conclusions.

This chapter commences with a presentation of United States data bearing sex differences in depressive phenomena, including treatment facility usage data and community surveys of untreated persons. Each section includes a critical analysis of methodological problems and implications of results. A second major section briefly reviews the concept of illness behavior and presents research bearing on its various components in an attempt to assess sources of gender differences in the phases of illness behavior germane to depression. Finally, the chapter concludes with an analysis of several of the major theories that have been offered to account for gender differences in the etiology of depressive phenomena.

Sex Differences in Diagnosed Treated Cases

Overview of Results

One source of information on potential sex differences comes from analysis of persons who are diagnosed and treated in public or private facilities for some form of depression. Most such investigations based on record-keeping have been done in Western industrialized nations. Weissman and Klerman (1977) present the most comprehensive and frequently cited review of such studies and uncovered a dozen United States studies and nearly twice as many studies from other countries. Their review concluded that a 2:1 sex ratio of women to men diagnosed as depressed was fairly typical for industrialized countries (except Finland and Norway). A more recent survey of United States national facility usage data (1969-1973) reported by Belle and Goldman (1980) found a consistent preponderance of women diagnosed as depressed, although actual F:M ratios vary by type of facility, specific diagnosis, and age. Similar results for 1975 United States data were reported by Vischi, Jones, Shank, and Lima (1980) in a compilation of facility usage figures.

Methodological Considerations

Although the results are fairly consistent, the meaning of the facility utilization data is by no means obvious. Any conclusions that might be drawn must be considered in the context of the methodological adequacy of such investigations and in terms of the implications of data based on persons who seek treatment. The latter issue is addressed in a later section.

Two of the chief methodological requirements of facility usage studies are (*a*) appropriateness and comprehensiveness of the samples for the conclusions drawn and (*b*) reliability and validity of the diagnoses reported. Relatively few of the United States studies on which Weissman and Klerman's (1977) conclusions are based meet the comprehensiveness criterion. For instance, Rice and Kepecs (1970) merely reported increased MMPI D-scale values among women referred for psychological testing in one hospital. Tarnower and Humphries (1969) report sex differences in persons treated with electroconvulsive therapy in one facility. Neither study was based on random sampling or controlled for demographic or referral factors as well as gender differences in the male and female groups. The earliest of the United States studies reported by Weissman and Klerman reported sex differences based in part on only 16 cases of "neurotic depression" (Cooper, Lemkau, & Tietze, 1942). Finally, it should be noted that the representativeness of nearly every sample of facility usage reported in the United States in the past 40 years is undermined by the exclusion of children and persons over age 65. Any conclusions about true sex differences in diagnosis and treatment of depression must be considered applicable only to young and middle-aged adults.

Not only must every study based on treated cases be evaluated for the appropriateness of its database but also issues of adequate diagnosis must be considered. There is a virtually universal difficulty across studies reported prior to the mid-1970s, based on the considerable heterogeneity of usages of various terms such as *reactive depression*, *neurotic depression*, *psychotic depression*, *involutional melancholia*, and *manic-depression*, among other terms. Not only do most of the studies fail to report reliability data on diagnostic practices but also several raise quite serious questions about the validity of diagnoses reported. For example, Tarnower and Humphries (1969) simply adopted the term *depression* as their way of coping with diagnostic problems and admitted that there were "a few schizophrenics" in their patient sample.

Cooper *et al.* (1942) questioned the diagnostic adequacy of their own work and suggested that they viewed manic-depressive and neurotic disorders as basically similar. Also, Pedersen, Barry, and Babigian (1972) reported sex differences in psychotic depression in cases in a county psychiatric register but warned that this was probably an incorrect diagnosis for many (and indeed removed 28% of the sample on the basis of post hoc judgments). Finally, Paykel, Klerman, and Prusoff (1970) did report diagnostic reliability data in their carefully executed study of depression incidence in various treatment settings. However, their criteria are not ones currently accepted for the diagnosis of major depressive disorder and, in fact, seem to emphasize affective, expressive, and self-deprecation symptoms that may be more characteristic of depression in women than in men (Hammen & Padesky, 1977; Padesky & Hammen, 1981).

Implications of Treatment Utilization Studies

As this brief review suggests, a sampling of American studies reported in the widely cited Weissman and Klerman (1977) review of sex differences uncovers rather major flaws in design and conclusions. The data are simply not unequivocal on the question of whether more women than men are depressed when they are treated in facilities.

Yet, even if there were dozens of comprehensive and diagnostically rigorous reviews of patient status, such data would fall short of answering questions of true incidence and prevalence of depression in women and men. Data on cases in treatment obviously underestimate true rates of depressive disorders, since many who are afflicted do not seek treatment (e.g., Brown & Harris, 1978; Weissman & Myers, 1978). Also, as Turns (1978) observes, treatment rates are especially inadequate indicators of true rates of depression compared with schizophrenia, for example, since the former is especially likely to include many misdiagnosed or undiagnosed cases and because of high rates of spontaneous remission for depression.

Many considerations besides symptomatology affect entry into treatment and diagnosis, and these factors themselves may be determined in part by gender. Such factors as symptom recognition and expression, coping, and help-seeking will be discussed in a later section.

Sex Differences in Community Surveys of Depression

Overview of Results: Depression Scales

Since facility utilization studies fall short of indicating the true rates of occurrence of depression, an alternative epidemiological tool has been the community survey. In such approaches, a random sample of individuals representing the demographic characteristics of the community as a whole completes standardized assessment procedures. By far the most common procedure involves administration, usually in interview format, of a brief symptom checklist or rating scale that involves relatively little judgment or inference on the part of the interviewer.

In their recent reviews of such surveys, Weissman and Klerman (1977) and Goldman and Ravid (1980) report about 10 such studies, and several additional surveys of United States communities are now available (Frerichs, Aneshensel, & Clark, 1981; Sayetta & Johnson, 1980). Virtually all reported that women's scores on depression symptom scales were higher than those of men or that a larger proportion of women than men scored in the highest ranges. On the other hand, however, in the studies where interactions of various demographic variables were assessed, it is clear that findings of overall sex differences are sharply modified by their interactions with age, marital status, education, income levels, and diverse other demographic factors (Amenson & Lewinsohn, 1981; Frerichs *et al.*, 1981; Ilfeld, 1977; Markush & Favero, 1974; Radloff, 1980; Sayetta & Johnson, 1980).

The large-scale studies concur that it is generally the young adult, relatively uneducated, formerly married women employed in low-income jobs who report the most depression. Women in higher-status occupations and relatively educated women, for example, do not typically report more depression than their male counterparts. Similarly, in circumscribed studies in which demographic factors are relatively homogeneous, representing young, never married, middle-class college students, sex differences in degree or frequency of depression symptoms have not been observed (Chevron, Quinlan, & Blatt, 1978; Funabiki, Bologna, Pepping, & Fitzgerald, 1980; Hammen & Padesky, 1977; Oliver & Burkham, 1979; Padesky & Hammen, 1981; Parker, 1979).

Methodological Comments on Studies Using Scales

The existence of complex interactions of gender and other demographic factors on depression levels modifies the overall conclusion of some researchers that women are more depressed than men. An even more significant interpretive factor is the question of the validity of the instruments themselves for drawing conclusions about depression. Several of the studies employ scales that are not comparable or that clearly involve anxiety symptoms or other complaints that are not directly generalizable to depression; some use scales of dubious psychometric adequacy. Probably the most extensively studied scale, the Center for Epidemiological Studies-Depression (CES-D) scale, includes items drawn from various clinically validated self-report scales of depression and has the advantage of offering comparability across studies. One disadvantage, however, is that the scale is heavily loaded with affective symptoms whereas other features of the syndrome of depression are minimally sampled. Thus, the meaning of various score levels is elusive. Many researchers have been appropriately cautious in ascribing meaning to scores, noting that the instruments do not provide diagnoses, that scores may fluctuate with transitory mood states, and that depression symptoms may be secondary to other psychological or even physical disturbance. Therefore, although it is possible to use scale scores comparatively to describe relative levels of the construct in various demographic groups, the clinical implications in terms of impairment of functioning and personal distress, or even in the implication of depression, are not clear. Craig and Van Natta (1979) conclude from their study of CES-D scores in the community that the most marked sex differences appear to result from women's greater admission of transitory symptoms of depressed affect, whereas men and women were about equally likely to report evidence of a more enduring depressive syndrome. Research employing follow-up testing, such as that currently underway in Los Angeles (Frerichs *et al.*, 1981) may provide a much needed way of evaluating persistence of depression measured by the CES-D.

Other methodological pitfalls in surveys of depressive symptoms have been noted by Goldman and Ravid (1980). These include unknown refusal rates in the community surveys (Hogarty & Katz, 1971), small sample size (Schwab, Brown, & Holzer, 1968), and failure to report statistical comparisons between groups (Markush & Favero, 1974). Acknowledging some of these and other problems, Parker (1979) takes strong exception to the conclusion presented in the Weissman and Klerman (1977) review of community surveys. He states that "examination of the source material from the cited [Weissman & Klerman] United States studies shows that depression was not measured in some studies, that it can only be inferred in others, that sex differences were not examined in some studies and not found in others [Parker, 1979, p. 128]."

Community Surveys Using Diagnostic Interviews

In view of the methodological and interpretive questions raised thus far about epidemiological research in depression, it is apparent that what is needed is surveys of randomly sampled communities where diagnostic interviews are conducted by trained interviewers and are based on widely accepted, reliable, and valid diagnostic criteria. Fortunately, at least one such study has been published that pertains to affective disorders in the United States. Weissman and Myers (1978) reported the results of Research Diagnostic Criteria-based interviews of a longitudinal follow-up sample ($N = 511$) of a group representative of the population of New Haven, Connecticut. They found no statistically significant sex differences in current major or minor depression. They did, however, report a significant excess of women for lifetime prevalence of major and minor depression. Two interpretive comments should be noted, however. One is that the authors themselves urge caution in accepting the validity of lifetime prevalence data based on retrospective report. Second, women reported significantly higher rates of grief reaction (major depressive reactions following bereavement), which the authors note could be due in part to women's greater risk for bereavement owing to their greater longevity.

One other study warrants mention because of its use of Research Diagnostic Criteria for affective disorders in a community survey. Amenson and Lewinsohn (1981) found a significantly higher proportion of women than men currently diagnosed as experiencing a major or minor depression. However, their sample was a nonrandom, volunteer sample in which only 10% of those contacted participated, and it was composed mostly of women (69%). Interestingly, however, Amenson and Lewinsohn found that cases of depression occurred equally often in men and women who had never before been depressed. The sex differences they observed in diagnoses were accounted for by an excess of women who had been depressed previously. The investigators infer that women are not more susceptible than men to becoming depressed, but do experience more recurrence of depression.

Summary and Implications of Community Survey Studies

Studies using symptom scales suggest that women report more depressive complaints than do men, but only in certain demographic groups. Generally speaking, poor, uneducated, formerly married young adult women report more such symptoms than do their male counterparts. The scales typically assess only transient symptomatology that is possibly reflective more of demoralization than of clinical depression. More studies are needed that investigate the meaning of such transient symptoms. One investigation that assessed persistence as well as prevalence of symptoms argued that clinical significance can be attributed only when persistence occurs, and in such cases men and women were nearly equally likely to be considered depressed (Craig & Van Natta, 1979).

The most meaningful kind of study to answer questions of true prevalence of clinical depression is the community diagnosis survey. Only one such random sample design has been reported to date for United States incidence of depression, and it found no statistically significant sex differences in current depression (Weissman & Myers, 1978).

Sex Differences in Illness Behavior Factors Affecting Depression

People do not just "have" depression in the same way that someone "has" chicken pox. To the extent that the strict form of the medical model of psychopathology implies universal symptoms, course, and identifiable pathogens as in chicken pox, it may mislead us into ignoring the complex social, cultural, and political context in which a psychiatric disorder is judged to occur. Mechanic's (1970) concept of illness behavior and societal reaction considers such factors, and these seem especially relevant to the possible sources of differences between men and women in rates of treatment for depression and in depression symptom reporting. For example, illness behavior includes pain recognition and expression, receptivity to the use of medical and psychiatric services, and willingness to seek release from normal obligations and responsibilities. Societal reaction includes the responses of others to the individual that shape the ill person's behavior and that include labeling processes.

In the following section, four aspects of the illness behavior processes leading to depression treatment-seeking or symptom-reporting are discussed. It is hypothesized that sex differences that affect some of these processes contribute significantly to observed sex differences in depression.

Symptom Experience and Self-Labeling

Do men and women equally experience, recognize, and admit to the phenomena of depression? The experience question cannot be answered since it is inextricably bound to the other dimensions and to the procedures used to measure it. One can ask, however, whether the sexes are equally accurate in labeling depression, and the answer appears to be yes. Female and male college students (Padesky & Hammen, 1981) and community residents (Amenson & Lewinsohn, 1981) report equal convergence between subjective ratings of depression and objective questionnaire ratings of symptomatology for women and men.

Another question pertains to possible differential willingness to admit to depressive experiences. No extensive data are available to resolve this question. Phillips and Segal (1969) argued that women's greater reporting of psychiatric complaints in an interview reflected men's culturally shaped reluctance to admit unpleasurable feelings rather than actual differences in occurrence, but their data did not directly address this issue. Clancy and Gove (1974), on the other hand, found no sex differences in ratings of the social desirability of symptoms and concluded that reporting bias is not a factor in women's reported greater frequencies of distress. However, owing to the wording of their measure of undesirability, the ratings could have reflected general cultural stereotypes rather than personally relevant judgments. King and Buchwald (1981) tested the hypothesis that men are more likely than women to refuse to admit depressive symptoms by comparing self-reported depression scores under private and public disclosure conditions. They found no evidence that men report less depression than women as a function of disclosure condition. However, they did find that the sex of the examiner affected reports of depressive symptoms.

Perhaps the most provocative indirect data on admission of depressive symptoms come from studies such as those of Rosenkrantz, Vogel, Bee, Broverman, and Broverman (1968), who found that socially desirable traits included such masculine identified items (relevant to depression) as "not excitable in a minor crisis," "hides emotions," "never cries," "very self-confident," and the like. Hammen and Peters (1978) found that persons simulating a depressed role were viewed by others as showing significantly less masculine traits on the Rosenkrantz *et al.* dimensions. Thus, to the extent that depressive symptoms may violate sex role standards for men, the latter may be less willing to report them on scales of symptomatology.

A related issue concerns the recognition by others of depressive symptomatology in a friend or relative. In this regard, depression may be somewhat different from other serious psychopathology such as psychosis. The alien and bizarre features of schizophrenia are relatively quickly recognized and not tolerated, and men and women have approximately equal likelihood of diagnosis and treatment for this severe disorder (Belle & Goldman, 1980). Yet most depressive syndromes present much more ambiguous features in terms of impairment of functioning and extent to which individuals, supported by Judeo-Christian cultural standards, believe that symptoms are under volitional control. Thus, a decision to interpret someone's distress as problematic and requiring treatment may be strongly affected by sex role and other cultural standards.

Symptom Expression and Others' Reactions

Even if men and women were to experience equal instances of depression, it is possible that their modes of symptoms expression would differ and lead, in turn, to different consequences. For example, Hammen and Padesky (1977) and Padesky and Hammen (1981) found that although male and female college students did not differ in degree of depressive symptomatology as measured on two different standardized self-report questionnaires, they displayed somewhat different patterns. For instance, moderately depressed men were especially likely to report on the Beck Depression Inventory an inability to cry, various somatic concerns, social withdrawal, and a sense of failure. It was speculated that whereas women's more affectively expressive presentation of depression might be defined by self and others as depression, men's experiences could be seen as based on overwork or physical ailments. Byrne, Boyle, and Pritchard (1977) also found symptom differences in depressed male and female inpatients, with women displaying more symptoms that could be construed as sex role appropriate, such as helplessness and crying. Funabiki *et al.* (1980), in a survey of the phenomenology of depressive experiences and coping, also found sex differences in the ways college men and women expressed depression. Finally, Craig and Van Natta (1979) reported data from a community survey that indicated women's greater admission of transitory affective symptoms of depression but little difference between the sexes on persistent syndrome features of depression.

Another consideration is the response of others to a person's expression of symptoms. On this question the data are sparse but fairly consistent: Depression elicits negative reactions and judgments from others, and more so for men than women. Hammen and Peters (1977) found that persons described in a vignette as depressed were seen as significantly more impaired and less desirable if they were men rather than women (with actual content of the description held constant). Moreover, depression elicited sharper sex differences in rejection than did two other forms of psychological dysfunction. In an additional study simulating actual interviews, Hammen and Peters (1978) found that depressed role-players again were more often rejected and seen as more impaired than nondepressed persons, especially depressed men interacting with women. Howes and Hokanson (1979) found that women simulating depression elicited more supportive comments than did men enacting depression, as part of a larger investigation of reactions to depressed persons. Taken together, the data suggest that depressed men might be especially likely to elicit negative reactions from others—a social reaction that could have the effect of discouraging men from airing depressive complaints with the same freedom that women appear to experience. Amenson and Lewinsohn (1981) offer a similar speculation, observing that the excess of diagnosable depression in women in their sample arose from recurring episodes, whereas men and women who had never been depressed before showed the same rates of first episode.

Coping Behaviors

Data exist for samples of college students indicating that women more freely verbalize (or write) their depressive feelings (Funabiki *et al.*, 1980) and discuss them with friends than do men (Funabiki *et al.*, 1980; Padesky & Hammen, 1981). If these results can be generalized to other populations they imply that women's coping with depression may include complaining and receiving social support—behaviors compatible with both symptom expression in interviews and questionnaires as well as in treatment-seeking.

There is no evidence that the sexes differ in the overall adequacy of their coping responses to stressful situations (Astor-Dubin & Hammen, 1981; Padesky & Hammen, 1978). However, there is some suggestion of different typical modes of coping with stressful events and feelings of depression. For example, Astor-Dubin and Hammen (1981) found that men tended to use more cognitive strategies than women, who used more behavioral strategies.

Finally, it should be noted that men's relatively higher rates of drug and alcohol abuse have been hypothesized as stemming in part from coping with depression, suggesting that the male coping mode obscures the true incidence of depression in men. Although provocative, the accuracy of this speculation remains to be established through studies that appropriately analyze the causal sequence.

Help-Seeking and Labeling

Treatment facility usage data clearly indicate that women seek treatment more frequently for emotional disturbances (such as neurotic disorders and affective disorders) than men do (e.g., Belle & Goldman, 1980). It is also well established that women visit medical doctors more frequently than men do, and seek health care proportionately more frequently than men do for the same conditions (National Center for Health Statistics, 1980).

In a survey of medical help-seeking and mild depression, Selzer, Paluszny, and Carroll (1978) found that women factory workers' mild depression symptoms were correlated with absenteeism. Although open to other interpretations, these data suggest both greater help-seeking in women and greater help-seeking associated with symptoms of depression.

Finally, in a study of young adults' reactions to depression, Padesky and Hammen (1981) found women significantly more likely than men to report actual and hypothetical help-seeking from others for depression. Coie, Pennington, and Buckley (1974) found that women were more likely than men to recommend professional assistance for a variety of psychological problems presented in hypothetical situations. Taken together, results from these studies argue for women's greater willingness to seek treatment for symptoms of depression, as well as other problems, than men. The interpretation of women's more frequent diagnosis and treatment for depression in facility usage studies must therefore consider their greater acceptance of this mode of coping as an alternative to the interpretation of actual greater incidence of depression.

The possibility also exists that excessive rates of diagnosed depression in women reflect a bias in clinician judgments, possibly stemming in no small measure from the long-standing belief among clinicians that depression is a woman's disorder. The few studies that exist on possible diagnostician bias in general report conflicting outcomes (Zeldow, 1978). However, no studies were located that reported rates of diagnosis of depressed men and women in comparison to some concurrent criterion of depression.

Treatment utilization data reflect not only psychiatric distress and willingness to seek help but also availability of resources. It has been argued that women's higher facility usage in general may stem in part from an ability to take time for treatment because they are relatively unemployed or underemployed compared with men. On the other hand, as Brown and Harris (1978) reported, women who are not working but have small children at home who limit their treatment access may be underrepresented in treatment for depression.

Summary and Implications of Illness Behaviors Associated with Depression

Data from a small but growing number of studies suggest that gender differences exist in several realms that affect depressive illness behaviors. Since many depressive symptoms appear to violate sex role norms of masculinity, women may more freely complain of unpleasant feelings and concerns before eliciting negative reactions from others. Men's depressive experiences may take somewhat different forms that, speculatively, may be equally distressing but lead to different interpretations and outcomes. It is clear that women more freely seek help from friends and professionals for depressive phenomena, just as they more freely seek medical treatment for the same conditions men experience.

Such factors should not be considered as artifacts detracting from real depression. They are part of the illness behavior of depression, and such factors appear to contribute in various degrees to the form of psychological dysfunction experienced by any group.

Theories of the Etiology of Sex Differences in Depression

The review of actual data on sex differences has cast some doubt on the universality and magnitude of alleged sex differences in depression. Moreover, the review of illness behavior factors associated with depression may restrict the interpretation placed on any apparent preponderance of women among the depressed. Nonetheless, numerous theories have appeared over the years that attempt to "explain" sex differences in depression. Several of these will be explored with the goal of analyzing the status of causal factors that extend our understanding of depression in both women and men.

Radloff and Rae (1979) have made a useful distinction between susceptibility factors and precipitating factors in the origins of depression. Several of each of these are discussed in the next subsection; *susceptibility factors* include biological and learned psychological mechanisms, and *precipitating factors* include life stress events including episodic as well as more enduring conditions.

Biological Theories

It seems reasonable that a biological explanation of sex differences would at best consist of a weak effect or an interactive effect with other variables, since the incidence of depression in women is sharply affected by demographic factors rather than a main effect across all groups of women.

One version of a biological theory relevant to women is genetic, suggesting X-chromosome linked transmission of depression that, if by a single dominant gene, would affect more women than men. Although genetic theories of affective disorders in general have received empirical support (see review by Depue & Monroe, 1979), the X-linked theory has received only mixed support. A related theory of qualitative differences in type and etiology of depression (e.g., early onset female depressive spectrum versus late onset male pure depressive disease [Winokur, 1973]) requires further empirical support in independent laboratories.

Female endocrinology has been cited as a possible source of women's high rates of depression, as suggested by depressive reactions to oral contraceptives (e.g., review by Parry & Rush, 1978), premenstrual distress, and postpartum depression phenomena. However, the existence of such depressive conditions independent of possible preexisting situations or psychological factors remains to be demonstrated (e.g., Goldzieher, Moses, Averkin, Scheel, & Taber, 1971). Even if biochemically valid linkages between female hormones and neurotransmitter substances affecting mood are established, it appears that postpartum, premenstrual, and oral-contraceptive-related depression phenomena are quite mild and transitory.

Sociological Theories

Several social scientists (e.g., Bernard, 1972; Chesler, 1972; Gove & Tudor, 1973) have taken note of the relatively high rates of mental illness among women and have asserted that women's restricted social roles in this society may be responsible. They argue that the comparatively frustrating and less rewarding roles available to women predispose them to various forms of psychological maladjustment as expressions of their discontent and deprivation. Data supporting this contention such as that reported by Gove and Tudor (1973) showing, for example, that married women report more symptoms than married men, have been criticized by Dohrenwend and Dohrenwend (1974) as having systematically excluded indications of psychopathology such as personality disorder, in which men commonly have been found to be more numerous. Recent reviews of community surveys (Goldman & Ravid, 1980) and treatment utilization (Belle & Goldman, 1980) suggest that sex differences in psychopathology vary greatly by diagnosis, consistent with the Dohrenwends' (1969) position that it is not a matter of women's lives being more productive of pathology than those of men. Rather, "[the data] imply that each sex tends to learn a different style with which it reacts to whatever factors produce psychological disorder [Dohrenwend & Dohrenwend, 1969, p. 24]."

It does appear that relatively disadvantaged groups are more frequently treated for psychiatric conditions, as shown by especially high rates of facility utilization for low-income groups of both men and women (e.g., Belle, 1980). The broad assertion, however, that being female occasions the high rates of psychopathology as a result of restricted roles or disadvantaged status does not appear to be useful or valid. A growing body of research on possible linkages between women's roles (e.g., traditional and nontraditional roles of women and men, dual roles for women) and depression has yielded complex and sometimes contradictory results and conclusions (Aneshensel, Frerichs, & Clark, 1981; Radloff, 1975; Radloff & Rae, 1979; Rosenfield, 1980; Rothblum, in press). Whether women show an excess of depression compared with men in similar role situations or whether the sexes are similar under similar circumstances remains unclear at this time. What is clear, on the other hand, is that current role-related social stressors (such as marital status, financial condition, parenthood, employment situation, and neighborhood condition) *are* associated with depressive symptomatology. Ilfeld's (1977) community survey of depression symptoms and current social stressors cogently illustrates the need to move away from simplistic sex differences toward analyses aimed at uncovering conditions under which anyone exhibits symptomatology. For instance, he found that simple demographic status, including sex, accounted for only 8% of the variance in depression, whereas the current social stressors accounted for 25%.

The emphasis on social stressors has led to a more specific and potentially useful variant of the women's roles hypothesis of sex differences in psychopathology. According to this argument, women's lives may contain more of the stressors that are thought to be precipitants of depression; men and women may be equally depressed in response to life stresses, but women experience more of the stressful events. Radloff (1975; 1980; Radloff & Rae, 1979) explored this hypothesis by defining stressors in demographic terms such as income, education, occupational level, health status, and the like. She found evidence in a community survey using the CES-D scale that women were indeed exposed to more of the situational stressors than were men; yet statistical controls for such differences did not eliminate women's higher depression scores, implying additional causal factors.

Another line of research bearing on life stress as a precipitant of women's depression has quantified stress levels in terms of event occurrence, or *life-change units*. The relatively few studies that have examined sex differences in stress event occurrence, however, have most commonly failed to find sex differences in reported stress (Markush & Favero, 1974; Sarason, Johnson, & Siegel, 1978; Steele, 1978; Uhlenhuth, Lipman, Balter, & Stern, 1974). Makosky (1980) has argued, however, that life event schedules in common use underrepresent the stressful events that women frequently experience. Thus, any conclusions about differences in stressful conditions of men's and women's lives must await better methods for sampling and scaling individuals' stressful event experiences.

Another possibility is that women and men experience similar numbers and types of stressors, but may perceive and react differently to them. For example, Horowitz, Schaefer, Hiroto, Wilner, and Levin (1977) found that women's ratings of the stressfulness of hypothetical personal events from standard life event questionnaires were significantly higher than those of men. Similarly, Parker (1979) found that women reported significantly greater probabilities that they would become depressed following certain events than did men. In particular, women indicated that relationship problems and loss of self-esteem supports would be depressing. Rothblum (in press) argues a similar point based on her review of sex roles and depression: Negative social or interpersonal experiences appear to increase risk of depression, and women are apparently socialized to be particularly affected by interpersonal events.

Overall, the data suggest that women evaluate events as more stressful and possibly experience as stressful certain events not typically included on stress questionnaires or viewed by men as upsetting. In the absence of further research, the implications of such results are hard to establish. For instance, it is unclear whether women differ from men in certain coping capabilities or supports, thus rendering them more vulnerable to experiencing distress than men, or whether women's stressors, if objectively quantified, would be found to be greater than men's. An additional alternative is, of course, that women are freer in the expression of their distress or demoralization over stressful events and circumstances than men are.

Psychological Theories

Several theories of intraindividual determinants of depression have implications for possible gender differences in the etiology of affective disturbances. Psychodynamic formulations of depression tended to emphasize self-esteem deficiencies stemming from interpersonal dependency or excessively high standards of achievement and harsh self-evaluation. In general, inadequate research methodologies have characterized relevant investigations (Chodoff, 1974). The most recent psychodynamic research in this tradition (e.g., Blatt, D'Afflitti, & Quinlan, 1976; Chevron *et al.*, 1978) claimed to find evidence of separate dependency and self-criticism factors in a depressive experiences questionnaire, with women scoring higher on the former and men scoring higher on the latter. Dependency factors scores were not significantly correlated with concurrent measures of depression, however, casting some doubt on the utility of the formulations as potential determinants of depression in men and women. More contemporary versions of the social reinforcement (Lewinsohn, 1974) and achievement and self-evaluation (Rehm, 1977) models of depression have not articulated any basis for systematic sex differences.

The current intraindividual model of depression that does appear to have implications for potential sex differences in depression is the learned helplessness model (Seligman, 1975) and its most recent attributional reformulation (Abramson, Seligman, & Teasdale, 1978). Seligman and colleagues view depression as helplessness induced by perceiving lack of contingency between responses and outcomes and argued that an attributional style of interpreting the causes of the uncontrollability as internal, stable, and global, elicits the symptoms of depression.

Although the vast majority of studies in the voluminous learned helplessness literature have not examined possible sex differences in the hypothesized cognitive mediators, several authors have speculated that the learned helplessness "style" is prototypically a female one. Radloff (1980; Radloff & Rae, 1979), for example, cites circumstantial evidence from studies of sex role socialization that suggests women may learn less effective instrumental coping behaviors than do men and therefore experience more helplessness. However, the few studies that directly examined sex differences in induced helplessness have detected no differences (e.g., Abramson, Garber, Edwards, & Seligman, 1978; Klein, Fencil-Morse, & Seligman, 1976). Baucom and Danker-Brown (1979) found that not only were feminine sex-typed persons susceptible to helplessness inductions but also masculine-typed persons showed the effect as well, whereas androgynous and undifferentiated sex-typed persons seemed less affected.

Research specific to attributional styles has found that women's causal ascriptions do, in fact, differ in the depressive direction from those of men. College women or school girls, for instance, were found to attribute achievement failure more to internal (ability) sources than did males, and attributed success to external causes (Dweck & Goetz, 1978; Ickes & Layden, 1978). Such cognitions appear to negatively affect task persistence and expectations of future mastery. On the other hand, studies specifically relating attributional cognitions to depression have typically not assessed sex differences. One study that did analyze for gender effects failed to find any differences between men's and women's cognitions about the causes of their personal recent stressful events (Hammen, Krantz, & Cochran, 1981).

Etiology of Sex Differences: Summary and Conclusion

Nearly every theory of the etiology of depression could be found to have some implications for potential sex differences. It is equally clear, however, that no theory to date is supported by an empirical database unequivocally establishing the significance of gender as a moderator of the etiological factor. It is even possible that pursuit of knowledge about the etiology of sex differences in depression as an end in itself may be misdirected if, in common with much research in sex differences, it yields no theoretical explanation of mechanisms by which gender has an effect. Hypotheses of endocrinological differences, greater life stresses, more learned helplessness experiences, and the like provide the illusion but not the substance of explanations of the causes of sex differences in depression.

Indeed, if there is a unifying theme in this chapter it is that research in sex differences has yielded overly simple conclusions in terms of the magnitude, universality, and meaning of observed differences between men's and women's depression. Perhaps if the question can be reframed as the study of the conditions under which people, both men and women, are especially likely to experience, express, and seek help for depression, even greater advances will be made.

References

Abramson, L., Garber, J., Edwards, N., & Seligman, M. Expectancy changes in depression and schizophrenia. *Journal of Abnormal Psychology*, 1978, *87*, 102-109.

Abramson, L., Seligman, M., & Teasdale, J. Learned helplessness in humans: Critique and reformulation. *Journal of Abnormal Psychology*, 1978, *87*, 49-74.

Amenson, C., & Lewinsohn, P. An investigation into the observed sex differences in prevalence of unipolar depression. *Journal of Abnormal Psychology*, 1981, *90*, 1-13.

Aneshensel, C., Frerichs, R., & Clark, V. *Family roles and sex differences in depression*. Unpublished manuscript, 1981.

Astor-Dubin, L., & Hammen, C. *Sex differences in coping with depression*. Unpublished manuscript, University of California, Los Angeles, 1981.

Baucom, D., & Danker-Brown, P. Influences of sex roles on the development of learned helplessness. *Journal of Consulting and Clinical Psychology*, 1979, *47*, 928-936.

Belle, D. Who uses mental health facilities? In M. Guttentag, S. Salasin, & D. Belle (Eds.), *The mental health of women*. New York: Academic Press, 1980.

Belle, D., & Goldman, N. Patterns of diagnoses received by men and women. In M. Guttentag,

S. Salasin, & D. Belle (Eds.), *The mental health of women*. New York: Academic Press, 1980.

Bernard, J. *The future of marriage*. New York: Bantam, 1972.

Blatt, S., D'Afflitti, J., & Quinlan, D. Experiences of depression in normal young adults. *Journal of Abnormal Psychology*, 1976, *85*, 383-389.

Brown, G., & Harris, T. *Social origins of depression: A study of psychiatric disorder in women*. New York: Free Press, 1978.

Byrne, D. G., Boyle, D., & Pritchard, D. Sex differences in response to a self-rating depression scale. *British Journal of Social and Clinical Psychology*, 1977, *16*, 269-273.

Chesler, P. *Women and madness*. New York: Doubleday, 1972.

Chevron, E., Quinlan, D., & Blatt, S. Sex roles and gender differences in the experience of depression. *Journal of Abnormal Psychology*, 1978, *87*, 680-683.

Chodoff, P. The depressive personality: A critical review. In R. Friedman & M. Katz (Eds.), *The psychology of depression: Contemporary theory and research*. Washington, D.C.: Winston, 1974.

Clancy, K., & Gove, W. Sex differences in mental illness: An analysis of response bias in self-reports. *American Journal of Sociology*, 1974, *80*, 205-216.

Coie, J., Pennington, D., & Buckley, H. Effects of situational stress and sex roles on attributions of psychological disorder. *Journal of Consulting and Clinical Psychology*, 1974, *42*, 559-568.

Cooper, M., Lemkau, P., & Tietze, C. Complaint of nervousness and the psychoneuroses: An epidemiological viewpoint. *American Journal of Orthopsychiatry*, 1942, *12*, 214-223.

Craig, T., & Van Natta, P. Influence of demographic characteristics on two measures of depressive symptoms. *Archives of General Psychiatry*, 1979, *36*, 149-154.

Depue, R., & Monroe, S. The unipolar-bipolar distinction in the depressive disorders: Implications for stress-onset interaction. In R. A. Depue (Ed.), *The psychobiology of the depressive disorders: Implications for the effects of stress*. New York: Academic Press, 1979.

Dohrenwend, B. P., & Dohrenwend, B. S. *Social status and psychological disorder: A causal inquiry*. New York: Wiley, 1969.

Dohrenwend, B. P., & Dohrenwend, B. S. Social and cultural influences on psychopathology. *Annual Review of Psychology*, 1974, *25*, 417-452.

Dweck, C. S., & Goetz, T. Attributions and learned helplessness. In J. Harvey, W. Ickes, & R. Kidd (Eds.), *New directions in attribution research* (Vol. 2). Hillsdale, New Jersey: Erlbaum, 1978.

Frerichs, R., Aneshensel, C., & Clark, V. Prevalence of depression in Los Angeles County. *American Journal of Epidemiology*, 1981, *113*, 691-699.

Funabiki, D., Bologna, N., Pepping, M., & Fitzgerald, K. Revisiting sex differences in the expression of depression. *Journal of Abnormal Psychology*, 1980, *89*, 194-202.

Goldman, N., & Ravid, R. Community surveys: Sex differences in mental illness. In M. Guttentag, S. Salasin, & D. Belle (Eds.), *The mental health of women*. New York: Academic Press, 1980.

Goldzieher, J., Moses, L., Averkin, E., Scheel, C., & Taber, B. Nervousness and depression attributed to oral contraceptives: A double blind, placebo controlled study. *American Journal of Obstetrics and Gynecology*, 1971, *111*, 1013-1020.

Gove, W., & Tudor, J. Adult sex roles and mental illness. *American Journal of Sociology*. 1973, *78*, 812-835.

Hammen, C., Krantz, S., & Cochran, S. Relationships between depression and causal attributions about stressful life events. *Cognitive Therapy and Research*, 1981, *5*, 351-358.

Hammen, C., & Padesky, C. Sex differences in the expression of depressive responses on the Beck Depression Inventory. *Journal of Abnormal Psychology*, 1977, *86*, 609-614.

Hammen, C., & Peters, S. D. Differential responses to male and female depressive reactions. *Journal of Consulting and Clinical Psychology*, 1977, *45*, 994-1001.

Hammen, C., & Peters, S. D. Interpersonal consequences of depression: Responses to men and women enacting a depressed role. *Journal of Abnormal Psychology*, 1978, *87*, 322-332.

Hogarty, G., & Katz, M. Norms of adjustment and social behavior. *Archives of General Psychiatry*, 1971, *25*, 470-480.

Horowitz, M., Schaefer, C., Hiroto, D., Wilner, N., & Levin, B. Life event questionnaire for measuring presumptive stress. *Psychosomatic Medicine*, 1977, *39*, 413-431.

Howes, M., & Hokanson, J. E. Conversational and social responses to depressive interpersonal behavior. *Journal of Abnormal Psychology*, 1979, *88*, 625-634.

Ickes, W., & Layden, M. A. Attributional styles. In J. Harvey, W. Ickes, & R. Kidd (Eds.), *New directions in attribution research* (Vol. 2). Hillsdale, New Jersey: Erlbaum, 1978.

Ilfeld, F. Current social stressors and symptoms of depression. *American Journal of Psychiatry*, 1977, *33*, 508-516.

King, D., & Buchwald, A. Sex differences in subclinical depression: Administration of the Beck Depression Inventory in public and private disclosure situations. *Journal of Personality and Social Psychology*, 1982, in press.

Klein, D. C., Fencil-Morse, E., & Seligman, M. E. P. Learned helplessness, depression and the attribution of failure. *Journal of Personality and Social Psychology*, 1976, *33*, 508-516.

Lewinsohn, P. M. A behavioral approach to depression. In R. Friedman & M. Katz (Eds.), *The psychology of depression: Contemporary theory and research*. Washington, D.C.: Winston/Wiley, 1974.

Makosky, V. Stress and the mental health of women: A discussion of research and issues. In M. Guttentag, S. Salasin, & D. Belle (Eds.), *The mental health of women*. New York: Academic Press, 1980.

Markush, R. E., & Favero, R. V. Epidemiological assessment of stressful life events, depressed mood, and psychophysiological symptoms—A preliminary report. In B. S. Dohrenwend & B. P. Dohrenwend (Eds.), *Stressful life events: Their nature and effects*. New York: Wiley, 1974.

Mechanic, D. Problems and prospects in psychiatric epidemiology. In E. Hare & J. Wing (Eds.), *Psychiatric epidemiology*. London and New York: Oxford Univ. Press, 1970.

National Center for Health Statistics. *Office visits by women: The national ambulatory medical case survey, United States, 1977*. National Health Survey, Series 13, No. 45 (U.S. Public Health Service Publication No. 80-1796). Hyattsville, Maryland: Author, 1980.

Oliver, J., & Burkham, R. Depression in university students: Duration, relation to calendar time, prevalence, and demographic correlations. *Journal of Abnormal Psychology*, 1979, *88*, 667-670.

Padesky, C., & Hammen, C. *Knowing and doing: Coping response patterns in depressed and nondepressed college students*. Paper presented at the meetings of the Western Psychological Association, San Francisco, California, April 1978.

Padesky, C., & Hammen, C. Sex differences in depressive symptom expression and help-seeking among college students. *Sex Roles*, 1981, *7*, 309-320.

Parker, C. Sex differences in non-clinical depression. *Australian and New Zealand Journal of Psychiatry*, 1979, *13*, 127-132.

Parry, B., & Rush, A. J. *Oral contraceptives and depressive symptomatology: Biological mechanisms*. Unpublished manuscript, 1978.

Paykel, E., Klerman, G., & Prusoff, B. Treatment setting and clinical depression. *Archives of General Psychiatry*, 1970, *22*, 11-21.

Pedersen, A., Barry, D., & Babigian, H. Epidemiological considerations of psychotic depression. *Archives of General Psychiatry*, 1972, *27*, 193-197.

Phillips, D., & Segal, B. Sexual status and psychiatric symptoms. *American Sociological Review*, 1969, *34*, 58-72.

Radloff, L. Sex differences in depression: The effects of occupation and marital status. *Sex Roles*, 1975, *1*, 249-265.

Radloff, L. Risk factors for depression: What do we learn from them? In M. Guttentag, S. Salasin, & D. Belle (Eds.), *The mental health of women*. New York: Academic Press, 1980.

Radloff, L., & Rae, D. Susceptibility and precipitating factors in depression: Sex differences and similarities. *Journal of Abnormal Psychology*, 1979, *88*, 174-181.

Rehm, L. P. A self-control model of depression. *Behavior Therapy*, 1977, *8*, 787-804.

Rice, D., & Kepecs, J. Patient sex differences and MMPI changes—1958 to 1969. *Archives of General Psychiatry*, 1970, *23*, 185-192.

Rosenfield, S. Sex differences in depression: Do women always have higher rates? *Journal of Health and Social Behavior*, 1980, *21*, 33-42.

Rosenkrantz, P., Vogel, S., Bee, H., Broverman, I., & Broverman, D. Sex-role stereotypes and self-concepts in college students. *Journal of Consulting and Clinical Psychology*, 1968, *32*, 287-295.

Rothblum, E. Sex role stereotypes and depression in women. In V. Franks & E. Rothblum (Eds.), *The stereotyping of women: Its effects on mental health*. New York: Springer, in press.

Sarason, I. G., Johnson, J. H., & Siegel, J. M. Assessing the impact of life changes: Development of the life experiences survey. *Journal of Consulting and Clinical Psychology*, 1978, *46*, 932-946.

Sayetta, R., & Johnson, D. *Basic data on depressive symptomatology: United States, 1974-75*. National Health Survey, Series 11, No. 216 (U.S. Public Health Service Publication No. 80-1666). Hyattsville, Maryland: National Center for Health Statistics, 1980.

Schwab, J., Brown, J., & Holzer, C. Sex and age differences in depression in medical inpatients. *Mental Hygiene*, 1968, *52*, 627-630.

Seligman, M. E. P. *Helplessness: On depression, development, and death*. San Francisco, California: Freeman, 1975.

Selzer, M., Paluszny, M., & Carroll, R. A comparison of depression and physical illness in men and women. *American Journal of Psychiatry*, 1978, *135*, 1368-1370.

Silverman, C. *The epidemiology of depression*. Baltimore, Maryland: Johns Hopkins Univ. Press, 1968.

Steele, R. Relationship of race, sex, social class, and social mobility to depression in normal adults. *Journal of Social Psychology*, 1978, *104*, 37-47.

Tarnower, S., & Humphries, M. Depression: A recurring genetic illness more common in females. *Diseases of the Nervous System*, 1969, *30*, 601-604.

Turns, D. The epidemiology of major affective disorders. *American Journal of Psychotherapy*, 1978, *32*, 5-19.

Uhlenhuth, E., Lipman, R., Balter, M., & Stern, M. Symptom intensity and life stress in the city. *Archives of General Psychiatry*, 1974, *31*, 759-764.

Vischi, T., Jones, K., Shank, E., & Lima, L. *The alcohol drug abuse and mental health national data book*. Rockville, Maryland: ADAMHA, 1980.

Weissman, M. *Letter to the Editor. Newsweek*, Sept. 9, 1980.

Weissman, M., & Klerman, G. Sex differences and the epidemiology of depression. *Archives of General Psychiatry*, 1977, *34*, 98-111.

Weissman, M., & Myers, J. Affective disorders in a U.S. urban community. *Archives of General Psychiatry*, 1978, *35*, 1304-1311.

Winokur, G. Diagnostic and genetic aspects of affective illness. *Psychiatric Annals*, 1973, *3*, 6-19.

Zeldow, P. Sex differences in psychiatric evaluation and treatment. *Archives of General Psychiatry*, 1978, *35*, 89-93.

7

IHSAN AL-ISSA

Gender and Schizophrenia

Schizophrenia is one of the most extensively studied types of psychopathology. Its severity and its association with hospitalization and stigmatization have motivated much research on its etiology, particularly on the interaction between genetic and environmental factors. However, most published research on schizophrenia in major psychological and psychiatric journals tends either to employ predominantly male subjects or else to leave the sex of the subject unspecified in the collection and analysis of data (Cash, 1973; Wahl, 1977). This bias in subject selection may raise the question whether results can be generalized from one sex to the other. In a review of research on psychological deficit in schizophrenia, Buss and Lang (1965) have observed that discrepancies that occur among many studies that are otherwise comparable may be due to the neglect of controlling for the sex of subjects. This chapter reviews research on sex differences in the incidence, symptomatology, premorbid adjustment, and outcome of schizophrenia as well as its etiology in order to demonstrate that ignoring the sex of subjects may confound results and hinder their interpretation. Furthermore, schizophrenic patients are a heterogeneous group, and consideration of sex may reduce such heterogeneity. Also, information on the interaction between the sex of patients and socially prescribed gender role behavior or schizophrenic symptoms may contribute to biological and social theories of schizophrenia.

ISBN: 0-12-050350-6

Sex Differences in the Rates of Schizophrenia

Data from the United States (Rosenthal, 1970, 1977) and Britain (Wing, 1978) reveal no overall sex differences in the hospital admission for schizophrenia. However, the age pattern for hospital admission is different for males and females (Rosenthal, 1970). In childhood, the ratio of boys to girls is about 2.5:1; in early adolescence, it is about 2:1. Thereafter, the gap between the sexes narrows until it closes in the middle to late thirties. By the late fifties, about two new female cases are admitted for every male (Rosenthal, 1970). This age pattern of admission, which is based on pre-World War II data in the United States, is evident in the admission to state and county mental hospitals, private mental hospitals, and outpatient psychiatric services between 1969 and 1972, as reported by Belle and Goldman (1980). Also, a similar age pattern was found for the rates of admission for schizophrenia among immigrants in the United States (Malzberg, 1969) and in nine countries across four continents (WHO, 1973). Community studies that include both treated and untreated cases reported by Dohrenwend and Dohrenwend (1969) reveal no consistent sex differences in schizophrenia. Some studies show higher rates of schizophrenia among females, whereas other studies indicate higher rates among males. Murphy (1977, 1982) has demonstrated that when ethnic background is taken into consideration in examining sex differences, both hospital admission and community studies are inconsistent. The data reported by Murphy are discussed in a later section on etiology.

One possible explanation of the sex-age pattern in schizophrenia is that it is an artifact of a general trend in which all admissions to mental hospitals reveal a preponderance of young males and older females. However, analysis of admission statistics indicates that the age-sex pattern is specific to schizophrenia (Forrest & Hay, 1972; Lewine, 1980). Lewine (1980) has suggested that the onset of schizophrenia may occur at the same age for males and females but that male patients are less tolerated and are therefore more quickly hospitalized than female patients. If this is true, the interval between age of onset and admission is expected to be shorter for male than for female patients. Lewine (1980) found that females tend to have later onset as well as later hospitalization than males, giving no support to this hypothesis. Data on onset of patients' symptoms that are obtained from family members and other persons in the patients' environment may, of course, be inaccurate. However, because of the difficulty of ascertaining initial symptoms of patients, there seems to be a systematic error in which the age of onset is more likely to be given too high for both sexes.

The age-sex pattern may also be accounted for, in part, by diagnostic differences between males and females. Lewine (1980), for example, found that sex differences in the age of onset and hospitalization are not evident among paranoid schizophrenic patients. Similarly, Forrest and Hay (1972) found that sex differences in the age of onset are inflated by a large number of depressed females in their forties with paranoid delusions who are given the diagnosis of schizophrenia. They also observed that almost all female patients who are first admitted under the age of 20 with the diagnosis of schizophrenia have had their diagnosis changed later to personality disorder or manic-depressive disorder. These diagnostic trends may reduce the number of female schizophrenics at early adulthood but substantially increase it later.

Finally, the age-sex pattern of schizophrenic breakdown may be the result of stresses that impinge on males and females at different life stages. Noreik and Odegaard (1967) have pointed out that male stresses, which are predominantly related to the occupational role, occur earlier than female stresses, which involve young children, home, and husband. They hypothesized that changes in the Norwegian economy from unemployment and economic crisis in the 1930s, which might have affected young men, to the relative prosperity of the 1950s, should have brought about a change in the age of early onset of male schizophrenia. Their data reveal that the age-sex pattern of schizophrenic breakdown remained constant during these two historical periods, giving no support to the occupational stress hypothesis. The stress hypothesis would suggest that young men not only have a high rate of schizophrenia but also have high rates of other types of mental illness. However, young women tend to have a higher rate of depression than young men (Radloff, 1975), suggesting sex differences in the form of reaction to stress. Men not only have an early onset of schizophrenia but they also have a more severe form of it, which could be the result of stress as well as biological susceptibility. The evidence that an early type of schizophrenia with a poor prognosis is more prevalent among males than females across cultures would give weight to the genetic-biological hypothesis (WHO, 1979). However, conclusions about factors associated with the age-sex pattern in schizophrenic breakdown should await further research data.

Marital Status and Schizophrenia

There are more single males and married females among schizophrenic patients (Eaton, 1975; Farina, Garmezy, & Barry, 1963; Forrest & Hay, 1972). There are at least three hypotheses put forward to explain the relationship between marital status and schizophrenia. First, there is the selection hypothesis which suggests that schizophrenia makes marriage less likely for males than for females because males are expected to initiate the process involved in marriage (e.g., courtship) (Farina *et al.*, 1963). Second, there is the stress hypothesis, which postulates that married men are protected against schizophrenia because marriage is less stressful for them than for women. Finally, it has been suggested that single status may be associated with more ready entry into treatment than married status.

In considering the rates of first hospitalization for schizophrenia among the never-married, the widowed, and the married, the data reported by Eaton (1975) support both the selection and the stress hypothesis. For example, although the rates of the widowed is significantly lower than that of the never-married giving support to the selection hypothesis, their rates are also higher than the married suggesting the effects of stress in widowhood. Other data reveal that the rates of schizophrenia in widowhood could rise by stresses following bereavement (Birley & Brown, 1970). Brown and Birley (1968) also found that independent events (out of the patients' control and not brought about by the illness) that tend to precede schizophrenic breakdown are higher among single than married patients. Further evidence in support of the stress hypothesis is the finding by Eaton (1975) that the rates among widowed males are higher than for widowed females, which suggests more stress in widowhood among males than females. However, these data must be interpreted with caution because widowers in general are more likely to remarry than widows, which leaves a relatively large number of unstable widows unmarried.

Studies of the characteristics of spouses of schizophrenics give some support to the selection hypothesis. For example, Planansky and Johnson (1967) found that among married male schizophrenics, the wives were more active in pursuing their husbands during courtship than the wives of normal males. Furthermore, the normal wives of schizophrenics tend to be more resourceful and higher in intelligence than the normal husbands of schizophrenic women (Lane, 1967). In the consideration of the selection hypothesis, it should be recognized that male patients have their schizophrenic breakdown at an earlier age than females, decreasing their opportunity to get married.

Sex differences in the rate of readmission of schizophrenics into mental hospitals may account for the high rates of single males and married females in hospitals. Watt and Szulecka (1979) found that although the percentage of readmission of married males and females is equal, single male readmission is significantly higher than single females or married males. Married females, on the other hand, are readmitted more frequently than single females. The widowed also tend to stay longer in hospital than the married (Eaton, 1975).

Thus, the evidence suggests that in addition to selective factors, stress and the differential use of health facilities could account for the relationship between marital status and schizophrenia. Follow-up studies are needed to partial out the relative effects of these three factors. With recent changes in gender roles, stereotypical concepts of the parts that males and females are expected to play in spouse selection may no longer be valid for explaining the relationship between marital status and schizophrenia.

Gender Role and Schizophrenic Symptoms

Clinical observation of symptoms and behavior of schizophrenic patients may provide information about deviation from gender role in schizophrenia that might, in turn, play a part in the hospitalization of men and women or might influence treatment, eventual discharge from hospital, and rehospitalization. In this section, I first deal with hallucinations and delusions that are usually considered major symptoms in schizophrenia. Second, I discuss clinical observations of general behavioral patterns of schizophrenic patients as well as research revealing reversal of gender role and gender identity. The implication of reversal of gender roles for treatment is also outlined.

Hallucinations and Delusions

A survey of hallucinations in 1934 by Sherman and Sherman (cited in Lucas, Sainsbury, & Collins, 1962) indicates that they are more common among women than men. However, a more recent study reveals no sex differences among hospitalized patients (Zigler & Phillips, 1960). Similarly, a community study of a southeastern county in the United States shows that only slightly more women report visual and auditory hallucinations than do men (11.7% of all women and 9.8% of all men) (Schwab, 1977). In a study of preadolescent schizophrenic children, Portell (1970) found no significant differences in the frequency of hallucinations (59% of boys aged 12-14 and 58% of girls aged 10-12 reported hallucinations).

Schizophrenic females tend to have more delusions than males (Lucas *et al.*, 1962). The greatest sex differences in delusions occur between ages 40 and 50, when the incidence in the female is twice that in the male (Swanson, Bohmert, & Smith, 1970). Busse and Pfeiffer (1973) reported that paranoid psychoses of old age are markedly higher among females in all studies reviewed, with males accounting for only from 5% to 25% of patients with this diagnosis. It is also believed that there are characteristic features of the clinical picture of female schizophrenia after the menopause that include not only sexual delusions but also great pressure to talk and affective symptoms (Wing, 1978).

Lucas *et al.* (1962) found that schizophrenic women, particularly those who are married, tend to have significantly more sexual delusions, whereas schizophrenic men tend to exceed women in frequency of delusions of inferiority. An analysis of grandiose delusions indicates that those of males tend to contain significantly more themes related to authority and power, whereas those of females tend to include more themes related to wealth, social status, and skill. The contents of sexual delusions indicate that paranoid sexual ideas such as of imposed intercourse were greater in the females, particularly those who were single. Delusions of being married, betrothed, pregnant, and of having children also had a higher incidence in females, but again they were more frequent in the single than in the married patients. The only delusional content that occurred more in males than in females was, in the single, of masturbation and, in the married, of the spouse's infidelity.

Todd and Dewhurst (1955) also found that delusions of jealousy occur in both sexes, but they are more frequent and far more dangerous in males. They suggested that the wives' decreased sexual interest or the husband's impotence are major factors in the development of delusions of jealousy in the male. Disparity in the sexual ability of the couple is another critical factor—an elderly husband married to a much younger wife, for example. The content of sexual delusion in general also appears to reflect sexual inhibitions and sexual demands regarding the two sexes in society; for example, the greater restrictions on intercourse for single females as compared with single males, the greater pressure on married women than on married men to conform, and the more explicit condemnation of masturbation in men (Lucas *et al.*, 1962).

In contrast to Western studies, Weinstein (1962) found that sexual ideas are not very frequent in the delusions of native women in the Virgin Islands. Weinstein thought that the low rate of sexual delusion among native women is related to social expectations; they are not apt to gain their ends by playing the part of the helpless female or by acting in a seductive fashion. Also, the Virgin Islanders do not structure the environment in terms of sex as do other cultures; this does not mean that they are less active sexually in a physical way, but that the biological fact of sex does not determine social role to so great an extent.

Murphy (1967) suggested that cultural response to delusions can vary with the sexual status of the person. Many societies do not tolerate the delusions of widows because they are mistrusted (it is believed that they are a threat to the marital ties of neighbors, acquaintances, and friends). In the French-Canadian villages studied by Murphy, the communities were helpful to their deluded young men but not to their young women. Young women suspected of delusions were driven deeper into them if they were of a somatic nature or sent into exile if they were paranoid. Cross-culturally, discrimination against deluded women seems to depend on the type of psychiatric treatment practiced in societies. When exorcism of delusions is practiced, there seems to be no discrimination regarding who will be treated. However, where a sacrifice or other expenses are involved, a family may be willing to pay for the treatment of a son but not for that of a daughter or a wife (Murphy, 1967).

Reversal of Gender Role and Gender Identity

Cheek (1964) found that schizophrenic men tend to be more passive and withdrawn than normal men, whereas schizophrenic women appear more active and domineering than their normal counterparts. Clinical observations on hospital wards and in psychotherapy have particularly reported differential levels of aggression and sexuality among males and females, with schizophrenic women being more sexual and more aggressive than schizophrenic men (Chesler, 1972; Schulz & Kilgalen, 1969; Weich, 1968). Mayer-Gross, Slater, and Roth (1960) described "a flare-up of sexuality," excessive masturbation, and promiscuity in young schizophrenic women. A study of patients in three mental hospitals in Britain indicates that there is more violent behavior among those female patients who are predominantly schizophrenic (Fottrell, 1980). A community study of Puerto Rican families on the island by Rogler and Hollingshead (1965) revealed that schizophrenic husbands tend to withdraw and become dependent on their wives. The schizophrenic wives, on the other hand, become belligerent and defy their husbands. The authors noted that the behavior of the schizophrenic male is incompatible with normal *machismo*, which emphasizes strength of character, dominance, and independence. The behavior of the female schizophrenic is inconsistent with cultural expectations of humble, deferential, and conforming behavior.

Stevens (1970) found that schizophrenic women have a relatively high rate of illegitimacy (19.1% among schizophrenics, 7.5% among depressive patients, and 12.7% in the general population in London). However, the illegitimate births of schizophrenic women were the result of a serious relationship rather than a casual sexual encounter. Furthermore, the clinical impression given of schizophrenic women as "immoral" is inconsistent with the evidence, which indicates that these patients tend to give a more strict and somehow more extreme moral judgment on social issues than do schizophrenic men and normal men and women (Holzberg, 1963).

Selective factors may explain sex differences in the behavior of hospitalized schizophrenic patients. It is quite possible that overactive, aggressive females and underactive, withdrawn males are hospitalized more readily than those whose behavior is socially acceptable. Also, the prevalence of more violence and destructive behavior among females than males not only in hospitals but also in prisons (Mitchell & Murphy, 1975; Walker, 1965) may raise the question whether institutionalization might be responsible for sex differences in the behavior of patients. The aggression of schizophrenic women appears to be specific (e.g., during contact with the staff) and may not be generalized to other situations. For example, studies of jointly admitted mothers and their babies indicate that the aggression of schizophrenic women is not evident during interaction with their babies; they do not show a tendency to harm their babies and they even avoid the babies when they feel hostile (Baker, Morison, Game, & Thorpe, 1961; Weiss, Grunebaum, & Schell, 1964).

The overactive, aggressive schizophrenic females may bring more disturbance, attract more attention in the hospital, and therefore require more disciplinary treatment such as aversive therapy than their male counterparts (Al-Issa, 1980; Chesler, 1972; Ludwig, Marx, Hill, & Browning, 1969; Modlin, 1963). Discharge from hospital also tends to be associated with a decrease in the masculinity score of schizophrenic women (Distler, May, & Tuma, 1964; McKeever, May, & Tuma, 1965). Distler *et al.*, for example, found that schizophrenic women are more likely to be discharged from hospital if they show a feminine pattern of high anxiety and low ego strength than if they reveal a masculine pattern of low anxiety and high ego strength. Angrist and associates (Angrist, Dinitz, Lefton, & Pasamanick, 1961; Angrist, Lefton, Dinitz, & Pasamanick, 1968) found that rehospitalized female patients tended to be married women who performed less well on domestic work than other expatients who were not rehospitalized. Another group of these rehospitalized women were symptom-free and performed their domestic role as adequately as other expatients, but family friction and masculine behavior such as alcohol abuse and sexual activity played a part in their readmission.

In addition to clinical studies, self-report inventories are used in the study of reversal of gender role. McClelland and Watt (1968) gave a role preference test to normals and to schizophrenic patients of both sexes. They found that schizophrenic males liked to play feminine roles (angel, fashion designer, sister, witch, secretary, a cow) more often than normal males. As compared with normal females, schizophrenic females more often preferred to play masculine roles (Lord, scientist, brother, devil, policeman, bull). A replication of this study by LaTorre and Piper (1979) confirmed the tendency of schizophrenic patients to prefer opposite-sex roles, although the role preference scores are significantly correlated with length of hospitalization for females but not for males. Using only male patients, Kokonis (1973) found that schizophrenic males reveal less interest in male activities such as football, climbing, and parachuting than do their normal counterparts. Using the McClelland and Watt role preference test, Ecker, Levine, and Zigler (1973) found no significant difference between normals and schizophrenics, throwing some doubt on the hypothesis of reversal of gender role in schizophrenia. Role preference tests are based on stereotyped notions about the interests of males and females and may not be reliable from one situation to the other or from one group to the other.

McClelland and Watt (1968) also used satisfaction with certain parts of the body as an index of gender identity. They asked normals and schizophrenics of both sexes to express their degree of satisfaction with and concern about body parts that are considered feminine (relevant to appearance such as lips, hips, eyelashes, etc.) and masculine (relevant to strength such as shoulders, hands, etc.). They found that as compared with normal women, normal men were less concerned with body parts related to appearance (feminine) and more concerned with body parts related to strength (masculine). Schizophrenic men, however, revealed the opposite trend; they were, like normal women, more concerned about how they looked than about their strength. Schizophrenic women simply showed less concern than normal women for all aspects of their bodies, whether masculine (strength) or feminine (appearance). Jaskar and Reed (1963) reported that hospitalized psychiatric female patients were less happy with their bodies than were a control group of normal females. Appearance is important for the female, and it is understandable that long-term institutionalization may result in alienation from one's own body. However, it is not very clear how long-term institutionalization changes the body image of male patients. A study by Ecker *et al.* (1973) did not find changes in body image among recently hospitalized schizophrenics and suggests that these changes may be specific to chronic patients.

Another approach to the study of disturbance in gender identity in schizophrenia uses drawings of the human figure. It is assumed that the first figure drawn by a subject is the subject's unconscious perception of himself or herself. Thus, if the first figure drawn by the subject is that of the opposite sex, then it is concluded that the subject identifies with the opposite sex (Swensen, 1968). A review of studies using the Draw-a-Person Test to investigate sex identity reveals that schizophrenic patients tend to confuse sex identity in their drawings (LaTorre, 1976). However, when schizophrenic patients were compared with surgical patients, no difference between the drawings of the two groups was discernible (Smith, 1953), raising the question that patients, in general, because they are under stress, may produce poor human figures; human figures of poor quality tend to obliterate sex differentiation (Swensen, 1968). Male patients tend to draw poorer pictures than female patients, which may reflect the severity of their illness rather than gender role disturbance (Biller & Poey, 1969). There is also a tendency of males to draw their own pictures more than females (Money & Wang, 1966). Furthermore, the validity of projective techniques as a measure of gender identity has not been established.

Masculinity-femininity scales are also used for assessing disturbance in gender role and gender identity. Kayton and Biller (1972) gave Gough and Heilbrun's (1965) Adjective Checklist and the Gough Femininity Scale (Gough, 1966) to paranoid schizophrenics, neurotics, and normals. The diagnostic groups were significantly higher on femininity than the control group, suggesting a reversal of gender role not only in schizophrenia but also in neurosis among male patients. Using the Bem Sex-Role Inventory, LaTorre and Piper (1979) found that, as compared with normals, schizophrenic males obtained lower scores on masculinity, whereas schizophrenic females received lower scores on femininity. Reed (1957), however, found no significant difference between normal and psychotic females on the masculinity-femininity scale of Minnesota Multiphasic Personality Inventory (MMPI Mf) scale. Using the MMPI Mf scale, Petzel and Gynther (1969) also found that both schizophrenic males and females obtained normal masculinity-femininity scores. Thus, findings that schizophrenic patients show reversal of gender role on masculinity-femininity scales are inconsistent.

Studies of gender role and gender identity in schizophrenia are mostly based on the conception of masculinity and femininity as bipolar rather than orthogonal dimensions. They tend to ignore persons who can be either high on both masculinity and femininity (androgynous) or low on both (undifferentiated) (Spence, Helmreich, & Stapp, 1975). They also give little consideration to the possibility that under situational and social changes, rigid gender-typing and inability to adopt behavior of the opposite sex can also be maladaptive (Bem, 1975) and could result in schizophrenic breakdown (Murphy, 1982). Also, reversal of gender roles and gender identity are not specific to schizophrenia but are also associated with other disorders such as neurosis (Kayton & Biller, 1972) and transsexualism (Green, 1975). It is still not clear whether gender role deviation is pathogenic to schizophrenia or is one of many social factors that might bring the person in contact with psychiatric service and result in hospitalization. Of course, gender role reversal such as aggression of the female and withdrawal of the male may be only coincident to and quite independent of schizophrenia.

Sex Differences in Premorbid Adjustment and Prognosis

It is consistent with sex differences in symptomatology that females tend to develop reactive schizophrenia whereas males tend to develop the process type of the disorder (Allon, 1971; Lane, 1968). Heterosexual interest and the presence of affect and delusions in females are more compatible with reactive schizophrenia, less impairment, and better prognosis.

Females tend to have a better premorbid adjustment because they tend to be older, married and, if not housewives, to have higher occupational levels than males (Chapman, Day, & Burstein, 1961; Farina, Garmezy, Zalusky, & Becker, 1962; Zigler, Levine, & Zigler, 1977). Indeed, studies reveal that, in contrast to hospitalized men, hospitalized women are less noticeably different from the normal population on the five variables making up the Phillips-Zigler index (i.e., age, education, marital status, occupation, and employment history). However, premorbid adjustment appears to be more predictive of outcome for males than for females (Farina *et al.*, 1962). The relationship between marital status and outcome is also stronger in males than in females (Farina *et al.*, 1963; Norris, 1956; Odegaard, 1946, 1953). Moreover, since many women tend to be housewives, the occupational measure of premorbid adjustment is expected to be less sensitive to variations among women than men, and therefore less predictive of prognosis in women. Similarly, Schooler (1963) found that degree of involvement with others is significantly related to hospitalization of male, rather than female, schizophrenics. These sex differences in the criteria for premorbid adjustment and prognosis have led to the use of different norms and cutoff scores to categorize patients as to premorbid history (Kokes, Strauss, & Klorman, 1977).

A follow-up study by Prentky, Lewine, Watt, and Fryer (1980) has revealed that sex differences in prognostic signs are not specific to schizophrenia, but are generally evident among hospitalized psychiatric patients (schizophrenics, personality disorder, neurotics, depressive psychotics). They reported sex differences in negative prognostic signs for length of hospitalization and global outcome. For males, long duration of hospitalization is associated with adult avoidance of others and with orderliness, as observed by teachers in school. In the female, poor outcome as measured by length of hospitalization is predicted by premature parental death and the presence of perplexity and confusion at first hospitalization (low adult social competence is predictive of poor outcome for both sexes). Poor global outcome (outcome is rated as *good, fair, poor*) is predicted by the presence of hallucinations and adult avoidance of others in the male and by perplexity, good conduct in school, and internal family conflict in the female.

Prognostic differences and better outcome in females do not seem to be an artifact of criterion measurement of premorbid adjustment (e.g., marital status, heterosexual contacts) but reflect true sex differences. For example, when measures of psychosocial functioning that exclude marital status are used, females continue to show less severe schizoid tendencies (Rosen, Klein, & Gittelman-Klein, 1971; Rosen, Klein, Levenstein, & Shahinian, 1968). A follow-up study by Huber, Gross, Schuttler, and Linz (1980) has revealed that schizophrenic females show better social recovery than males; they are more fully employed at their previous occupational level than their male counterparts. Females generally tend to make a better social and occupational adjustment after hospital discharge (Raskin & Dyson, 1968) and have a significantly lower relapse rate than males (the rate for schizophrenic men is double that for women [Vaughn & Leff, 1976]).

Sex Differences in the Etiology of Schizophrenia

The Genetic-Environmental Hypothesis

Rosenthal (1962) reported higher concordance rates for females than males in both monozygotic and dyzygotic same-sexed twins. Similarly, the number of pairs of mother-daughter and sister-sister is larger than father-son or brother-brother (symbionic psychosis and *folie à deux* are more prevalent among women than men). High rates of concordance among women would suggest that genetic factors are more often involved in the schizophrenic breakdown of females than in males. However, if women are indeed more genetically predisposed to schizophrenia than men, higher rates of schizophrenia are expected not only among females with schizophrenic siblings but also among all schizophrenics (as noted earlier, a higher rate of schizophrenia among women in the general population has no support). Indeed, Rosenthal (1962) himself has argued in favor of environmental influences to explain concordance rates. He suggested that identification with same-sex family members may be stronger in females than in males and that the psychosis of one female partner is the result of living with the other female sibling who has already developed psychosis. However, the hypothesis that identification with same-sex family members is stronger in females than in males has not received empirical support (Maccoby & Jacklin, 1974). Against the identification hypothesis is also the finding that in symbionic psychosis the influence of the partners is mutual even though the influence of one partner may predominate over the other. Moreover, the psychosis in both partners is much more likely to develop simultaneously rather than having the psychosis of one emerging after that of the other (Bleuler, 1978). Data showing that women predominate both as induced and inducers in symbionic psychosis (Bleuler, 1978) are against the hypothesis that women are more susceptible to suggestion than men.

Bleuler (1978) has raised methodological questions against early studies of the rates of concordance of female patients. Data used in these studies may be biased because they are based on hospital admission, which is dependent on numbers of beds that may be allocated differently for men and women. Schizophrenic females are also more likely to be the inhabitants of chronic wards because the number of chronic males is reduced by their tendency to have a higher rate of mortality in hospital and a better chance of redischarge after rehospitalization (Rosenthal, 1961). Watt and Szulecka (1979) found a higher rate of rehospitalization among married females aged 45 and older than among their male counterparts. The excess of chronic female patients may, therefore, substantially increase the probability that investigators come across female siblings in a mental hospital. Indeed, studies that used consecutive admissions rather than chronic hospital inmates, reveal that female pairs (twins, siblings) are no more concordant than male pairs (Bleuler, 1978; Gottesman & Shields, 1972), thus supporting the view that the previous findings were due to methodological factors rather than to real differences between the sexes (see discussion by Lewine, 1979; Samuels, 1978, 1979). Yet, these studies indicate that there are more women than men among schizophrenics with schizophrenic siblings (Bleuler, 1978). Thus, it is not that girls are more likely than boys to become schizophrenics with female than with male siblings, but that girls with brothers or sisters are more likely to become ill together than boys are. It appears that the presence of disturbed persons in the home regardless of their sex is more related to the development of schizophrenia in women than in men.

Another finding that suggests a sex-linked transmission of schizophrenia is the preponderance of schizophrenics among mothers, rather than fathers, of schizophrenics. However, this trend is a result of the larger number of married schizophrenic females. Family studies also provide evidence against the sex-linked hypothesis in schizophrenia (Gottesman & Shields, 1976). For example, the offspring of male schizophrenics are as often schizophrenic as those of female schizophrenics. Similarly, paternal half-siblings of index schizophrenic adoptees are as often schizophrenic as maternal half-siblings.

Studies suggest that environmental factors are more involved in the development of schizophrenia in females than males (Bleuler, 1978). Early parental loss and broken homes occur more often in the histories of schizophrenic women than in schizophrenic men or in the general population. Hilgard and Newman (1963) reported that there is significant maternal death among schizophrenic women between the ages of 3 and 5 as compared with schizophrenic men and normal controls. However, they found that early loss is not specific to schizophrenia, but is prevalent among alcoholic and neurotic women. The tendency of women to have more early loss than men is also found in depression (Beck, 1967; Birtchnell, 1970; Hill & Price, 1967).

In general, schizophrenic women are more likely to be influenced by adverse childhood backgrounds than are schizophrenic men. Bleuler (1978) has observed that, among sisters of schizophrenics coming from stressful childhood backgrounds, there are more schizophrenics than among brothers of schizophrenics coming from the same backgrounds. Girls who become schizophrenic more often live together with a schizophrenic mother or a schizophrenic stepparent, particularly a stepmother, than their male counterparts. The association between changes in the course of the illness and the death of a parent is stronger in schizophrenic women than men. Traumatic experiences such as the loss of a lover, husband, or other person with whom they have close emotional ties are more often associated with deterioration in the mental health of women than of men. Similarly, improvement tends to take place in the aftermath of contact with somebody they love. The involvement of environmental factors as well as the course and outcome of schizophrenia in women is compatible with their tendency to have a high rate of the reactive form of the disorder, as discussed earlier.

Since data indicate that sex is not relevant to the rates of schizophrenia except in the age of onset (Gottesman & Shields, 1976), it is useful to hypothesize that the excess of the disorder in one sex or the other in community studies may reflect cultural factors in general and gender role in particular. Murphy (1982), for example, reported an excess of female schizophrenics among French-Canadian villagers, but not in a comparable group of Anglo-Saxon Protestants. The rates for French-Canadian females were also significantly higher than for Anglo-Saxon, Protestant females, but the rates for the males were not significantly different from each other in these two communities. In examining the demographic characteristics of the French and Anglo-Saxon, Protestant communities (e.g., economic base, mean income, sex ratio, age structure) he found a striking similarity between the two groups, and thus these factors cannot account for the results. Selective factors related to hospitalization are also excluded because both hospitalized patients and those living in the community were used in the study. Similarly, there was no noticeable difference in the roles carried out by females in the two communities; both carried out the roles of parent, spouse, farmer's wife, retailer, and shop assistant as in any other agricultural community. The women in both communities were slightly more educated than the men because of the tendency of that generation of females to stay longer at school. Thus, the actual life situation and actual roles do not appear to be different enough to provoke such different rates of prevalence among French families. However, when the ideals held for womanhood were examined, Murphy found marked differences between the two communities. In the older, French Catholic tradition, a woman is expected to be a good mother, religious, a loyal spouse, a hard worker, and subordinate to her husband. In the present generation of females, however, she has also learned from school that she should exploit her superior education and her abilities, a teaching that is incompatible with the older idea of subordinate status. On the other hand, the Anglo-Saxon, Protestant females are not exposed to the same conflict, but are left free to dominate their husbands, to become career women, or to simply take the role of a subordinate wife. Murphy put forward the hypothesis that cultural conflicts that are brought about by modern education or by old-fashioned men may explain excessive breakdown among French Canadian females.

Hospital admission data in Canada reported by Murphy (1977) reveal that the association between educational level and sex differences in schizophrenia varies from one ethnic background to the other. For example, among British Canadians, males with a low level of education have a much higher rate of schizophrenia than their female counterparts; at a high level of education, the sex difference becomes small and almost diminishes. Among Dutch Canadians, however, a high level of education tends to be related to high rates of schizophrenia for females but relatively low rates for males. Murphy put forward a sociocultural hypothesis to explain sex differences among British Canadians and Dutch Canadians. Sex differences among British Canadians could be related to the privileged status of the group and its expectations of preferential treatment. He observed that British women with a low level of education benefit from having English as their mother tongue and thus find employment very easily (as saleswomen, telephone operators, and so on). In contrast, British Canadian men with a low level of education do not benefit from the preferential treatment of their subculture because of a tendency among Canadian employers to prefer unskilled workers to be from other ethnic groups that are less demanding and less challenging of their authority. Thus the relatively high rate of unemployment of the British Canadian men with a low level of education could have contributed to hospital admission for schizophrenia. With a high level of education, however, both British Canadian males and females benefit from their privileged position, which may reduce their risk for schizophrenic breakdown. In an attempt to explain the high rate of hospital admission among Dutch Canadian females with a high level of education, Murphy suggested that employment tends to provide these women with less satisfaction than it gives their male counterparts. This is particularly true for those women whose work outside the home is in conflict with the ideal prescribed for females in the Dutch culture.

Physiological and Biological Sex Differences

An early review by Duffy (1962) reveals that, in normal subjects, most physiological measures show either no differences between the sexes or a higher degree of arousal on the part of females. Sex differences in the physiological reactions of schizophrenic patients have not been extensively studied. Gunderson, Autry, Mosher, and Buchsbaum (1974), for example, have briefly referred to the data on the evoked responses collected by Shagass, which revealed that chronic schizophrenic females are more responsive than males. They noted that restricted responsiveness, which is reported earlier in schizophrenic patients, seems to hold only for males. In a doctoral dissertation, Watts (1968) found that schizophrenic females, particularly those in the paranoid category, tend to give larger galvanic skin responses (GSRs) than their male counterparts (in contrast to these data, Graham, Cohen, and Schmavonian [1966] found that with normal subjects, females obtain lower GSRs than males).

Mednick, Schulsinger, Teasdale, Schulsinger, Venables, and Rock (1978) reported that autonomic nervous system measures are differently associated with the etiology of schizophrenia in the sexes. Among high-risk subjects (those whose mothers are schizophrenic), they found that a high percentage of GSRs and a fast rate of recovery are associated with the development of schizophrenia in males but not in females. Repeated studies by Venables have failed to find differences between schizophrenic and normal females in autonomic responsivity, thus supporting the view that GSRs may not be relevant to the development of schizophrenia in females. However, the Mednick *et al.* sample is less representative of female than male schizophrenics because the subjects are between 20-30 years old and may not include the typical female patient, who tends to have a later onset. Furthermore, the sex distribution of schizophrenic index parents, in this study as well as in the majority of genetic risk research, is biased in selecting schizophrenic mothers who differ from schizophrenic fathers on many characteristics (onset, symptoms, premorbid adjustment, etc.) (Lewine, Watt, & Grubb, 1981). Mednick *et al.* have, however, speculated that the physiological data may explain sex differences in the manifestation of schizophrenia, particularly its severe form in the male. Based on Mednick's learning interpretation of schizophrenia, they noted that boys who have an abnormally high reactive autonomic nervous system are often forced by society to suppress their emotionality and therefore any response, such as irrelevant thoughts and bizarre behavior, that avoids emotionally arousing stimuli will be reinforced and quickly learned. Fast autonomic nervous system recovery also provides a strong reinforcement for, and increases the probability of, such avoidance responses. This type of avoidance learning situation tends to isolate the male schizophrenic and increase his withdrawal. On the other hand, since girls are allowed to express their emotions, they are less influenced by autonomic nervous system factors and consequently do not resort as often as boys to avoidance behavior and the development of a withdrawn form of schizophrenia. The Mednick *et al.* interpretation is largely based on the traditional stereotypical views of expressive behavior as more acceptable for the female than for the male.

Studies of the platelet monoamine oxidase activity (MAO) reveal that males have lower levels than females in both normals and schizophrenics (Murphy, Wright, Buchsbaum, Nichols, Costa, & Wyatt, 1976; Robinson, Davis, Nies, Ravaris, & Sylvester, 1971; Zeller & Davis, 1980). Since low MAO levels are observed in chronic rather than acute schizophrenia or schizo-affective disorders (Buchsbaum, Coursey, & Murphy, 1980; Wyatt, Potkin, Bridge, Phelps, & Wise, 1980), it may only contribute to severe schizophrenia (e.g., process schizophrenia), which is characteristic of the male schizophrenic.

However, conclusions about the relationship between sex, MAO, and schizophrenia are confounded by the fact that higher levels of MAO in females are not specific to schizophrenia, but are observed in other types of psychopathology (e.g., depression) and in normal populations. Furthermore, the level of MAO activity in the adult female varies with the menstrual cycle, being highest just before ovulation and lowest in the postovulatory period (Belmaker, Murphy, Wyatt, & Lorieux, 1974). Nevertheless, one piece of evidence reported by Murphy, Belmaker, Buchsbaum, Martin, Ciaranello, and Wyatt (1977) indicates that the relationship between MAO activity level and psychopathology may be different in males and females. In a group of normal subjects, they found that low MAO males tend to have higher profiles on the MMPI than high MAO males. However, no association exists between MMPI profiles and MAO with low or high MAO females. There seems to be a relatively greater amount of psychopathology in low MAO males who have T-scores higher than 70 for hypomania, psychopathic deviation, and schizophrenia but this was not true of the females. These biochemical data, as well as the physiological findings, reinforce the view that different forms of schizophrenia in males and females may arise from different underlying etiology.

Childhood Antecedents of Schizophrenia

It is traditionally believed that the shy, introverted, and seclusive personality characterizes both male and female preschizophrenic children (Wittman, 1948). However, more recent retrospective studies based on school records indicate sex differences among preschizophrenic children (Watt, 1978; Watt & Lubensky, 1976; Watt, Stolorow, Lubensky, & McClelland, 1970). Preschizophrenic girls are seen as more shy, insecure, and overinhibited than normal girls and preschizophrenic boys. On the other hand, preschizophrenic boys are described as negativistic, egocentric, unpleasant, and antisocial. However, they are no more introverted than normal boys. With age, these preschizophrenic boys become more unpleasant, aggressive, self-centered, and defiant of authority. Thus, retrospective studies do not show gender role reversal; they are consistent with the stereotype of boys as aggressive and girls as expressive.

In contrast to retrospective data, follow-up studies do not support the view that shyness and withdrawal in childhood are predictive of the development of later schizophrenia. Antisocial behavior appears to be predictive of schizophrenia in both sexes. In a group of predominantly male subjects, Robins (1966) described the typical preschizophrenic as a boy who is usually referred to the clinic for antisocial, rather than withdrawn, behavior. Hafner, Quast, and Shea (1975) found that, in contrast to internalizing girls (shy, withdrawn, and overcontrolled), externalizing girls (antisocial, aggressive, and undercontrolled) tend to be given the diagnosis of schizophrenia as adults. Although the diagnosis of externalizing males in adulthood does not support a higher incidence rate for schizophrenia, Hafner *et al.* noted that externalizing males who are usually sent to correctional institutions could have been hospitalized for schizophrenia.

A follow-up of a group of aggressive children by Morris, Escoll, and Wexler (1956) reveals that antisocial behavior may be even more predictive of adult psychosis in girls than in boys. They found that although the ratio of boys to girls in their group was 2.5:1, the ratio of those who became psychotic was reversed, 6:7. There was also more sexual acting out among girls than boys who became psychotic. Again, shyness and withdrawn behavior in childhood were not predictive of adult schizophrenia (Michael, Morris, & Soroker, 1954, 1957).

Mednick *et al.* (1978), in a follow-up of high-risk children, found that factors associated with later schizophrenia in the female are different from those in the male. In the female, schizophrenic breakdown is negatively associated with the age of onset of the mother's illness, a finding consistent with other studies indicating that the degree of the mother's illness is related to schizophrenia in women but not in men (Gardener, 1967). However, factors such as early parental separation, prenatal or birth complications, and autonomic nervous system responsivity and recovery were related to later schizophrenia in the male but not in the female. The age of onset of the mother's illness is indirectly related to schizophrenia in the male only because it produces separation from the mother. In contrast, separation from the mother is not significantly related to schizophrenia in the female. Also, the amount of separation experienced by boys—but not by girls—is negatively related to the patients' socioeconomic status. Mednick *et al.* suggested that this finding could mean that the experiences of boys who are separated from their parents are of poorer quality than those of girls. Mednick *et al.* found that, among girls, mothers' early onset of schizophrenia was associated with low verbal IQ, disturbed and peculiar word associations, and adult thought disorder. Among boys, it was only associated with psychopathy in adulthood, raising the possibility that marriage with criminals by schizophrenic women may be more predominant in early onset mothers.

Overall, studies demonstrate that antisocial behavior in childhood is predictive of adult schizophrenia in both sexes and particularly in females. However, the Mednick *et al.* data on high-risk children indicate that there are sex differences in the factors associated with later development of schizophrenia.

Summary

There are no sex differences in the rates of hospital admission for schizophrenia. However, there is a sex-age pattern, with males admitted at an earlier age than females. Sex differences in the age of admission is not a general trend for all types of mental illness but is specific to schizophrenia. Men seem to have an earlier onset of schizophrenia than females. It is possible that men and women experience stresses related to schizophrenia at a different stage of life. Three hypotheses have been put forward to explain the predominance of single males and married females among schizophrenics: the selection hypothesis, the stress hypothesis, and the differential use of health facilities. A combination of factors may account for the relationship between marital status and schizophrenia.

Women report more delusions than men. There is no sex difference in the frequency of hallucinations. Clinical observations and test results suggest that hospital schizophrenic patients show gender role reversal. However, selective factors may bias these data by bringing the withdrawn, submissive male and the aggressive, assertive female to the hospital. Research on gender identity reversal in schizophrenia is also inconclusive.

It is consistent with sex differences in symptomatology that females have been found to have better premorbid adjustment and prognosis as well as better adjustment after hospital discharge. They also tend to have more reactive schizophrenia than men. There is no evidence that one sex is more predisposed to schizophrenia than the other. Early studies reported higher rates of concordance (twins, siblings) for female patients. One hypothesis put forward to explain this trend is that identification with same-sex family members is stronger in females than males. However, the differential identification hypothesis has not received empirical support. There are more chronic females than males in hospitals, which may increase the probability that investigators would come across pairs of related females more often than males. Indeed, later studies that use consecutive admissions rather than chronic hospital inmates reveal no sex differences in concordance rates. They do, however, indicate that the presence of disturbed persons in the home, regardless of their sex, is more related to the development of schizophrenia in women.

Schizophrenic breakdown is associated with environmental factors in women more than in men (early parental loss, broken homes, and having a schizophrenic parent). The quality of the relationship with a lover, husband, or other person with whom they have close emotional ties seems to influence the course of illness in some women. Cross-cultural studies reveal that conflicts associated with the ideals prescribed by the culture may be associated with schizophrenic breakdown of both males and females.

Little attention has been given to the study of sex differences in physiological responses of schizophrenic patients. Available data in this area does not reveal a consistent trend. However, a study of high-risk children indicates that autonomic nervous measures are more predictive of schizophrenic breakdown in males than in females. Lower levels of platelet monoamine oxidase activity in males may be related to the prevalence of the severe type of schizophrenia in men. Studies of childhood antecedents of schizophrenia demonstrate that antisocial behavior is predictive of the illness in both sexes. However, there are sex differences in other factors associated with later development of schizophrenia.

References

Al-Issa, I. *The psychopathology of women.* Englewood Cliffs, New Jersey: Prentice-Hall, 1980.

Allon, R. Sex, race, socioeconomic status, social mobility, and process-reactive ratings of schizophrenics. *Journal of Nervous and Mental Disease,* 1971, *153,* 343-350.

Angrist, S., Dinitz, S., Lefton, M., & Pasamanick, B. Rehospitalization of mental patients. *Archives of General Psychiatry,* 1961, *4,* 363-370.

Angrist, S., Lefton, M., Dinitz, S., & Pasamanick, B. *Women after treatment: A study of former mental patients and their normal neighbors.* Englewood Cliffs, New Jersey: Prentice-Hall, 1968.

Baker, A. A., Morison, M., Game, J. A., & Thorpe, J. G. Admitting schizophrenic mothers with their babies. *Lancet,* 1961, *2,* 237-239.

Beck, A. T. *Depression: Clinical, experimental and theoretical aspects.* New York: Harper & Row, 1967.

Belle, D., & Goldman, N. *Patterns of diagnoses received by men and women.* In M. Guttentag, S. Salasin, & D. Belle (Eds.), *The mental health of women.* New York: Academic Press, 1980.

Belmaker, R., Murphy, D., Wyatt, R. J., & Lorieux, D. L. Human platelet monoamine oxidase changes during the menstrual cycle. *Archives of General Psychiatry,* 1974, *31,* 557-560.

Bem, S. L. Sex role adaptability: One consequence of psychological androgyny. *Journal of Personality and Social Psychology,* 1975, *31,* 634-643.

Biller, H. B., & Poey, K. An exploratory comparison of sex-role related behaviors in schizophrenics and nonschizophrenics. *Developmental Psychology,* 1969, *1,* 629.

Birley, J. L. T., & Brown, G. W. Crises and life changes preceding the onset and relapse of acute schizophrenia: Clinical aspects. *British Journal of Psychiatry,* 1970, *116,* 327-333.

Birtchnell, J. Early parent death and mental illness. *British Journal of Psychiatry,* 1970, *116,* 281-288.

Bleuler, M. *The schizophrenic disorders—Long-term patient and family studies.* New Haven, Connecticut: Yale Univ. Press, 1978.

Brown, D. W., & Birley, J. L. T. Crisis and life changes and the onset of schizophrenia. *Journal of Health and Social Behavior,* 1968, *9,* 203-214.

Buchsbaum, M. S., Coursey, R. D., & Murphy, D. L. Schizophrenia and platelet monoamine oxidase: Research strategies. *Schizophrenia Bulletin,* 1980, *6,* 375-384.

Buss, A. H., & Lang, P. J. Psychological deficit in schizophrenia 1. Affect, reinforcement and concept attainment. *Journal of Abnormal Psychology,* 1965, *70,* 2-24.

Busse, E. W., & Pfeiffer, E. *Mental illness in later life.* Washington, D.C.: American Psychiatric Association, 1973.

Cash, T. F. Methodological problems and progress in schizophrenia research: A survey. *Journal of Consulting and Clinical Psychology,* 1973, *40,* 278-286.

Chapman, L. J., Day, D.,& Burstein, A. The process-reactive distinction and prognosis in schizophrenia. *Journal of Nervous and Mental Disease,* 1961, *133,* 383-391.

Cheek, F. E. A serendipitous finding: Sex roles and schizophrenia. *Journal of Abnormal and Social Psychology,* 1964, *69,* 392-400.

Chesler, P. *Women and madness.* Garden City, New York: Doubleday, 1972.

Distler, L. S., May, P. R., & Tuma, A. H. Anxiety and ego-strength as predictors of response to treatment in schizophrenic patients. *Journal of Consulting Psychology,* 1964, *28,* 170-177.

Dohrenwend, B. P., & Dohrenwend, B. S. *Social status and psychological disorders.* New York: Wiley, 1969.

Duffy, E. *Activation and behavior.* New York: Wiley, 1962.

Eaton, W. W. Marital status and schizophrenia. *Acta Psychiatrica Scandinavica*, 1975, *52*, 320-329.

Ecker, J., Levine, J., & Zigler, E. Impaired sex-role identification in schizophrenia expressed in the comprehension of humor stimuli. *Journal of Psychology*, 1973, *83*, 67-77.

Farina, A., Garmezy, N., & Barry, H. Relationship of marital status to the incidence and prognosis of schizophrenia. *Journal of Abnormal and Social Psychology*, 1963, *67*, 624-630.

Farina, A., Garmezy, N., Zalusky, M., & Becker, J. Premorbid behavior and prognosis in female schizophrenic patients. *Journal of Consulting Psychology*, 1962, *26*, 56-60.

Forrest, A. D., & Hay, A. J. The influence of sex on schizophrenia. *Acta Psychiatrica Scandinavica*, 1972, *48*, 49-58.

Fottrell, E. A study of violent behavior among patients in psychiatric hospitals. *British Journal of Psychiatry*, 1980, *136*, 216-221.

Gardener, G. G. Role of maternal psychopathology in male and female schizophrenics. *Journal of Consulting Psychology*, 1967, *31*, 411-413.

Gottesman, I. I., & Shields, J. *Schizophrenia and genetics: A twin study vantage point*. New York: Academic Press, 1972.

Gottesman, I. I., & Shields, J. Rejoinder: toward optimal arousal and away from original din. *Schizophrenia Bulletin*, 1976, *2*, 447-453.

Gough, H. G. A cross-cultural analysis of the CPI femininity scale. *Journal of Consulting Psychology*, 1966, *30*, 136-141.

Gough, H. G., & Heilbrun, A. B. *Joint manual for the adjective check list and the need scales for the ACL*. Palo Alto, California: Consulting Psychologists Press, 1965.

Graham, L. A., Cohen, S. I., & Shmavonian, B. M. Sex differences in autonomic responses during instrumental conditioning. *Psychosomatic Medicine*, 1966, *28*, 264-271.

Green, R. Adults who want to change sex; adolescents who cross-dress; and children called "sissy" and "tomboy." In R. Green (Ed.), *Human sexuality: A health practitioner's text*. Baltimore, Maryland: Williams and Wilkins, 1975.

Gunderson, J. G., Autry, J. H., Mosher, L. R., & Buchsbaum, S. Special report: Schizophrenia, 1974. *Schizophrenia Bulletin*, 1974, *9*, 16-54.

Hafner, A. J., Quast, W., & Shea, M. J. The adult adjustment of one thousand psychiatric and pediatric patients: Initial findings from a twenty-five year follow-up. In R. D. Wirt, G. Winokur, & M. Roff (Eds.), *Life history research in psychopathology* (Vol. 4.). Minneapolis: Univ. of Minnesota Press, 1975.

Hilgard, J., & Newman, M. F. Parental loss by death in childhood as an etiological factor among schizophrenic and alcoholic patients compared with non-patient community sample. *Journal of Nervous and Mental Disease*, 1963, *137*, 14-28.

Hill, O. W., & Price, J. S. Childhood bereavement and adult depression. *British Journal of Psychiatry*, 1967, *113*, 743-751.

Holzberg, J. D. Sex differences in schizophrenia. In H. Beigel (Ed.), *Advances in sex research*. New York: Harper & Row, 1963.

Huber, G., Gross, G., Schuttler, R., & Linz, M. Longitudinal studies of schizophrenic patients. *Schizophrenia Bulletin*, 1980, *6*, 592-605.

Jaskar, R. O., & Reed, M. R. Assessment of body image organization of hospitalized and non-hospitalized subjects. *Journal of Projective Techniques*, 1963, *27*, 185-190.

Kayton, R., & Biller, H. B. Sex-role development and psychopathology in adult males. *Journal of Consulting and Clinical Psychology*, 1972, *38*, 208-210.

Kokes, R. F., Strauss, J. S., & Klorman, R. Premorbid adjustment in schizophrenia. Part II. *Schizophrenia Bulletin*, 1977, *3*, 186-213.

Kokonis, N. D. Parental dominance and sex-role identification in schizophrenia. *Journal of Psychology*, 1973, *84*, 211-218.

Lane, E. A. The intelligence of spouses of schizophrenics. *The Psychological Record,* 1967, *17,* 477-481.

Lane, E. A. The influence of sex and race on process-reactive ratings of schizophrenics. *Journal of Psychology,* 1968, *68,* 15-20.

LaTorre, R. A. The psychological assessment of gender identity and gender role in schizophrenia. *Schizophrenia Bulletin,* 1976, *2,* 266-285.

LaTorre, R. A., & Piper, W. E. Gender identity and gender role in schizophrenia. *Journal of Abnormal Psychology,* 1979, *88,* 68-72.

Lewine, R. R. J. Sex differences in schizophrenia: A commentary. *Schizophrenia Bulletin,* 1979, *5,* 4-6.

Lewine, R. R. J. Sex differences in age of symptom onset and first hospitalization in schizophrenia. *American Journal of Orthopsychiatry,* 1980, *50,* 316-322.

Lewine, R. R. J., Watt, N., & Grubb, T. W. High-risk-for-schizophrenia research: Sampling bias and its implications. *Schizophrenia Bulletin,* 1981, *7,* 273-280.

Lucas, C. J., Sainsbury, R., & Collins, G. A social and clinical study of delusions in schizophrenia. *Journal of Mental Science,* 1962, *108,* 747-758.

Ludwig, A., Marx, A. J., Hill, P. A., & Browning, R. M. The control of violent behavior through faradic shock: A case study. *Journal of Nervous and Mental Disease,* 1969, *148,* 624-637.

Maccoby, E. E., & Jacklin, C. N. *Psychology of sex differences.* Stanford, California: Stanford Univ. Press, 1974.

McClelland, D. C., & Watt, N. F. Sex-role alienation in schizophrenia. *Journal of Abnormal Psychology,* 1968, *74,* 226-238.

McKeever, W. F., May, P. R. A., & Tuma, A. H. Prognosis in schizophrenia: Prediction of length of hospitalization from psychological test variables. *Journal of Clinical Psychology,* 1965, *21,* 214-221.

Malzberg, B. Are immigrants psychologically disturbed? In S. C. Plog & R. B. Edgerton (Eds.), *Changing perspectives in mental illness.* New York: Holt, 1969.

Mayer-Gross, W., Slater, E., & Roth, M. *Clinical psychiatry.* London, England: Cassell, 1960.

Mednick, S. A., Schulsinger, F., Teasdale, T. W., Schulsinger, H., Venables, P. H., & Rock, D. R. Schizophrenia in high-risk children: Sex differences in predisposing factors. In G. Serban (Ed.), *Cognitive defects in the development of mental illness.* New York: Brunner/Mazel, 1978.

Michael, C. M., Morris, D. P., & Soroker, E. Follow-up studies of shy, withdrawn children. 1. Evaluation of later adjustment. *American Journal of Orthopsychiatry,* 1954, *24,* 743-754.

Michael, C. M., Morris, D. P., & Soroker, E. Follow-up studies of shy, withdrawn children. 2. Relative incidence of schizophrenia. *American Journal of Orthopsychiatry,* 1957, *27,* 331-337.

Mitchell, G., & Murphy, J. B. A survey of female patients in Carstairs State Hospital. *British Journal of Psychiatry,* 1975, *127,* 445-447.

Modlin, H. C. Psychodynamics in the management of paranoid states of women. *Archives of General Psychiatry,* 1963, *8,* 263-268.

Money, J., & Wang, C. Human figure drawing. 1: Sex of first choice in gender-identity anomalies, Klinefelter's syndrome and precocious puberty. *Journal of Nervous and Mental Disease,* 1966, *143,* 157-162.

Morris, H. H., Escoll, P. J., & Wexler, R. Aggressive disorders in childhood—A follow-up study. *American Journal of Psychiatry,* 1956, *112,* 991-997.

Murphy, D. L., Belmaker, R. H., Buchsbaum, M., Martin, N. F., Ciaranello, R., & Wyatt, R. J. Biogenic amino-related enzymes and personality variations in normals. *Psychological Medicine,* 1977, *7,* 149-157.

Murphy, D. L., Wright, C., Buchsbaum, M., Nichols, A., Costa, J. L., & Wyatt, R. J. Platelet and plasma amino oxidase activity in 680 normals: Sex and age differences and stability over time. *Biochemical Medicine,* 1976, *16,* 254-265.

Murphy, H. B. M. Cultural aspects of the delusion. *Studium Generale,* 1967, *20,* 684-692.

Murphy, H. B. M. *Male/female differences in psychiatric morbidity; their use in transcultural studies.* Paper presented at IX Congreso Latinamericano di psiquiatria (APAL), La Habana, Cuba, February 1977.

Murphy, H. B. M. Culture and schizophrenia. In I. Al-Issa (Ed.), *Culture and psychopathology.* Baltimore, Maryland: Univ. Park Press, 1982.

Noreik, K., & Odegaard, O. Age at onset of schizophrenia in relation to socio-economic factors. *The British Journal of Social Psychiatry,* 1967, *1,* 243-259.

Norris, V. A statistical study of the influence of marriage on the hospital care of the mentally sick. *Journal of Mental Science,* 1956, *102,* 467-486.

Odegaard, O. New data on marriage and mental disease: The incidence of psychoses in the widowed and the divorced. *Journal of Mental Science,* 1953, *99,* 778-785.

Odegaard, O. Marriage and mental illness: A study in social psychopathology. *Journal of Mental Science,* 1946, *92,* 35-59.

Petzel, T. P., & Gynther, M. S. A comparison of psychiatric diagnosis and behavioral classification as criteria for differentiating psychiatric patients. *Journal of General Psychology,* 1969, *80,* 219-227.

Planansky, K., & Johnson, R. Mate selection in schizophrenia. *Acta Psychiatrica Scandinavica,* 1967, *43,* 397-409.

Portell, J. Hallucinations in pre-adolescent schizophrenic children. In W. Kemp (Ed.), *Origin and mechanisms of hallucinations.* New York: Plenum, 1970.

Prentky, R. A., Lewine, R. J., Watt, N. F., & Fryer, J. H. A longitudinal study of psychiatric outcome: Developmental variables vs. psychiatric symptoms. *Schizophrenia Bulletin,* 1980, *6,* 139-148.

Radloff, L. Sex differences in depression. *Sex Roles,* 1975, *1,* 249-265.

Raskin, M., & Dyson, W. L. Treatment problems leading to readmission of schizophrenic patients. *Archives of General Psychiatry,* 1968, *19,* 356-360.

Reed, M. R. Masculinity-femininity dimension in normal and psychotic subjects. *Journal of Abnormal and Social Psychology,* 1957, *55,* 289-294.

Robins, L. N. *Deviant children grown up.* Baltimore, Maryland: Williams and Wilkins, 1966.

Robinson, D. S., Davis, J. M., Nies, A., Ravaris, C. L., & Sylvester, D. Relation of sex and aging to monoamine oxidase activity of human brain, plasma and platelets. *Archives of General Psychiatry,* 1971, *24,* 536-539.

Rogler, L. H., & Hollingshead, A. B. *Trapped: Families and schizophrenia.* New York: Wiley, 1965.

Rosen, B., Klein, D. F., & Gittelman-Klein, R. The relationship between age of first psychiatric treatment contact, marital status and premorbid social adjustment. *Journal of Nervous and Mental Disease,* 1971, *152,* 17-22.

Rosen, B., Klein, D. F., Levenstein, S., & Shahinian, S. P. Social competence and post-hospital outcome. *Archives of General Psychiatry,* 1968, *19,* 165-170.

Rosenthal, D. Sex distribution and the severity of illness among samples of schizophrenic twins. *Journal of Psychiatric Research,* 1961, *1,* 26-36.

Rosenthal, D. Familial concordance by sex with respect to schizophrenia. *Psychological Bulletin,* 1962, *59,* 401-421.

Rosenthal, D. *Genetic theory and abnormal behavior.* New York: McGraw-Hill, 1970.

Rosenthal, D. Searches for the mode of genetic transmission in schizophrenia: Reflections and loose ends. *Schizophrenia Bulletin,* 1977, *3,* 268-276.

Samuels, L. Sex differences in concordance rates of schizophrenia: Finding or artifact? *Schizophrenia Bulletin*, 1978, *4*, 14-15.

Samuels, L. Reply to Lewine. *Schizophrenia Bulletin*, 1979, *5*, 8-10.

Schooler, C. Affiliation among schizophrenics: Preferred characteristics of the other. *Journal of Nervous and Mental Disease*, 1963, *137*, 438-446.

Schulz, C. G., & Kilgalen, R. K. *Case studies in schizophrenia*. New York: Basic Books, 1969.

Schwab, M. E. A study of reported hallucinations in a southeastern county. *Mental Health and Society*, 1977, *4*, 344-354.

Smith, E. A study of sex differentiations in drawings and verbalizations of schizophrenics. *Journal of Clinical Psychology*, 1953, *8*, 183-185.

Spence, J. T., Helmreich, R., & Stapp, J. Ratings of self and peers on sex-role attributes and their relation to self-esteem and conceptions of masculinity and femininity. *Journal of Personality and Social Psychology*, 1975, *32*, 29-39.

Stevens, B. Illegitimate fertility of psychotic women. *Journal of Biosocial Science*, 1970, *2*, 17-30.

Swanson, D. W., Bohmert, P. J., & Smith, J. A. *The paranoid*. Boston, Massachusetts: Little, Brown, 1970.

Swensen, C. H. Empirical evaluation of human figure drawings: 1957-1966. *Psychological Bulletin*, 1968, *70*, 20-44.

Todd, J., & Dewhurst, K. The Othello syndrome. *Journal of Nervous and Mental Disease*, 1955, *122*, 367-374.

Vaughn, C. E., & Leff, J. P. The influence of family and social factors on the course of psychiatric illness. *British Journal of Psychiatry*, 1976, *129*, 235-237.

Wahl, O. F. Sex bias in schizophrenia research: A short report. *Journal of Abnormal Psychology*, 1977, *86*, 195-198.

Walker, N. *Crime and punishment in Britain: The penal system in theory, law and practice*. Edinburgh, Scotland: Edinburgh Univ. Press, 1965.

Watt, D. C., & Szulecka, T. K. The effect of sex, marriage and age at first admission on the hospitalization of schizophrenics during two years following discharge. *Psychological Medicine*, 1979, *9*, 529-539.

Watt, N. F. Patterns of childhood social development in adult schizophrenics. *Archives of General Psychiatry*, 1978, *35*, 160-165.

Watt, N. F., & Lubensky, A. W. Childhood roots of schizophrenia. *Journal of Consulting and Clinical Psychology*, 1976, *44*, 363-375.

Watt, N. F., Stolorow, R. D., Lubensky, A. W., & McClelland, D. C. School adjustment and behavior of children hospitalized for schizophrenia as adults. *American Journal of Orthopsychiatry*, 1970, *40*, 637-657.

Watts, W. *Semantic conditioning and generalization in schizophrenia*. Unpublished doctoral dissertation, University of California, Los Angeles, 1968.

Weich, M. J. Behavioral differences between groups of acutely psychotic (schizophrenic) males and females. *Psychiatric Quarterly*, 1968, *42*, 107-122.

Weinstein, E. A. *Social aspects of delusions: A psychiatric study of the Virgin Islands*. New York: Free Press, 1962.

Weiss, J. L., Grunebaum, H. U., & Schell, R. E. Psychotic mothers and their children. *Archives of General Psychiatry*, 1964, *11*, 90-98.

Wing, J. K. Clinical concepts of schizophrenia. In J. K. Wing (Ed.), *Schizophrenia: Towards a new synthesis*. New York: Academic Press, 1978.

Wittman, P. Diagnostic and prognostic significance of the shut-in personality type as a prodromal factor in schizophrenia. *Clinical Psychology*, 1948, *4*, 211-214.

World Health Organization (WHO). *Schizophrenia: An international pilot study of schizophrenia.* Geneva, Switzerland: Author, 1973.

World Health Organization (WHO). *Schizophrenia: An international follow-up study.* Chichester, England: Wiley, 1979.

Wyatt, R. J., Potkin, S. G., Bridge, T. P., Phelps, B. H., & Wise, C. D. Monoamine oxidase in schizophrenia: An overview. *Schizophrenia Bulletin,* 1980, *6,* 199-207.

Zeller, A., & Davis, J. M. Protein content and monoamine oxidase activity in platelets. *Schizophrenia Bulletin,* 1980, *6,* 267-274.

Zigler, E., Levine, J., & Zigler, B. Premorbid social competence and paranoid-nonparanoid status in female schizophrenic patients. *Journal of Nervous and Mental Disease,* 1977, *164,* 333-339.

Zigler, E., & Phillips, L. Social effectiveness and symptomatic behaviors. *Journal of Abnormal and Social Psychology,* 1960, *61,* 231-238.

8

IRIS GOLDSTEIN FODOR

Gender and Phobia

> In assessing the aetiology of phobias in man we need to account for their general features. Phobias do not occur randomly with respect to all situations and people. Rather, phobias tend to occur in particular situations, at certain ages, with a sex bias, with other clusters of psychiatric symptoms and in selected personality backgrounds [Marks, 1969, p. 72].

Recent theoretical research and clinical writing have characterized clinical phobias as primarily a female disorder (Brehony, 1982; Brehony & Geller, 1981; Fodor, 1974). In spite of the overrepresentation of females and the underrepresentation of males in the phobia literature, there have been few attempts to explore the variables relevant to this sex difference.

This chapter will survey the clinical, research, and theoretical literature on phobia in order to shed light on the issue of sex differences among phobias of different categories. Sex role socialization variables and social learning theory will be highlighted toward reaching an understanding of the disproportionately large number of women and the small number of men who present themselves for treatment with phobias.

Definition

The diagnostic classification manual of the American Psychiatric Association, DSM III (American Psychiatric Association, 1980), places *phobia* under anxiety disorders and defines it as follows: "The essential feature is a persistent

ISBN: 0-12-050350-6

and irrational fear of a specific object, activity or situation that results in a compelling desire to avoid the dreaded object, activity, or situation (the phobia stimulus) [p. 225]." The phobic disorders are further characterized according to DSM III as simple phobia, social phobia, and agoraphobia. See Table 8.1 for a fuller description of the three types of phobias.

Characteristics of the Various Types of Phobias

Agras, Sylvester, and Oliveau (1969) report the incidence of phobia to be 6.3 per 1000. From an examination of Table 8.1, we see the different representations of males and females for the various phobic disorders. Whereas females slightly outnumber males for social phobias, they are overrepresented in the population of simple phobics and agoraphobics.

Agoraphobia, which is the most common phobia, has received the most attention in the psychiatric literature. Generally, social phobias are infrequently discussed in that literature unless they are extreme cases. Instead, social phobics represent populations typically seen in counseling centers and community clinics and are discussed in the counseling and behavioral literature under the topics of test and performance anxiety and social skills deficits. One might characterize simple and social phobias as developmental disorders, in that they typically begin in childhood or adolescence. Social phobias, in particular, appear to involve avoidance of situations involving evaluation of mastery and competency, issues typical of adolescence. Agoraphobia, on the other hand, appears to occur in young, married adults who do not have a prior psychiatric history and who have, for the most part (unlike simple phobics), mastered their childhood fears and are beginning to assume their appropriate adult roles. Hence, agoraphobia could be considered a disruptive disorder in contrast to simple and social phobias.

Simple Phobias

Simple phobias typically involve one specific fear and have a high incidence among females. Animal phobias, the most common of the simple phobias, are reported to have the highest representation of females of any phobic disorder (95% female incidence). Simple phobias can be considered developmental in that they originate in childhood and often lead to a lifetime habit of avoiding the phobic stimuli. People seek help only when the phobia interferes with other aspects of their lives. For example, I was consulted by a young woman from the city with a butterfly phobia. She usually avoided trips to the country, but she had just begun a relationship with a young man who enjoyed weekends in the country. In order to maintain the relationship, at age 25 she consulted a therapist for help with the phobia.

TABLE 8.1
Description of Phobias[a]

	Simple phobia	Social phobia	Agoraphobia
Frequency	Common	Common (8% of phobics)	Fairly common (5% of population)
Sex incidence	More common in females (In particular, animal phobiac: 95% female, 5% male.)	More equal sexual distribution: 60% female, 40% male.	75-85% female, 15-25% male.
Phobic symptomology	A persistent, irrational fear and desire to avoid an object or situation. Most common involve animals, claustrophobia (fear of closed spaces), and acrophobia (fear of heights).	Persistent, irrational fear and desire to avoid situations in which the individual may be exposed to the scrutiny of others. Marked anticipatory anxiety occurs if the individual is confronted with the necessity of entering into such a situation. Common social fears involve fears of speaking or performing in public, taking examinations, eatin in public.	A marked fear of being in public places from which escape might be difficult or help not available in case of sudden incapacitation. Normal activities are increasingly restricted as the fears or avoidance behaviors dominate the individual's life. (Examples of feared situations include busy streets, tunnels, crowded stores, elevators, or public transportation. Often these individuals insist that a family member or friend accompany them when they leave home. May or may not be accompanied by anxiety attacks
Age of onset	Varies, most animal phobias begin in childhood	Late childhood or early adolescence	mid-twenties.

[a] This table is adapted from American Psychiatric Association, Diagnostic and Statistical Manual of Mental Disorders, Third Edition, Washington, D.C., APA, 1980; Fodor, 1974; Marks, 1969.

SEX, AGE, AND CHILDHOOD FEARS

In many respects, simple phobias can be viewed as a retention of childhood fears so common to both sexes. Generally, researchers studying children's fears are in agreement that boys and girls are similar in the frequency and intensity of fears. Children are most frequently afraid of the supernatural, being alone in the dark, strange places, being lost, attack or danger of attack by animals, bodily injury, and falling ill (Jersild, Marhey, & Jersild, 1933; Jersild & Holmes, 1935).

Macfarlane, Allen, and Honzik (1974), in their comprehensive study of childhood fears, found different levels of fearfulness for boys and for girls at different age levels. A peak of fearfulness occurred for girls at age 3 (67%), and for boys at age 3½ (56%). Another peak occurred for boys and girls at age 11 (40% and 52%, respectively). However, by age 13, only 4% of the boys still reported fears, as compared to 21% of the girls. Data from fear survey scales confirm that boys and men from adolescence onward generally admit to fewer fears than girls (Maccoby & Jacklin, 1974; Sarason, Davidson, Lighthall, Waite, & Ruebush, 1960).

As children get older, there is a decline in reports of fear of animals, of the dark, and of the supernatural. By sixth grade, fears of school and social relations show an increase, with boys reporting a higher incidence of these fears than girls (Angelinio, Dollins, & Mech, 1956; Croake, 1969; Lapouse & Monk, 1959).

SEX ROLE INFLUENCES

One might speculate that simple phobias, which are more common among females, may be a retention and exaggeration of the childhood fears that are normal for most people. Marks (1969) addresses the issue of the lowered incidence of fears in men as follows:

> A mixture of influences is again at work here, including greater masculine aggression due to androgens and social learning, differential exposure of the sexes to particular situations, and differences in their social obligations. All of these will mould the opportunity for contact with the phobic situation, the quality of this contact and the vigour with which fear in that situation will be overcome [pp. 75-76].

Although biological differences between men and women may account for some of these differences, what is striking in reviewing the work on childhood fears is the similarity of fear development in boys and girls up to adolescence. It would appear that the socialization of children might be more relevant than androgens in influencing fear and development among the sexes. Hoffman (1972), in a review of the socialization literature on mastery of fears, concludes that "mastery exploration can alleviate fear, but girls are not reinforced for this type of mastery . . . there is a differential sex role message about mastery of fears presented to males and females [p. 147]."

If we examine the sex role messages presented to males and females by the media, we see a clear differentiation of role (Unger, 1979; Weitz, 1977). For example, a NOW (National Organization of Women) task force studied the messages widely used in children's readers. They found that girls are portrayed as helpless and incompetent and as yielding to their fears, whereas boys are featured as either mastering their fears or as already competent and brave. Girls express fears three times more often than boys. The following are examples from the readers (*Dick and Jane as Victims: Sex Stereotyping in Children's Readers*, Expanded 1975 Edition. Women on Words & Images, P.O. Box 2163, Princeton, NJ 08540).

> Fearfulness: *"Cries of fright came from the women and children around her."*
> Bravery: *"He felt a tear coming into his eye, but he brushed it away with his hands, boys eight years old don't cry."*
> Contrast between the sexes: *"Oh, Raymond, boys are so much braver than girls." "Roger's mother wept afraid that her son would be eaten, but Roger was a brave boy."*

The most frequent theme for boys is daring and overcoming fear through suppression or perseverance, whereas girls' fearfulness or inadequacies further enhance the boys image of success: "Boys struggle with and subdue fears of horses, heights, crawly things, the dark and even a buffalo stampede. . . . . When two little girls stand on chairs and shriek for their younger brother to rescue them from a frog it is in the best feminine tradition [*Dick and Jane as Victims*, 1975, p. 30]."

TREATMENT OF SIMPLE PHOBIAS

The behavioral treatment of simple phobias typically involves some form of anxiety management and exposure to the feared stimuli (Marks, 1969; Wolpe, 1958). In many respects, exposure treatments are similar to the bravery training that most boys engage in to master their fears and could be viewed as an antidote to allowing girls and women to avoid mastery, remaining hysterical and dependent on males for rescue.

Social Phobias

TYPES OF SOCIAL PHOBIAS AND THEIR CLINICAL FEATURES

Social phobics avoid situations where they might be subjected to evaluation and social scrutiny. These phobias are more likely to begin in adolescence than other phobias, and males and females are more equally represented (F to M, 3:2) [Marks, 1969].

People with social phobias are most likely to come for therapy when they are under environmental pressure to face the feared situation. Often, the presenting complaint is less often a phobia than an anxiety state (anticipatory anxiety often approaching panic about a situation that can no longer be avoided).

Social phobics are typically seen by therapists for the following types of problems: (*a*) test and performance anxiety, (*b*) social anxiety or shyness (which involves avoidance of social interaction situations), (*c*) assertiveness problems (involving inhibition of behaviors of self-expression in social situations, and (*d*) extreme introversion (these persons are totally shy and introverted and their entire life revolves around avoidance of socially evaluative situations). There has been little discussion in the literature about sex differences among social phobics. We shall separately discuss two of the most common types of social phobias—those related to achievement pressures (test and performance anxiety) and those related to social situations (anxiety about social interactions).

PERFORMANCE ANXIETY

Research on performance anxiety has focused on test anxiety (anticipatory anxiety about taking examinations) and fears of success and failure in achievement situations.

TEST ANXIETY: SOME MALE-FEMALE DIFFERENCES

Generally, girls and boys do not show differences on self-report of test anxiety until the fourth grade. From then on, girls score considerably higher on test anxiety measures than boys, whereas boys have higher "lie" scores on these scales (Sarason, Davidson, Lighthall, Waite, & Ruebush, 1960).

College students represent the majority of patients seeking therapy for test anxiety. There are few reports of sex differences. I have studied over 50 self-referred test anxious college students who show a sex ratio similar to that reported for other social phobics (F to M, 27:23). However, when I examined the personality traits of these students, I discovered two major personality styles with varying incidences among the sexes. Most of the students exhibited an obsessive compulsive style (75%), and this style was equally represented by males and females. A smaller number (25% of the students) exhibited a hysterical style, and females here considerably outnumbered males (F to M, 8:3).

The obsessive compulsive style of test anxiety typically occurred in good students who were very tense, studied all the time (and worried about knowing enough (the more compulsive), or worried so much they obsessed (the obsessive).

CASE EXAMPLE

Steven is a perfectionist whose obsessive worry interferes with his ability to sit down and study for an exam. He engages in some ritualistic behavior for anxiety relief, but under the stress of not having time to study, often far in advance of an exam, he becomes increasingly anxious, approaching a panic state. For days before the exam, he often cannot sleep.

A smaller number of students, mostly female, exhibited the hysterical style. These were mainly *B* and *C*-average students who were more often avoiders of studying and preparing for exams. They became increasingly anxious, often approaching panic just prior to the examination date. Of interest regarding this large female group was the high incidence of concern about technical or scientific subjects.

CASE EXAMPLE

Mary: *Mary avoids all contact with her books and puts worry about the exam out of her mind until the last minute. At the point where avoidance is no longer possible, she becomes inceasingly anxious and disorganized, and often does not show up to take the exam* [Fodor & Lief, 1980].

FEAR OF SUCCESS AND FEAR OF FAILURE

There exists a vast literature on the fear of success in women. Unger (1979) reports that fear of success (fear of social rejection by high-achieving women) may be the most cited research in psychology texts. In reviewing the issues relevant to fear of success, Unger (1979) says, "A variety of different studies indicate that members of both sexes view achievement as a male characteristic [p. 365]." There also exists a comparable, older literature on fear of failure that studies primarily male issues of achievement. Thus, it would appear that for both sexes performance anxieties relate to sex role expectations about achievement.

TREATMENT OF PERFORMANCE ANXIETIES

A variety of behavioral techniques have been developed as treatments for performance anxieties. Central to all these treatments are training in anxiety management and support for confronting the situation. Often patients, prior to facing the feared situation in real life, prepare themselves in fantasy using techniques of desensitization developed by Wolpe (1958). For example, I treated a married, young, woman artist who appeared to have a fear of success that interfered with working effectively. First, she was trained in relaxation techniques. Next she drew up a list (hierarchy) of situations she feared, if successful. This list included such items as having a show at a gallery, a favorable review in the *New York Times*, her husband's faculty colleagues congratulating her after a lecture while he looks on, etc. Then these scenes were presented while she relaxed. In this way, she was able to begin to view success positively and was able to resume productive work.

SOCIAL ANXIETIES: SOCIAL SKILLS AND ASSERTIVENESS TRAINING

Social skills training that focuses on shaping competent social behaviors via modeling, role play, and behavior rehearsal is a growing field. Most of the clinical work in the area has been conducted with patients with marked deficits (extremely introverted or schizoid people) and college students who come for help to develop competencies for age-appropriate social situations. Male college students, in particular, report to college counseling centers for dating anxiety, reflecting the pressure still existing for young men to take the initiative in dating (Machlowitz, 1981).

CASE EXAMPLE: SOCIAL SKILLS TRAINING (HAL)

Hal has anxieties about talking with women. He is often unsure how to begin conversation. He feels so lost when he goes to a party . . . one has to do so much sorting . . . he isn't sure what the other person wants to hear . . . he worries about being boring.

In order to shape up conversational skills, Hal is instructed to talk with the therapist about the weather, recent news, etc. Through reviewing these tapes and repeated exposure and practice to group situations, which include taking the risk in talking to new women, Hal learns to develop social conversation skills (Fodor, 1980).

There is also a growing literature on assertiveness training, which teaches self-expressive behaviors and ways of combating anxiety about negative evaluation and the consequences of behaving more assertively. Most of this work (about three-fourths of the more than 700 studies) has been done with women. Since many women have been trained to believe behaving assertively (a male trait) is incompatible with being feminine, assertiveness training is often construed as remediation training for women for traditional sex role programming (Fodor, 1980; Jakubowski-Spector, 1973; Wolfe & Fodor, 1975).

Agoraphobia

Agoraphobia, the most frequently occurring clinical phobia, has received the most attention in both the psychoanalytic and behavioral literature (Marks, 1969). Generally, there is agreement that agoraphobia represents a coherent clinical syndrome with similarity of symptoms from person to person and with similar profiles reported from various social classes and ethnic groups (Hallam,

1978; Marks, 1969, 1970). From surveying the results of the published research on agoraphobics on over 2500 patients, I find that women consistently outnumber men, 3:1 (Brehony, 1982; Fodor, 1974; Marks, 1969).

Agoraphobia has often been referred to as the housewives disorder due to the high incidence of young, married females reporting the problem. In trying to understand more about agoraphobia, we need to address the following: Why is there a high preponderance of agoraphobics among females? What special condition predisposes the few males represented to become agoraphobic? What are the differences between male and female agoraphobics? What is special about the mid-twenties and the newly married state to account for the onset? How might we account for the success of behavioral treatment?

CLINICAL FEATURES OF AGORAPHOBIA

Female: *The patient was chronically anxious and feared death or sudden illness if she went out on the street, on trains, in cars or to the theatre or church. She had reached the point at which she could not perform any of her duties and was helpless. Her husband had to remain home with her and even then she continued to be frightened.*

Male: *Separated from his wife . . . had pains in his chest, fear of heart disease, loss of appetite . . . weakness and insomnia. He was afraid to go to his office. He stayed at home, would not travel by train, car and avoided friends . . . then the patient went to live in the hospital and would not walk out of sight of the hospital* [Terhune, 1949, p. 167].

From clinical discussions of the syndrome, several patterns become apparent. The first involves what Goldstein and Chambless (1978) call *the fear of fear*—worry about the physical symptoms breaking through and leading to panic attacks. Second, there are avoidance behaviors. What agoraphobics fear most are not the feared objects themselves (closed spaces, tunnels), but the "trappedness" in these situations that relates to anxiety about losing control (becoming hysterical) and manifesting the physical symptoms (dizziness, seating, hyperventilation, nausea, etc.) with no escape or help available. A third feature is the lack of development of self-sufficiency. Agoraphobics appear to lack the skills to control themselves when they panic or to function competently as adults in coping with the outside world (Fodor, 1974; Goldstein & Chambless, 1978; Marks, 1969, 1970).

ASSOCIATED OTHER PSYCHIATRIC AND PHYSICAL SYMPTOMS

Although there are reports of higher rates of anxiety, neuroticism, and depression among agoraphobics as compared to social and simple phobics, no sex differences are noted (Burglass, Clarke, Henderson, Kreitman, & Presley, 1977; Hallam, 1978; Marks, 1970; Roth, 1959).

There are also reports of a high incidence of physical illness and hypochrondriacal symptoms. Roth (1959) reports that the most frequent precipitating stress among men (50% of cases) and the second commonest in women (17% of the cases) was physical illness, particularly among older patients. Furthermore, there are also consistent reports of hypochondriacal symptoms, particularly among male agoraphobics (Burglass *et al.*, 1977; Finberg-Orter & Fodor, 1981). For example, Jassin (1980) found that agoraphobics scored higher on the hypochondriacal scale of the Minnesota Multiphasic Personality Inventory (MMPI) than anxiety neurotics and depressives, with male agoraphobics showing the highest hypochondriacal scores of all.

THEORIES OF AGORAPHOBIA

Psychoanalytic Theory. There are many conflicting, confusing discussions of phobia in the psychoanalytic literature. The traditional psychoanalytic view of phobia is that it represents conflict over repressed sexual and aggressive impulses. Defense mechanisms are utilized as avoidances against these dangerous impulses, which leads to the development of phobia: for example, the fear of going out of the house is conceptualized as representing an unconscious sexual exhibitionism (Fenichel, 1945). More recent work stresses ego defects (Weiss, 1966) and separation anxiety (Bowlby, 1973). Generally, there has been little in the psychoanalytic writing to provide a basis for understanding why women are so much more likely to develop these symptoms than men, although Bowlby's (1973) views of attachment behavior may have special relevance for women.

Behavioral Theories. Generally, most behavioral theorists have not directly addressed the issue of sex differences in phobias. Classical conditioning theory views phobias as representing autonomically conditioned responses to classes of feared stimuli. Avoidance behaviors are viewed as anxiety reducing (Wolpe, 1958). However, there has not been much work in conditioning theory to specify why females are more prone to develop avoidance behaviors than are males.

Social Learning Theory and Sex Role Expectations. Social learning theory, which stresses social factors in the development, reinforcement, and maintenance of behaviors, may have more applicability to understanding agoraphobia than other behavioral theories.

There is a tendency in our culture to teach and reinforce differential sex role expectations for males and females. Thus, males are expected to exhibit traits of aggressiveness, independence, coolness, objectivity, adventurousness, and ambition, whereas females are expected to exhibit their opposite—passivity, emotionality, subjectivity, submissiveness, excitability, dependency, lack of adventurousness, etc. (Broverman, Broverman, Clarkson, Rosenkranz, & Vogel, 1972).

In the clinical literature, agoraphobics are described as having the personality traits of passivity, dependency, avoidance, and nonassertiveness more often than other neurotics (Andrews, 1966; Marks, 1970); and these traits are descriptive of male as well as female agoraphobics.

On self-report questionnaires, female agoraphobics achieve more stereotypically feminine scores than do normals and anxiety neurotics (Jassin, 1980). In addition, females who are high-scorers for agoraphobic traits are also reported to be high-scorers for stereotypic feminine traits as well (Brehony, 1982). Although agoraphobic males do not show any stereotypic pattern, they are reported to achieve higher scores for hysterical traits on the MMPI as compared to anxiety neurotics and normals (Jassin, 1980).

Social Learning Theory and Socialization of Agoraphobics. Social learning theorists such as Bandura (1969) and Mischel (1970) suggest that parental and societal reinforcement as well as modeling are important influences in the socialization of children. Researchers on socialization conclude that girls are not reinforced for autonomy. Hoffman (1972) summarizes this research as follows:

> a) since the little girl has less encouragement for independence b) more parental protectiveness c) less cognitive and social pressure for establishing an identity separate from the mother d) less mother-child conflict which highlights this separation, she engages in less independent exploration of her environment . . . continues to be dependent upon adults for solving her problems [p. 147].

Using these concepts from social learning theory, we might speculate that children who later become agoraphobics are socialized more like females in our culture and get a stronger dose of this experience. That is, they are allowed to retain childhood fears, are reinforced for dependency (overprotected) and, following modeling theory, may have been subjected to less effective, even phobic, parental models.

CHILDHOOD FEARS AND SOCIAL PHOBIA AMONG AGORAPHOBICS

There are conflicting reports of high frequency of childhood fears in agoraphobics. However, Burns and Thorpe (1977), in reviewing this work, suggest that the high recall of childhood fears was similar to the rates reported by Lapouse and Monk (1959) for normal children. Furthermore, there is no difference noted for recall of childhood fears among male and female agoraphobics. Thus, agoraphobics would appear to have patterns of childhood fears similar to those of normals.

School phobia, which could be considered a childhood version of agoraphobic and social phobia, appears with equal frequency among boys and girls (M to F, 49:51) (Gordon & Young, 1976). Generally, there are reports of high incidences of school phobia and/or fears of going to school in clinical studies of agoraphobics (over 30% of agoraphobics reported childhood school phobia in studies by Burns and Thorpe [1977]; Solyom, Beck, Solyom, & Hugel [1974]). Berg (1976), however, reported the same proportion of childhood history of school phobia (1:5) among agoraphobics as among neurotic controls. What is clear from the research is that, whereas boys and girls are equally likely to be school phobic, 20-30% of child school phobics develop adult symptoms of agoraphobia and/or neurosis. Since agoraphobics are primarily females, one might speculate that school phobic males may be more likely to end up as social phobics or neurotics. More research in follow-up of child school phobics appears to be indicated.

PARENTAL PROTECTIVENESS

Most clinical writers reviewing histories of agoraphobics neglect to mention parental or paternal overprotectiveness but stress maternal overprotectiveness as a factor in promoting dependency and phobias in both males and females (Andrews, 1966; Bowlby, 1973; Roth, 1959; Webster, 1953). However, Solyom *et al.* (1974) reported inconclusive results from a research scale developed to measure overprotectiveness in mothers of agoraphobics. However, the mother's anxiety score was positively correlated with the prevalence of fears in the agoraphobic.

For the most part, there are few differences reported in the clinical literature pattern of maternal overprotectiveness for males and females. Roth (1959) describes women and their mothers as "close, intense and often excluded contact outside the immediate circle [p. 592]." He describes the men as children as "overprotected by their mothers and—often their mother's pet [p. 592]."

PHOBIC DISORDERS IN OTHER FAMILY MEMBERS

There are reports in the clinical literature of a high rate of phobic disorders for relatives of agoraphobics. Solyom *et al.* (1974) reports that 34% of his sample had phobic mothers, whereas only 6% had phobic fathers. Finberg-Orter and Fodor (1981), in their survey of published case histories, report that phobic mothers were mentioned for 39% of the females and 11% of the males. Other relatives are also reported to have a high incidence of phobics, for example, 17% are reported by Burglass *et al.* (1977) to have a phobic brother.

THE ONSET OF AGORAPHOBIA

Adults usually become agoraphobic in their mid-twenties, a few years into their marriage. Terhune (1949) views the development of phobias as related to the pressures to be independent in apprehensive, dependent, immature persons. In trying to account for the 3:1 ratio of female to male agoraphobics, we need to keep in mind that agoraphobic symptoms are more consistent with the traditionally defined female sex role and are at variance with the male sex role.

FEMALE ADULT ROLE EXPECTATIONS

Even today, most researchers suggest the importance of the mother-wife role as proper for women (Unger, 1979; Weitz, 1977). As we have noted, agoraphobic women have been socialized as child-women: overprotected, dependent, stereotypically female, often with a phobic maternal role model. Being an adult requires adult competencies that these women have often not yet developed. Under the normal stress of the housewife (or homeworker) role, or perhaps linked to the wish to escape from that role as well, these young women feel trapped since they are ill prepared to actualize or even fantasize other possibilities. Furthermore, since avoidance has often been a lifetime pattern, under stress these women appear to sink further into an exaggeration of the stereotypically feminine role by becoming even more helpless, hysterical, and dependent. These fearful behaviors are then reinforced by significant others in the woman's life as consonant with her sex role (Goldstein & Chambless, 1978).

CASE EXAMPLE

Ms. A, 21, feeling trapped at home, children a burden, wishes to flee her marriage but knows cannot. On stressful day she feels anxious and dizzy in a crowded department store. Soon, after standing on line in the supermarket, she feels dizzy. Gradually, the anxiety attacks increase in frequency and are unpredictable. Anxiety is alleviated by avoiding crowds, stores, shopping. The husband who was too busy to listen to her complaints is suddenly pressed into service to do the shopping and the phobia becomes consolidated.

MARITAL RELATIONSHIPS

Many writers have argued that the marital relationship, particularly the feeling of being trapped in the marriage, assertiveness issues, and reinforcement of the phobia by the spouse are factors in the etiology and maintenance of agoraphobia (Fodor, 1974; Goldstein & Chambless, 1978; Symonds, 1971; Wolpe, 1970).

A review of much of the literature on marital factors for women shows that the findings are not clearcut. Many studies divide female agoraphobics into groups with functional and dysfunctional marriages and do indeed find a group of dysfunctional relationships and neurotic spouses that appear to relate to the maintenance of the phobia, but there are often many reports of functional, nondistressed marriages and nondistressed, nonneurotic spouses as well (Agulnik, 1970; Goodstein & Swift, 1977; Hafner, 1977; Hafner & Phil, 1977; Torpy & Measey, 1974).

Sexual functioning within the marriage, while problematic for some women agoraphobics, seems to show a similar pattern to that reported for females with other neurotic disorders (Burglass *et al.*, 1977; Hafner, 1977; Marks, 1969).

ROLE OF HOUSEWIFE (HOUSEWORKER)

There is some evidence to suggest that the role of housewife (houseworker) rather than the marital relationship is problematic for agoraphobics. Marks and Herst (1970), in their large-scale survey of agoraphobics, report that only 22% of the women were employed outside the home. They further divided the 88% of the sample who were full time housewives into those who were discontented (wanted to work outside the home but did not; $N = 561$) and compared them to those who were content only with housework ($N = 202$) and found the discontented housewives were more symptomatic, more agoraphobic, and needed more help for their phobias than the contented housewives.

MALE AGORAPHOBICS

Male agoraphobics, like their female counterparts, are reported to be dependent, to come from families with maternal overprotectiveness, often with a phobic member, and to lack many of the same personal and social competencies the females lack. They are also more likely to suffer from physical illness prior to the first agoraphobic episode and are reported to be hypochondriacal. Most importantly, unlike female agoraphobics, the personality patterns and symptoms of agoraphobia, particularly the hysterical, dependent personality style and staying at home, are in direct variance with prescribed sex role behavior for a male.

Sex Role Expectations for Males. Young adult males are still under more pressure than young females to function competently in the outside world. They must achieve in the world of work and in marriage and will additionally have the primary burden of economic support (Weitz, 1977).

CASE EXAMPLE

Mr. H, youngest of a large, first-generation American family, works for his oldest brother in a stressful family business. His mother has just moved in with his wife and daughter and there is much bickering at home. Leaving work on a particularly stressful hot day, feeling annoyed and anxious, the train is more crowded and slower than usual and he feels dizzy. Next week, while waiting for the train on a similar hot and stressful day, he notices chest pains and worries that he may be having a heart attack and might pass out on the train. He begins to take taxis but the stress continues and he becomes more and more anxious about leaving the house until all he can do is stay at home.

Marital Relationships. Given the low incidence of male agoraphobia, there have been few studies of relevant marital issues. In the clinical literature there is a suggestion, contrary to the mixed findings for females, of marital stress. For example, Liotti and Guidano (1976), from clinical interviews with 15 Italian male agoraphobics and their spouses, report the following pattern relating to the phobia: The wives become more assertive and the husbands become more anxious and aggressive. Then the symptom develops and the wives respond by becoming more protective and supportive.

Other Findings Relevant for Male Agoraphobics. Work pressures for male agoraphobics have not been studied. It would seem plausible that male agoraphobics suffer from the double stress of work and home. Arrindell (1980) reports from studying the pattern of factors on the Fear Survey Scale that male agoraphobics scored high for "being criticized by people in authority" and "being watched working." Goldstein and Chambless (1980) report that male agoraphobics generally have less severe disabilities because familial and societal pressures mitigate against men becoming dependent and helpless. Jassin (1980) speculates that agoraphobic-prone males may fall into the anxiety neurotic category because for men avoidance becomes a luxury they literally cannot afford, and it is also possible they may be found in the alcoholic category as well (Chambless & Goldstein, 1980).

TREATMENT OF AGORAPHOBIA

Traditional psychoanalytic therapies have not worked for agoraphobics. The 1970s saw the development of behavioral treatments as well as auxilliary pharmacological treatments for agoraphobia. The latter may be particularly helpful in alleviating some of the depressive symptoms. However, behavioral treatments appear to be the most systematically studied and the most successful for agoraphobics (Goldstein & Chambless, 1980; Marks, 1978).

Behavioral treatments vary from standard desensitization with relaxation (see Case Example for fear of success), anxiety management, exposure (confronting the feared situation alone), and cognitive restructuring (working on the underlying belief systems that maintain the phobia). Marks (1978) suggests that exposure therapists are the most effective interventions for the alleviation of the phobia, whereas Fodor (1974) and Goldstein and Chambless (1980) advocate utilization of expanded behavior procedures to change the dependent avoidance personality patterns. This expanded therapy for female agoraphobics could also be construed as feminist therapy in that by transcending traditional sex role programming, it provides for independence training (mastery and confronting) in contrast to the familial dependency training (hysteria and avoidance).

CASE EXAMPLE: TREATMENT OF AGORAPHOBIA

Treatment plan for Ms. A., the agoraphobic housewife:

Anxiety management: Ms. A. is taught self-monitoring procedures to recognize early phases of stress and anxiety. Relaxation procedures (deep-breathing techniques and visual imagery) are also presented for use during exposure therapy.

Exposure: *Ms. A. prepared a list of her feared situations (grocery store, department store, driving on highway, etc.) and gradually begins to encounter these situations alone for increasing periods of time.*

Cognitive strategies: *Through self-monitoring of thoughts, Ms. A. begins to view herself differently, as someone who can control her anxiety and develop coping strategies. (Examples include: "be brave, independent, I can handle myself and stand a bit of anxiety," etc.).*

Developing other competencies: *Other routes out of the wife-mother role are explored. First, she is encouraged to find childcare, then to take courses, and finally she prepares for employment outside the home. Or often, she is just encouraged to look for employment immediately.*

Marital therapy: *Although the marriage is not troubled in this case, it is important to enlist the husband's support for Ms. A. to function more independently outside the home and to be available for any couple work as needed.*

Treatment plan for Mr. H.:

A similar approach would be utilized for Mr. H. However, since he is already employed, he would be encouraged to return to work as soon as possible. Alternative employment possibilities would also be explored. Further work on assertiveness to help him confront his older brothers and to taking more responsibility in finding another home for the mother as well as dealing with marital issues is also indicated. The wife may also need help to support his more independent functioning as well.

Summary

This chapter has surveyed the clinical, research, and theoretical literature on phobia, underscoring sex role socialization and social learning factors in order to understand why a disproportionately large number of women and a small number of men come for treatment of phobias. An outline of the different faces of the categories of phobias (simple, social, and agoraphobia) was given with regard to etiology, clinical features, sex differences and treatment. Particular attention was given to agoraphobia. Sex role messages presented by the media were examined, as were the different environmental expectations put on boys as opposed to girls for mastery of and exposure to feared situations. Behavioral treatments were examined for the various types of phobias, and clinical illustrations were provided.

Acknowledgments

Author acknowledges the assistance of Bonny Finberg-Orter, New York University and Lorna Rhone, New York University for research assistance.

References

Agras, S., Sylvester, D., & Oliveau, D. The epidemiology of common fears and phobias. *Comprehensive Psychiatry*, 1969, *10*(2), 151-156.

Agulnik, P. The spouse of the phobic patient. *Journal of Psychiatry*, 1970, *117*, 59-67.

American Psychiatric Association. *Diagnostic and statistical manual of mental disorders* (3rd ed.). Washington, D.C.: Author, 1980.

Andrews, J. D. Psychotherapy of phobias. *Psychological Bulletin*, 1966, *66*, 455-480.

Angelino, H., Dollins, J., & Mech, E. Trends in the fears and worries of school children as related to socio-economic status and age. *Journal of Genetic Psychology*, 1965, *89*, 263-276.

Arrindell, W. Dimensional structure and psychopathology correlates of the Fear Survey Schedule (FSSIII) in a phobic population: A factoral definition of agoraphobia. *Behavioral Research and Therapy*, 1980, *18*, 229-242.

Bandura, A. *Principles of behavior modification*. New York: Holt, 1969.

Berg, I. School phobia in the children of agoraphobic women. *British Journal of Psychiatry*, 1976, *128*, 86-89.

Bowlby, J. *Attachment and loss* (Vol. 2): *Separation, anxiety, anger*. New York: Basic Books, 1973.

Brehony, A. Women and agoraphobia: A case for the etiological significance of the feminine sex role stereotype. In V. Franks & E. Rothblum (Eds.), *Sex role stereotypes and women's mental health*. New York: Springer, 1982.

Brehony, A., & Geller, E. Agoraphobia: An appraisal of research and a proposal for an integrative model. In R. M. Eisler, P. M. Miller (Eds.), *Advances in behavior modification* (Vol. 11). New York: Academic Press, 1981.

Broverman, I. K., Broverman, D. M., Clarkson, F., Rosenkranz, P., & Vogel, S. Sex role stereotypes: A current appraisal. *Journal of Social Issues*, 1972, *28*, 59-78.

Burglass, D., Clarke, J., Henderson, A. S., Kreitman, N., & Presley, A. S. A study of agoraphobic housewives. *Psychological Medicine*, 1977, *7*, 73-86.

Burns, L. E., & Thorpe, G. L. The epidemiology of fears and phobias. *International Medical Research*, 1977, *5*, 1. (Supplement 5)

Chambless, D. L., & Goldstein, A. J. Anxieties: Agoraphobia and hysteria. In A. Brodsky & R. Hare-Mustin (Eds.), *Women and psychotherapy*. New York: Guilford, 1980.

Croake, J. W. Fears of children. *Human Development*, 1969, *12*, 239-247.

Dick and Jane as Victims: Sex stereotyping in children's readers. Princeton, New Jersey: Women on Words and Images, 1975.

Fenichel, O. *The psychoanalytic theory of neurosis*. New York: Norton, 1945.

Finberg-Orter, B., & Fodor, I. G. *A survey of published case histories of male and female agoraphobics.* Unpublished manuscript, 1981.

Fodor, I. G. The phobic syndrome in women: Implications for treatment. In V. Franks & V. Burtle (Eds.), *Women in therapy.* New York: Bruner/Mazel, 1974.

Fodor, I. G. The treatments of communication problems with assertiveness training. In A. Goldstein & E. Foa (Eds.), *Handbook of behavioral interventions.* New York: Wiley, 1980.

Fodor, I. G., & Lief, J. *Personality patterns among test anxious college students.* Unpublished manuscript presented at annual meeting of National Association of School Psychologists, April 1980.

Goldstein, A. J., & Chambless, D. L. A reanalysis of agoraphobia. *Behavior Therapy,* 1978, *9,* 47-59.

Goldstein, A. J., & Chambless, D. L. The treatment of agoraphobia. In A. J. Goldstein & E. G. Foa (Eds.), *Handbook of behavioral interventions.* New York: Wiley, 1980.

Goodstein, R., & Swift, K. Psychotherapy with phobic patients: The marriage relationship as the source of symptoms and focus of treatment. *American Journal of Psychotherapy,* 1977, 31(2), 284-293.

Gordon, D. A., & Young, R. D. School phobia: A discussion of etiology, treatment and evaluation. *Psychological Reports,* 1976, *39,* (3, Pt. 1), 783-804.

Hafner, R., The husbands of agoraphobic women and their influence on treatment outcome. *Digest of Neurology and Psychiatry,* 1977, 438.

Hafner, R. J., & Phil, M. The husbands of agoraphobic women and their influence on treatment outcome. *British Journal of Psychiatry,* 1977, *131,* 289-294.

Hallam, R. S. Agoraphobia: A critical review of the concept. *British Journal of Psychiatry,* 1978, *133,* 314-319.

Hoffman, L. Early childhood experiences and women's achievement motives. *Journal of Social Issues,* 1972, *29*(2), 120-155.

Jakubowski-Spector, P. Facilitating the growth of women through assertiveness training. *The Counseling Psychologist,* 1973, *4,* 76-86.

Jassin, S. A comparison of agoraphobics, anxiety neurotics, and depressive neurotics using the MMPI and the Beck Depression Inventory. Unpublished dissertation, Temple University, Pensylvania, 1980.

Jersild, A. T., Marhey, F. V., & Jersild, C. L. *Children's fears: Dreams, wishes, daydreams, likes, dislikes, pleasant and unpleasant memories.* New York: Columbia Univ. Press, 1933.

Jersild, A. T., & Holmes, F. B. *Children's fears.* (Child Development Monographs, No. 20.) New York: Columbia Univ. Press, 1935.

Lapouse, R., & Monk, M. Fears and worries in a representative sample of children. *American Journal of Orthopsychiatry* 1959, *24,* 803-818.

Liotti, G., & Guidano, V. Behavioral analysis of marital interaction in agoraphobic male patients. *Behavior Research and Therapy,* 1976, *14,* 161-162.

Maccoby, E. E., & Jacklin, C. N. *The psychology of sex differences.* Stanford, California: Stanford Univ. Press, 1974.

Macfarlane, J., Allen, L., & Honzik, M. A. *Developmental study of the behavior problems of normal children.* Berkeley: Univ. of California Press, 1954.

Machlowitz, M. In dating, men remain the more troubled sex. *New York Times,* April 30, 1981.

Marks, I. *Fears and phobias.* London, England: Heinemann, 1969.

Marks, I. Agoraphobic syndrome: Phobic anxiety state. *Archives of General Psychiatry,* 1970, *23,* 538-553.

Marks, I. Exposure treatments: Clinical studies in phobic, obsessive compulsive and allied disorders in W. S. Agras (Ed.), *Behavior therapy in clinical psychiatry* (2nd ed.). Boston, Massachusetts: Little, Brown, 1978.

Marks, I. M., & Herst, E. R. *Social Psychiatry,* 1970, *5*(1), 16-24.

Mischel, W. Sex-typing and socialization. In P. Mussen (Ed.), *Carmichael's manual of child psychology* (Vol. 2). New York: Wiley, 1970.

Roth, M. The phobic anxiety and depersonalization syndrome (abridged). *Proceedings of the Royal Society of Medicine,* 1959, *52,* 587-594.

Sarason, S., Davidson, K., Lighthall, F., Waite, R., & Ruebush, B. *Anxiety in elementary school children.* Westport, Connecticut: Greenword, 1960.

Sarason, I. *Test anxiety: Theory, research and applications.* Hillsdale, New Jersey: Erlbaum, 1980.

Solyom, L., Beck, P., Solyom, C., & Hugel, R. Some etiological factors in public neurosis. *Canadian Psychiatric Association Journal,* 1974, *19*(1), 69-79.

Symonds, A. Phobias after marriage: Women's declaration of dependence. *The American Journal of Psychoanalysis,* 1971, *31,* 144-152.

Terhune, W. The phobic syndrome: A study of 86 patients with phobic reactions. *Archives Neurological Psychiatry,* 1949, *62,* 162-172.

Torpy, D., & Measey, L. G. Marital interaction in agoraphobia. *Journal of Clinical Psychology,* 1974, *30,* 351-354.

Tucker, W. I. Diagnosis and treatment of the phobic reaction. *American Journal of Psychiatry,* 1956, *112,* 825-830.

Unger, R. *Female and male: Psychological perspectives.* New York: Harper & Row, 1979.

Webster, A. S. The development of phobias in married women. *Psychological Monographs,* 1953, *67*(17).

Weiss, E. Psychodynamic formulation of agoraphobia. *The Psychoanalytic Forum,* 1966, *1*(4), 378-386.

Weitz, S. *Sex roles: Biological, psychological and social foundations.* London and New York: Oxford Univ. Press, 1977.

Wolfe, J. L., & Fodor, I. G. A cognitive-behavioral approach to modifying assertive behavior in women. *Counseling Psychologist,* 1975, *5*(4), 45-52.

Wolpe, J. *Psychotherapy by reciprocal inhibition.* Stanford, California: Stanford Univ. Press, 1958.

Wolpe, J. Identifying the antecedents of an agoraphobic reaction: A transcript. *Journal of Behavior Therapy & Experimental Psychiatry,* 1970, *1,* 229-304.

IV

Gender and Personality Disorders

9

JOY LELAND

Gender, Drinking, and Alcohol Abuse

Why do some poeple abuse alcohol whereas others do not? We search for clues by comparing those who do with those who do not. Men are more apt to abuse alcohol than women, so that would seem to present a promising opportunity for investigating the puzzle of problem drinking. However, the magnitude of the differences that make this a promising natural experiment also have discouraged researchers from taking advantage of it. To tap a pool of female problem drinkers large enough for statistical analysis, general population samples must be larger than would be necessary to obtain a comparable pool of men; even in clinical populations, small numbers of potential female subjects have discouraged gender comparisons. Furthermore, the higher prevalence of problem drinking in men than in women has made it seem prudent to concentrate limited resources where the need appeared more urgent. But the situation is changing now, due to the influence of the women's movement and other factors. We are beginning to get some data that allow us to compare North American male and female alcohol use and abuse—their antecedents, manifestations, and consequences.

Gender Differences in the Prevalence of Alcohol Use and Abuse, over Time and Population Subgroups

The notion that women are catching up with men in both drinking and drinking problems seems to be gaining premature acceptance. With increasing frequency, we encounter statements in the literature that assume, or infer from

ISBN: 0-12-050350-6

isolated items of evidence, that this is the case. But repetition alone should not be allowed to establish fact. Authors who directly and comprehensively assess a broad spectrum of evidence concerning gender ratio trends find no support for the assumption that gender differences are disappearing in either alcohol use or abuse (Clark & Midanik, 1981; Ferrence, 1980; Schuckit & Morrissey, 1976). A summary of the pertinent data is shown in Table 9.1. A current estimate, derived by combining those from a variety of recent, independent general population surveys, indicates that in North America about 120 men drink for every 100 women who do. This gender ratio has prevailed for years, not exceeding random error limits or presenting a consistent linear trend even within these limits during this period in adults (Ferrence, 1980, pp. 82-83). Levels of use are slightly higher for both sexes in Canada than in the United States, but gender ratios are similar (Ferrence, 1980, p. 75; Robins & Smith, 1980, p. 212). Prevalence rates are higher in youth than in adults but, again, the gender ratios are about the same or only slightly lower (Ferrence, 1980, p. 75; Robins & Smith, 1980, p. 212).

More recent data have suggested that drinking may be increasing faster in females than males, among both adults and high school students (Ferrence, 1980, pp. 75-81, 84, 113). However, these short-term gender ratio decreases would have to continue through several more series to make an impressive case. The slight decrease in gender ratios among youth could merely reflect a change in customary behavior specific to young people, which may not persist into adulthood.[1]

The heavier the drinking level reported, the greater the disproportion of males over females, as shown in the gender ratio column of Table 9.1. The similarity of current gender ratios between youth and adults at higher consumption levels raises doubts that female drinking patterns are on the verge of becoming more like males at the higher levels of use. The relative immunity of women to drinking problems is confirmed by survey data (both general and special populations, both cross-sectional and longitudinal), as well as by a variety of less direct measures (Robins & Smith, 1980, pp. 215, 229). However, note that among people who take 60 or more drinks per month, the proportion of women reporting some problem equaled that of men in the 1979 survey (gender ratio 96:1, see Table 9.1).

Less direct problem-drinking measures produce gender ratio estimates ranging from 1.68 to 17.00, M to F. Overall, however, the estimates are remarkably similar among comparable independent sources of data, both in the United States and in Canada. The best current estimate indicates that there

[1] Perhaps related to reduction of drinking age in some states, which would likely affect females more than males, since females are generally more conforming to societal rules (Clark, 1964).

TABLE 9.1
Prevalence of Alcohol Use and Abuse, North American Adults

	Males (%)	Females (%)	M to F[a]
Drinkers			
U.S., 1979	75	60	1.25:1
U.S., 1967	80	64	1.25:1
U.S., 1971-1979, range 8 samples	76-70	61-53	1.40-1.21:1
U.S. & Canada, 1939-1979, range 35 samples	87-65	77-45	1.56-1.09:1
Heavier drinkers, variously defined			
U.S., 1979	14	4	3.50:1
U.S., 1967	13	2	6.50:1
U.S., 1971-1979, range 8 samples	22-14	6- 3	6.00-3.00:1
U.S. & Canada, 1960-1978, range 35 samples	40- 6	18- 1	7.44-2.18:1
Problem drinkers, variously defined:			
U.S., 1979, total sample	17.7	7.4	2.39:1
U.S., 1979, drinkers	23.6	12.4	1.90:1
U.S., 1979, 60+ drinks/month, (unweighted average)	44.5	46.5	.96:1
U.S. & Canada, 1960-1978, average 9 samples,	18	7	2.57:1
range 9 samples	43- 4	21- 1	8.00-1.80:1
Serious problem drinkers			
U.S., 1971-1976, range of averages, 7 samples	15-10	5- 3	3.33-3.00:1
U.S., 1967	15	4	3.75:1

Data from Cahalan (1970, p. 119), Clark and Midanik (1981, pp. 56-57), and Ferrence (1980, pp. 82-83, 87-90).

[a] The range of gender ratios are the extremes of those calculated for each of the samples and do not correspond to the indicated extremes of prevalence rates. Except where otherwise indicated, percentages are of total population of men or of women.

are three men who are problem drinkers for every woman. Gender ratios are a bit higher (about 4:1, M to F) when based on measures more likely to reflect the population of clinically defined alcoholics, such as alcohol-related deaths and alcoholic psychosis. The proportions of alcohol-abusing male and female patients vary decidedly with the type of institution reporting, reflecting general, rather than alcohol patient-specific, sex differences in referral patterns. Gender ratios are highest for alcohol-related offenses, reflecting the high ratios for most criminal behavior in the general population (Ferrence, 1980, p. 113).

So far, there is no compelling evidence that problem-drinking gender ratios are decreasing over time (Ferrence, 1980, p. 112). They have been stable over two decades for heavy use, problem drinking, deaths from alcoholic cirrhosis, and other alcohol-related mortality measures. Some morbidity measures do suggest an impending decline in problem-drinking gender ratios, but none has developed so far. Gender ratios for public intoxication are not declining, but those for driving under the influence are, probably due to increased driving (and hence risk) by women. Given the lack of evidence that gender ratios of alcohol use and abuse are converging, it is fascinating to explore how the idea has achieved such currency among general readers and professionals, alike. (For some thoughts on this, see Ferrence [1980, pp. 115-118]).

Among subgroups of the population, the prevalence of alcohol use and abuse varies greatly, as does the relative prevalence between the sexes. There are fewer drinkers among older people than younger people in the United States (see Table 9.2, panel [*a*]). Comparisons of cross-sectional general population data over time suggest that the decrease over age groups reflects a moderation of drinking with age more than historical, generational differences. Both drinking and heavy drinking peak at later ages for women than for men and then decline steadily in both sexes. The average male problem drinker is 10 years older than his general population counterpart, whereas the average female problem drinker is 1 year older than her counterpart.

Currently, the proportion of male to female drinkers is about the same in the married, the unmarried, and the general populations (see Table 9.2, panel [*b*]). Females contribute disproportionately to drinkers among the divorced or separated. In heavy drinkers, the proportion of males to females is high among the unmarried, especially among the divorced or separated. The latter contrasts with the current gender ratios for drinkers and with 1960s data for heavy drinkers indicating that *females,* not males, contribute disproportionately to divorced or separated drinkers (discussed in Leland, 1982). If the earlier pattern reflected a tendency for husbands of heavy drinkers to abandon the marriage more frequently than wives in a corresponding situation, the more recent figures may reflect a change.

Other recent survey data on women (Johnson & Aavedal, 1980), unfortunately without comparable information on men, shows higher risk of heavy drinking in separated than in divorced women; thus it would be desirable to separate these categories in analyses. The same study reported a heavy-drinking rate over twice as high among female heads of households as among wives and a 68% higher proportion of heavy drinkers among employed women than among housewives. In clinical samples, alcoholic women are employed at higher rates (ranging from 50% to 100% higher in most studies) than their general population counterparts (Knupfer, 1980, p. 160). Other recent general population surveys (Johnson, Armor, Polich, & Stambul, 1977) confirm similar results for problem and heavy drinkers (plus providing comparisons to men). In both sexes, problem- and heavy-drinking rates are higher among the unemployed. On the other hand, employed married women, but not men, have higher rates of problem and heavy drinking than single women

TABLE 9.2
Prevalence of Alcohol Use and Abuse among U.S. Adult Population Subgroups

	Drinkers			Heavier drinkers		
	M (%)	F (%)	M to F	M (%)	F (%)	M to F
a. Age						
18-20	95	69	1.38:1	10	4	2.50:1
21-34	84	77	1.09:1	19	5	3.80:1
35-49	73	65	1.12:1	16	8	2.00:1
50-64	69	49	1.41:1	11	3	3.67:1
65+	59	40	1.47:1	8	2	4.00:1
b. Marital status						
General population			1.25:1			3.50:1
Married drinkers	71	60	1.18:1	17	5	3.40:1
Unmarried drinkers	75	60	1.25:1	23	6	3.83:1
Never married	87	71	1.23:1	31	8	3.87:1
Divorced or separated	74	74	1.00:1	29	6	4.83:1
Widowed	65	35	1.86:1	11	3	3.67:1
c. Income						
Under $4000	63	32	1.97:1	19	-.5	-
$4000-$9999	64	56	1.15:1	21	5	4.20:1
$10,000-$24,999	77	62	1.24:1	21	7	3.00:1
$25,000 +	85	82	1.04:1	21	6	2.62:1
d. Education						
Less than 7 years	50	12	4.17:1	12	4	3.00:1
7-11 years	71	47	1.51:1	21	7	3.00:1
12 years	74	64	1.16:1	23	5	4.60:1
13-college grad	84	79	1.06:1	21	5	4.20:1
Grad school	87	85	1.02:1	20	12	1.67:1
e. Ethnicity						
Blacks	70	51	1.37:1	14	7	2.00:1
Whites	75	61	1.23:1	21	5	4.20:1
Hispanics	79	69	1.14:1	43	10	4.30:1
f. Religion						
Protestant	64	43	1.49:1	14	4	3.50:1
Fundamentalist						
Catholic	91	77	1.18:1	31	8	3.87:1
Liberal Protestant	76	68	1.12:1	20	5	4.00:1
No religion	82	79	1.04:1	22	9	2.44:1
Jewish	61	72	.85:1	6	4	1.50:1
g. Region						
New England	92	75	1.23:1	27	8	3.77:1
Mid-Atlantic	78	71	1.10:1	21	5	4.20:1
East N Central	76	65	1.17:1	22	8	2.75:1
West N Central	68	56	1.21:1	21	3	7.00:1
S Atlantic	64	41	1.56:1	12	-	-
East S Central	51	24	2.12:1	18	3	6.00:1
West S Central	78	53	1.47:1	23	8	2.87:1
Mountain	65	59	1.10:1	25	13	1.92:1
Pacific	90	80	1.12:1	24	6	4.00:1

Data from Clark and Midanik (1981, pp. 58-59, 65-70).

or housewives not in the labor force. All these results belie the stereotype of the female alcoholic as a "hidden housewife"; for additional evidence contradicting this folk notion, see Ferrence (1980, pp. 105-109, 114-118).

General population surveys since 1965 have shown that people of higher income and education are more likely to drink but to experience fewer drinking problems than people of lower status who drink (Clark & Midanik, 1981, p. 35). Heavy drinking (60+ drinks per month) is less closely associated than normal drinking with education and income (see Table 9.2, panels [*c*] and [*d*]). Currently, drinking gender ratios are similar for blacks and whites, whereas those for heavier drinking are about twice as high for whites as blacks (see Table 9.2, panel [*e*]). The difference between the sexes among blacks was even lower in the 1960s (the problem drinking gender ratio was 1.09 to 1, M to F ([Cahalan, Cisin, & Crossley, 1969, p. 48]), suggesting that some moderation has occurred in black women drinkers' tendency to be heavy drinkers, if they drink at all. Among the various religions, drinking gender ratios vary considerably and correspond more closely to the relative abstinence orientation of the sect than heavier drinking gender ratios (see Table 9.2, panel [*f*]). Degree of urbanization, city size, and alcohol attitudes of the predominant religion contribute to regional differences in drinking; the effects differ between the sexes (see Table 9.2, panel [*g*]), and comparisons to 1960 data (Cahalan *et al.*, 1969, p. 38) indicate regional shifts over time.

Gender Differences in the Antecedents of Problem Drinking[2]

Problem drinking runs in families. Recently, progress has been made toward disentangling the relative contributions of inheritance from those of environment. Evidence of a genetic component in male problem drinking is accumulating from studies of twins, adopted children, and half-siblings (Swinson, 1980, pp. 223-262).[3] Unfortunately, the twin studies included no

[2] Items were selected for inclusion in this "antecedents" section for convenience rather than according to any conviction that they are established predictors of drinking problems for either sex. For example, it is not at all clear whether either spouse's alcohol abuse is an antecedent or, alternatively, a consequence of the other's and, therefore, that discussion could have been included in the latter section, rather than this one; marital instability, covered in the "prevalence" section, could have been included in either the "antecedents" or the "consequences" sections.

[3] The principal findings are: (*a*) higher concordance of problem drinking rates in identical (54%) than in fraternal (32%) male twins; (*b*) problem-drinking rates four times as high in adopted male children born to an alcoholic parent as in those born to nonalcoholic parents, when both sets had been separated from the biological parent within 6 weeks of birth; (*c*) an alcoholic biological parent was identified among 62% of alcoholic half-siblings, but only 20% of nonalcoholic half-siblings, even though the same proportion of each group was actually raised by an

females, and the half-siblings studies did not separately analyze the data for the small number of females in the samples. The adoption study results for females were much less conclusive than for males and suggested that environmental factors may be more important in the development of problem drinking among women than among men.

Psychiatric disorders, as well as problem drinking, tend to run in families and particularly in the families of alcoholics, suggesting the possibility of a common genetic antecedent. There have been indications that females who experience early onset of depressive illness have significantly more alcoholic male relatives than do late onset females suffering from the same affliction, but these results have not been confirmed in subsequent studies; the significance of this finding for sex differences in problem drinking has not been clearly established, having been interpreted differently by different researchers. Psychiatric illness in parents and other relatives is more common in female than in male alcohol abusers (Boothroyd, 1980, p. 312). So far, there is no conclusive evidence that the coincidence of alcoholism and psychiatric disorders in the same family has a genetic basis (Swinson, 1980, p. 258).

Studies of a possible association between alcoholism and various genetic markers have not yet produced convincing positive results. Gynecological problems constitute a risk factor for problem drinking that is unique to women (Wilsnack, 1980, p. 25). There is no evidence of sex differences in alcohol metabolism rates. Alcohol absorption does differ; women attain higher peak blood alcohol levels than men for the same dose of alcohol because they have a lower proportion of body fluid to fat and thus a smaller volume in which to absorb a given amount of alcohol. Also, peak blood alcohol levels vary over the menstrual cycle, which suggests that hormones may also contribute to sex differences in alcohol absorption (Mello, 1980, p. 270). It is not yet clear how higher peak blood alcohol levels could be logically associated with lower rates of drinking and drinking problems in women than in men; if there is a connection, it presumably would be based on a theory of avoidance of aversive reactions. Although it seems likely that genetic components in the development of problem drinking eventually will be firmly established, environmental influences will remain important. One basis for this inference is the fact that a considerable proportion of people who develop alcohol problems have no family history thereof.

A number of apparent antecedents of alcohol use and abuse have been identified in the family environment. Longitudinal studies show that both males and females are more likely to drink if their parents do (Robins & Smith,

---

alcoholic parent. Most of the data indicating a genetic component in male problem drinking have come from studies in Scandinavia; their representativeness of other gene pools remains to be tested.

1980, p. 223). Females who are alcoholics are more likely than alcoholic males to have alcoholic fathers (Mello, 1980, p. 269) and, in general, females seem more vulnerable than males to the impact of alcoholism among relatives (Armor, Polich, & Stambul, 1978, p. 66; Cotton, 1979); this fits with an earlier suggestion that female drinking is more influenced by environmental factors than is male. A biological parent who abuses alcohol is an even more reliable predictor of problem drinking in males than is growing up with an alcohol-abusing parent figure (Mello, 1980, p. 271). Male relatives of alcoholics more frequently exhibit alcoholism, whereas female relatives of alcoholics have a greater tendency toward depression (Cotton, 1979). From this, it has sometimes been inferred that alcoholism and depression are sex-specific manifestations of the same underlying tendencies (Schuckit, 1973).

Several familial characteristics other than drinking behavior and mental illness also appear to increase the risk of heavy or problem drinking in offspring (see review in Leland, 1982). In general, drinking problems in offspring are associated with deficits in parental group maintenance and socialization methods or models; lower-class children are especially vulnerable to these effects. The more a family's rituals are disrupted by an alcoholic, the more likely alcoholism is to occur in the child's generation (Wolin, Bennett, & Noonan, 1979).

The absence of parental role models may be as damaging as poor models. Gomberg's (1979) review indicates that female problem drinkers exhibit even more early deprivation of parents than males. On the other hand, Cahalan *et al.* (1969) found an absent parent effect only among people aged 45 years or older, and then only among males. Problem drinking, but not other forms of psychopathology, occurs disproportionately in the last-born child, especially in large families; this pattern is clearer for males than for females. Older sisters, rather than older brothers, predominate in the families of male alcoholics (see review in Leland, 1982). Peer influence appears to exert even stronger influences than parental models and, again, even more so for girls than for boys (Robins & Smith, 1980, p. 223). Women who use alcohol heavily or who abuse it are more likely than other women to be married to or to live with a problem-drinking man (Wilsnack, 1980, pp. 17–18). The overall picture suggests that girls conform more than boys to family and peer influences in the development of their drinking behavior. In both sexes, problem drinking seems to be more closely associated with such environmental influences than with the drinkers' own personal characteristics.

So far, no pattern of personality characteristics appears to reliably predict alcohol problems in either men or women (Beckman, 1976; Mello, 1980, pp. 268, 272). Results of longitudinal studies of the personal characteristics of alcohol abusers (reviewed in Robins & Smith, 1980, pp. 224–226) are confusing. Some studies found that antisocial behavior in childhood predicts problem drinking in both sexes. Others found such associations among males, only, with neurotic and depressive symptoms in childhood more typical of females who become alcohol abusers. This would reinforce the suggestion that alcoholism is more often secondary to depression in women than in men (Schuckit, 1973; Winokur & Clayton, 1968) since sociopathy is more common than affective disorder among men. On the other hand, if alcohol acts as a depressant in women, as it does in men (Mello, 1980, p. 292), drinking would not seem to serve a positive function for women, who already are inclined to be depressed, so we would have to hypothesize that negative consequences can actually reinforce drinking; there are some indications that this could be the case (Mello, 1980, p. 288). Furthermore, males are more likely to use alcohol to cope with depression and anxiety; females prefer psychotropic drugs (Ferrence, 1980, p. 109).

For nearly four decades, studies of problem drinkers in treatment have reported that females are more likely than males to begin abusing alcohol in response to discrete, stressful life events such as the "empty nest" situation (Knupfer, 1980, pp. 149-150, 164). (This could be another indication that women's drinking is more sensitive to environmental influences than men's; or, perhaps, women are just more apt to report such events as rationalizations.) On the other hand, this generalization is contradicted by Morrissey (1980), whose large-sample retrospective study indicated that males were much more likely than females to associate a major life-change event with their first alcohol problems and slightly more likely to associate the initiation of problem drinking with such an event.

The notion that sex roles influence patterns of alcohol use and abuse has been a prominent theme in recent alcohol studies (see review by Leland, 1982, of which the following discussion is a summary). There are potential sex role implications in many of the findings reported here so far, particularly familial factors. The research that more directly approaches this subject has taken a curious course. Sex roles are implicated in two prominent general theories of drinking—the power and the dependency theories. Other investigations of the association have tended to ignore two potentially fruitful avenues in favor of one whose significance is more restricted.

The power theory (McClelland, Davis, Kalin, & Wanner, 1972) proposes that in societies where men (but not women) are expected to be strong, independent, aggressive achievers, men reach for alcohol as a convenient instrument to enhance their power feelings, interpreting the boost in levels of adrenalin and energy that alcohol produces as a sensation of increased strength. The theory could be expanded to account for men's tendency to drink more than women; women are not expected to be powerful and hence have less need for alcohol as a reinforcer of power feelings. According to the dependency theory (Bacon, 1974), in societies where the open expression of dependent behavior is severely restricted among men, males must hide their dependency needs. Alcohol creates feelings of warmth, comfort, security, acceptance, and infantile omnipotence that allow the drinker to escape for a while society's demands for self-reliance and to briefly satisfy yearnings to feel dependent. In corresponding life situations, it is assumed that women are allowed, and even encouraged, to act dependent. Thus, women experience less conflict over dependency needs than men and have less motive to drink.

Both theories sound plausible and can accommodate drinking differences between men and women, but they pose three dilemmas. First, they propose opposite motives for drinking; clearly, both cannot be right. Second, they assume opposite effects for alcohol; obviously a first step is to find out which, if either, effect alcohol actually produces—power or dependency. Third, the assumptions about sex roles that are intrinsic to the logic of both theories are largely based on untested conventional wisdom. Thus, so far the sex role implications of the two theories remain no more than tantalizing hypotheses.

More direct investigations of sex roles and drinking have neglected comparisons between cultures, and between sexes in the same culture, in favor of a curiously narrow preoccupation with the covariation between alcohol abuse and sex role conflict within the female sex. The principal issues and findings are summarized here. Alcohol use and abuse in adult women is weakly associated with some kind of sex role conflict, variously measured and defined, in all the studies;[4] the data on younger women are less clear. The kind of sex role conflict varies among the studies, so perhaps the magnitude is the crucial element. Sex role conflict is likely a more complex construct than we have assumed, since recent research suggests that high levels of both male and female traits are associated with a low incidence of alcohol problems, whereas undifferentiated people, who weakly exhibit both sets of traits, are more apt to be impaired. The nature of the connection between sex role conflict and female drinking remains obscure. The idea that drinking makes women feel more "womanly" and thus provides a motive for drinking (Wilsnack, 1974) is far from established. Alcohol abusers may have different motives from normal drinkers; the same could be true of older women versus younger ones. Sex role conflict is unlikely to provide a general explanation for drinking (a notion I recently heard Wilsnack call "a straw [wo]man"), since the studies show that many normal drinkers, but not even a majority of problem drinkers (much less all of them), exhibited such conflict. Some evidence suggests that sex role conflict may merely represent a special case of general identity conflict as a factor in drinking.

If women's roles really are changing significantly, the potential effects on female problem drinking might offset each other. Relief from stress caused by

[4] Boothroyd (1980, p. 311) reaches the opposite conclusion.

confusing roles could reduce female alcohol problems, whereas increased consumption incidental to increased drinking opportunities, stress related to the job, or conflicting demands from multiple roles could increase drinking problems (Wilsnack, 1980, p. 23). Even these meager conclusions remain highly tentative, since the assumptions about how women do and should behave, as reflected in tests of sex role conflict, have little or no empirical foundation. They have merely distinguished male from female subjects in past tests. The tests may reflect folk notions peculiar to the test devisor's own cultural, subcultural, familial, and individual experience. They show bias toward including pathological extremes in measures of femininity, but not of masculinity (Knupfer, 1980, pp. 157-158). Actual sex role norms must be delineated much more decisively before sex role conflict can be defined. Variations among social classes and ethnic groups complicate this task. Status inferiority is a dimension of sex role differences whose significance deserves more attention (Knupfer, 1980, p. 156).

Gender Differences in Drinking Patterns and Contexts

Public drinking, which is associated with greater consumption and social consequences than private drinking, is more common in men than in women (Gomberg, 1976, p. 139). However, this may be changing as female roles alter (e.g., increasing employment [Knupfer, 1980, p. 140; Wilsnack, 1980, p. 16]). Harford (1977, p. 295) has shown that the male preponderance of public drinking holds true only for bars, not restaurants. The tendency for problem-drinking women, more than men, to drink with their spouses (Gomberg, 1976, p. 139; Harford, 1977, p. 293) probably is related to the tendency toward more private drinking in women. Females drink with men more than men drink with women, and women consume more when drinking with men than they do with their own sex (Wilsnack, 1980, p. 17).

Private drinking by females does not, however, support the frequent assertion that women hide their drinking or do more solitary drinking than men (Ferrence, 1980, p. 108). Problem-drinking women are about as likely as men to report having their most recent drink alone (gender ratio 1.13:1, F to M), according to Cahalan's data (1970, p. 128). Nearly twice as many male as female heavy drinkers report they most often drink alone (Cahalan *et al.*, 1969, p. 88); the gender ratio (3.8:1, M to F) was even higher in Harford's (1977, p. 293) study.

Women's drinking is more likely to be concentrated, and even confined, to weekends than is men's. Women drink more frequently at mealtimes and on special occasions than men, who report drinking in association with a wider variety of events (Harford, 1977, p. 292). The duration of drinking events does not significantly differ between the sexes and is highly correlated with the amount consumed in both sexes, though women consistently drink less per event than men (Harford, 1977, p. 291). Binge drinking often has been reported as more frequent in men than in women (Knupfer, 1980, p. 140), but a 1979 United States survey shows the same gender ratio (1.25:1, M to F) as for drinking in general (Clark & Midanik, 1981, p. 73). Overall, consumption levels vary similarly with drinking context in both sexes, though females drink consistently less than men in all settings (Harford, 1977, p. 294).

It frequently has been claimed that problem drinking develops more quickly, though at a later age, in women than in men, as evidenced by their tendency to come to treatment after shorter periods of alcohol abuse than men (Wilkinson, 1980, p. 334). This sometimes has been invoked as evidence of greater susceptibility to the physical and social consequences of alcohol in females than in males. Alternatively, it could merely reflect a sex difference in general willingness to acknowledge the need for, and to ask for, help (Knupfer, 1980, p. 140), and does not necessarily indicate more rapid development of problem drinking in women than in men. As mentioned earlier, although retrospective studies have shown a somewhat later onset of alcohol problems in women than in men, this has not been confirmed in longitudinal studies, which provide a better test (Robins & Smith, 1980, pp. 216, 218). Longitudinal studies do show that for both men and women, the earlier drinking begins, the more likely it will lead to drinking problems.

From the limited data available, spontaneous remission occurs in both sexes, but the decline occurs sharply at a younger age (about 50) among women and more gradually for men, where "maturing out" may not happen until as late as 70 years (Cahalan, 1970, p. 137).

Gender Differences in the Consequences of Drinking and Alcohol Abuse

Overall, women may be more vulnerable than men to the physical effects of alcohol. In general population studies, "health problems" in association with alcohol use are about twice as often reported by women as men (Cahalan, 1970; Clark & Midanik, 1981, p. 62). Many clinical studies indicate equivalent or greater physical illness, often at younger ages, in women than in men, despite the women's lower alcohol intake and shorter problem-drinking histories (Wilkinson, 1980, pp. 336-338). However, the degree of differential female vulnerability varies with specific alcohol-related illnesses. It seems pretty clear that problem-drinking females exhibit disproportionate rates of alcoholic cirrhosis, Wernicke-Korsakoff syndrome, and deficiencies of iron and folate. Men, on the other hand, exhibit disproportionate amounts of alcoholic cardiomyopathy and chronic lung disease, although it is difficult to isolate the effects of alcohol from those of smoking. In addition, some studies have reported disproportionate male rates of delirium tremens, alcohol-induced hypertension, alcoholic pancreatitis, and peptic ulceration but disproportionate female rates of alcoholic ketoacidosis and degenerative diseases of the nervous system; however, this evidence is not well established (Wilkinson, 1980, pp. 355-358).

Among all these disorders, a constitutional difference between the sexes has been well demonstrated only for alcoholic cirrhosis and alcoholic cardiomyopathy; in the remainder, environmental differences such as relative exposure to drinking, beverage choice, drinking style, nutrition, and use of other drugs are currently thought to be more important, though constitutional differences may eventually be discovered to account for the observed sex differences in prevalence (Wilkinson, 1980, pp. 342, 350, 358). Perhaps the most striking gender difference in the consequences of heavy drinking centers around fetal alcohol syndrome—a constellation of physical and mental birth defects that are strongly associated with maternal alcohol abuse during pregnancy (National Institute on Alcohol Abuse and Alcoholism, 1978, pp. 2-12). If women heed the warnings, this could increase sex differences in problem drinking rates.

Some studies have found that alcohol impairs the performance of females more than males on tests of delayed (but not immediate) recall and of reaction time. Delayed recall was not related to females' menstrual cycle phase, which conforms to general findings on performance tests among normal women. In contrast, reaction time *was* related to menstrual cycle phase, but maximum impairment did not consistently occur during the phase when blood alcohol levels are supposed to be highest (the premenstrual) (Mello, 1980, pp. 282-285).

Negative mood does predominate during the premenstrual period, but does not necessarily impair performance (Mello, 1980, pp. 283-284). Sustained alcohol abuse is consistently associated with negative mood in men and is often, but not invariably, reported by normal drinkers in experimental settings, though the reported threshold dose varies (Mello, 1980, pp. 286-287). These and other findings belie one item of conventional wisdom: that alcohol's effects on mood are primarily experienced as positive. Thus, mood improvement cannot be invoked as a motive for excessive drinking (Mello, 1980, p. 287).

In men, increases in aggression, sexual response, sociability, and even laughter and eating are related only to the *expectancy* that alcohol has been consumed and occur even when the "drink" contains none. This and much other evidence contradicts the notion that pharmacological effects of alcohol cause "disinhibition" (Social Research Group, in preparation). In women, the limited research results are more equivocal. Drinking alcohol decreases sexual response, whereas the expectancy of having consumed alcohol increases social anxiety, perhaps reflecting different experiences and/or beliefs regarding alcohol in men than in women (Lang, 1981).

In general populations, females have been living longer than males for over 100 years. Both biological and environmental factors are influential (Schmidt & Popham, 1980, p. 365). Problem-drinking males and females are more similar to each other in overall mortality than to males and females in the general population, with high rates of excess mortality in alcoholics of both sexes. Up to age 50, female alcoholics have higher death rates than males, but in the older age groups, the male mortality rate is so elevated it offsets the high female rates at younger ages, resulting in a lower overall female ratio over the entire life span; for every 100 deaths in male alcoholics, there are only 83 deaths in female alcoholics. In nonalcoholics, the corresponding male-female difference is much greater—54 female deaths for every 100 male deaths. Thus, the common experience of problem drinking considerably reduces the longevity advantage enjoyed by females in the general population (Schmidt & Popham, 1980, p. 369).

The same tendency toward equalizing death rates is exhibited for the major causes of death as well as in other apparently alcohol-related disorders. Where alcohol ingestion appears to be the primary cause of death (alcoholism, cirrhosis, violence), the same cause of excess death occurs in nearly equal proportions in alcoholic males and females. Where smoking is primary (e.g., lung cancer), the female proportion is much lower (24 female deaths to every 100 male). The alcoholic female's proportion of deaths also is low for heart disease (55 female deaths to 100 male deaths). The sex differences in mortality from lung cancer and heart disease together account for almost all the excess mortality in males. Since smoking rates of male and female alcoholics are almost equal, it seems highly likely that female hearts and lungs are constitutionally less vulnerable than male organs (Schmidt & Popham, 1980, pp. 373-376).

Death rates from all violent causes combined are about equal in male and female alcoholics, but males predominate in suicide whereas females predominate in deaths from accidental poisoning, which may in fact be masked suicide. In female alcoholics under 50, death rates equal or exceed male rates for all causes except violent death and heart disease. In female alcoholics over 50, only violent death rates exceed those for males (Schmidt & Popham, 1980, pp. 376-378).

Cirrhosis death rates in Canada are higher in female than in male alcoholics up to age 50 (1.25 females for every male); after that, the female rate is lower (.86 female deaths for every male) (Schmidt & Popham, 1980, p. 376). In contrast to these Canadian data, in the United States, the cirrhosis death gender ratio for all ages combined is 2.29:1, M to F (Johnson, 1979). When we compare this to a serious problem-drinking gender ratio of 4.0 males to every female, we see that United States women are disproportionately represented in deaths from this disorder. These apparent national differences in cirrhosis death gender ratios are puzzling; perhaps some environmental difference, such as choice of beverage, contributes. The other mortality findings from Canada (Schmidt & Popham, 1980) are much more similar to United States data.

Trends in mortality gender ratios show that male rates of alcohol-related deaths are becoming higher than female rates (arguing, again, against convergence in problem-drinking rates or, at least, suggesting that the development, if it is occurring, is too recent to show up in mortality figures). Many inferences about gender differences in the social consequences of problem drinking seem to be based more on presuppositions than on data, which is surprisingly scarce. Some studies report less adverse social consequences for women than for men; others suggest the contrary.

Men reported higher rates of all alcohol-associated problems, measured in general population surveys conducted in 1967 and 1978 (Clark & Midanik, 1981, p. 62) and in a separate series of eight surveys in the 1970s (Johnson, Armor, Polich, & Stambul, 1977), with a single exception; in the latter, more women than men reported a physician had warned them that alcohol was injuring their health. From the 1979 data, M to F gender ratios were: job problems (3.5:1); problems with friends (3:1); problems with law, police, accidents (2:1); problems with spouse (reported by only 2% of males and less than .5% of females).

However, the survey problem choices have been very narrow. For example, presumably drinking can interfere with household responsibilities for both men and women, but information has not been gathered on this or many other potential drinking-related problems (Wilsnack, 1980, p. 3). Furthermore, the problems covered in the surveys have been biased toward those for which males generally are at greater risk than females; surveys should control for general population sex differences in alcohol problems.

When controls for drinking levels are included, we get a different picture. In the 1979 survey, among people who drank more than 60 drinks per month, only .68 men reported social consequences for every woman who did (Clark & Midanik, 1981, p. 72). The women may have experienced more adverse consequences because of lower societal tolerance for female than male drinking at these levels or, alternatively, perhaps because they reached higher blood alcohol levels at the indicated intake levels. However, on the four individual items in the social consequences scale, rates for heavy drinkers were higher for females on only one—problems with friends and relatives (only .27 males for every female). Thus, this one item accounts for the entire gender difference on the combined consequences. Gender ratios were 1:1 for job problems and 1.23:1, M to F for problems with police and accidents. Incidentally, alcohol-related accidents may be a particular risk for recently separated or divorced women (Wilsnack, 1980, p. 25). Problems with one's spouse were reported by only 6% of the heavy-drinking males and none of the females in this category. This comparison would, of course, be more meaningful if marital status were controlled; only 6% of the women in this drinking category had a spouse to have trouble with (Clark & Midanik, 1981, pp. 65-72). Female adolescent heavy drinkers also reported fewer negative social consequences than their male counterparts (Wilsnak, 1980, p. 20). Reports of fewer negative social consequences in women support the frequent contention that women may be better insulated from the consequences of alcohol abuse, at least women of higher status who are not in the labor force (Wilsnack, 1980, p. 21).

On the other hand, data from a study that reports consequences for people who get drunk frequently (8 + drinks, 1 + times per week) suggest that social consequences are more severe for women than for men. Females disproportionately experienced seven of eight consequences listed. The only problem disproportionately reported by males was arrest for driving under the influence (Knupfer, 1980, p. 145). Perhaps this frequent intoxication measure tapped women with more severe drinking problems than the 60+ measure in the 1979 United States survey. Clinical data suggest that husbands of alcoholic women are more indifferent to their wives' problems and efforts to get treatment than are wives of alcoholic men (Knupfer, 1980, p. 151).

Elsewhere in the 1979 survey, we see that financial problems were almost as common in heavy-drinking females as males (gender ratio 1.1:1, M to F), whereas child-raising concerns were reported by only .3 males for every female (Clark & Midanik, 1981, p. 74). There are indications that drunkenness is more likely to be accepted as an excuse for bad behavior in men than in women (Knupfer, 1980, p. 146). Clearly, sex differences in the social consequences of drinking depend on the particular consequence being measured. Findings of high social consequences for at least some drinking problems among heavy-drinking females support the frequent assertion that such women are judged more harshly than their male counterparts.

We have seen claims of two countervailing societal responses to female drunkenness and problem drinking—relative protection versus relatively greater punishment. Perhaps both occur, and the resulting ambiguity probably exacerbates the problems some women have in coming to grips with alcohol. On balance, however, the current societal response continues to be far more negative for female than for male alcohol abusers (Knupfer, 1980, p. 144), regardless of whether this is translated into greater perceived social consequences for women than for men.

Given the preponderance of male over female problem drinking, it is clear that the most frequent social consequence of alcohol for women results not from their own drinking, but from that of others, principally husbands—a topic worthy of detailed discussion in itself (see, e.g., Orford, 1977).

Gender Differences in Treatment and Outcome

A majority of the men and women with drinking problems are never treated (Ferrence, 1980, p. 105). In earlier decades, women probably were underrepresented, relative to men, in treatment populations, but that no longer seems to be the case (Annis & Liban, 1980, p. 385). Gender ratios vary greatly by type of service but, over a broad range of services, the gender ratios are within the range of those for the prevalence of problem drinking (3:1, M to F) (Ferrence, 1980, p. 106).

Overall, women do as well in comparable treatment as men (Annis & Liban, 1980, p. 402), contrary to a persistent bromide in the literature. Data are scarce on the course of problem drinking, both with and without treatment, for both sexes; gender comparisons are even more rare. We can rarely be sure that treatment is responsible for the drinking behavior changes observed in treatment populations of either sex because of methodological problems such as failure to obtain pretreatment baseline measures or to use randomized control groups in evaluations (Annis & Liban, 1980, pp. 402-403).

So far, there is nothing we can say with confidence about sex differences in factors associated with treatment prognosis. Annis and Liban (1980, pp. 406-409) reviewed 11 studies that provide data on both sexes (under the headings of demographic, familial, drinking history, social relationship, physical complications, diagnosis, personality, pretreatment, and treatment factors). Most of the items examined were unrelated to outcome for either sex in any of the studies. Factors that were related to outcome for both sexes in some studies were unrelated or differentially related between the sexes in others (age, education, currently married, marital stability, use of protective drug, program completion). Factors that were related in a single study (underlying neurosis, psychopathy) were not investigated in other studies. The current picture is very confused, for males as well as females. Presenting characteristics of patients seem to be more closely linked to outcome than is the kind of treatment. Vannicelli (1980, pp. 6-8) has shown that sex role values of treatment personnel influence a client's comfort in the clinical situation. Clinicians, particularly female clinicians, see the female alcoholic as having a poorer prognosis than the male. Significant results are unlikely to emerge until evaluations control for differences within the presenting population and in the kind of treatment to which they are subjected; most programs use a shotgun approach that makes it impossible to tell what has helped, even if something has. Some treatment programs have been "tailored" to women in recent years, but there are no data available comparing outcome between the special programs and the traditional ones and no data indicating what has guided the choice of approaches that are supposed to be suited to women (except perhaps for the inclusion of childcare facilities). The meager information about the prevention of alcohol problems in women has been reviewed by Wilsnack (1980); I am unaware of any gender comparisons on this topic, so far.

The Future

This review has indicated that the natural experiment of gender differences in alcohol use and abuse will likely continue for some time and has identified characteristics where gender differences are unusually great, thus pinpointing appropriate subgroups for more controlled and intensive comparisons in the future. The resulting improvements in the data will allow us to begin exploring the implications of gender differences in drinking for prevention and treatment.

References

Annis, H. M., & Liban, C. B. Alcoholism in women: Treatment modalities and outcomes. In O. J. Kalant (Ed.), *Alcohol and drug problems in women*. New York: Plenum, 1980.

Armor, D. J., Polich, J. M., & Stambul, H. B. *Alcoholism and treatment*. New York: Wiley, 1978.

Bacon, M. The dependency-conflict hypothesis and the frequency of drunkenness: Further evidence from a cross-cultural study. *Quarterly Journal of Studies on Alcohol*, 1974, *35*, pp. 863-876.

Beckman, L. J. Alcoholism problems and women: An overview. In M. Greenblatt & M. A. Schuckit (Eds.), *Alcoholism problems in women and children*. New York: Grune & Stratton, 1976.

Boothroyd, W. E. Nature and development of alcoholism in women. In O. J. Kalant (Ed.), *Alcohol and drug problems in women*. New York: Plenum, 1980.

Cahalan, D. *Problem drinkers: A national survey*. San Francisco, California: Jossey-Bass, 1970.

Cahalan, D., Cisin, I., & Crossley, H. American drinking practices. *Monographs of the Rutgers Center of Alcohol Studies* (No. 6). New Brunswick, New Jersey: Journal of Studies on Alcohol, Inc., 1969.

Clark, W., & Midanik, L. *Alcohol use and alcohol problems among U.S. adults: Results of the 1979 national survey*. Berkeley, California: Social Research Group, 1981 (working draft).

Cotton, N. S. The familial incidence of alcoholism: A review. *Journal of Studies on Alcohol*, 1979, *40*(1), pp. 89-116.

Ferrence, R. G. Sex differences in the prevalence of problem drinking. In O. J. Kalant (Ed.), *Alcohol and drug problems in women*. New York: Plenum, 1980.

Gomberg, E. Alcoholism in women. In B. Kissin & H. Begleiter (Eds.), *Social aspects of alcoholism*. New York: Plenum, 1976.

Gomberg, E. Problems with alcohol and other drugs. In E. Gomberg & V. Franks (Eds.), *Gender and disordered behavior*. New York: Brunner/Mazel, 1979.

Harford, T. C. Social class and station. In F. Seixas (Ed.), *Currents in alcoholism: Psychiatric, psychological, social and epidemiological studies* (Vol. 4). New York: Grune & Stratton, 1977.

Johnson, P., Armor, D. J., Polich, S., & Stambul, H. *U.S. adult drinking practices: Time trends, social correlates and sex roles* (Report prepared for the National Institute on Alcohol Abuse and Alcoholism). Santa Monica, California: Rand Corporation, 1977.

Johnson, S. *Cirrhosis mortality among American Indian women: Rates and ratios, 1975 and 1976*. Paper presented to the Tenth Annual Medical Scientific Conference of the National Council on Alcoholism/American Medical Society on Alcoholism/Research Society on Alcoholism, Washington, D.C., April 1979.

Johnson, S., & Aavedal, M. Social factors of drinking patterns of U.S. women: Findings from the First Health and Nutrition Examination Survey, 1971-1973. Rockville, Maryland: National Clearinghouse for Alcohol Information, 1980.

Knupfer, G. Problems associated with drunkenness in women. In J. R. Deluca (Ed.), *Fourth special report to the U.S. Congress on alcohol and health*. Washington, D.C.: U.S. Department of Health and Human Services, 1980.

Lang, A. R. *Drinking and disinhibition: Contributions from psychological research*. Paper presented at the Workshop Conference on Alcohol and Disinhibition: The Nature and Meaning of the Link. (Sponsored by the Social Research Group and the National Institute on Alcohol Abuse and Alcoholism.) Berkeley, California: February 1981.

Leland, J. Sex roles, family organization and alcohol abuse. In J. Orford & J. Harwin (Eds.), *Alcohol and the family*. London, England: Croom Helm, 1982.

McClelland, D. C., Davis, W. N., Kalin, R., & Wanner, E. *The drinking man*. New York: Free Press, 1972.

Mello, N. K. Some behavioral and biological aspects of alcohol problems in women. In O. J. Kalant (Ed.), *Alcohol and drug problems in women*. New York: Plenum, 1980.

Morrissey, E. *Gender differences in the impact of life change on the development of drinking problems*. Paper presented at the annual meeting of the American Sociological Association, New York, August 1980.

National Institute on Alcohol Abuse and Alcoholism. Fetal alcohol syndrome: New perspectives. *Alcohol Health and Research World*, 1978, *2*(4), pp. 2-12.

Orford, J. Impact of alcoholism on family and home. In G. Edwards & M. Grant (Eds.), *Alcoholism: New knowledge and new responses*. London, England: Croom Helm, 1977.

Robins, L. N., & Smith, E. M. Longitudinal studies of alcohol and drug problems: Sex differences. In O. J. Kalant (Ed.), *Alcohol and drug problems in women*. New York: Plenum, 1980.

Schmidt, W., & Popham, R. E. Sex differences in mortality: A comparison of male and female alcoholics. In O. J. Kalant (Ed.), *Alcohol and drug problems in women*. New York: Plenum, 1980.

Schuckit, M. A. Depression and alcoholism in women. In *Proceedings, First Annual Alcoholism Conference of the National Institute on Alcohol Abuse and Alcoholism*. Washington, D.C.: US Gov. Printing Office, 1973.

Schuckit, M. A., & Morrissey, E. R. Alcoholism in women: Some clinical and social perspectives with an emphasis on possible subtypes. In M. Greenblatt & M. A. Schuckit (Eds.), *Alcoholism problems in women and children*. New York: Grune & Stratton, 1976.

Social Research Group. *Alcohol and disinhibition: The nature and meaning of the link*. Proceedings of a workship conference, February 1981. Berkeley, California: National Institute on Alcohol Abuse and Alcoholism. (in preparation)

Swinson, R. P. Sex differences in the inheritance of alcoholism. In O. J. Kalant (Ed.), *Alcohol and drug problems in women*. New York: Plenum, 1980.

Vannicelli, Marsha. *Sex-role values and bias in alcohol treatment personnel*. Paper presented at the symposium, Sex roles and Psychopathology, American Psychological Association, Montreal, Canada: September 1980.

Wilkinson, P. Sex differences in morbidity of alcoholics. In O. J. Kalant (Ed.), *Alcohol and drug problems in women*. New York: Plenum, 1980.

Wilsnack, S. C. The effects of social drinking on women's fantasy. *Journal of Personality*, 1974, *42*(1), pp. 43-61.

Wilsnack, S. C. Prevention of alcohol problems in women. In J. R. Deluca (Ed.), *Fourth special report to the U.S. Congress on alcohol and health*. Washington, D.C.: U.S. Department of Health and Human Services, 1980.

Winokur, G., & Clayton, P. Family history studies (IV): Comparison of male and female alcoholics. *Quarterly Journal of Studies on Alcohol*, 1968, *29*, pp. 885-891.

Wolin, S. J., Bennett, L. A., & Noonan, D. L. Family rituals and the recurrence of alcoholism over generations, *American Journal of Psychiatry*, 1979, *136*(4B), pp. 589-593.

10

LINDA S. FIDELL

Gender and Drug Use and Abuse

This chapter reviews sex differences and similarities in the use of substances that produce alterations in affect. Categories of such substances include illicit drugs (e.g., heroin, marijuana); psychotropic drugs (e.g., Valium) used both nonmedically and by prescription; over-the-counter (OTC) drugs (e.g., Compōz); and tobacco and alcohol.

There is a vast literature in the area of substance use and abuse, some of which focuses specifically on women or on sex differences (cf. the annotated bibliographies prepared by Glenn & Richards, 1974, or Green & MacDonald, 1976). Several excellent reviews of that literature, written from slightly different perspectives, are already available on which to build (e.g., Burt, Glynn, & Sowder, 1979; Kandel, 1980; Prather & Fidell, 1978; Suffet & Brotman, 1976). Therefore, only the most recent findings will be summarized here.

Although a great deal is to be learned by careful analysis of substance use in different countries (e.g., Cooperstock, 1976), this paper will concentrate on data from the United States. Similarly, important differences among users in ethnicity, social class, and the like (e.g., Kleinman & Lukoff, 1978) will be glossed over in an attempt to emphasize gender differences and similarities.

Even the decision to concentrate on sex differences in substance use in the United States is difficult because of the rather rapidly changing nature of the phenomenon. Cisin, Miller, and Harrell (1977) provide, among other information, an excellent summary of shifting patterns in drug abuse. The picture, unfortunately, indicates steadily increasing abuse in many categories of drugs

ISBN: 0-12-050350-6

between 1962 and 1977. Patterns of use of drugs obtained by prescription also shift. Rates of prescriptions for barbiturates and amphetamines, for instance, have decreased dramatically as both the limitations of their effectiveness and the extent of their adverse side effects have become more apparent. As the number of prescriptions for barbiturates declined, that for minor tranquilizers increased, at least into the mid-1970s.

As in many areas of social science, problems with clear definition of measures and lack of standardization in reporting results make comparisons among men and women in rates of use of substances difficult. Even the distinction between those who use and those who abuse mood-modifying substances is unclear. By tradition, those who got their drugs from a physician were *users* and those who got drugs from other sources were *misusers* or *abusers*. This distinction is now widely regarded as simplistic. Abuse of drugs obtained by prescription has been clearly documented, as has more or less casual and temporary use of even so dangerous a drug as heroin among military personnel in Vietnam. But although the distinction by source between use and abuse has proved unsatisfactory, no other distinction has universally replaced it. It seems clear, however, that the definition of abuse will have to include the personal consequences of use as well as the source, frequency, and duration of it. The National Institute on Drug Abuse, in addition to serving as a most helpful clearinghouse for information, is also actively trying to solve the problems of lack of standardization in data gathering (Nehemkis, Macari, & Lettieri, 1975) and analysis (Bentler, Lettieri, & Austin, 1976).

Gender and Extent of Use

Since the early 1970s, the National Institute on Drug Abuse has sponsored large-sample national surveys on drug abuse. Because of the sizes of the samples and the standardization in data collection, these surveys provide probably the best information available on the extent of use of various substances. Data from the 1979 survey have been used to estimate the extent of use by sex where possible. However, the report issued from the 1979 survey (Fishburne, Abelson, & Cisin, 1979) did not include a breakdown by sex for all categories of interest. Data from earlier national surveys, then, or secondary analyses by sex of them, were used as necessary. Not only are there difficulties in comparing rates of use by category of substance because data come from different years, but also some tables report *current use* (defined differently in different studies to mean "in past month" or "in past year") whereas others report *ever used* (in lifetime). Although current use is probably a more meaningful measure than lifetime use, the latter was reported here because data were more consistently available.

Illicit Drugs

Table 10.1 presents a breakdown by sex, age, and substance of use of illicit drugs as determined in the 1975–1976 national survey and reported in Burt *et al.* (1979). The percentage of lifetime users of these drugs, with the exceptions of marijuana and hashish, is low. As shown in Table 10.1, a greater percentage of men than women use drugs in almost every category. Although lifetime use of these drugs is higher for men, there are few sex differences in the current use of them, except for marijuana (where men have both higher current and lifetime use). Because more men have tried these drugs but are not necessarily currently using them, it must be that a higher percentage of women who ever try them remain users of them.

A further breakdown of these and other data from the national surveys reveals that men who are involved tend to use these drugs more heavily than do women. Thus, although use of illicit drugs is by no means the exclusive province of men, more men than women have tried the drugs, the sexes are involved with them in equal percentages at present, but men tend to take heavier or more frequent doses.

Psychotropic Drugs: Nonmedical Use

Psychotropic drugs are drugs such as the minor and major tranquilizers, the sedatives and hypnotics, the stimulants, and the antidepressants, that were developed and are used primarily to alter mood. Table 10.2 presents a breakdown by sex, age, and category of drug ever used as measured in the 1979 national survey (Fishburne *et al.*, 1979). As defined in the survey, *nonmedical use* refers to use where the intent is to satisfy curiosity, produce desirable mood alterations, or other, nonmedical, reasons. Sex differences are

TABLE 10.1
Percentage of Lifetime Users of Illicit Drugs by Sex, Age, and Category of Drug, 1975–1976

	Heroin	Other opiates	Cocaine	Hallucinogens	Inhalants	Marijuana	Hashish
Youths (12–17)							
Boys	.7	—	3.9	5.0	11.5	26.0	11.1
Girls	.4	—	2.9	5.2	4.7	18.6	8.1
Adults (18+)							
Men	1.8	7.2	5.8	6.4	4.9	28.7	13.6
Women	.6	3.6	2.5	3.5	1.9	14.5	6.1

From Burt *et al.* (1979).

TABLE 10.2
Percentage of Lifetime Users of Psychotropic Drugs for Nonmedical Purposes by Age, Sex, and Drug Category, 1979

	Stimulants	Sedatives	Tranquilizers	Analgesics
Youths (12-17)				
Boys	4	4	4	4
Girls	3	3	4	3
Young adults (18-25)				
Men	22	22	20	15
Women	15	12	11	9
Adults (26+)				
Men	8	5	4	4
Women	4	2	2	1

From Fishburne *et al.* (1979).

seen among young adults and adults, but not among youths. For each category of drug, a higher percentage of men is involved than women.

A household survey conducted in 1975-1976 of nonmedical drug use in New York State (New York State Division of Substance Abuse Services, 1978) provides further relevant detail. As for the illicit drugs, not only did a higher percentage of men than women use psychotropic drugs nonmedically but also they were more likely to be recurrent users or multiple-category users of them, with some exceptions. In the 25-45 year age categories, women were three to four times more likely than men to begin nonmedical use of tranquilizers and stimulants (diet pills).

The inclusion of the analgesics (pain killers) in Table 10.2 deserves comment. Many of them are a mix of analgesic and psychotropic substances in the same pill. Darvon (propoxyphene), for instance, is structurally related to methadone and is usually combined with aspirin. Other of the analgesics include tranquilizers and sedatives in the mix. Another category of drugs, the antispasmodics, are almost exclusively psychotropic. Because they are not defined as psychotropics, however, they are sometimes not included in surveys of psychotropic drug use. The total amount of psychotropic drug use, both medical and nonmedical, is underestimated by the exclusion of drugs in these categories.

Psychotropic Drugs: Medical Use

Use of psychotropic drugs by prescription shows a pattern of sex differences unlike that seen in the other categories (Table 10.3). Not only is a higher percentage of women involved with these drugs by prescription but also both

TABLE 10.3
Percentage of Lifetime Users of Psychotropic Drugs for Medical Purposes by Sex and Category of Drug, 1975-1976

	Stimulants	Sedatives	Tranquilizers	Any psychotropic
All ages				
Men	7	20	23	37
Women	17	33	38	55

Estimated from a frequency histogram in Burt *et al.* (1979).

the frequency and duration of their use tends to be higher than for men. Interestingly, prescription use of drugs for both women and men seems to be longer-term and more consistent than nonprescription use of them (Fidell, 1977).

Other sex differences were noted by Cooper (1977) in a report that focused on the sedative-hypnotic drugs. In almost every category of these—barbiturate hypnotic (Seconal), nonbarbiturate hypnotic (Quaalude), and benzodiazephine hypnotic (Dalmane) prescribed in 1975—women received about 62% of the prescriptions whereas men received 38% of them. The 2:1 ratio, F to M, for prescribing psychotropics of all kinds has been stable over the 1970s. Furthermore, the percentage of women who use these drugs is fairly constant over the 20-39, 40-59, and 60+ age categories. The percentage of men who use them is lower up to about the age of 60+, when sex differences tend to disappear.

Over-the-Counter (OTC) Mood Modifying Drugs

The prescription tranquilizers and stimulants have OTC counterparts in the form of drugs like Compōz and NoDoz. As reported in Burt *et al.* (1979), sex differences are not found in percentage of lifetime users of these drugs. Among youths (12-17), 6% of boys and 5% of girls have used them. In young adults (18-25), 14% of men and 10% of women have used them, whereas in adults (26+), 5% of men and 5% of women have. For all adults (18 years and over), 7% of men and 6% of women have ever used OTC mood modifiers.

The absence of sex differences in OTC use contrasts sharply with large sex differences in psychotropic drug use by prescription. Both kinds of use are legal, but medical use of psychotropics involves both stronger drugs and the cooperation of a physician.

Tobacco and Alcohol

Rates of *current* use of tobacco and alcohol were reported in Fishburne *et al.* (1979). As can be seen in Table 10.4, sex differences in percentage of current users of alcohol are present at least in the 18+ age categories, whereas sex differences in current users of cigarettes are not apparent. Not only is a higher percentage of men than women involved with alcohol, but also men tend to be more heavily involved as measured by amounts consumed.

Overview

Consideration of the data in Tables 10.1-10.4 leads to several conclusions. One of them is that there is a bulge in the percentage of nonmedical use among young adults (18-25), also apparent in numerous other sources not mentioned here, that will reverberate through the next several decades as they become adults and their lifetime use of drugs is assessed. The high percentage of young people who have come into contact with these substances illuminates a growing awareness that drug abuse is no longer a minority, inner-city problem.

The pattern of sex differences in substance use might make sense if the drugs were aligned along a continuum with the illicit drugs at one end (of illegality and strength), followed by nonmedical psychotropics (also illegal, but somewhat milder), OTC mood modifiers in the middle, and the psychotropic drugs used medically at the other end (legal, but also strong). The illicit drugs are in some sense the strongest, with the most negative personal and social consequences. Men use more of them than women but, with the exceptions of marijuana and hashish, the percentage who use them tends to be small. Men

TABLE 10.4
Percentage of Current Users by Sex, of Alcohol and Cigarettes, 1979

	Alcohol	Cigarettes
Youth (12-17)		
Boys	39	13
Girls	36	12
Young adults (18-25)		
Men	84	45
Women	68	40
Adults (26+)		
Men	72	41
Women	52	33

From Fishburne, *et al.* (1979)

also use psychotropic drugs nonmedically at a greater rate than women. For OTC mood modifiers and cigarettes, however, both legal and relatively safe (in the short run), sex differences are not apparent. At the legal, but strong, end of the continuum, on the other hand, women use the psychotropic drugs at a greater overall rate than men, and many more people are involved.

One is tempted to speculate that men do not need to get prescriptions for their strong drugs because they have other sources for them. Or, conversely, that women do not need to use illegal sources for strong drugs because they have an easily available source in the medical profession. Because of differences in the way surveys are conducted and the data are reported, it is impossible to determine if men or women are, on the whole, more involved with substances. If a kind of "seriousness of drug, by percentage of use" statistic could be generated, however, my guess is that the sexes would come out fairly equally. Alcohol, both legal and strong, does not fit along the continuum, but probably tips the balance in favor of overall heavier involvement on the part of men (cf. Mellinger, Balter, Parry, Manheimer, & Cisin, 1974).

The percentages listed in Tables 10.1-10.4 do not reveal the extent of the problem. Projected to a United States population of about 215 million people, each category represents tens of thousands, hundreds of thousands, or, in the case of prescribed psychotropics, millions of people who have been involved with mood modifying substances during their lifetimes. For many in all categories, use becomes abuse with attendant personal and social costs.

Gender and Characteristics of Users and Abusers

An enormous and bewildering array of studies has been conducted to determine the relationship between use of drugs and the demographic, personality, attitudinal, social, physiological, and familial characteristics of those who use and abuse various substances. Not only do the aforementioned differences in definitions of terms afflict those who would compare results but also the results themselves, when comparable, are often contradictory. With judicious selection from this array, one could support or refute almost any proposition concerning the relationship between gender and substance use.

Not only do methodologies differ widely, but also sampling in this area is difficult; a drug-abusing population, whether on heroin or Valium, is an unlikely group from which to draw a random sample. Thus, many studies of illicit drug abusers use as subjects people from treatment centers or prisons. Researchers interested in use of prescribed psychotropics also sometimes do purposive sampling from community mental health centers and the like. It seems probable that biases introduced by this kind of sampling have distorted most of this literature, including the portions dealing with sex differences and similarities.

Users and Abusers of Illicit Drugs and Nonmedical Psychotropics

This review summarizes gender differences and similarities from several recent publications, themselves summaries of gender differences (Burt *et al.*, 1979; Prather & Fidell, 1978; Suffet & Brotman, 1976). A published monograph (National Institute on Drug Abuse [NIDA], 1979), that compares heroin addicted women with addicted men and a group of nonaddicted women will also be included.

The woman who is frankly addicted to some drug and in treatment is somewhat less likely than her male counterpart to be using heroin and somewhat more likely to be using psychotropic drugs, however obtained. She was probably a year or so older than a male addict when she began using (Burt *et al.*, 1979), and she probably obtained her first drug from a man (66%), particularly if it was heroin (75%). The addicted man usually obtains his drugs from men, as well (NIDA, 1979).

She may have been somewhat less likely than her male counterpart, particularly if she is black, to have sought treatment. Once there, she is less likely to complete treatment or to be successfully treated, possibly because treatment centers are frequently ill-equipped to handle the special medical, child-related, and vocational needs of the female addict (Burt *et al.*, 1979).

The heroin addicted woman is likely to be white and, as a child, to have grown up in a blue-collar home (Prather & Fidell, 1978) that is most noteworthy because it is so normal (Binion, 1979). Although previous research had hypothesized a disrupted and troubled childhood for the heroin addicted woman, particularly in her social relationship with her mother (Prather & Fidell, 1978) or her sexual relationship with male members of her family (Densen-Gerber, 1973), careful work has revealed a very different picture. Binion (1979) found a remarkably normal childhood environment for the heroin addicted women she studied, where the girls felt secure and loved by both parents, but closer to their mothers. There were, however, some differences between heroin addicted and nonaddicted comparison women in the disciplinary techniques and the amount of alcohol used by parents, and in the tendency for the girl to have run away from home before age 16. These differences should not be overemphasized, however, in light of the similarity between heroin addicted and comparison women on so many other measures.

The heroin addicted woman is less likely to have completed high school than a comparison woman or an addicted man (Burt *et al.*, 1979). She usually does not recall being treated as special by any of her teachers and she is more likely to have quit high school because of pregnancy or drugs than a comparison woman (Binion, 1979). She is less likely than an addicted man to be gainfully employed (23% of women and 36% of men) and more likely to be economically dependent on others, on welfare, or engaging in prostitution. She is less likely than her male counterpart to have been arrested (27% of women, 57% of men) (Burt *et al.*, 1979).

The heroin addicted woman is more likely to have been married and to have had children than an addicted man (NIDA, 1979). She is likely now, however, to be widowed, separated, or divorced. She is less likely than an addicted man or a comparison woman to be in a meaningful relationship, but if she is in one, it probably is the same along many dimensions as that of the man or comparison woman. The heroin addicted woman's partner is more likely than partners of the others to be involved with drugs (Tucker, 1979).

Other than her mother, who is more likely to live close by and to offer considerable practical and social support, the heroin addicted woman reports having fewer friends than comparison women or addicted men. She also reports more numerous "problem relationships" than either of the other two groups, (Tucker, 1979). The social isolation from both male and female friends has been noted before (Suffet & Brotman, 1976) but must be evaluated in a context of considerable support from a mother with whom the heroin addicted woman maintains a close relationship (Tucker, 1979).

Many have concluded that the addicted woman in treatment is "sicker" than a corresponding man (Burt *et al.*, 1979). Certainly, she is more likely to have contemplated or attempted suicide. The heroin addicted woman reports more physical illness than addicted men or comparison women (Tucker, 1979). She has lower self-esteem than either of the others and feels that people look down on her more than on an addicted man (Colten, 1979). In terms of specific personality measures, the heroin addicted woman differs from the addicted man in that she is less assertive and Machiavellian and more depressed and anxious. She is unlikely to attribute to herself either strong masculine or strong feminine characteristics, and thus is defined as undifferentiated with regard to gender identity (Colten, 1979).

It should be stressed that the "average addicted woman" just described is probably very different from the younger female student who is using marijuana. The student using marijuana is probably living an unconventional lifestyle and holding unconventional attitudes. Whether or not the venture into use of this illicit drug has serious long-range consequences is a matter of considerable debate (Kandel, 1980).

Users and Abusers of Prescribed Psychotropics

Persons who are using and abusing psychotropic drugs obtained by prescription are likely to be older, richer, and more often white than those using illicit drugs. They are also more numerous than users of illicit drugs and they are much more likely to be female. The drug with which they are most likely involved is a tranquilizer such as Valium, for which 57 million prescriptions were written between May 1976 and April 1977 in the United States alone (NIDA, 1978*a*). Cooperstock (1980) reports that 33% of the women aged 45-59 in her sample had prescriptions for tranquilizers, compared to fewer than 10% of the men; four times as many women as men in the 20-29 age group had prescriptions.

The physicians who wrote these prescriptions are most often general practitioners or internists and less frequently psychiatrists and neurologists. The forces that promote physicians to prescribe psychotropic drugs are not totally understood. Although some have suggested that the prescribing is for the most part appropriate and conservative (Mellinger *et al.*, 1974), others have determined that physician bias, whether economically (Waldron, 1977) or socially motivated (Cooperstock, 1978), plays at least a part. Elsewhere, I have argued that an unfortunate congruence between physician expectations regarding women as patients and sex differences in the behavior of patients leads physicians to prescribe psychotropic drugs to women more often than to men (Fidell, 1980). Further evidence of physician bias will not be reviewed here.

One of the more important sex differences in medical behavior is the greater number of visits by women to physicians. Indeed, some (Cooper, 1977) have argued that this sex difference alone accounts for the differences in the rates of prescription of these drugs. Women, on average, make about 58% of all physician visits (more during the reproductive years) but receive between 62% and 73% (estimates vary) of the prescriptions for psychotropic drugs. Cooperstock (1979) concludes that differences in rates of visits do not alone account for the prescribing data, whereas Kravitz (1975) reports that if differences in rates of visits due to pregnancy and the longer life span of women are controlled using regression, sex differences in number of visits disappear. Chien and Schneiderman (1975) report no difference in visit rates between middle-class women and men if visits related to reproduction are eliminated. It is important to realize that visits by women due to pregnancy or for a routine gynecological examination are mostly visits made to a gynecologist by healthy women who would not be expected to need psychotropic drugs. Since gynecologists are not the leading prescribers, this expectation is confirmed. Why, then, do women get prescriptions for psychotropics at a rate of 2:1 from their internists and general practitioners?

Women seem to report more numerous mental and physical health symptoms than do men (Phillips & Segal, 1969; Weissman, 1976), and those who report more numerous symptoms are more heavily involved with psychotropic drugs (Fidell, 1977). As Cooperstock (1979) has noted, it is extremely hard to decide whether the difference in reporting behavior is associated with real or perceived differences in mental and/or physical health. Resolution of this issue is critical to determination of the legitimacy of drug prescribing and drug using practices.

Many theories attempting to explain more numerously reported symptoms have been offered. Weissman (1976) and Gove and Tudor (1973) have concluded that greater stress among women produces real sex differences in mental health. Clancy and Gove (1974) studied response bias as a factor in women's admission of more numerous mental health symptoms and found that sex differences increased when response bias was controlled, leading again to speculation of real sex differences in mental health. Phillips and Segal (1969) doubted that mental health is worse among women and concluded, instead, that women have greater permission, because of sex stereotypes, to admit to emotional difficulties. Certainly, the expectation created by the stereotype that women are more emotional and dependent is consistent with this view. Yet another explanation was offered by Coser (1975), who suggested that more numerous psychological symptoms are found among women because, as the socioemotional experts for themselves and their families, they are expected to monitor and report them. Another sex difference in illness behavior may also be related. The woman who reports to her physician (at least for psychiatric problems) is more likely to have talked over her symptoms with four or five female friends or kin before the visit (Horwitz, 1977). During these discussions, not only will she have practiced reporting symptoms but also she may have noticed others and have gained some information regarding possible diagnoses, treatments, and the like. A man on a visit is unlikely to have discussed his problems with anyone but his spouse, if at all, and may, as a consequence, be much less aware, or at least verbal, concerning what has happened to him.

If sex differences in mental health are "real," then greater use of psychotropic drugs by women is probably legitimate. If, however, differences in symptom presentation are a result of differences in the sex stereotype, physicians should be taught to expect persons of different sex to behave differently and to adjust their prescribing practices accordingly.

Two other relationships between health and heavy use of psychotropic drugs, usually tranquilizers, deserve mention. It seems likely (Borgman, 1973; Fidell, 1981) that some people become heavily involved with psychotropic drugs during the course of prolonged, but inconclusive, attempts at medical diagnosis. Physicians and patients should be aware of the special risks for drug abuse at this time. Second, some patients with serious but chronic health problems report that tranquilizers may be used to help them adapt to the sick role, a role that involves considerably more dependency than adults normally assume (Cooperstock & Lennard, 1979). Perhaps without the drugs, greater independence could be achieved, even among those who are chronically ill.

Differences in personality in self-esteem (Borgman, 1973; Fidell, 1977), neuroticism (on the Eysenck Personality Inventory), and gender differentiation (Fidell, 1977); in rates of psychosocial problems (Lynn & Davis, 1971); and in psychic distress (Mellinger *et al.*, 974) have all been found between those who use and do not use psychotropic drugs. Generally, those who use psychotropic drugs, and use them more heavily, tend to be more neurotic and undifferentiated, with lower self-esteem and more numerous personal and social problems. It is not known, however, whether these differences are a cause or an effect of greater drug use. As Cooperstock (1980) points out, use of psychotropic drugs on a regular basis is related to decrements in cognitive and motor performance. Is social performance involved, as well?

Cooperstock and Lennard (1979) also found, however, a strong relationship between the use of drugs and the need to adjust to life situations that are otherwise unbearable. For men, these situations tended to center around employment; for women, they center around home and family. None of the respondents seemed particularly pleased with their reliance on drugs to adjust to some aspects of their lives, but they saw the consequences of not using them as much worse. Whether or not these persons would have scored differently from nonusers on personality measures remains unknown, but from their perspective their problems were, for the most part, structural rather than personal.

Among middle- and upper-middle-class persons, psychotropic drug use is remarkably *un*related to other demographic variables. There is some evidence that persons of either sex who are retired, housewives, or unemployed tend to be users (Cooperstock, 1979) but, again, the direction of causality is uncertain (do sick people work less frequently, or do those who work less become sick; some analyses of my data suggest the former), and the relationship is small. Similarly, there is a weak relationship between drug use and disrupted marital situations (greater use among those who are divorced, separated, and widowed), but the direction of causality is uncertain.

There is some evidence in the literature and in my data that parental modeling is associated with a child's use of psychotropic drugs. The relationship appears to be stronger between mothers and daughters, with higher rates of use seen in daughters of mothers who used psychotropic drugs (Kleinknecht & Smith-Scott, 1977) or alcohol. Father's use of drugs or alcohol was also related, but less strongly.

There are few or inappropriate treatment centers for the middle-class adult who is abusing psychotropic drugs. Yet, symptoms of physical dependence can be produced with use of even a relatively safe drug such as Valium if 30-40 mg are taken daily for 3-4 months. Unfortunately, withdrawal symptoms from Valium mimic the anxiety-type symptoms for which it was probably originally prescribed, so that distinguishing between the withdrawal and a return of original symptoms is difficult. The National Institute on Drug Abuse

(NIDA, 1978*b*) estimates that 1-2 million Americans have prescription-drug-related dependencies. Furthermore, the minor tranquilizers have become a leading method of suicide. In the mid-1970s, approximately 110,000 women, many over age 30, appeared in hospital emergency rooms with accidental or intentional drug overdoses, particularly Valium in combination with alcohol (from DAWN III, 1974-1975, as cited in Burt *et al.*, 1979).

Summary and Conclusion

There are some notable similarities between those who use and abuse illicit drugs or nonmedical psychotropics and those who use and abuse psychotropics by prescription. It may be that ease of contacting sources is a stronger determinant of which category of drug a person becomes involved with than other considerations. For the relatively more affluent middle- and upper-middle-class person, a physician may be more available, whereas for others, "street" sources are easier to contact. But whatever the other characteristics of the source, for both men and women the sex of the source is likely to be male. Men, either as pushers or physicians, initiate the use of and supply drugs to both men and women.

Correlates of use of drugs of whatever kind among women include lower self-esteem, a personality that tends to be undifferentiated with respect to gender identity, numerous physical and mental health symptoms, more frequently troubled psychosocial interactions (including more broken marriages), unemployment, and more frequently attempted or completed suicide. Correlates of use of drugs among men are similar except that the normal sex differences in self-esteem, rates of employment, and the like seem to hold for the drug using and abusing population as well.

A notable sex difference among substance abusers is the availability of treatment. Many treatment centers are unattractive to women addicted to illicit drugs because they do not provide the special services women, especially mothers, need. For middle-class women on Valium, the same centers are totally inappropriate.

Overall, it would appear that drug abusing persons are less personally or socially advantaged than are their nonabusing counterparts, whether they remain within the middle class or lower. Women, as is generally true, appear to have more numerous problems than men, even if they are similar on such characteristics as class and type of drug used or abused. In other words, sex differences seem to remain even if the overlapping curves are shifted up or down an economic continuum. How much of what kind of a sex difference is real and how much is attributable to learned stereotypic behavior remains uncertain.

Acknowledgments

The author wishes to express her appreciation for the special help she received in gathering reference materials from both Dr. Louise Richards, research psychologist with the National Institute on Drug Abuse, and Marsha Farrell, a very talented student.

References

Bentler, P. M., Lettieri, D. J., & Austin, G. A. *Data analysis strategies and designs for substance abuse research* (National Institute on Drug Abuse Stock No. 017-024-00562-2). Washington, D.C.: US Gov. Printing Office, 1976.

Binion, V. J. A descriptive comparison of the families of origin of women heroin users and nonusers. In M. B. Hall (Ed.), *Addicted women: Family dynamics, self-perceptions, and support systems.* Services Research Monograph Series. (DHEW Publication No. [ADM] 80-762). Rockville, Maryland: National Institute on Drug Abuse, 1979.

Borgman, R. D. Medication abuse by middle-aged women. *Social Casework,* 1973, *54*(9), 526-532.

Burt, M. R., Glynn, T. J., & Sowder, B. J. *Psychosocial characteristics of drug-abusing women.* (DHEW Publication No. [ADM] 80-917). Rockville, Maryland: National Institute on Drug Abuse, 1979.

Chien, A., & Schneiderman, L. J. A comparison of health care utilization by husbands and wives. *Journal of Community Health,* 1975, *1,* 118-126.

Cisin, I., Miller, J. D., & Harrell, A. V. *Highlights from the national survey on drug abuse* (National Institute on Drug Abuse, Stock No. 017-024-00725-1). Washington, D.C.: US Gov. Printing Office, 1977.

Clancy, K., & Gove, W. Sex differences in mental health: An analysis of response bias in self-reports. *American Journal of Sociology,* 1974, *80*(1), 205-216.

Colten, M. E. A descriptive and comparative analysis of self-perceptions and attitudes of heroin addicted women. In M. B. Hall (Ed.), *Addicted women: Family dynamics, self-perceptions, and support systems.* Services Research Monograph Series. (DHEW Publication No. [ADM] 80-762). Rockville, Maryland: National Institute on Drug Abuse, 1979.

Cooper, J. R. *Sedative-hypnotic drugs: Risks and benefits.* (DHEW Publication No. [ADM] 78-592). Rockville, Maryland: National Institute on Drug Abuse, 1977.

Cooperstock, R. Current trends in prescribed psychotropic drug use. In R. J. Gibbins, Y. Israel, H. Kalant, R. E. Popham, W. Schmidt, & R. G. Smart (Eds.), *Research advances in alcohol and drug problems* (Vol. 3). New York: Wiley, 1976.

Cooperstock, R. Sex differences in psychotropic drug use. *Social Science and Medicine,* 1978, *12*(3), 179-186.

Cooperstock, R. A review of women's psychotropic drug use. *Canadian Journal of Psychiatry,* 1979, *24*(1), 29-34.

Cooperstock, R. Special problems of psychotropic drug use among women. *Canada's Mental Health,* 1980, *28*(2), 3-5.

Cooperstock, R., & Lennard, H. L. Some social meanings of tranquilizer use. *Sociology of Health and Illness,* 1979, *1*(3), 331-347.

Coser, R. L. Why bother? Is research on issues of women's health worthwhile? In V. Olesen (Ed.), *Women and their health: Research implications for a new era* (HEW Publication No. HRA 77-3138). Washington, D.C.: U.S. Department of Health, Education and Welfare, 1975.

Densen-Gerber, J. The woman's marathon. In J. Densen-Gerber (Ed.), *We mainline dreams: The Odyssey House story.* Garden City, New York: Doubleday, 1973.

Fidell, L. S. *Psychotropic drug use by women: Health, attitudinal, personality, and demographic correlates.* Paper presented at the annual meeting of the American Psychological Association, San Francisco, California, August 1977.

Fidell, L. S. Sex role stereotypes and the American physician. *Psychology of Women Quarterly,* 1980, *4*(3), 313-331.

Fidell, L. S. Sex differences in psychotropic drug use. *Professional Psychology,* 1981, *12*(1), 156-162.

Fishburne, P. M., Abelson, H. I., & Cisin, I. *National survey on drug abuse: Main findings, 1979.* Rockville, Maryland: National Institute on Drug Abuse, 1979.

Glenn, W. A., & Richards, L. G. *Recent surveys of nonmedical drug use: A compendium of abstracts.* Rockville, Maryland: National Institute on Drug Abuse, 1974.

Gove, W., & Tudor, J. F. Adult sex roles and mental illness. *American Journal of Sociology,* 1973, *78*(4), 812-835.

Green, D. E., & MacDonald, M. *Women and psychoactive drug use: An interim annotated bibliography.* Ontario, Canada: The Addiction Research Foundation, 1976.

Horwitz, A. The pathways into psychiatric treatment: Some differences between men and women. *Journal of Health and Social Behavior,* 1977, *18*(2), 169-178.

Kandel, D. B. Drug and drinking behavior among youth. *Annual Review of Sociology,* 1980, *6,* 235-285.

Kleinknecht, R. A., & Smith-Scott, J. Prevalence, sources and uses of tranquilizers among college students. *Journal of Drug Education,* 1977, *7*(3), 249-257.

Kleinman, P. H., & Lukoff, I. F. Ethnic differences in factors related to drug use. *Journal of Health and Social Behavior,* 1978, *19,* 190-199.

Kravitz, J. Sex differences in health care: Social survey research methods. In V. Olesen (Ed.), *Women and their health: Research implications for a new era* (HEW Publication No. HRA 77-3138). Washington, D.C.: U.S. Department of Health, Education and Welfare, 1975.

Lynn, L. S., & Davis, M. S. The use of psychotherapeutic drugs by middle-aged women. *Journal of Health and Social Behavior,* 1971, *12,* 331-340.

Mellinger, G. D., Balter, M. B., Parry, H. J., Manheimer, D. I., & Cisin, I. H. An overview of psychotherapeutic drug use in the United States. In E. Josephson & E. E. Carroll (Eds.), *Drug use: Epidemiological and sociological approaches.* Washington, D.C.: Hemisphere, 1974.

National Institute on Drug Abuse. *Top 26 problem drugs in the U.S.* (NIDA Capsules.) Washington, D.C.: Author, 1978. (a)

National Institute on Drug Abuse. *Women and prescription drugs.* (NIDA Capsules.) Washington, D.C.: Author, 1978. (b)

National Institute on Drug Abuse. *Addicted women: Family dynamics, self-perceptions, and support systems.* Services Research Monograph Series. (DHEW Publication No. [ADM] 80-762). Rockville, Maryland: Author, 1979.

Nehemkis, A., Macari, M. A., & Lettieri, D. J. (Eds.). *Drug abuse instrument handbook* (National Institute on Drug Abuse, Stock No. 017-024-00533-9). Washington, D.C.: US Gov. Printing Office, 1975.

New York State Division of Substance Abuse Services. *Drug abuse in New York State: A report on the nonmedical use of drugs among the New York State household population, 1978.* Albany, New York: Author, 1978.

Phillips, D. C., & Segal, B. E. Sexual status and psychiatric symptoms. *American Sociological Review,* 1969, *34,* 58-72.

Prather, J. E., & Fidell, L. S. Drug use and abuse among women: An overview. *The International Journal of the Addictions,* 1978, *13*(6), 863-885.

Suffet, F., & Brotman, R. Female drug use: Some observations. *The International Journal of the Addictions*, 1976, *11*(1), 19-33.

Tucker, M. B. A description and comparative analysis of the social support structure of heroin-addicted women. In M. B. Hall (Ed.), *Addicted women: Family dynamics, self-perceptions, and support systems*. Services Research Monograph Series. (DHEW Publication No [ADM] 80-762). Rockville, Maryland: National Institute on Drug Abuse, 1979.

Waldron, I. Increased prescribing of Valium, Librium, and other drugs: An example of the influence of economic and social factors on the practice of medicine. *International Journal of Health Services*, 1977, 7(1), 37-61.

Weissman, M. M. Depressed women: Traditional and nontraditional therapies. In J. L. Claghorn (Ed.), *Successful psychotherapy*. New York: Brunner/Mazel, 1976.

11

ANNE CAMPBELL

Gender and Crime

The Epistemology of Female Criminality and Psychopathology

It has become almost a truism to point out that psychopathology has assumed a far greater importance in the explanation of female criminality than it has in male criminality. The reasons for this are partly rooted in epistemological tradition, partly in the prevailing view of females as emotionally childlike, and, certainly, they are partly related to the fact that a criminal woman has denied not only the laws of society but the norms of her sex role. For many years, it was this latter deviance that provoked the most intense interest among both theoreticians and practitioners of criminal justice.

Lombroso and Ferrero (1895), fired by the contemporary fascination with genetics and natural selection, conducted studies of Italian criminals of both sexes. Male criminals were considered to be atavistic throwbacks to an earlier stage of evolution. This was evidenced by the presence of certain physical signs such as cranium size, moles, hairiness, and heavy musculature. Alas, a similar analysis of female criminals revealed an incidence of atavism of only 14%. Undeterred, they argued that this was because women were less evolved than men and consequently were not capable of degenerating so far. The small percentage of born female criminals they did find were characterized as particularly vicious—a fact that could be accounted for by their similarity to males: "Her maternal sense is weak because psychologically and an-

ISBN: 0-12-050350-6

thropologically she belongs more to the male than to the female sex [Lombroso & Ferrero, 1895, p. 153]." So began the tradition of viewing criminal women as pseudo-males, one which has continued to this day.

At the same time, Freud (1925/1973) was turning his attention to the psychology, rather than the anthropology, of women. In his famous *Biology as Destiny* thesis, he characterized women as naturally more passive and dependent than men. Woman's passivity is demonstrated by her role in the sexual act, and her dependence on male approval begins early, with her rivalry with her mother for the affection of her father. If, however, such a transfer of affection to the father should not occur, the girl is left in limbo, either desperately trying to attain male approval through promiscuity or rejecting it entirely in favor of homosexuality. Since, Freud noted, the formation of conscience is naturally impaired in the female, those girls who fail to turn their love to their father are free to commit any moral breach without guilt:

> In the absence of fear of castration the chief motive is lacking which leads boys to surmount the Oedipal complex. Girls remain in it for an indeterminate length of time; they demolish it late and even so, incompletely. In these circumstances the formation of the superego must suffer; it cannot attain the strength and independence which gives it cultural significance [Freud 1925/1973, p. 163].

So was laid the basis for the continued view of women as childlike and amoral, of women as *naturally* passive, of female criminality as equated with promiscuity, and of the importance of childhood as determining adult criminality. Both these fundamental orientations attracted much interest in the years that followed.

In the biology of crime, Lombroso and Ferrero (1895) set a tradition that many are still loath to relinquish. Cowie, Cowie, and Slater (1968), in a study of English approved schoolgirls, consider many variables, ranging from IQ and health through to family size, but ultimately come down in favor of a genetic explanation of female delinquency. With no supportive data of their own, they claim:

> It is more natural to suppose that the male-female difference, both in delinquency rates and in the forms that delinquency takes, would be closely connected with masculine and feminine patterns of development of personality. This again would be related to biological and somatic differences including differences in hormonal balance; and these would at the ultimate remove be derived from chromosomal differences between the sexes [Cowie *et al.*, 1968, p. 170].

They go on to claim that delinquent girls would be expected to show a higher rate of XXY genetic makeup. In evidence of this, they point to the fact that delinquent girls are large for their age, that psychiatrists have remarked on their masculine traits, and that prostitutes show high rates of homosexuality.

Studies of the chromosomal composition of female offenders has completely failed to support any such view (Kaplan, cited in Ferdon, 1971).

Another line taken by biological theorists is the relationship between crime and body type. Kretschmer (1925) and Sheldon, Hartt, and McDermott (1949) put forth the view that mesomorphs (muscular, heavy build) tended to be boisterous, aggressive, and undisciplined and, as such, were the predators in man's hunting history. Little wonder in contemporary society they were overrepresented in delinquent populations. Since the data offered in support of this view have been measurement of weight:height ratio, and given that these measures have been collected in community homes where the girls get little exercise, have high-carbohydrate diets, and are prone to depressive "food bingeing," it comes as no surprise that some authors have found many delinquent girls to be mesomorphic (Cowie *et al.*, 1968; Epps & Parnell, 1952; Richardson, 1969).

The biologists found a new avenue of exploration in female criminality—the relationship of crime to the menstrual cycle. The nature of the implied causality was never clear, but it was suggested that prior to and during menstrual periods, the disturbance of the hormonal system causes a host of misbehaviors, from clumsiness to crime. However, Dalton (1961), Epps (in Gibbens & Prince, 1962), and Healy (1925) were not able to offer substantial proof of such a link. If we were also to accept Pollak's (1961) suggestion that pregnancy and menopause are similarly hormonally disturbed times, we would predict a crime rate that hopefully we are never likely to witness.

The original confusion that Lombroso and Ferrero (1895) began between female gender and feminine behaviors or attitudes reemerged in the view that women who do not hold stereotypically female views must be psychologically disturbed (Cohen, 1955; Cowie *et al.*, 1968; Morris, 1964). Cochrane (1971) and Widom (1980) have investigated the extent to which criminal women tend to hold masculine values and self-concepts. In a time of shifting ideas of sex roles, many of the psychological tools employed are outdated. The failure of some writers to recognize social class as an important factor is also suspect. More importantly, those who began this school of thought are reactionary in their views and would like to see women revert to more passive and less unorthodox behavior (Cochrane, 1971; Hart, 1975). Those who oppose this view and attempt to show that criminal women are not, in fact, more masculine than controls are tacitly accepting the view that male and female attitudes *are* different, instead of turning their attention away from psychological factors and investigating the social and economic variables that have been long accepted as paramount in explanations of male crime.

Freud's legacy to female criminality has perhaps been even greater than Lombroso and Ferrero's. In the work of W. I. Thomas (1923/1967), we see biology as psychological destiny, with the female of the species at once revered and damned. In Thomas's scheme, human behavior is guided by wishes: the desire for new experience, for security, for response, and for recognition. These wishes correspond to features of the nervous system expressed in the universal instincts of anger, fear, love, and the will to gain power, respectively. However, a woman's need for response (love), Thomas assumed to be far greater than a man's. When appropriately controlled by society, this elevates women to earthly madonnas. When uncontrolled, it allows women to become promiscuous. In so doing, they lose the only worth that they have (their self-sacrificing love) and, consequently, Thomas argued, it was important for the prevention of delinquency to teach young girls sexual restraint. The themes of female criminality as entirely sexual, combined with the greater need for love among girls, not only stemmed naturally from Freud's writing but became a familiar theme right up to the present day.

Pollak (1961) continued the tradition of basing full-scale theories on the supposed inherent nature of women. His major thesis rested on the contention that the true rate of female criminality is masked by underreporting of female offenses, that the nature of their crimes is less detectable, and that women receive more leniency from the police and courts than men. All of these allegations (many of which have been shown to be true) stemmed from the fundamental presumption that women are inherently deceitful. Because of this, they are able to control men, instigate them to criminal activity, and, finally, murder them without detection. Their natural capacity for deceitfulness arises from their experience of the sexual act: "Not enough attention has been paid to the physiological fact that man must achieve an erection in order to perform the sex act and will not be able to hide his failure . . . Woman's body, however, permits such pretense to a certain degree and lack of orgasm does not prevent her ability to participate in the sex act [Pollak, 1961, p. 10]."

Blos (1957), Cowie *et al.* (1968), Konopka (1966), Morris (1964), Richardson (1969), Riege (1972), and many others have approached the female delinquent as driven by a need for love that has been denied. Konopka (1966) views this need for love as common to all adolescent girls and simply more visible in delinquents. Blos (1957) takes a Freudian line, arguing for the absence or inadequacy of the father figure in the girl's early life. The others view the disrupted home as having a particularly important role to play in female delinquency. All view delinquency in girls as implicitly sexual by noting the number of girls rather than boys institutionalized as being in need of supervision. This bias in the juvenile justice system has been examined and condemned by many writers (Campbell, 1981; Chesney-Lind, 1973; Sarri, 1976; Smart, 1977). The double standard that has been and still is applied to female sexuality is now visible, although most writers of the 1960s and before were quite unperturbed at institutionalizing girls for behavior that in males would be considered a sign of healthy development. Those writers who did not simply assume the equation of delinquency with sexuality often reinterpreted other crimes as sexual ones either in legal process (Chesney-Lind, 1973) or in psychological theory (Blos, 1957; Gibbens & Prince, 1962).

The particular importance of love to girls is justified in various ways. Many assumed it to be inherent in the female psyche. Others discussed maternal deprivation in terms of the absence of suitable role models. Cowie *et al.* (1968) noted the increased incidence of broken homes among female delinquents and concluded that girls required a greater impelling force from the environment (such as a disrupted family) because they were by nature more immune than boys to delinquency.

Only Smart (1977) made the observation that girls by virtue of their historical position as chattels have indeed needed love in a purely economic and material sense. Being loved guaranteed their continued role as daughter, wife, mother, or mistress on which their economic well-being depended. Cultural forces in socialization, education, literature, and social norms have conspired to encourage girls to spend a disproportionate amount of time in activities designed to promote the goal of being loved—cosmetic self-improvement, care-taking activities, and pursuing boyfriends or husbands (McRobbie, 1978). The importance of being loved does not lie in the genetic makeup of females, in their inherent nature, or in their delicate psyche, but in the social and cultural superstructure that has grown up around their economic position. The enduring stress that has been placed on the role of love and sexuality in the psychopathology of *female* criminality is more a reflection of its importance in society's view of women than as a causal factor in or expression of female crime.

Criminal Women and Psychopathology

The undue stress that has been placed on the role of psychopathology in female criminals has, in recent years, provoked controversy. Some of the arguments attack the importance of mental illness as a causal factor, others suggest that rates of apparent psychopathology in women criminals may be artifactual.

Denial of Relevance of Psychopathology

The view that psychopathology is irrelevant stresses female crime as a personally meaningful reaction to the same material and social factors as among men—poor housing, little education, and lack of opportunity. This view has perhaps understressed (even implicitly denied) that psychopathology plays any role. Less extremely, some writers argue that although psychopathology may be higher among the criminal population than among normals, the relative rates among men and women are not substantially different from those in the community. Evidence now suggests that women do have higher rates of mental illness than do men. Women are especially numerous in the categories of neuroses and depression, and relatively underrepresented in personality disorders and drug and alcohol addiction. This same pattern, it is argued, is reflected in the criminal population and therefore negates the role of psychopathology as an important causative factor in one sex rather than the other.

Crime and Psychopathology as Functionally Equivalent

It has been argued that the socialization process for boys allows for the acting-out of stress in the form of rough and tumble play, fighting, and so on, whereas girls learn to direct their aggression onto themselves (see Maccoby & Jacklin, 1974). That men seem to be overrepresented in the more visible forms of psychopathology and women in the more introspective ones (depression and neuroses) seems to confirm this. Bertrand (1973) has argued that mental illness may be the female functional equivalent of crime in males, resulting in the higher number of men in prison and women in psychiatric hospitals.

Differential Labeling

Work by Broverman, Broverman, Clarkson, Rosengrantz, and Vogel (1975) demonstrated that among clinicians, the concept of the healthy male approximated to that of healthy adult more closely than did healthy female. Even healthy women were described as more excitable in minor crises, more easily hurt, more emotional, and less independent than a healthy adult. The higher rate of mental illness among women may then be due to differential labeling by clinicians. This would be true in a prison setting as well as in the community—arguably more so, since female criminals by virtue of their rarity are more likely to be judged deviant than are males.

Differential Expression

Phillips and Segal (1969) similarly argue that women far more than men are willing to admit to illness. The male ethic still demands that men grin and bear it. Even in the context of a routine psychiatric screening interview in prison, women may be more likely to admit to symptoms that men might deny. Consequently, they would more frequently be diagnosed as mentally ill. Perhaps some of the debate may be answered by considering the rates of mental illness among female and male criminals respectively (bearing in mind, at the same time, the possible artifacts suggested by Phillips & Segal, 1969). However, before doing so, there are some important restrictions on the validity of the conclusions that can be drawn from such an exercise.

Any correlation between crime and psychopathology for either sex cannot indicate cause. Mental illness may occur as a response to admission to prison, rather than as a cause of criminality. The criminal act and the mental illness may be contemporaneous responses to a particular life stress. In the majority of cases, studies select an imprisoned population and then screen for psychopathology. (A few work in the reverse manner.) In neither sample are the two factors a priori discrete. Criminological studies have shown that the imprisoned population is not a random sample of the criminal population. Age, sex, race, employment, nature of the crime, and criminal history are all likely to affect the decision as to who goes to prison and who is released back into the community. Similarly, factors such as the patient's diagnosis, his dangerousness to himself and others, his ability to fend for himself, his age, and the extent to which the hospital can "cure" such an illness are likely to be important in deciding who is admitted to hospital on an inpatient basis. The studies, therefore, sample institution inmates. These may not be typical of most criminals or most victims of mental illness. Also, the two factors interact. Criminality may affect a decision as to whether or not to hospitalize a patient, just as psychopathology may affect a judge's decision as to an offenders disposal.

Levels of diagnostic reliability have frequently been shown to be low. For example, in studies reviewed by Widom (1978), levels of sociopathy in a female prison population vary from 2.2% to 65%. The variability in diagnostic criteria makes comparison of different studies very hazardous.

Gross figures on psychopathology among prison populations implicitly treat crime as a homogeneous phenomenon. It seems unlikely that sophisticated tax-defrauders are similar to rapists in motivation, attitudes, social demographic characteristics, and in the importance that psychopathology plays in their crimes. This clouds the issue of the precise relationship between forms of psychopathology and types of criminal behavior both within and between the sexes.

Changing policies regarding the disposition of offenders and the mentally ill make any comparison over time problematic. Biles and Mulligan (1973) have shown that where the mental hospital population is high, the prison population will be low, and vice versa. They suggest that "the data are consistant with the view, also canvassed by Penrose, that the relative use of mental hospitals or prisons for the segregation of deviants reflects different styles of administration [Biles & Mulligan, 1973, p. 279]." The trend in the United States in the latter half of the 1970s was to divert psychiatrically disturbed offenders from the criminal justice system to mental hospitals (Zitrin, Hardesty, Burdock, & Drossman, 1976). The interaction between the two agencies produces research and data collection problems of its own. For example, some mentally ill offenders are found unfit to plead and as such do not appear in conviction statistics at all. With these caveats in mind, we can turn to a consideration of the available data on crime, psychopathology, and gender.

Most writers agree that women have a higher rate of mental illness in the community than do men (Chesler, 1974; Gove & Tudor, 1973). Precisely how much higher depends on the criteria of mental illness used. Community survey studies based on responses to structured interviews give a low for men of 13.1% (Hare & Shaw, 1965) and a high of 31.0% (Bradburn & Caplovitz, 1965). For women, the rates vary between 22.9% (Hare & Shaw, 1965) and 54.0% (Bradburn & Caplovitz, 1965). Of the studies reviewed by Gove and Tudor (1973), the median for males is 20.3% and for women, 34.2%. However, community studies that have employed clinical evaluations have found male rates between 1.7% and 6.0% and female rates between 3.7% and 15.6% (see Gove & Tudor, 1973). These figures are perhaps most comparable to those derived from clinical evaluations of imprisoned men and women.

This higher female rate is substantiated by figures on admissions to mental hospitals. The rate of first admissions to mental hospitals in 1967 was 671 males per 100,000 population, compared to 834 females per 100,000. As recipients of psychiatric care in general hospitals, females exceed males by 3413 to 2029 per 100,000. Even studies of visits to private psychiatrists put women ahead by between 18% and 32% (all figures from Gove & Tudor, 1973).

Few studies have systematically investigated psychiatric morbidity in male and female criminals. Petrich (1976) reviews literature pertaining to general levels of morbidity in criminal populations. In imprisoned felons, early studies gave a wide range of figures, from 12% (Glueck, 1918) to 82% (Anderson, 1919). More recent studies would indicate that between 10% and 30% of all prison inmates manifest psychiatric illness (see review by Petrich, 1976). However, studies of jail populations (unincarcerated felons) have given figures of 4.6% (Petrich, 1976) through 18% (Bromberg & Thompson, 1937) to a high of 52% to 81% (Cloninger & Guze, 1970, 1973; Guze, Tuason, Gatfield, Stewart, & Picken, 1962). The high variability of such figures clearly casts doubt on their reliability and suggests important differences in the application of diagnostic criteria by the different researchers. With respect to females particularly, early studies report psychiatric morbidity rates in female prisoners of 21% to 28% (Epps, 1951), 55% (Pailthorpe, 1932), and 73%

(Glueck, 1918). More recent studies have offered figures of 48.9% (Woodside, 1962) to 100% (Cloninger & Guze, 1970).

The most meaningful data come from studies in which the same authors have investigated male and female populations. Petrich (1976) investigated 102 males and 20 females in a metropolitan county jail. The males received a total of 212 diagnoses (a mean of 2.08 diagnoses per man) whereas the females received 33 diagnoses (a mean of 1.65 per woman). This would suggest a higher rate of psychiatric morbidity among males. However, studies by Guze and his associates (Guze, Goodwin, & Crane, 1969; Guze *et al.*, 1962) and by Cloninger and Guze (1970, 1973) investigated 223 men and 66 women on parole in Missouri. Men received 310 diagnoses ($\overline{X} = 1.39$) to women's 142 ($\overline{X} = 2.15$), indicating a higher rate of psychiatric illness in females. In the Cloninger and Guze (1970) study, every woman received at least one diagnosis, which would suggest a very liberal use of diagnostic criteria.

We can also investigate the extent to which the *pattern* of psychological disturbance among criminal men and women relates to that in the community. The results of three studies are reported in Table 11.1. The first column gives the percentages of males and females in each diagnostic category and thus indicates the typically male and female disorders in the community. The results from Petrich and the studies by Cloninger and Guze give the percentage of offenders within each sex receiving the various diagnoses. Both studies find, as would be expected from the general population, a higher rate of depression among women and of antisocial personality-psychopathy in men. Both studies found a reversal of the national trend with respect to alcoholism, with criminal women showing higher rates than men. This may well be the result of the criminal justice system sanctioning women more severely for the kinds of public offenses associated with drunkenness. Rates of schizophrenia, neurosis, and drug abuse fluctuate in the two studies. The results also indicate that neurotics are underrepresented in the criminal, as compared to the psychiatric, population, but criminals do show high rates of alcoholism, drug addiction, and antisocial personality. The role of schizophrenia in criminality is unclear from these studies.

A final route in attempting to piece together the scant information on criminality and psychiatric illness is by looking at studies that have investigated criminal arrest rates of psychiatric patients. The most relevant data for the present discussion are those concerning arrests *prior* to hospitalization, if we assume that hospital discharge implies that the original problem is either cured or in remission.

Rappeport and Lassen (1966) compared the arrest rates of 2129 female patients in 1959 for 5 years prior and subsequent to hospitalization. They

TABLE 11.1
Rates of Psychopathology in the Community and in the Criminal Population by Sex and Diagnoses

	General hospitals 1966-1968 (Incidence of diagnosis)				Jail population (Petrich, 1976)		Felons (Cloninger & Guze, 1970, 1973)	
	Absolute nos. cases (male and female)	Percentage of total	Percentage of category female	Percentage of category male	Percentage of all females so diagnosed	Percentage of all males so diagnosed	Percentage of all females so diagnosed	Percentage of all males so diagnosed
Female disorders								
Neuroses	378,289	24.9	70	30	5	2	11	12
Schizophrenia	158,689	10.5	61	39	25	31	1.5	1
Depression[a]	58,975	3.9	64-69	31-36	15	0	6	0
Secondary depression	—	—	—	—	20	17	—	—
Male disorders								
Antisocial or psychopathic personality[b]	143,142	9.4	40	60	33	45	65	73
Drug addiction	11,004	.1	36	64	15	51	26	5
Alcohol addiction	69,183	4.6	25	75	30	26	47	43

Data from Petrich (1976) and Cloninger and Guze (1970, 1973).
[a] Includes manic and psychotic.
[b] Includes all personality disorders.

argue that female patients have a higher rate of aggravated assault than the general population. However, prior to hospitalization, significant differences appear on only two of the five annual comparisons. Subsequent to hospitalization, arrest rates rise, with four out of five comparisons significant. However, there are few differences between patients and the general population with respect to murder, robbery, burglary, and larceny.

Of all those arrested prior to hospitalization, 41% were alcoholics, 41% schizophrenics. There were no arrests among those diagnosed as acute brain syndrome, psychophysiological reactions, personality trait disturbances, or sociopathic personality. The absence of these last two categories from those arrested is particularly surprising in light of Cloninger and Guze's claim to have found sociopathy in 65% of imprisoned women. Perhaps courts are more willing to accept schizophrenia as a basis for hospitalization than personality disturbance or sociopathy (although by no means all of the patients were admitted because of committing a crime). To keep these figures in perspective, it is important to note that arrest rates were much lower for female patients than for male patients. The highest arrest rates were 14% for females, 52% for males.

Zitrin *et al.* (1976), in their study of criminal behavior in mental patients, find precisely opposite results. Compared to the population at large, sex differences in crimes committed by mental patients showed that women patients were underrepresented in the categories of assault and burglary, although somewhat overrepresented in robbery. Although mental patients were found to be arrested for crimes at a higher rate than the general population in major United States cities, in some cases their crime rate was lower than that for the catchment area of the hospital to which they were admitted (notably for murder and robbery). Significance levels are not given, and absolute arrest rates are not broken down by sex.

Steadman and Halfon (1971) studied the arrest and diagnostic categories of women involved in the repercussions of the Baxstrom case. The Baxstrom case involved individuals who had been placed in hospitals for the criminally insane and had served beyond the maximum prison sentence for their crime. They were then transferred to state mental institutions. Proportionately more women than men were originally convicted of offenses against public health and morals and miscellaneous offenses such as vagrancy, intoxication, and disorderly conduct. Diagnoses showed more men than women to be suffering from paranoid schizophrenia (41.7% versus 21.3%) and other forms of schizophrenia (36.2% versus 34%), whereas women outnumbered men in psychosis with mental deficiency (21.3% versus 7.5%) and psychopathy (11% versus 9%). This psychopathy figure is once again substantially lower than that claimed by Cloninger and Guze (1970). Cloninger and Guze's criteria for a diagnosis of sociopathy rested on the individual displaying two of the following characteristics in addition to a history of trouble with the police: excessive fighting, school delinquency, poor job record, a period of wanderlust, being a runaway, or a history of prostitution (Guze, 1976). In a group of criminal women, such a set of criteria appear to be tautological. Also, a diagnosis of uncomplicated sociopathy was only given to 19% of the women.

The figures we have examined lead, sadly, to the conclusion that any conclusion would be premature on the basis of the available data. The absence of control groups in many of the studies and the variability of the diagnostic criteria account for the wild fluctuations in the figures. We must still await comprehensive data using male and female populations both within prison and the community with appropriate controls for social class and other important demographic characteristics. A tentative hypothesis might be that the pattern of psychopathology among male and female criminals parallels that found in the community although the actual numbers of both sexes evidencing psychopathology might be higher. Even such a finding would have to be qualified with the caveat that rates of apparent mental illness in women both in the community and in prison may be artifactual and reflect more about diagnostic practices and the female stereotype than about the causes of crime.

Smart (1977) offers a warning against too hastily accepting a pathological model of crime that some of the researchers here reviewed might do well to consider. A mental illness model presumes criminal action to be "irrational, illogical and without meaning to the actor [Smart, 1977, p. 147]"; it focuses attention on individual treatment rather than societal change and, perhaps most importantly, it views the socioeconomic structure of society as having little or no meaning for the offender. Other theoretical positions are available that attend to these factors, and it is to these that we now turn.

Other Approaches to Female Crime

In many Western countries, the crime rate for women has been increasing even faster than that for men (Adler, 1975; Simon, 1975). This is particularly true of robbery, larceny, burglary, fraud, and gun possession. Rates of violence among women have also risen, but much less dramatically.

In 1975, Adler published *Sisters in Crime*, a book in which she suggested that the increase in female crime rates may be related to the fact that women are taking a much more active part in society and new opportunities for crime have opened up as a result. Since that time, the majority of research and theorizing in the area of female crime has addressed itself to this issue. Much of the work has attempted to show that criminal women are not in fact "liberated" and that the women's movement is therefore an insufficient explanation of their criminal behavior. Measures of "liberation" have included demographic information on marriage, children, and employment, questionnaires on values, life goals, and social etiquette. Adler (1980) has stated that such measures are irrelevant since *liberation,* in her original argument, referred not to subjective experience or to expressed attitudes but to opportunities for crime in women's day-to-day lives. Similarly, her thesis by its nature depends on longitudinal data showing that women's lives are relatively more open to criminal opportunity than they were two decades ago. Such data are extremely difficult to collect after the fact. The problem is compounded by the fact that crime statistics over the years are not necessarily comparable. Definitions of criminal behavior change, and police practices toward women (among others) have probably altered. For example, the rate of cautioning might have dropped and the rate of prosecution might have risen. Women may simply have become involved in more "visible" crimes than heretofore. The question, therefore, of the link between female crime and women's emancipation is likely to remain unsolved, at least at an empirical level. It is probably fair to say that most studies suggest that female criminals are not as "liberated" in their attitudes as are middle-class controls. The relevance of such a finding is unclear, and it does not address the issue of whether criminal women are relatively more emancipated than they were 20 years ago.

At a political level, however, the question is likely to rage for some time. Feminists have objected strongly to the emphasis that Adler's work has placed on women as criminals rather than as victims and to both the suggestion that liberation may entail antisocial or negative repercussions and the stress that has been placed on the causes of female crime rather than to the prejudicial treatment of female criminals in the criminal justice system (Loving & Olson, 1976).

Other research has dissected the particular position of women in the community and has attempted to show that differences in sex role, socialization practices, and self-concept may lie at the heart of the lower crime rate of women. Such research usually includes some reference to the changes that we are currently experiencing in these spheres and suggests that the result may well be the increase we now witness in female crime rates. Cassel and Clayton (1961), Cochrane (1971), Maas (1966), and Widom (1980) have looked at the self-concept of female offenders. Although Cochrane (1971) found that they were "outside the normal limits of female behavior [p. 78]," the other studies reported that prisoners were not, on the whole, any more masculine than were the controls.

Hoffman-Bustamante (1973) and Simon (1975) have analyzed female crime in terms of the social roles occupied by women and the extent to which they can be exploited for criminal purposes. The high shoplifting rate among women can be seen in terms of the fact that in their day-to-day lives, women are more exposed to this temptation than are men. Conversely, their low rate of involvement in burglary may well be due to the facts that until recently women went out alone at night less often than men and that in the course of their upbringing they would be less likely to acquire the necessary skills. The middle-class woman who handles family finances is more likely to commit credit card offenses or to forge checks than her working-class counterpart. Similarly, female embezzlers are often middle-class women who steal from charities—which are rarely audited. The pattern of homicide among women shows that the victims (lovers, husbands, children) as well as the modus operandi (household implements such as knives or poison and guns that do not require any physical strength) were closely tied to the female role (Ward, Jackson, & Ward, 1968).

Attention has also been paid to the traditional differences in socialization given to the two sexes. The greater protectiveness accorded to females has meant that they spend less time outside the home and so are less often open to the temptations and opportunities that face boys (Adler, 1975). Also, it is argued that females are reared to be more conforming to the moral codes of society. However, evidence reviewed by Al-Issa (1980) suggests that girls and boys are very similar in their moral development. Other writers (Cloward & Ohlin, 1960; Morris, 1964) have suggested that girls' goals are often related to affectional relationships whereas boys are raised to seek status in a wider society. Consequently, girls more often come to the attention of juvenile courts for their sexual behavior whereas boys appear more often because of criminal offenses. As has already been pointed out, such differences now appear to be more related to double standards of sexual behavior in society than to the actual rates of promiscuity of boys and girls. Juvenile girls in the United States and Britain show an even higher rate of involvement in crime than their older counterparts. Research that has been conducted into prostitution has pointed to the economic motives that seem more important than pathology. At the same time, other authors were noting the new economic stress that has been placed on women. The increase in women as heads of households, the breakdown of marriage, and the declining economic condition have all made it harder for some sections of the female population to make ends meet. This, they argue, accounts for the increase in crimes for profit by females.

These arguments share certain common factors. They implicitly address the increase in female crime over recent years and attempt to explain it in terms of concomitant changes in the position of women. They also, with the exception of Hoffman-Bustamante and Smart, tend to see the dependent variable—crime—as a homogeneous phenomenon. In general, they fail to consider the already available theories of male crime as possibly applicable to women. Last, very few of the prevailing theories have a sufficiently strong data base to permit any evaluation of their worth.

The concentration on sex differences seems to have blinded us to the importance of social class as an important factor in crime. Class differences in crime rates are one of the most consistent findings across cultures. There is evidence that they may, in part, be artifactual. Vaz (1967), for example, has argued that many middle-class teenagers commit crimes for which they are either not apprehended or not charged and, in the field of adult crime, self-report and victimization studies certainly suggest that most white-collar crime goes undetected (see Hood & Sparks, 1970). Nevertheless, the bulk of detected offenders are working-class.

This single fact has, in the area of male crime, been at the heart of many theoretical schools. Miller (1958) has examined working-class values and has suggested that delinquent behavior, rather than being deviant, may be highly conforming to these focal concerns. Cohen (1955) and Cloward and Ohlin (1960) have examined the stress that the American Dream has placed on those who have little hope of success in the conventional world. Cohen suggests that such youths band together and invert the values of the middle-class in a process of reaction formation. Cloward and Ohlin, by contrast, argue that the value of money and prestige is accepted, but that the conventional means of attaining them is rejected. Hirschi (1969) has suggested that delinquent youths have become estranged from those social institutions that encourage them to have a stake in conformity—school, family, and employment. Without such ties, they are free to drift into delinquency.

We now understand much about *male* working-class values, lifestyles, and pressures. By contrast, we know very little indeed of the lives that working-class women face and the values and attitudes that they carry with them. At the heart of any explanation of female crime should be a solid descriptive and empirical base of knowledge related to this issue. Only with this is it possible to evaluate important issues: Is criminal behavior really seen to be at odds with femininity? Is crime a reaction to working-class female life or is it an accepted part of it? How do the families and neighbors of criminal women view, evaluate, and justify criminal activity? Does such crime really constitute a challenge to the middle-classes or is it a short-term solution to stresses (emotional or financial)? With such an empirical base, it would be possible to evaluate whether theories of male crime (strain, subcultural, and control theories) have any validity for women. It is largely because of the political posturing of those who study the issue that many have been reluctant to apply tested male theories to women. Whether women need their own sex-specific theory should be an empirical issue, not one based on a priori assumptions. It seems most likely that class differences have a more profound effect on criminal behavior than do sex differences.

Second, the interest in female crime is now sufficiently well developed to allow us to stop considering female crime as a homogeneous phenomenon.

The motivations that lie behind a wife who knifes her husband to death are not likely to have much in common with those of a girl who is truant from school, a woman who earns her living by systematic shoplifting, or a female terrorist who kidnaps a diplomat as a political statement. Once again, we badly need detailed studies of particular issues. We need to understand what such women are saying, both at a personal and a theoretical level as well as at a political one. Until we do, it is small wonder that results are so contradictory. Widom's (1978) review of the applicability of personality theories to female crime indicates the chaotic array of results that come from assuming that all female criminals are the same.

Last, the issue of whether the late 1970s did or did not see an increase in female crime and whether or not this is related to women's positions should be put aside. The question is unanswerable. We do not have comparable data on either of these issues over the time span in question. Even if a correlation could be demonstrated, the causal link would still remain in doubt. Were both the result of some third, unmeasured factor? Did criminal women alert others to the mutability of the female role or was it the other way around? As fascinating as these questions are, they are never likely to be answered.

Just as attention in the study of male criminality has turned toward listening to the accounts of criminal men and recognizing crime as a potentially rational response to material circumstances, so it is time that the same courtesy is accorded to women. Before we hasten to dismiss them as mentally ill, deviant from their sex role, or in the forefront of the sexual revolution, we should take the time to listen to them. Before theory and rhetoric should come understanding.

References

Adler, A. *Sisters in crime*. New York: McGraw-Hill, 1975.

Adler, A. *The relationship between the feminist movement and crime rates among women: Causal, correlational or what?* Paper delivered at the annual meeting of the American Society of Criminology, San Francisco, California: November 1980.

Al-Issa, I. *The psychopathology of women*. Englewood Cliffs, New Jersey: Prentice-Hall, 1980.

Anderson, V. V. Mental disease and delinquency. *Mental Hygiene*, 1919, *3*, 177-198.

Bertrand, M. A. *The insignificance of female criminality in the light of the hegemonic conceptions of sexual roles and the privatization of women*. Paper delivered at the first conference of the European Group for the Study of Deviance and Social Control, Florence, Italy, 1973.

Biles, D., & Mulligan, G. Mad or bad—The enduring dilemma. *British Journal of Criminology*, 1973, *13*, 275-279.

Blos, P. Preoedipal factors in the etiology of female delinquency, *Psychoanalytic Studies of the Child*, 1957, *12*, 229-242.

Bradburn, N., & Caplovitz, D. *Reports on happiness*. Chicago, Illinois: Aldine, 1965.

Bromberg, W., & Thompson, C. B. The relation of psychosis, mental defect and personality types of crime. *Journal of Criminal Law and Criminology*, 1937, *28*, 70-89.

Broverman, I. K., Broverman, D. M., Clarkson, E. E., Rosengrantz, P. S., & Vogel, S. R. Sex role stereotypes and clinical judgements of mental health. *Journal of Consulting and Clinical Psychology*, 1975, *34*, 1-7.

Campbell, A. *Girl delinquents*. Oxford, England: Blackwell, 1981.

Cassel, R. N., & Clayton, J. A preliminary analysis of certain social self-concepts of women in a correctional institution. *Sociology and Social Research*, 1961, *45*, 316-319.

Chesler, P. *Women and madness*. London, England: Allen Lane, 1974.

Chesney-Lind, M. Judicial enforcement of the female sex role; the family court and the female delinquent. *Issues in Criminology*, 1973, *8*, 43-46.

Cloninger, C. R., & Guze, S. B. Psychiatric illness and female criminality: The role of sociopathy and hysteria in the antisocial woman. *American Journal of Psychiatry*, 1970, *127*, 303-311.

Cloninger, C. R., & Guze, S. B. Psychiatric disorders and criminal recidivism. *Archives of General Psychiatry*, 1973, *29*, 266-269.

Cloward, R. A., & Ohlin, L. E. *Delinquency and opportunity*. Glencoe, Illinois: Free Press, 1960.

Cochrane, R. The structure of value systems in male and female prisoners. *British Journal of Criminology*, 1971, *12*, 73-79.

Cohen, A. K. *Delinquent boys: The culture of the gang*. Glencoe, Illinois: Free Press, 1955.

Cowie, J., Cowie, B., & Slater, E. *Delinquency in girls*. London, England: Heinemann, 1968.

Dalton, K. Menstruation and crime. *British Medical Journal*, 1961, *2*, 1752-1753.

Epps, P. A preliminary study of 300 female delinquents in Borstal institutions. *British Journal of Delinquency*, 1951, *1*, 187-197.

Epps, P., & Parnell, R. W. Physique and temperament of women delinquents compared with women undergraduates. *British Journal of Medical Psychology*, 1952, *25*, 249-255.

Ferdon, N. M. Chromosomal abnormalities and antisocial behaviour. *Journal of Genetic Psychology*, 1971, *118*, 281-292.

Freud, S. Femininity. In J. Strachey & A. Richards (Eds.), *New introductory lectures in psychoanalysis*. Harmondsworth, England: Penguin, 1973. (Originally published, 1925 and 1931)

Gibbens, T. C. N., & Prince, J. *Shoplifting*. London, England: Institute for the Study and Treatment of Delinquency, 1962.

Glueck, B. A study of 608 admissions to Sing Sing prison. *Mental Hygiene*, 1918, *2*, 85-151.

Gove, W. R., & Tudor, J. F. Adult sex roles and mental illness. *American Journal of Sociology*, 1973, *78*, 812-835.

Guze, S. B. *Criminality and psychiatric disorders*. London and New York: Oxford Univ. Press, 1976.

Guze, S. B., Goodwin, D. W., & Crane, J. B. Criminality and psychiatric disorders. *Archives of General Psychiatry*, 1969, *20*, 583-591.

Guze, S. B., Tuason, V. B., Gatfield, P. D., Stewart, M. A., & Picken, B. Psychiatric illness and crime with particular reference to alcoholism: A study of 223 criminals. *Journal of Nervous and Mental Disorders*, 1962, *134*, 512-521.

Hare, E. H., & Shaw, G. K. *Mental health on a housing estàte*. London and New York: Oxford Univ. Press, 1965.

Hart, T. *The new adolescent offender*. Paper presented at the Institute for the Study and Treatment of Delinquency Spring Conference, London, England, April 1975.

Healy, W. A review of some studies of delinquents and delinquency. *Archives of Neurology and Psychiatry*, 1925, *14*, 25-30.

Hirschi, T. *Caüses of delinquency*. Berkeley: Univ. of California Press, 1969.

Hoffman-Bustamante, D. The nature of female criminality. *Issues in Criminology*, 1973, *8*, 117-136.

Hood, R., & Sparks, R. *Key issues in criminology*. New York: McGraw-Hill, 1970.

Kretschmer, E. *Physique and character*. New York: Harcourt, 1925.

Konopka, G. *The adolescent girl in conflict.* Englewood Cliffs, New Jersey: Prentice-Hall, 1966.
Lombroso, C., & Ferrero, W. *The female offender.* London, England: Fisher Unwin, 1895.
Loving, N., & Olson, L. *Proceedings of the National Conference on Women and Crime.* Washington, D.C.: National League of Cities and United States Conference of Mayors, 1976.
Maas, J. P. Cathexes toward significant others by sociopathic women. *Archives of General Psychiatry,* 1966, *15,* 516-522.
Maccoby, E., & Jacklin, C. N. *The psychology of sex differences.* Stanford, California: Stanford Univ. Press, 1974.
McRobbie, A. *Working-class girls and the culture of femininity.* Unpublished masters thesis, Birmingham University, England, 1978.
Miller, W. B. Lower class culture as a generating milieu of gang delinquency. *Journal of Social Issues,* 1958, *14,* 5-19.
Morris, R. Female delinquency and relational problems. *Social Forces,* 1964, *43,* 82-89.
Pailthorpe, G. W. *What we put in prison and in preventative and rescue homes.* London, England: Williams and Norgate, 1932.
Petrich, J. Rate of psychiatric morbidity in a metropolitan county jail population. *American Journal of Psychiatry,* 1976, *133,* 1439-1444.
Phillips, D. L., & Segal, B. E. Sexual status and psychiatric symptoms. *American Sociological Review,* 1969, *34,* 58-72.
Pollak, O. *The criminality of women.* New York: Barnes, 1961. (Originally published, 1950)
Rappeport, J. R., & Lassen, G. The dangerousness of female patients: A comparison of the arrest rate of discharged psychiatric patients and the general population. *American Journal of Psychiatry,* 1966, *123,* 413-419.
Richardson, H. *Adolescent girls in approved schools.* London, England: Routledge & Kegan Paul, 1969.
Riege, M. Parental affection and juvenile delinquency in girls. *British Journal of Criminology,* 1972, *12,* 55-73.
Sarri, R. C. Juvenile law: How it penalizes females. In L. Crites (Ed.), *The female offender.* Lexington, Massachusetts: Heath, 1976.
Sheldon, W. H., Hartt, E. M., & McDermott, G. *Varieties of delinquent youths.* New York: Harper, 1949.
Simon, R. J. *The contemporary woman and crime.* Bethesda, Maryland: National Institute of Mental Health, 1975.
Smart, C. *Women, crime and criminology: A feminist critique.* London, England: Routledge & Kegan Paul, 1977.
Steadman, H. J., & Halfon, A. The Baxstrom patients: Backgrounds and outcomes. *Seminars in Psychiatry,* 1971, *3,* 376-385.
Thomas, W. I. *The unadjusted girl.* New York: Harper, 1967. (Originally published, 1923)
Vaz, E. (Ed.). *Middle class juvenile delinquency.* New York: Harper, 1967.
Ward, D. A., Jackson, M., & Ward, R. E. Crimes of violence by women. In D. J. Mulvihill & M. M. Tumin (Eds.), *Crimes of violence* (Vol. 13). Washington, D.C.: US Govt. Printing Office, 1968.
Widom, C. S. Toward an understanding of female criminality. *Progress in Experimental Personality Research,* 1978, *8,* 245-308.
Widom, C. S. *Sex roles and crime.* Paper presented at the 88th Annual Conference of the American Psychological Association, Montreal, Canada, 1980.
Woodside, M. Instability in women prisoners. *Lancet,* 1962, *2,* 928-930.
Zitrin, A., Hardesty, A. S., Burdock, E. I., & Drossman, A. K. Crime and violence among mental patients. *American Journal of Psychiatry,* 1976, *133,* 142-149.

V

Gender and Mind–Body Problems

12

HANS J. EYSENCK

Gender, Genes, and Psychopathology

Other chapters in this book have dealt with psychopathology in the psychiatric sense, that is, as mental illness (schizophrenia, manic-depressive illness), drug abuse, neurosis, and psychopathy. In this chapter my intention is to use the term in quite another sense, more psychological and indeed behavioristic. Behavior may be (and often is) regarded as pathological in a nontechnical, nonpsychiatric sense when it departs from normality; this is the statistical definition of abnormality (Eysenck, 1960). Thus, complete sexual abstinence would be regarded by many as abnormal and indeed pathological; so would excessive indulgence in extramarital affairs, nymphomania, etc. The notion of abnormality or pathology as unusual or rare behavior at the ends of some form of normal distribution is sometimes qualified by denoting one end of the distribution as desirable and only labeling the undesirable end as abnormal and pathological. When we apply these notions to gender differences, we come face to face with the fact that expectations, distributions of behavior, attitudes and reactions, and social roles are rather different for the two sexes; the question that arises is, of course, whether these differences are natural, that is, produced partly or entirely by biological causes, or whether they are social, that is, produced by social precepts enjoining certain roles on otherwise neutral members of the two sexes. Gomberg and Franks (1979) present a good summary of research favoring the latter view; so do Birke, Faulkner, Best, Janson-Smith, and Overfield (1980), Mischel (1966), Wesley and Wesley (1977), and Safilios-Rothschild (1977). The opposite view is taken by CIBA

ISBN: 0-12-050350-6

(1979), Dörner (1972), Gray (1971), Mitchell (1979), Schlegel (1966), and Symons (1979). A more balanced view is taken by Cook and Wilson (1977), Eysenck and Wilson (1979), Feldman and MacCulloch (1980), Hutt (1972), Lloyd and Archer (1976), Maccoby and Jacklin (1975), Money and Ehrhardt (1972), and Richards (1980).

The purely social position is often taken by sociologists; the purely biological by medical workers concerned with hormone secretion, and by workers in animal laboratories. Few would acknowledge supporting a truly 100% position either way, but recognition of opposing views is often little but lip-service to scientific rectitude. The writer has suggested that no unified, realistic psychology is possible without an explicit recognition that human beings are biosocial animals (Eysenck, 1980a, 1980b). Human behavior cannot be understood only in terms of social factors, role playing, and modeling; neither can human behavior be understood solely in terms of biological determinants, instincts, and genes. In recent years, advocates of a purely social role for humans have been more aggressive in denying the importance of biological factors; few biologists would claim that physiological biochemical, hormonal, and other such factors *exclusively* determined human conduct or sexual differentiation in behavior. However, in practice writers like Symons (1979) do seem to press unduly for a much more important part to be played by the genes than the evidence warrants, and although his approach is interesting and ingenious, it leaves out too much material to be convincing. Most likely, biological and social factors have in the past worked in unison to overcome the natural diversity to be found within each sex; society has tended to insist on men and women playing roles that they were in any case predisposed (on the average) to play by virtue of their biological nature. This, at least, is the conclusion come to by Eysenck and Wilson (1979) after a review of the evidence, and it is a view supported by most reviewers who have taken cognizance of all the wide range of evidence now available.

What is the connection between this controversy and psychopathology? The answer is relatively simple. Let us suppose that male-female differences in behavior, sex roles and social conduct generally are entirely due to precepts enjoined on them by society; arbitrary rules imposed by the dominant sex, for the most part. In this case, any other set of arbitrary rules (such as complete sexual equality in the sense of identity) could with equal ease be adopted by society, and an entirely different type of behavior would now become acceptable. Behaviors acceptable under the old rules would now be labeled *pathological,* and behavior once considered pathological would now be entirely acceptable. This assumption of cultural relativism is indeed made by many modern writers; it suggests omnipotence on our part in changing the rules of the social game. If we wish females to be aggressive, sexually promiscuous, and masculine in their behavior, then all we would have to do is to change the rules of their upbringing and the role structure in our society. Similarly, males could easily be led into ways of acting resembling those now more usual in women. Or, of course, we could engineer a unisex society in which both sexes would indeed act in an identical manner, outside the obvious limitations of their physical sexual characteristics.

If, however, the sociobiological view is nearer the truth, then any such attempt to force behavioral change on a population of men and women innately predisposed to act along the lines at present modeled by their parents and supported by society would lead to truly psychopathological behavior, that is, behavior contrary to the biological predisposition of men and women, respectively. Such unnatural behavior could lead to serious mental disorientation, unhappiness, and mental disorder, if persisted in. We shall see that there is much evidence to support such a view and that, accordingly, the path of those who wish to change social attitudes in respect to gender differentiation is bestrewn with difficulties and problems. Yet, clearly, they are right in maintaining that present practices are often unjust, discriminatory, and frustrating, particularly to women. A possible compromise solution to this problem will be suggested at the end of this chapter.

Before turning to a consideration of the evidence, it may be useful to point out limitations of the survey here undertaken. Other chapters contain reviews of the biological evidence on hormonal effects and more general reviews of specific role-playing and modeling factors in our society. I shall concentrate on a small number of studies that I believe support strongly the generalization outlined above; no review of all the available literature is attempted because so much has been written on these topics that a whole chapter could be filled just with references to these writings. Hence I have concentrated on particularly impressive studies that seem to be free from the objections to which so many published works are subject. Of the available alternatives, this seemed to be the most useful to readers of a book such as this.

In addition, I have concentrated on methodological issues, not only on substantive ones. The reason for this, of course, is that complex and difficult questions such as those investigated here cannot be answered at all except by the use of special designs and techniques that are outside the realm of the usual type of psychological study. Adherents of one or other of the opposing extreme views often simply use *interpretations* of agreed facts as evidence for their beliefs; thus the fact that men and women in our society tend to differ in their sexual attitudes (Eysenck, 1976) is often interpreted in terms of role-playing by sociologists and in terms of genetic determination by biologists. Clearly, the facts are equally compatible with both types of interpretation; they post the question, but do not answer it.

One last point before we turn to a detailed consideration of methodology and findings. It would be an error, equally frequently committed by feminists as by antifeminists, to believe that biological interpretations of behavior differences associated with gender necessarily support the status quo. The leap from fact to prescription might be permissible for the lower animals, but it is impermissible in human beings where the existence of society has introduced a new force that is expressly designed to promote changes in the behavior of *homo sapiens* that may go counter to their instinctual preferences but that are demonstrably useful for the greater health and happiness of the majority. It is reasonable to argue for the existence of genetic forces tending in the direction of harem formation in human males (Symons, 1979); it is not reasonable to argue that the existence of such forces either legitimizes the practical execution of such natural desires or makes impossible social control over the marriage customs of males and females outlawing such practices. Simple arithmetic shows that not only may harem formation frustrate large numbers of women desirous of monogamous partnership; clearly, if a harem consists of one man marrying four women (as allowed by Mohammedan law), then 75% of all men will have to make do without any women at all! Clearly, the drive toward harem formation, although perhaps natural and genetically advantageous to the harem-owning male, is disadvantageous for the majority, and hence subject to social control. Whether such control is desirable in any particular instance is, of course, subject to democratic debate; the possibility of control is not ruled out by the existence of biological determinants that are never strong enough to override all social considerations (Eysenck & Wilson, 1979).

When Society Changes Sex Roles

The argument of those who take a social learning view of sex differences in behavior (Mischel, 1966) is clearly that social pressure and reinforcements determine the roles that men and women play and that our current practices are simply a reflection of the pressures brought to bear by society on boys and girls growing up in that society. An ideal ground for testing such an hypothesis would of course be the discovery of a society that encouraged an entirely different set of values, preferably one opposed to those currently held by most Western cultures. Such societies do exist, although they tend to be rather small and isolated. In particular, we may regard the Israeli kibbutz, in the words of Beit-Hallahmi and Rabin (1977), "as a social experiment and as a child-rearing laboratory [p. 532]," and ask ourselves whether children growing up with pressures entirely different and indeed opposed to those governing the bringing up of children in our society do indeed show such very different behaviors as might be expected on the basis of the social learning theory.

In this section we will concentrate on the work of Spiro (1979), for several reasons. In the first place, he observed the growth of the kibbutz for many years, having made detailed studies some 30 years ago (Spiro, 1955, 1958). In the second place, Spiro started out as a clear adherent of the social learning view; hence he cannot be accused of antifeminist prejudice. In the third place, his findings are replicable, in the sense that other observers of different kibbutzim have found much the same results (Beit-Hallahmi & Rabin, 1977; Hazleton, 1977; Padan-Eisenstark, 1975; Shazar, 1975; Tiger & Shepher, 1975). The facts, therefore, are hardly in dispute, and Spiro supplies an interpretation and account that is so clear, unbiased, and reasonable that a brief summary will suffice to give an outline of the major outcomes of this experiment.

Spiro (1979) studied in particular Kibbutz Kiryat Yedidim, and concerned himself in the main with the attitudes and behavior evinced by the sabras, the native-born young men and women forming the succeeding generation to the original pioneers. He also studied a sample of sabras in six other veteran kibbutzim, two from each of the three major kibbutz federations. The adults Spiro studied in 1975 were the children he had studied in 1951. Spiro devoted his attention to a large number of topics all of which are relevant to this chapter, including sex roles in work, parenting, governance, marriage, attitudes to the family, femininity, and play.

The kibbutzim were founded on socialist and egalitarian principles, including the principle of sexual equality; work, in particular, was equally distributed between the sexes, so that women would take an equal part in the backbreaking work on the land, driving tractors, etc., and men would take an equal part in the general housekeeping. A special effort was made to destroy the family because of its traditional and conservative influence; marriage was discouraged or outlawed, children did not live with their parents but were brought up by caretakers, and quite generally an effort was made to make the kibbutz rather than the family the center of the child's value system. There was a strong drive to get women to take part in the government of the kibbutz and to make them give up all those practices of femininity, such as personal adornment and differential dress, so characteristic of Western society.

What were the effects? Attitude to work is the first item looked at by Spiro (1979). At the beginning, there had been a clear distinction between farm work (important) and service work (unimportant), with men and women sharing in both. This has completely changed; sexual specialization in the economy has come to be regarded as a natural and indeed a desirable state of affairs. The identity meaning of sexual equality, as interpreted by the pioneer women, has been changed to an equivalence meaning. Farm work is now mostly done by men, service work by women; there has been a complete turnabout to the kind of pattern characteristic of Western society. Equally important with the notion that women would work together with men on the same jobs was the expectation that the emancipation from domestic work would enable them to participate equally with men in political activities and to share leadership positions in the kibbutz equally with men. However, right from the beginning, leadership positions have been disproportionately held by males, and this disproportion has continued and even increased. Some committees, indeed, have a preponderantly female membership, but this is usually in relation to what are now considered appropriate female activities, such as the child care committee, library committee, high school committee, health committee, and clothing committee. Even when they are present on committees, women seldom assume leadership roles, and even on committees on which they constitute a majority they seldom serve as chairpersons.

This underrepresentation of women in the running of the kibbutz also holds for extra-kibbutz political and leadership activities. As Tiger and Shepher (1975) have pointed out, for the entire federation, males constitute 84% of the participants in economic public service, 71% of the leadership positions of the federation, and 78% of the political activists (1975, p. 91). Others have found the same (Shain, cited in Spiro, 1979; Talmon-Garber, 1965). Even the insistence of one of the federations that at least one-third of the membership of its administrative committees and other governing bodies should be made up of women could not be met because few women were willing to serve. In spite of long-continued propaganda from birth onward, women are more concerned with their families, whereas men are more concerned with community affairs. This outcome of a planned reversal of sex attitudes was extremely disappointing to the original members of the kibbutz, who had confidently expected that the changes introduced in the traditional marriage and family systems would produce political consequences as well. As Spiro (1979) points out, the pioneers were not necessarily wrong in viewing the women's emotional involvement with the family as an obstacle to the development of political motivation; rather, they underestimated the strength of this involvement, and its possible genetic basis.

One of the most symbolic events signaling a reversal in the kibbutz of the original drive toward sexual equality is the restoration of the traditional terms of reference for the spouse. In the 1950s, women would refer to their spouses as "my friend" or "my man." Today "my husband" is used by all women, including the most radical of the early feminists. Also symbolic of this counter-revolution are the return of the traditional wedding and the public celebration of marriage. In the early days, marriage consisted simply of the granting of a joint room to the couple, and there were no public celebrations of any kind. Legal ceremonies were only involved after the couple decided to have children, and the ceremonies were never held in the kibbutz itself. Now, marriage customs are the same in the kibbutz as they are generally in the Western world—there are public receptions, official announcements, congratulations in the newspapers, and a legal ceremony conducted by a rabbi.

Many important changes are associated with this resurrection of the traditional marriage bond. The *unit of consumption,* as Spiro so quaintly terms it, has shifted from the group to the domestic family, and coincidental with this there has been a dramatic increase in the budget allocated for housing, furniture, clothing, and other consumer goods for the family rather than, as before, for communal institutions and public places such as a clubhouse. The decision to devote public resources to the private consumption of married couples rather than to collective consumption in communal institutions is one of the most dramatic changes in the kibbutz and a tribute to the recognition of the importance of the marriage bond and the family. Where previously the communal dining room was the center of social life, now it is a private apartment.

Marriages now occur earlier; being a spinster beyond one's teenage years is regarded as a misfortune for women; divorce is now frowned on; and general moral attitudes are probably stricter than in Western countries. All these changes have taken place within one generation and mark a complete reversal of all the modeling and indoctrination to which the young sabras were exposed.

It is in accordance with these changes that stress on family life by women has dramatically increased. Spiro (1979) presents some data to show that in recent public opinion surveys questioning respondents about the relative importance of work, family, public activities, study, and hobbies, most men ranked work as first in importance, whereas women chose family. Women came to be much more involved in the family than in work, and much more dependent upon it for personal fulfillment. Even the women in the parent generation, now grown old, had reverted to type. Kibbutz women in general have ceased to view the care of and concern for their children as an obstacle to female emancipation, and regard it as an important source of personal fulfillment; they look on their maternal orientation as biologically determined and natural. Accompanying this change in orientation, there has also been a tremendous increase in the birth rate, which has more than doubled in one generation.

A battle is still going on for the right to have the children live with their parents all the time, an idea directly contradictory to all the traditional wisdom of the kibbutz. Mothers (and fathers too) feel deprived in having their children reared in communal sleeping quarters, and only the investment of money and energy in the construction of units in the past prevents the change from being made immediately. Clearly, the pioneers underestimated the strength of maternal (and paternal) feelings, or those of the children themselves; by neglecting biology, they introduced social changes that led to considerable suffering on the part of parents and children alike.

Another area in which traditional feminine values were downgraded by the kibbutz pioneers was feminine adornment. Early beliefs in the notion that equality with males involved becoming like males and minimizing sexual dimorphism have disappeared; nowadays women are again actively interested in feminine fashions, sexual attractiveness, and fashionable clothing. Together with this goes interest in jewelery, cosmetics, perfume, feminine hairdos, beauty parlors, and all the other artificial aids to feminine beauty. Making her person attractive is valued as highly by the female sabra as is making the home attractive and generally being interested in domesticity. Indeed, femininity as revealed in attitudes among kibbutz women is now more strongly marked than in Israeli women generally.

Of particular interest in demonstrating the strength of noncultural factors in behavior is Spiro's (1979) account of the origins of sexual shame. The pioneers believed that attitudes and orientations to sexual behavior and sexual anatomy were culturally determined and that if children were raised in a permissive and enlightened environment, with boys and girls living together, becoming acquainted with each others' bodies and viewing nudity as natural, then the exposure of sex organs would not be likely to give rise to shame and other bourgeois reactions. Accordingly, boys and girls were brought up to use the same toilets, dress and undress in each others' presence, walk about in the nude in their dormitories, shower together in the same shower room, and so on. Apparently the system worked perfectly well until the beginning of puberty in the girls, "at which time the very girls who had been raised in a sex-blind environment developed intense feelings of shame at being seen in the nude by the boys (Spiro, 1979, p. 98)." The girls indeed rebelled against the rules, insisted on showering separately from the boys, and undressed in private. Mixed showers had finally to be abandoned, and unisex bedrooms had to be introduced. Thus these children developed a sense of sexual shame "not as a result of, but in opposition to, the cultural values of their learning environment (Spiro, 1979, p. 99)." This is an important demonstration of the strength of biological factors when placed in opposition to cultural determinants and social learning.

Equally interesting in many ways are Spiro's (1979) accounts of the play activity of children observed by him. Boys were found to prefer to play with large toys, using strenuous, muscular activity, whereas girls preferred artistic-imaginative fantasy behavior. "Altogether, muscular-physical activity is a male dimension, while artistic-imaginative activity is a female dimension of play (Spiro, 1979, p. 76)." Thus, even in preschool children, boys and girls exhibited important sex differences in behavior, and Spiro asks how these sexual differences could be determined by culture when the boys and girls were raised in the same learning environment, when their socialization had been uniform, when they had been taught the same plays and games, and when the persons involved in the socialization process, that is, parents and nursery teachers, were committed to the abolition of sex differences in behavior. "Since, in this kind of cultural regime, it would be unlikely for these differences to have been culturally determined, it is much more likely that they were determined by precultural motivational differences between the sexes (Spiro, 1979, p. 76)."

What conclusions may we draw from Spiro's (1979) study and from the others that have conducted similar investigations of the effects of kibbutz enculturation (Beit-Hallahmi & Rabin, 1977; Tiger & Shepher, 1975)? It is difficult to reconcile the findings with a social learning theory that rules out genetic and biological factors completely. The rather naive views of the early pioneers have been decisively disproved, and it is difficult to interpret the results other than in terms of a strong biological predetermination of males and females to act differentially and to adopt different social roles *regardless of indoctrination*. Spiro (1979) discusses many criticisms that can be, or have been, made in this connection and shows that these do not invalidate the findings or the conclusions. It is possible to point out that the kibbutz is not completely isolated from the outer world and that possibly the children may have received messages from the outer world contradicting those received from their mentors. This is true, but surely irrelevant. Reinforcements were being administered within the kibbutz, and the precepts received from their parents, minders, and others were very much more direct and powerful than any possible voices from the outside. Traditionally, small, isolated groups sharing a common ideology have been particularly resistant to the acceptance of messages from the outside, and this by itself should have ensured the maintenance by the sabras of the original kibbutz philosophy.

Of particular interest is the general trend of the findings; they are not confined to one kibbutz, but tend to be replicated in the majority, if not all. There are, of course, degrees of reversal, ranging from what one might consider overcompensation to relatively small regression, particularly in very ideologically oriented kibbutzim. But the trend is universal and cannot be explained on social learning grounds. Thus, what might be considered a direct experiment in modeling or social learning has produced results more strongly favorable to the biological view than might have been thought possible. It is not suggested, of course, that these results demonstrate cultural, social, and learning reinforcement factors to be completely impotent; that would be a misreading of the results. No one doubts the great importance of such influences; all that is asserted is that they do not determine human conduct 100% and are in disregard of biological predisposing factors.

Sexual Behavior, Personality, and Genetics

The study discussed in the last section dealt directly with the effects of social training on gender-linked behaviors. In this section we shall deal with the genetic links between gender-associated behavior and sex, as mediated by personality. The argument is inevitably a rather complex one because direct genetic experimentation encounters the same difficulty in contrasting men and women as it does in contrasting two different races. Orthodox types of genetic experimentation or argumentation are therefore inappropriate and a rather indirect design has to be substituted. Let us first consider the actual differences between men and women insofar as sexual attitudes, beliefs, and behaviors are concerned, as these are found in our society.

In several large-scale studies using questionnaires of sex attitudes and behavior on thousands of British men and women, the writer found very marked sex differences on a number of items (Eysenck, 1976). The 27 of these giving the largest differences are listed in Table 12.1; these will be seen to reinforce the popular conceptions of differences between men and women in regard to sexual practices. There are strong differences between the sexes on items relating to pornography (with males more approving), orgies (with males more approving), voyeurism (with men more approving), and prostitution (with men again more approving). Impersonal sex, too, is very much more typical of males, as is strength of sexual excitement, premarital sex, and promiscuity in general. Masturbation is more a male pasttime, according to these results, and men are less prudish in general and feel less guilt about sex. On the other hand, contentment with their sex lives is more marked among women than among men, possibly an unexpected result.

Figure 12.1 shows the scores of men and women on a masculinity-femininity index that was constructed from the sex attitudes inventory and includes the 40 most diagnostic items. The differences in libido (the term is here used simply to refer to the content of the scales and has no psychoanalytic meaning) are clearly marked, with the mean value for the women below 20, for the males just below 30. Equally apparent, however, is a certain degree of overlap; a small portion of males score below the female mean, a small portion of women score above the male mean.

The subjects of this particular study were students, similar in age and obviously more knowledgeable than average about, and concerned with, modern views about sexual equality, the modeling of gender roles, and other theories concerning social learning factors in the causation of sex differences. Nevertheless, the differences are very large and clearly marked. Other groups were also tested, including large samples of nonacademic adult males and females (Eysenck, 1976), and these gave very similar results. Taken together with many other studies carried out in different countries (e.g., Daly & Wilson, 1979), and referred to in this book, we may take it for granted that even in this day and age sex differences are very large in this area.

The fact that these differences in attitude exist does not, of course, by itself tell us very much about their origin. There may be a biological determination, possibly through differential hormonal secretions, or a more general genetic determination, possibly involving other bodily systems as well. Or else, the differences might have been produced by social learning, role-playing, and

TABLE 12.1
Percentage Endorsement Differences between Males and Females on 27 Items of the Sexual Attitude Scale

	M-F differences
If you were invited to take part in an orgy, would you: (a) accept it? (b) refuse?	57
I like to look at pictures of nudes	53
I like to look at sexy pictures	53
The thought of a sex orgy is disgusting to me	−47
If you were invited to see a "blue" film would you: (a) accept? (b) refuse?	43
It is all right to seduce a person who is old enough to know what they are doing	38
I believe in taking my pleasures where I find them	37
If you were offered a highly pornographic book, would you: (a) accept it? (b) refuse it?	36
It doesn't take much to get me excited sexually	35
Buttocks excite me	34
I get excited sexually very easily	33
I think about sex almost every day	32
Seeing a person nude does not interest me	−32
Sex without love ("impersonal sex") is highly unsatisfactory	−31
I do not need to respect a woman, or love her, in order to enjoy petting and/or intercourse with her	31
Prostitution should be legally permitted	−30
If you had a chance to see people making love, without being seen, would you take it?	29
Pornographic writings should be freely allowed to be published	27
It is better not to have sexual relations until you are married	−25
Sometimes the woman should be sexually aggressive	24
I get pleasant feelings from touching my sexual parts	24
Something is lacking in my sex life	24
There should be no censorship, on sexual grounds, of plays and films	34
Conditions have to be just right to get me excited sexually	−22
I find the thought of a coloured sex partner particularly exciting	21
The opposite sex will respect you more if you are not too familiar with them	−21
All in all I am satisfied with my sex life	−20

From Eysenck, 1976.

other, similar factors. The data reviewed in the last section make this an unlikely explanation, but direct evidence would be desirable in order to come to a more definitive conclusion.

The hypothesis tested by Eysenck (1976) may be stated as follows:

1. Men and women show marked personality differences that are genetically determined and that define a general personality factor of masculinity-femininity.

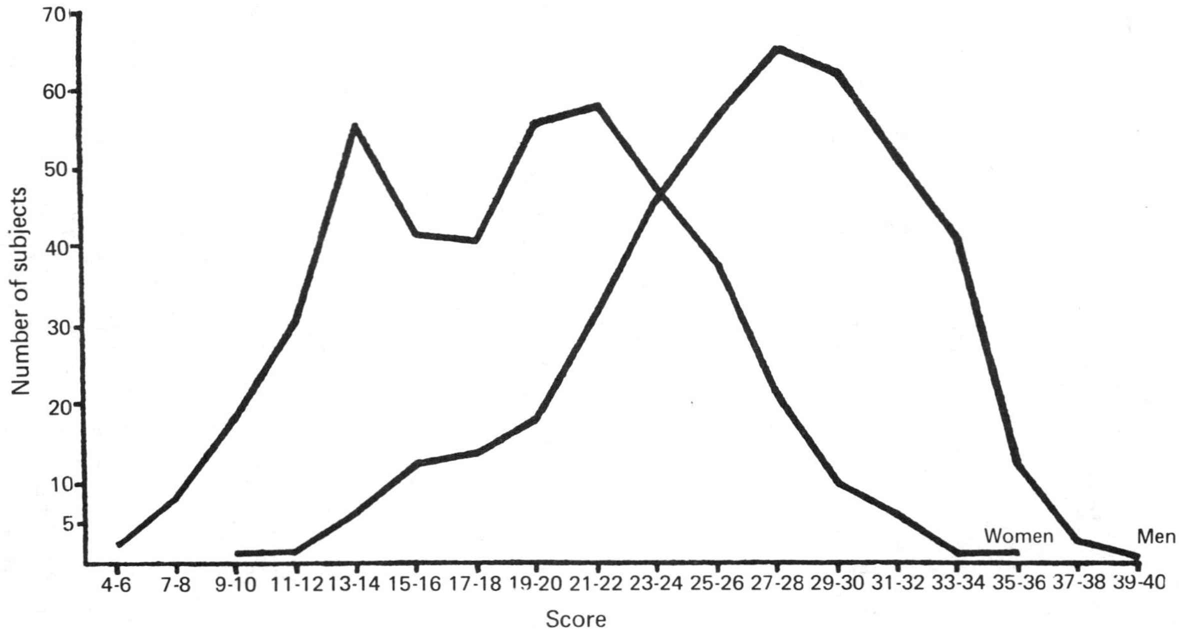

FIGURE 12.1. ***Distribution of scores on the libido (masculinity-femininity) scale (From Eysenck, 1976).***

2. This factor extends way beyond the simple sexual adjustment and sexual attitudes discussed so far and covers many other areas of social life.
3. This masculinity-femininity factor is largely determined by genetic influences and has a high heritability.
4. These genetic determinants work at least in part through the androgen-estrogen system.
5. The personality factor of masculinity-femininity constitutes a continuum, and on this continuum, men overlap with women, very much as they do in relation to their sexual attitudes.
6. The sexual attitudes of females having a high score on this masculinity-femininity index are similar to those of males in general, and the attitudes of males having low scores on this masculinity-femininity index are similar to those of women in general.

We will go on to discuss the various parts of the argument in turn.

There are three major personality factors that emerge from factor analytic studies of traits, namely extraversion-introversion, neuroticism-stability, and psychoticism-superego (Eysenck & Eysenck, 1976; Royce, 1973). All of these show sex differences; thus, males tend to be somewhat more extraverted than females, females somewhat more emotional-neurotic than males. However, these differences are relatively small; it is when we come to psychoticism-superego that really large differences occur. The nature of this factor, as disclosed by the most highly loading items in the questionnaire, is related to aggressiveness, egocentricity, impersonal attitudes, lack of care for others, lack of empathy, lack of personal feeling for others, and general coldness. This general factor has been referred to as P (for psychoticism) because it was originally suggested by the early German descriptions of members of the psychotic *Erbkreis,* that is, the peculiarities of behavior of relatives of schizophrenics and manic-depressives. It was found that these included a much larger number than expected of psychopaths, criminals, alcoholics, odd-balls, schizoid people, and others who, although not in the psychiatric sense insane, nevertheless showed behavior in some ways similar to psychotic people.

The questionnaire constructed to measure this dimension did indeed discriminate psychotics, psychopaths, criminals, drug addicts, and others from normals and it also correlated with degree of psychotic disorder within psychotic groups. It has also been found to correlate with the amount of serotonin metabolites like 5HIAA, monoamine oxydase platelets, and leucocyte antigens like HLA-B27, known to be related to schizophrenia; furthermore, P is related to male (androgen) hormones, and may thus serve as a masculinity-femininity personality factor postulated in our paradigm (Eysenck & Eysenck, 1976), particularly as males have much higher P scores than females.

In a large-scale genetic study of monozygotic and dizygotic twins, Eaves and Eysenck (1977) found strong evidence for the heritability of this trait in both men and women, the heritability being 81% when correction is made for unreliability of measurement. We thus have here a measure of personality that differentiates very clearly between males and females (with males having scores about twice as high as females), that is linked with male and female hormones, that shows genetic determination of individual differences, and that may be invoked as a possible intermediary to explain the observed differences in sexual attitudes between males and females.

Returning to the topic of sexual attitudes, we may now contrast high P scoring males and females with low P scoring males and females. It is found that high P scorers are clearly opposed to current morality and customs, wishing to do away with marriage, favoring polygamy, and considering premarital sex to be all right. They have a realistic, not an idealistic, view of sex, believe that romantic love is an illusion, do not think it disgusting to see animals having sex, believe in taking pleasure where they can find it, believe that tenderness in sex is not important, and that faithfulness in marriage is silly. High-scorers are very permissive, believe that pornography should be freely available, do not object to four-letter swear words being used in mixed company, are not disturbed by seeing necking in public, do not think that sex orgies are disgusting, consider sex play among children to be harmless, do not consider virginity important, have their first intercourse early, and get excited sexually very easily. In addition, women with high P scores are not keen on having babies, and quite generally there is an endorsement of so-called perverted practices. This general list reads very much like the general male, as opposed to the general female, attitude to sex.

The correlations between P and the libido scale are indeed quite high, both for males and females. In the student population, for instance, they are $r = .54$ and $r = .74$, both significant at the $p < .001$ level. There is thus close correspondence between the sexual attitudes of high P scoring men and high P scoring women, as compared with low-scoring men and low-scoring women, and both high-scoring males and high-scoring females on the P scale have views similar to males, as compared with females. Thus, so far the results bear out the paradigm. It is also of some interest that extraversion, too, correlates with the libido score, both for males and females, the correlations being $r = .31$ and $r = .30$. Both are significant at the $p < .01$ level, and it will be remembered that males on the whole tend to have higher extraversion scores than females and that extraversion, too, has a strong genetic basis (Eaves & Eysenck, 1975).

There is so far no direct evidence of the influence of genetic factors on sexual attitudes. Martin and Eysenck (1976) have carried out such an analysis.

They found that, with respect to libido, additive genetic factors play a very strong part for men, whereas for women cultural influences seem to be more important. When corrections were made for unreliability in the male sample, the heritability of libido reached 67%. These empirical findings agree well with the theoretical work of Dawkins (1976), Symons (1979), and Trivers (1972), who argue, in essence, that the behavior of an animal, like its body, has evolved in order to promote the survival of the genes carried in each of its cells and that the instincts of the individual are not concerned only with his or her own personal survival but with the welfare of all the relatives and descendants with whom some of his or her genes are held in common. With this is associated the concept of *parental investment,* that is, the idea that because the two sexes invest differently in their offspring, therefore their behavior, in the service of the "selfish gene," is very different. In mammals, the male only has to invest a small amount of time in courtship and copulation, whereas the female has to devote a great deal of additional time and energy to pregnancy, childbirth, and lactation. As a result, the male is, at least in theory, capable of producing a far larger number of offspring than the female; his reproductive success can be greatly increased by mating with a large number of different females, but the female has little to gain by mating with many different males. Her main interest is in the survival of the children that she does bear.

Another important factor is that the human female produces only a few hundred eggs in the course of her lifetime, whereas the male produces literally millions of potentially fertile sperm with each ejaculation. It follows that the woman is much more likely to be concerned about the fate of her eggs than is the man about the fate of his spermatozoa; a women's chances of reproducing her genes are tied up with a small number of eggs, but a single male could practically fertilize millions of women.

Symons (1979) argues persuasively that these factors are responsible for the polygynous nature of man, the competition among males for access to females, the reticence of females concerned with investigating the quality of the male to have sex with, and other features of the male-female difference in sexual attitudes and behavior we noted previously. The arguments are well presented by Symons, whose book should be consulted for details; here we can only note that he provides a theory that encompasses and explains the findings noted in this section. The theory itself is completely biological and genetic; it is therefore only partial and leaves out important social factors. Thus, we have noted that for males the heritability of the libidinal factor is very strong, but for females it is much weaker; society, and the roles it decrees women should play, apparently takes on much more importance in the case of females than males. Thus, the purely biological picture painted by Trivers

(1972) and Symons (1979) has to be supplemented by sociological, social learning, and other types of environmentalist theories.

The Argument from Universality

Methodologies for deciding between social learning theories and theories involving genetic, in addition to social, causes in the determination of sex differences in behavior can be derived from the concept of *universality*. If there are no genetic causes at all for the creation of male-female differences, then a look at a large number of different societies and cultures should present us with a great variety of different formalizations of such differences. If, however, there are genetic causes that are at least in part responsible for the observed differences in our own culture, then one would expect these differences to be found in most, if not all, other cultures as well. Polygyny, the hypothetical genetic background for which has already been mentioned, may be used as one such example. George Murdock's *Ethnographic Atlas* (1976) summarizes data on 849 societies; of these, 709 are polygynous and only 4 are polyandrous, that is, permit women more than one husband. On a chance basis, we would expect as much polyandry as polygyny. The gigantic disproportion would then be interpreted as evidence for a causal biological or genetic factor, leading to legislative and other social activity in support of these biological determinants (Daly & Wilson, 1979).

Universality, as in this case, may not be quite complete, for various reasons. Thus, a male desire for polygyny may conflict with the obvious rights and wishes of the males who would be deprived of mates because of the multiple marriages of a small number of privileged males. Most advanced societies have trodden this path of social control, and the male desire for polygamy now takes the different form of greater marital infidelity, use of prostitutes, etc. A given biological constraint may issue in different forms of social conduct that also serve the same fundamental aim but accommodate themselves to the pressure of other needs and drives.

A good example of the argument from universality is Goldberg's (1977) book, *The Inevitability of Patriarchy*. *Patriarchy* is defined as any system of organization (political, economic, industrial, financial, religious, or social) in which the overwhelming number of upper positions in hierarchies are occupied by males. In contradistinction to patriarchy, which refers only to suprafamilial levels of organization, Goldberg defines *male dominance* as authority in familial and dyadic relationships.

Goldberg (1977) in his book demonstrates that "patriarchy is universal [p. 26]." Different societies have shown great differences in developing various types of political, economic, religious, and social systems, but "there has never been a society which failed to associate hierarchical authority and leadership in these areas with men [Goldberg, 1977, p. 26]." As he states, there is not now, nor has there ever been, a society that even remotely failed to associate authority and leadership in suprafamilial areas with the male.

This does not mean that there have not been queens in some societies, or women in leadership positions; the point made is simply that the great majority of leadership positions are occupied by males. There have been four cases of women obtaining the highest positions of authority in a democracy (Israel, India, Sri Lanka, and England), but even in these societies authority is still overwhelmingly associated with the male, and the overwhelming number of upper hierarchical positions are still occupied by males. Goldberg (1977) used detailed figures to show what the position is now even in those countries that are the most advanced theoretically, at least as far as feminist movements are concerned. In his view, the number of women in the United States Congress is derisory, as is that of women in the British Parliament; furthermore, the numbers are decreasing rather than increasing. There are very few women in positions of power and leadership in the financial and business world in these countries, or on the European continent.

The position is no different in countries with an ideological commitment to sexual equalization in the hierarchies of authority, or which have made strong attempts to equalize sexual distribution in government. In Sweden, all 13 Ministers with portfolios are male; in Cuba, only 1 of the 21 Ministers and none of the members of the Political Bureau and the secretariat of the Communist Party are females. In Israel, less than 5% of the cabinet ministers are female, and well under 10% of the Members of Parliament. In Communist China, as Goldberg points out, at the time of writing his book 13 of the 14 leaders of the Standing Committee of National People's Congress, all 17 members of the State Council, and all 67 Heads of the general ministries were men, in spite of that country's commitment to equalization in sexual representations since the revolution. All but one of the members of the Polit Bureau were men at the time, the only exception being the widow of Mao Tse Tung, who has, of course, since fallen from favor. In the Soviet Union, too, 96.9% of the members of the central committee were men at the time Goldberg was writing his book. It is clear that not only is patriarchy universal, but that it is equally marked in countries theoretically favoring equality and, as in the Soviet Union, denying the theoretical relevance of biology to behavior.

Male dominance, as Goldberg (1977) points out, " is somewhat more difficult to define and reveal because the *institutional manifestation* of the psychophysiological differentiation relevant to male dominance is only almost universal, rather than universal [p. 37]." Goldberg goes into much detail to support his case of universality of male dominance from anthropological studies; it is not the point to follow him in this.

There have, of course, been many attempts to contradict his thesis, but as he points out, these have universally failed. Even Margaret Mead (1973), often cited as holding the opposite opinions, acknowledged in her review of Goldberg's book that "men have always been the leaders in public affairs and the final authorities at home [p. 48]."

Goldberg's third argument relates to the universality of *male attainment*. As he points out, certain primitive societies, such as the Bamendas, the Hopi, the Iroquois, the Mbuti Pygmys, or the Nayars, are quoted as exceptions to the universality of male dominance. But these alleged exceptions are simply societies that associate with *women* tasks or functions that *we* associate with *men*. In other words, what is defined as important in a society tends to be associated with males, that which is unimportant (with the exception of maternal roles for females) is associated with females. There is no universal agreement on what is regarded as important or unimportant, but the correlation between importance of function and maleness is universal. This point again is recognized by Margaret Mead when she writes: "In every known human society, the male's need for achievement can be recognized. Men may cook, or weave or dress dolls or hunt humming birds, but if such activities are appropriate occupations of men, then the whole society, men and women alike, vote them as important. When the same occupations are performed by women, they are regarded as less important [Mead, 1970, p. 168]." Goldberg (1977) adds that the roles filled by males are, of course, not necessarily more important to the society's survival, or whatever criterion may be used to measure importance; what is involved is merely the *status* accorded to these roles by society. To use his example, business executives are not more important than nurses, but they are given higher status and are usually male. The medical profession is accorded higher status in the United States than in the Soviet Union, and, correspondingly, far more doctors in the United States are male, compared to the Soviet Union, where a majority is female.

The case made by Goldberg (1977) is a strong one, particularly when seen in relation to all the other available evidence. Thus, he refers directly to the biological evidence relating behavior to hormones, the type of proof discussed in another chapter in this book and hence not dealt with here. The failure of the kibbutz-type indoctrination to alter the types of dominance behavior dealt with by Goldberg is another type of support for his hypothesis. The sex-related personality traits of dominance, assertiveness, etc. would also tend in the same direction. No single type of proof in science is, of course, absolute; one's judgment has to take into account the congruence of different types of approaches and the results obtained by the use of different methodologies. It is this congruence that is so notable in this field, all approaches leading to the conclusion that male-female differences in behavior are not entirely due to role-playing consequent on some kind of social learning experiences, but are fundamentally *prepared* (in Seligman's [1971], phrase), that is, a biologically determined tendency to condition or learn certain types of responses to certain types of situations more readily than others. *Preparedness* is the half-way house to instinct, as it were, and probably a better explanation of the facts than the outmoded concept of instinct itself.

The Avoidance of Psychopathology

Psychopathology is often (though not invariably) the consequence of frustration, conflict, and mismatching of expectation and reality (Eysenck, 1977). If that be so, then mistaken interpretations of gender identification in the psychological sense, that is, erroneous assumptions about the biological or social nature of sex differences in behavior, may easily lead to frustration, conflict and hence psychopathology. If there is a conflict between social norms and preparedness, that is, the biological pressure, exerted through genetic channels, toward sex-specific types of behavior, then there is a likelihood of increased psychopathology; if there is agreement, then the likelihood of psychopathology is reduced. It is for this reason that it is so important to carry out researches and experiments in this field; only sound knowledge will enable us to arrive at the optimal approximation of social teaching and biological determination. A good example of failure to make these two agree is the unexpected appearance of shame in the kibbutz experiment mentioned in a previous section, in which boys and girls were taught to disregard sexual dimorphism, yet, quite unexpectedly, girls at the onset of puberty refused to obey the social learning to which they had been exposed and insisted on separation from boys and avoidance of shared nudity. It is not too hypothetical to conclude that had the authorities insisted on their doctrinal approach, strong neurotic reactions might have been produced in at least a portion of the girls involved.

This general thesis might be taken as support for the status quo in our society, and indeed the insistence on biological factors (even though far from excluding social factors) has often been taken to mean just that. Such a view is mistaken; it disregards entirely another, equally important, facet of the evidence, namely, the appearance of very large differences in behavior and attitudes within as well as between the sexes, also conditioned in part by biological factors. We have documented this in relation to differences in libido; however, evidence is available in relation to all the other sex-associated differences we have noted. Some women are more dominant, ruthless, aggressive, egocentric, libidinous, and impersonal than most men; some men are more empathic, caring, nutritive, kind, and loving than most women. Any social rules that we may wish to introduce in order to ameliorate psychopathology and to eliminate some of its causes, as far as possible, therefore face two possibly contradictory demands; they should be in line with biologically determined differences between the sexes but they must also take into account within-sex differences that often go counter to between-sex differences. It is this biologically determined contradiction that is responsible for many of the problems and difficulties that face lawmakers in any advanced (or even primitive) society.

A society legislating for the majority of men and women would inflict possible psychopathology on the quite sizable minority whose prepared (biologically determined) behavior ran counter to that of the majority of their sex. Rules barring women from university study, from leading roles in commerce and industry, from political endeavor and voting, or from the professions clearly fall into this group; it may be that the majority of women do not care all that much for these activities, but obviously many do, and to deprive them of the possibility of behaving in a manner contrary to that characteristic of the majority would clearly be not only discriminatory but liable to lead to frustration and hence psychopathology. Modern governments are steadily advancing to an equal rights position that minimizes the possibilities of such conflict-frustration-pathology by insisting on the rights of the individual, whether male or female, rather than using broad classifications related to gender that, though on the whole probably related to biological determination, are too inclusive to be useful any longer. As John Stuart Mill already maintained in the last century, the role of the state should not be that of curtailing a person's freedom of choice on grounds of sex or anything else; it should be to enhance his or her freedom of choice and defend it against prejudice and bias. We can and should investigate the importance of the factors that determine male and female behavior and contrast, in particular, social and biological factors but, when it comes down to individuals, the only kind of reply that science can give to questions about male or female behavior most congruent with social desirability is that given originally by Dr. Samuel Johnson to a similar question: "Which man? Which woman?" The partial homogeneity of gender groups hides considerable divergence, and it is scientifically as well as socially wrong to discuss one without paying attention to the other; both are vitally important aspects of reality.

This generalization, of course, applies not only to governments and their possibly restrictive rules that militate against feminine equality (in the *equivalence*, not the *identity* sense of the word); it applies equally to the many trendsetters and leaders of thought who attempt to persuade and even coerce girls and women into disregard of sexual dimorphism and who often try to persuade women to adopt what are usually thought of as masculine roles in a search for identity, rather than equivalence. If there were no biological constraints involved, such pressure would be harmless, in that it would simply contrast one arbitrary set of norms with another. But as we have seen this is not so; existing sex roles are not allocated to men and women on a random or accidental basis, but they follow, to some extent at least, biologically prepared lines that apply to the majority of (though not all) men and women. Persuasion to adopt roles that go counter to these biologically determined types of behavior may lead to unhappiness and psychopathology for those men and women prepared, biologically, to follow the socially determined patterns of behavior. It is possible that some, at least, of current unhappiness and psychopathology among men and women alike may be due to the intellectual adoption of attitudes that negate biological determinism. It is paradoxical that many of the behaviors advocated for women by feminists are, in fact, masculine in nature, go counter to the biological pattern for feminine behavior, and are thus likely to lead to more psychopathology than would more traditional behavior. Direct investigation of these suggested possibilities is rare; it would seem socially of considerable importance to study these predictions from the general theory here developed.

References

Beit-Hallahmi, B., & Rabin, A. I. The kibbutz as a social experiment and as a child-rearing laboratory. *American Psychologist*, 1977, *32*, 532-541.

Birke, L., Faulkner, W., Best, S., Janson-Smith, D., & Overfield, K. (Eds.). *Alice through the microscope*. London, England: Virgo, 1980.

CIBA Foundation Symposium. *Sex, hormones and behaviour*. Oxford, England: Excerpta Medica, 1979.

Cook, M., & Wilson, G. *Love and attraction*. Oxford, England: Pergamon, 1977.

Daly, M., & Wilson, M. *Sex, evolution and behaviour*. London, England: Duxbury, 1979.

Dawkins, R. *The selfish gene*. London and New York: Oxford Univ. Press, 1976.

Dörner, G. *Sexualhormonabhängige Gehirndifferenzierung und Sexualität*. Berlin and New York: Springer-Verlag, 1972.

Eaves, L., & Eysenck, H. J. The nature of extraversion: A genetical analysis. *Journal of Personality and Social Psychology*, 1975, 32, 102-112.

Eaves, L., & Eysenck, H. J. Genotype-environmental model for psychoticism. *Advances in Behaviour Research and Therapy*, 1977, *1*, 5-26.

Eysenck, H. J. (Ed.). *Handbook of abnormal psychology*. London, England: Pitman, 1960.

Eysenck, H. J. *Sex and personality*. London, England: Open Books, 1976.

Eysenck, H. J. *You and neurosis*. London, England: Temple Smith, 1977.

Eysenck, H. J. The bio-social model of man and the unification of psychology. In A. J. Chapman & D. H. Jones (Eds.), *Models of man*. Leicester, England: British Psychological Society, 1980. (a)

Eysenck, H. J. The bio-social nature of man. *Journal of Social and Biological Structures*, 1980, *3*, 125-134. (b)

Eysenck, H. J., & Eysenck, S. B. G. *Psychoticism as a dimension of personality*. London, England: Hodder & Stoughton, 1976.

Eysenck, H. J., & Wilson, G. *The psychology of sex*. Toronto, Canada: Dent, 1979.

Feldman, P., & MacCulloch, M. *Human sexual behavior.* New York: Wiley, 1980.

Goldberg, S. *The inevitability of patriarchy.* London, England: Temple Smith, 1977.

Gomberg, E. S., & Franks, V. *Gender and disordered behavior: Sex differences in psychopathology.* New York: Brunner/Mazel, 1979.

Gray, J. Sex differences in emotional behavior in mammals including man: Endocrine bases. *Acta Psychologica,* 1971, *35,* 29-40.

Hazleton, L. *Israeli women.* New York: Simon and Schuster, 1977.

Hutt, C. *Males and females.* New York: Penguin Books, 1972.

Lloyd, B., & Archer, J. *Exploring sex differences.* New York: Academic Press, 1976.

Maccoby, E., & Jacklin, C. *The psychology of sex differences.* London and New York: Oxford Univ. Press, 1975.

Martin, N. G., & Eysenck, H. J. Genetic factors in sexual behavior. In H. J. Eysenck (Ed.), *Sex and personality.* London, England: Open Books, 1976.

Mead, M. *Male and female.* New York: Penguin Books, 1970.

Mead, M. Review of S. Goldberg: The inevitability of patriarchy. *Redbook,* 1973, p. 48.

Mischel, W. A social-learning view of sex differences in behavior. In E. Maccoby (Ed.), *The development of sex differences.* Stanford, California: Stanford Univ. Press, 1966.

Mitchell, G. *Behavioral sex differences in nonhuman primates.* New York: Van Nostrand-Reinhold, 1979.

Money, J., & Ehrhardt, A. A. *Man and woman, boy and girl.* Baltimore, Maryland: Johns Hopkins Univ. Press, 1972.

Murdock, G. *Ethnographic atlas.* Pittsburgh, Pennsylvania: Univ. of Pittsburgh Press, 1967.

Padan-Eisenstark, D. Image and reality: women's status in Israel. In R. Rohrlich-Leavitt (Ed.), *Women cross-culturally.* The Hague, The Netherlands: Mouton, 1975.

Richards, J. R. *The sceptical feminist.* London, England: Routledge & Kegan Paul, 1980.

Royce, J. The conceptual framework for a multi-factor theory of individuality. In J. Royce (Ed.), *Multivariate analysis and psychological theory.* New York: Academic Press, 1973.

Safilios-Rothschild, C. *Love, sex, and sex roles.* Englewood Cliffs, New Jersey: Prentice-Hall, 1977.

Schlegel, W. S. *Die Sexualinstinkte des Menschen.* Munich, W. Germany: Rutten & Loening Verlag, 1966.

Seligman, M. Phobias and preparedness. *Behavior Therapy,* 1971, *2,* 307-320.

Shazar, R. (Ed.). *The plough woman.* New York: Hazel, 1975.

Spiro, M. *Kibbutz: Venture in utopia.* Cambridge, Massachusetts: Harvard Univ. Press, 1955.

Spiro, M. *Children of the kibbutz.* Cambridge, Massachusetts: Harvard Univ. Press, 1958.

Spiro, M. *Gender and culture: Kibbutz women revisited.* Durham, North Carolina: Duke Univ. Press, 1979.

Symons, D. *The evolution of human sexuality.* London and New York: Oxford Univ. Press, 1979.

Talmon-Garber, Y. Sex role differentiation in an egalitarian society. In T. E. Lawell, J. H. Burma, & S. H. Gronson (Eds.), *Life in society.* Glenview, Illinois: Scott Foreman, 1965.

Tiger, L., & Shepher, J. *Women in the kibbutz.* New York: Harcourt, 1975.

Trivers, R. L. Parental investment and sexual selection. In B. Campbell (Ed.), *Sexual selection and the descent of man.* Chicago, Illinois: Aldine, 1972.

Wesley, F., & Wesley, C. *Sex-role psychology.* New York: Human Sciences Press, 1977.

13

IHSAN AL-ISSA

Gender, Hormones, and Psychopathology

In Chapter 12, Eysenck discussed the relative influence of genetic and environmental factors on gender roles. This chapter presents, by providing evidence on the influence of genetic factors in general and biological factors in particular, research on the relationship between prenatal and postnatal hormones and sexual dimorphism. At an early stage of development, the embryo's genetic sex (the XX or XY chromosomal combination) initiates sexual dimorphism by determining whether the embryo's undifferentiated gonads become ovaries or testes. If the embryo has a Y chromosome, the gonads differentiate into testes that will produce androgen. However, if the embryo has two X chromosomes, the gonads differentiate into ovaries. Any further development of the reproductive structures is dependent on the presence or absence of androgen rather than on the direct effect of the genetic sex of the fetus. Thus, a complete morphological differentiation (the shape of the external genitalia) into a male requires the presence of a Y chromosome and androgen, whereas differentiation into a female occurs in the presence of two X chromosomes and the absence of androgen. It appears that the differentiation of the reproductive anatomy of the female takes place in the total absence of fetal ovarian hormones. Of course, hormones continue to exert their influence on the differentiation of physical appearance during puberty.

Although the biological origin of sex differences in physical characteristics is rarely questioned, sexually dimorphic behavior that is traditionally classified as masculine or feminine is often attributed to socialization and to the differential

ISBN: 0-12-050350-6

treatment of boys and girls. However, the universality of gender role differences and the difficulty of eradicating such differences even under social pressure would suggest the influence of biological factors (see Eysenck, Chapter 12, this volume). In addition to their influence on physical appearance, sex hormones are involved in the organization of the brain, which seems to determine sexually dimorphic behavior. This chapter deals with research on the influence of prenatal and postnatal hormones, especially androgen, on sexually dimorphic mating and nonmating behavior that is traditionally incorporated in gender roles. Both animal and human research are covered. Furthermore, the relationship between hormones and the development of gender identity is discussed. Finally, the chapter deals with the possible behavioral and emotional influences of female hormones during the menstrual cycle, postpartum, and the menopause as well as during the use of oral contraceptives.

Hormones and Animal Behavior

Experimental work with animals reveals that hormonal levels, particularly androgen, at critical periods during early development affect both mating and nonmating behavior. Pregnant female guinea pigs injected with testosterone have genetic female offspring that are morphologically (e.g., genitalia) and psychosexually masculinized (Diamond & Young, 1963; Phoenix, Goy, Gerall, & Young, 1959). The mature animal also becomes sensitive to male rather than to female hormones. The level of aggression and the sexual behavior of these female hermaphrodites are like those of the male guinea pig. Mounting increases with androgen, whereas lordosis (a downward arching of the back in response to the male's mounting) is absent even following the administration of estrogen or progesterone. In the rat, the critical period for brain differentiation and organization occurs neonatally rather that prenatally, making it possible to manipulate directly the hormonal environment of the offspring. Male rats castrated after birth tend to respond to estrogen or progesterone by lordosis, much as do genetic females (Phoenix, Goy, & Resko, 1968). In contrast, female rats treated with testosterone during the critical period demonstrate an inhibition of female sexual behavior and an increase in male intromission patterns (mounting with vigorous pelvic thrusts, followed by a backward fall) (Harris & Levine, 1965; Young, Goy, & Phoenix, 1964). These neonatally androgenized females have lost their attractiveness to and are less frequently mounted by males than untreated females even when they were administered estrogen (Pfaff & Zigmond, 1971).

Sexually dimorphic nonmating behavior such as wheel running, emergence, and open-field behavior are also affected by the presence or absence of testosterone. Females neonatally treated with testosterone react more like males, whereas males castrated at the critical period behave much more like females than their untreated male controls. (Normal female rats emerge more frequently with shorter latencies than male rats. They are also more active, cover a greater area, and drop fewer fecal boluses in open field test than do males [Harris, 1964; Swanson, 1967].) Male mice castrated before puberty fail to display aggressive behavior as compared with normal male mice (Beeman, 1947). Neonatal administration of androgen to female mice raises adult aggression, particularly when further testosterone treatments are given in adulthood (Edwards, 1969; Edwards & Herndon, 1970). Female rhesus monkeys treated by testosterone engage in rough-and-tumble play, chasing, and threatening behaviors that are normally displayed by males (Goy, 1970; Young *et al.*, 1964).

Androgen tends to sensitize brain structures that mediate aggressive behavior to the action of testosterone in adulthood. Neonatal androgenization of male or female mice results in fighting sooner than mice not androgenized when both groups were given testosterone (Von Saal, Svare, & Gandelman, 1976). On the one hand, Gray (1971) believes that aggression is enhanced by the presence of circulating androgen only in animals that have differentiated sexually as males. On the other hand, Edwards (1969) suggests that since female mice tend to display aggressive behavior under appropriate conditions, it seems that androgen in infancy is not necessary for the development of neural mechanisms for aggression, but rather that they affect the sensitivity of these mechanisms to androgenic stimulation in adulthood.

Many of the animal studies using androgen during the critical period of brain differentiation have been replicated in studies using estrogen (Reinisch, 1974). For example, estrogen tends to masculinize the behavior of both castrated male and normal female rodents in the same manner that was demonstrated with androgen. However, feminine patterns of behavior develop in normal females with the presence of ovaries because, in contrast to testes, ovaries do not seem to play a role during the critical period of sexual differentiation (Reinisch, 1974).

The effect of hormones depends on the dosage used. The timing of the intervention is also important since the critical periods for hormonal effect on genital anatomy and on the central nervous system seem to differ. That hormones definitely influence sexually dimorphic behavior does not exclude the role of experience in the development of animals (Beach, 1974). For example, sexual and play behavior are shown to be influenced by rearing conditions in rhesus monkeys (Goy & Goldfoot, 1974). Similarly, the social environment in which a rat pup is reared influences the development of normal social behavior (Gruendel & Arnold, 1974). McEwen (1976) has demonstrated that experience may influence hormonal levels; rhesus monkeys that are subjected to defeat by dominant males show a decrease in testosterone, but when these defeated animals are exposed to female companions, their testosterone level returns quickly to normal. In general, the lower the animal on the phyletic scale, the more likely that its prenatally determined behavior is stereotyped and less affected by later experience. In higher primates and, particularly, human beings, the behavior is more open to postnatal influences. Thus, the animal evidence on hormonal influences does not exclude the role of social learning on behavior (Bandura, 1969), but it indicates that hormones merely lower the threshold for such behavior.

Hormones and Human Behavior

Sexually dimorphic behavior in animals seems to have its counterpart in human beings. The finding that male aggression is universal not only among animals but also among humans seems to suggest strongly the involvement of biological factors (Gray, 1971; Maccoby & Jacklin, 1974; Rohner, 1976).

In his review of the literature, Rohner (1976) presented evidence in support of the biological rather than the enculturation hypothesis, which attempts to explain sex differences in aggression exclusively on the basis of learning. He rejected the hypothesis suggesting that sex differences in aggression result from social pressures that encourage more aggressive behavior in boys than in girls. Rohner cites evidence showing that, in 75% of a world sample of societies, both boys and girls are encouraged or equally allowed to be aggressive (Barry, Josephson, Lauer, & Marshall, cited in Rohner, 1976). Maccoby and Jacklin (1974) also pointed out that boys receive as much punishment for aggression as girls, or even more, and on the basis of punishment alone, they would be expected to have as much fear of performing aggressive acts. A second enculturation hypothesis discussed by Rohner (1976) states that sex differences in the division of labor produce sex differences in aggression. Data against this hypothesis reveal that boys who are assigned the same domestic tasks as girls are still more aggressive than girls, even though these boys are less aggressive than boys who do more "aggressive" chores. Rohner noted that a biosocial mechanism is needed to explain why boys around the world are assigned tasks that lead to greater aggression than girls. From the available evidence, he concluded that there is a biological predisposition for males to behave more aggressively than females, although this differential in readiness to respond aggressively is subject to substantial modification through learning and experience.

Taking into consideration research on hormonally induced aggression in animals as well as the dominance of man throughout history and across cultures, Goldberg (1973) argued that biological factors may lead to patriarchy and the dominant relationship between the sexes (see Chapter 12, this volume). However, several arguments have been put forward against the biological hypothesis of human aggression. For example, a frequently cited study by Mead (1935) describes three New Guinea tribes in which gender roles appear to be inconsistent with a biological explanation. Among the Arapesh tribe, both men and women exhibited feminine behavior, being cooperative, gentle, and nonaggressive. In contrast, Mead observed that among the Mundugumor tribe, both men and women are equally aggressive and competitive. In a third tribe, the Tchambuli, however, gender roles are reversed, with women engaging in fishing, trade, and production and men in arts and other nonutilitarian pursuits. There are also exceptions to the animal findings. In the golden hamster, for example, the female is more aggressive than the male (Phoenix *et al.*, 1968). In evaluating this evidence, Goldberg (1973) pointed out that the findings of Mead or of Phoenix *et al.* do not refute the biological basis of sex differences. He indicated that Mead's conclusions regarding the plasticity of gender roles do not follow from her description of the three tribes. Mead herself has noted that the three tribes described by her do not disprove the existence of sex differences. In fact, her description of the Tchambuli boys as cruel and aggressive (e.g., killing a victim and hanging the head in a ceremonial house as a trophy) is consistent with other findings on male aggression. Goldberg also argued that animals that reveal sex reversal in aggressive behavior also show similar tendency in body size, with the female larger than the male. This size reversal would suggest that the hormonal development of the entire central nervous system of these animals such as in the hamster is the reverse of that found in other experimental animals.

Due to ethical considerations, research involving the manipulation of the prenatal environment has used nonhuman subjects. However, in the following section, I discuss human sex hormone abnormalities that yield data similar to those obtained with animals. These abnormalities may be caused by an excess of androgen such as in the androgenital syndrome in the genetic males and females and progestin-induced excess of androgen in genetic females. Abnormalities could also be caused by a deficiency in the amount of and reaction to sex-appropriate hormones as in Turner's syndrome individuals and androgen insensitivity syndrome in genetic males. Another human research area to be discussed is the investigation of the fluctuation and changes in female hormones during the menstrual cycle, menopause, pregnancy, and childbirth and during the use of oral contraceptives, on the one hand, and emotional behavior, on the other. Finally, I discuss sex hormones in relation to sexual orientation. (Hormones and sexual functioning are discussed by Heiman & Verholst, Chapter 14, this volume.)

Sex Hormone Abnormalities

The Androgenital Syndrome

In the androgenital syndrome, the hormonal abnormality consists of an increase in the production of androgen by the adrenal cortex. The excess of fetal androgen results in the virilization of the female fetus as well as in an accelerated puberal development because the same prenatal adrenal androgen that creates the hermaphroditic sex organs continues to exert the same influence postnatally. A life-long cortisone therapy is used to control the excess of androgen in addition to early surgical feminization of external genitalia. However, prior to 1950, there was no cortisone therapy for the androgenital syndrome, and these women become masculinized prenatally and postnatally.

Both treated and untreated genetic females with the androgenital syndrome were followed up by Ehrhardt, Epstein, and Money (1968) and Ehrhardt, Evers, and Money (1968). These girls were described by their mothers and by themselves as tomboys during childhood. They had high levels of energy with strong interest in outdoor physical activities. They showed little interest in girls' activities such as doll play and dresses. As compared with a control group, a larger number of them (eight versus one control) were ambivalent about their female gender identity. The patient group also revealed less concern about marriage and child care and more interest in careers than the controls. The treated group whose excessive androgen is controlled after birth show the same results as the untreated group, suggesting that tomboyish behavior and interests are due to prenatal rather than postnatal effects.

Ehrhardt, Evers, and Money (1968) found that *some* of the untreated females who were postnatally masculinized and living as virilized women manifested little behavior that could be considered more masculine than feminine. These data would suggest that gender role and gender identity are not determined by postnatal levels of androgen. They also show that a permanent prenatal hormonal effect on the brain that will mediate dimorphic sexual behavior is selective by being dependent on factors such as the timing and the amount of fetal androgen exposure.

Although girls with the androgenital syndrome reveal tomboyish behavior such as high level of activity, they tend to show less aggression and dominance than boys or normal females (Money & Schwartz, 1976). A. G. Kaplan (1980) pointed out that these female patients behave more like an androgynous rather than a typical masculine person. She concluded that a slight to moderate excess of androgen, particularly in females, tends to be associated with gender role flexibility.

Money and Ehrhardt (1972) observed that a genetic female with the androgenital syndrome raised as a female but not surgically corrected or hormonally treated may develop an ambiguous gender identity or one that is compatible with her masculine anatomy rather than with her assigned, female sex. They noted, however, that premature masculinization by itself does not predestine the hermaphroditic child living as a girl to differentiate either an ambivalent or a masculine gender identity. The development of female gender identity depends on the consistency of the experience of being reared as female, particularly during the early years of the onset of language acquisition at around 18 months until the age of 3 or 4. This early period in the development of gender identity is so important that sex reassignment imposed during these formative years or later is rarely successful. Money and Ehrhardt (1972) report cases of matched pairs of hermaphrodites who are chromosomally, gonadally, and diagnostically the same (e.g., genetic females with the androgenital syndrome) but they have the opposite sex assignment, biographical history, and gender identity. These cases may develop socially and vocationally in opposite manners to the extent that it is difficult to gather any clues about their medical histories.

Progestin-Induced Hermaphroditism

Women are sometimes given synthetic progestins in order to prevent threatened miscarriages, but these drugs tend to act like testosterone and result in some of the women giving birth to partially virilized babies. Genetic females of these pregnancies exhibit masculinized external genitalia quite similar to those found in girls with androgenital syndrome. However, they do not show premature virilization, but exhibit normal feminization at puberty. Menstruation and ovulation occur without any treatment. Since these genetic females, like those with the androgenital syndrome, are reared as girls, they would show the possible effects of prenatal hormonal masculinization on behavior even in the presence of social feminization (i.e., being reared as girls) and in the absence of social masculinization (i.e., without being reared as boys). A study by Ehrhardt and Money (1967) indicates that progestin-masculinized girls are tomboyish in behavior. They show interest in vigorous athletic activity and functional clothing rather than in self-adornment and the rehearsal of maternalism in doll play. They also show more concern with achievement and career than with marriage. They tend to respond to visual erotic stimuli in a manner similar to men (tomboyish females objectify the figure in the picture). These traits could be easily assimilated into a male gender identity should these prenatally androgenized chromosomal and gonadal females be assigned and reared as males.

In a study by Reinisch and Karow (1977), it was found that a group of males and females whose mothers were treated with intermediate amounts of progestin and minimum dosages of estrogen, were more independent, individualistic, self-assured, self-sufficient, and sensitive than an untreated group on the Cattell Personality Questionnaires. In contrast, subjects whose mothers were treated with minimum amounts of progestin with maximum dosages of estrogen were more group-oriented, group dependent, and less independent or self-assured. In another study, Reinisch (1981) compared males and females whose mothers were administered synthetic progestin with same-sex siblings unexposed to the drug on a test measuring potential for aggression. Progestin-exposed females had a mean score almost double that of their sisters. Similarly, the progestin-exposed males exhibited double the score of their brothers. However, these significant differences between the treated and untreated groups were found in physical rather than verbal aggression. As expected from previous research, the aggression scores of the unexposed males were significantly higher than those of the unexposed females.

It has been suggested that maternal knowledge of the medical treatment and awareness of the clinical status of the offspring (e.g., surgical feminization early in life) may have exposed the children to different socialization experiences than controls or made the mothers more willing to admit cross-sex behavior. However, Reinisch and Karow (1977) noted that many of the mothers in their study could not recall that they had taken medication except vitamins during pregnancy. Ehrhardt (1973) found that even in extreme cases, when the effect of the prenatal hormones were genital, morphological changes such as in the androgenital syndrome or in progestin-induced hermaphroditism, there was no consistent difference between patients and controls in maternal attitude toward their daughters' behavior.

The time of administration of the pregnancy-maintaining drugs is a crucial variable. Kester, Green, Finch, and Williams (1980) found that when the drug stilbestrol is given in the first trimester, it tends to have more masculine outcomes in boys, such as less cross-dressing, more boys as playmates, and more interest in sports. There was, however, no consistent pattern for those exposed after the first trimester.

Androgen Insensitivity Syndrome (Testicular Feminization)

In the androgen insensitivity syndrome, a genetic and gonadal male (XY male) has the external sex appearance and sexual rearing of a female. The patient cannot utilize endogenous or exogenous androgen because of a genetically transmitted defect that blocks, at the cellular level, the intake of androgen by the target organs. Money, Ehrhardt, and Masica (1968) studied the personality characteristics and the gender identity of 10 patients with this syndrome. They found that the majority of their patients strongly desired marriage and had little interest in outside jobs. These patients tended to play with dolls and other girls' toys in childhood. They were exclusively feminine in their gender role and gender identity, revealing no tomboyish behavior. The masculine genetics of the patients has not resulted in any masculinized behavior. Money *et al.* (1968) concluded that the XY chromosomal constitution does not carry a genetic code that directly influences psychological traits and behavior but that the mediation between genetics and behavior is hormonal, instead.

Money and Ehrhardt (1972) pointed out that in the androgen insensitivity syndrome the prenatal hormone effects on the chromosomal males cannot be distinguished from the postnatal cultural effects (i.e., social feminization) since the baby is born with female genitalia and assigned and reared as a girl. However, there are cases of incomplete forms of the androgen insensitivity syndrome in which there is partial prenatal androgen failure resulting in ambiguous genitalia at birth followed by rearing as a boy. Although these cases of partial androgenization are rare, they seem to be associated with the opposite of tomboyism even though they are reared as boys rather than girls.

Turner's Syndrome

Turner's syndrome (XO) individuals are similar to androgen insensitivity syndrome (XY) individuals in several respects. In both syndromes, the fetus is not a genetic female (XX). Since the children have not been exposed to androgen prenatally, they develop female external genitalia and are reared as females. Because they do not have two X chromosomes, neither group has ovaries.

Fifteen patients with Turner's syndrome were studied by Ehrhardt, Greenberg, and Money (1970). As compared with controls, the patients were more passive during fights in childhood. They were also more likely to withdraw in a fight rather than to defend themselves or to start a fight. Their interest was in doll play rather than in outdoor activities. In general, they showed the opposite of tomboyish behavior and differentiated a female rather than a male gender identity. This study of Turner's syndrome demonstrates that in order to differentiate a postnatal feminine gender role or gender identity is neither dependent on prenatal gonadal hormones (estrogen or androgen) acting on the brain nor is it dependent on the presence of a second X chromosome.

Adult Hormones and Gender Role

In contrast to the influence of prenatal hormonal abnormalities on gender role, the relationship between levels of circulating hormones in adulthood and sexually dimorphic behavior is not consistent. Whereas some studies found that levels of plasma testosterone are related to self-report measures of aggression in normal males (Persky, Smith, & Basu, 1971) and to violent crimes in prisoners (Moyer, 1974), others did not show such a relationship (Beach, 1965). Since social situations such as stress tend to increase androgen level (Kreuz, Rose, & Jennings, 1972), the direction of causality in the relationship between hormones and behavior in adults is not clear.

Sex differences in sexually dimorphic behavior seem to decrease or even reverse in some individuals with age (Guttman, 1975). These behavioral changes may be the result of age-related hormonal levels that have masculinizing effects in women and feminizing effects in men (Marcus & Korenman, 1976).

Hormones and Sexual Behavior: Human Research

Estrogen is necessary for the maturation as well as the maintenance of the female reproductive tracts (the size of the vagina and the maintenance of the structure and lubrication of the vaginal lining). On the other hand, androgen is required for fetal development as well as for the maturation and maintenance of the size and function of the male reproductive tract. An extreme reduction of these hormones can interfere with adequate sexual functioning (Ledwitz-Rigby, 1980). Libido, however, seems to be controlled by androgen in both males and females. Thus, if a male is castrated before puberty, libido fails to develop. After puberty, castration may not be followed by loss of libido if the adrenal gland provides sufficient androgen. In contrast to men, women do not lose their libido with the loss of ovaries because their adrenals are the usual source of androgen.

Yet, it is difficult to establish direct relationships between sexual drive and function, on the one hand, and hormone levels circulating in the blood, on the other. Excessive sexual behavior is not significantly correlated with excessive hormone levels. For example, the plasma testosterone levels in rapists (i.e., sexual aggression) tend to be within the normal range (Rada, Laws, & Kellner, 1976). Similarly, a high frequency of coitus and masturbation do not correlate with elevated hormone levels. However, such correlation is wrongly inferred from the finding that low libido in hormonally deficient people may be increased after hormonal supplementation (Money, 1980).

The administration of high doses of estrogen or progesterone (in the treatment of prostate cancer with estrogen or progesterone, the treatment of male sex offenders with antiandrogens) tends to have castrating effects by suppressing ejaculation, reducing or suppressing erection, and decreasing or abolishing sex drive. These effects can be reversed by withdrawal of the drug (Money, 1980). Kester *et al.* (1980) found that male subjects who had been exposed prenatally to synthetic progesterone had a lower rating on sexual drive along with a later onset of intercourse in adulthood than the normal controls. The natural progesterone subjects reported more problems with erectile failure than nonexposed subjects. The authors suggested that progesterone and progestin treatment may interfere with the activity of endogenous testosterone during sexual differentiation. Antiandrogenic effects of progesterone have been reported in rats (Kinel & Maqueo, 1965). Progestin is also used as a chemical castrator in the treatment of sex offenders (Walker, 1977). However, the mechanism that mediates the effects of these female hormones is still unclear (Kester *et al.*, 1980).

Hormones and Sexual Orientation

Animal work reviewed earlier in this chapter demonstrates that prenatal or perinatal levels of androgen are related to sexual orientation in general and to sexual inversion in particular. Early hormonal treatment also sensitizes the animal to the effects of hormones in adulthood. These findings of prenatal and postnatal hormonal effects on animals were extrapolated to human sexual orientation, especially in the etiology and treatment of homosexuality.

Consistent with the animal data is the suggestion by Dörner (1976) that in genetic males, androgen deficiency during the hypothalamus differentiation phase of the brain will result in a female differentiation of the brain with a neuroendocrine predisposition for bisexuality or homosexuality. In genetic females, on the other hand, an excess of androgen during the hypothalamus differentiation phase leads to a male differentiation in the brain and a neuroendocrine predisposition for bisexuality or homosexuality. Cases of hormonal abnormalities should provide an experiment in nature to throw light on Dörner's theory. However, the evidence in this area appears to be negative (Money & Ehrhardt, 1972). For example, prenatal androgenization of genetic females or partial androgen insensitivity in genetic males does not determine or predispose to homosexuality. Money and Ehrhardt conclude that in cases involving prenatal hormonal disturbance, it is the gender the child is reared in that determines heterosexual orientation.

Hormones affect morphological fetal development as well as sexual dimorphism of body build in puberty. If hormones also affect sexual orientation, it is expected that there would be an association between body build and sexual orientation. Prenatal androgen level seems to influence the shape of the pelvis. Whereas the male pelvic outlet tends to be narrow, the female pelvic outlet is rather broad. However, there is a variation in the shape of the pelvis with an overlap between the sexes. That is, some men may have broader pelvic outlets than women and vice versa. Figure 13.1 shows the measurement of the width of pelvic outlets for men and women, with narrower outlets

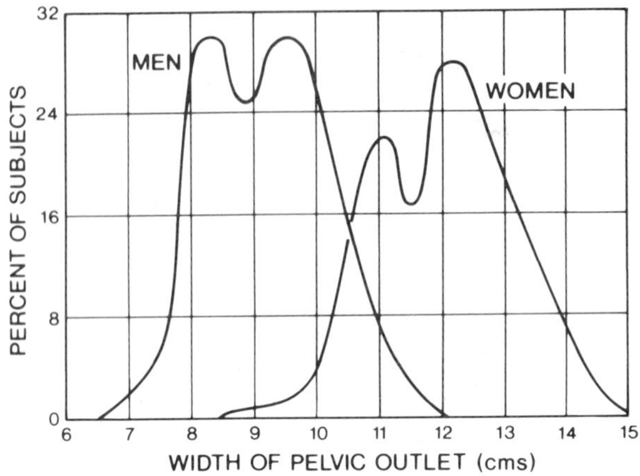

FIGURE 13.1. ***Distribution of pelvic shapes for men and women (From Eysenck, 1976).***

characterizing most men and wider outlets characterizing most women. Schlegel (1962, 1966) found a significant shift in the shape of pelvic outlets of homosexual males in the direction of females. In addition to the relationship between pelvic shape and homosexuality, Schlegel postulated that if both pelvic shape and masculine and feminine behavior are determined by prenatal hormones, it is expected that pelvic shape would be associated with masculinity-femininity. He found that individuals (males and females) with a male-type pelvis (narrow shape) tend to exhibit masculine behavior, whereas those with a female-type pelvis (wide shape) tend to exhibit feminine behavior. On the one hand, a masculine-type pelvis is associated with leadership, activity, and dominance in both sexes. On the other hand, a feminine-type pelvis correlates with empathy, suggestibility, and compliance.

There is a striking similarity between the distribution of pelvic shapes in men and women in Figure 13.1 and the distribution of sexual attitudes and behavior in Figure 12.1 except that in the latter, men are on the right and women on the left. This would suggest that a narrow pelvic outlet may be associated with masculine sexual attitudes, whereas a wide pelvic outlet may be related to feminine sexual attitudes. Figures 13.1 and 12.1 reveal that there is overlap between men and women in both the shape of the pelvis and in sexual attitudes. That is, there are some men whose pelvic outlets and sexual attitudes are similar to those of the average female, and there are some women whose pelvic outlets and sexual attitudes are similar to those of the average male. How far these similarities in pelvic shapes and sexual attitudes reveal common underlying hormonal influences needs further research.

Coppen (1959) reported lower shoulder:pelvis ratios in homosexual than in heterosexual males. This result was replicated by Evans (1972), who also found that homosexual subjects were less muscular than normal controls. Kenyon (1968) found that lesbians tend to be heavier, with bigger busts and waists than married women. Griffiths *et al.* (1974) reported a larger stature in lesbians than in a group of mothers. However, differences in body build disappear when body height is controlled. Thus, it appears that there is no specific body build that is unique to lesbians.

Meyer-Bahlburg (1980) observes that differences in body build may not necessarily imply a neuroendocrine basis for male homosexuality. She points out that nonmasculine body build may bring about a poor self-image for a male that may in turn increase the risk for many behaviors (nonassertive, passive, submissive), including homosexuality. In conclusion, she indicates that body build is unlikely to be a major determinant of sexual orientation although it may be a contributing factor in some subgroups of homosexuals. The animal and human data seem to suggest that both body build and sexually dimorphic behavior, which may include sexual orientation, are influenced by prenatal hormones.

Adult Hormones and Sexual Orientation

Early studies with male homosexuals revealed that they have lower testosterone levels than heterosexuals (Kolodny, Jacobs, Masters, Toro, & Daughaday, 1972; Loraine, Adamopoulos, Kirkham, Ismail, & Dove, 1971). However, subsequent studies that employed careful subject selection procedures and multiple blood sampling did not find decreased testosterone levels in homosexuals (Brodie, Gartrell, Doering, & Rhue, 1974; Parks, *et al.*, 1974). Against the hormonal hypothesis in male homosexuality is the finding of Friedman, Wollesen, and Tendler (1976) that a pair of monozygotic twins discordant for sexual orientation had the same, normal blood levels of testosterone. There is also no correlation between testosterone levels and the preferred role (passive, active, alternately passive and active) in sexual activities (Doerr, Kockott, Vogt, Pirke, & Dittmar, 1973). Similarly, testosterone is not associated with the degree of effeminacy in gender role among male homosexuals (Pillard, Rose, & Sherwood, 1974).

Overall, studies reveal that most male homosexuals tend to have testosterone levels within the normal range of male samples from the general population (Meyer-Bahlburg, 1980). Although early studies with lesbians indicated elevated testosterone levels (Griffiths *et al.*, 1974; Loraine *et al.*, 1971), the majority of lesbians do not seem to be different from heterosexual women. There is still a possibility that testosterone levels may contribute to the sexual orientation of some subgroups of both homosexual males and females (Meyer-Bahlburg, 1980).

If sexual orientation is the expression of prenatal brain differentiation, as suggested by Dörner (1976), it cannot be changed by hormonal treatment in adulthood but should involve prenatal manipulations or hypothalamic surgery in adulthood. However, psychosurgery with homosexuals seems to reduce the overall sexual drive rather than change sexual orientation (Valenstein, 1973). Similarly, hormonal treatment of homosexual males has received little success. Surgical castration seems to decrease sexual activity and the libido of male homosexuals as well as heterosexuals without changing sexual orientation (Bremer, 1958; Cornu, 1973). Results obtained with synthetic hormones that suppress the production of testosterone or reduce its effectiveness are the same as those from surgical castration (Money, 1970; Murray, Bancroft, Anderson, Tennent, & Carr, 1975). Finally, hypogonadism in both males and females is associated with hyposexuality rather than with sexual orientation (Meyer-Bahlburg, 1977).

Female Hormones and Psychiatric Disturbance

The cyclic nature of female hormones (estrogen and progesterone) raises the question whether there are behavioral changes associated with their fluctuation. Particular attention has been given to the relationship between emotional or psychiatric disturbance, on the one hand, and the menstrual cycle, menopause, pregnancy, childbirth, and the ingestion of oral contraceptives on the other.

Early studies of women at the premenstrual phase of the cycle have reported mood disturbance (Moos *et al.*, 1969; Silbergeld, Brast, & Noble, 1971) and increases in crime (Dalton, 1961; Morton, Addition, Addison, Hunt, & Sullivan, 1953), suicide (Dalton, 1959; MacKinnon, MacKinnon, & Thompson, 1959; Tonks, Rack, & Rose, 1968), accidents (Dalton, 1960), and hospital admission for mental illness (Dalton, 1959; Janowsky, Gomey, Castelnuovo-Tedesco, & Stone, 1969). It is assumed that there is a causal relationship between low levels of hormones and a wide spectrum of deviant behavior. This assumption has, however, been questioned on both methodological and theoretical grounds. Two critical reviews of the literature by Parlee (1973) and Sommer (1973) have noted methodological problems such as the selection of subjects and the interpretation of data based on self-report. Patients, for example, are used without normal controls. The extent to which the biological state of the women (independent variable) is causally related to affective states and other dependent variables is not well established. Studies are also inconsistent in finding premenstrual negative mood (Ruble & Brooks-Gunn, 1979). Negative affect reported by random samples of normal menstruating women is significantly lower than that reported by female psychiatric patients. In these random samples, affective changes during the menstrual cycle are not greater than mood changes resulting from other factors in the person's everyday life. Ruble and Brooks-Gunn (1979) concluded that although some women experience affective and behavioral problems associated with the menstrual cycle, the number of these women is relatively small.

Sommer (1973) reported a discrepancy between subjective reports that demonstrate impairment in behavior during menstruation and objective measures that indicate negative effects. The finding that suicidal behavior is a feature of the premenstrual cycle has not been confirmed (Buckle, Linnane, & McConacky, 1965; Holding & Minkoff, 1973). Moos (1969) also found no consistent reaction during menstruation from one woman to the other; whereas some women experienced mainly dysmenorrhea with no mood disturbance, others complained of mood disturbance without pain or cramps.

It has been suggested that behavioral disturbance during the premenstrual and menstrual periods may only appear in women who are predisposed toward such behavior in the first place. Coppen and Kessel (1963) found that the presence of premenstrual symptoms such as irritability, depression, tension, nervousness, and anxiety are related to high neuroticism scores on the Maudsley Personality Inventory. However, a group of psychologically and physically healthy females reported by Persky (1974) show no increase in depression, hostility, and anxiety during the premenstrual period. Other studies also indicate that premenstrual symptoms tend to appear in emotionally unstable, rather than well-adjusted, women (Kashiwagi, McClure, & Wetzel, 1976; Paulson, 1961; Rees, 1953; Schuckit, Daly, Herrman, & Hineman, 1975; Smith & Sauder, 1969). Those women who report physical discomfort and mood symptoms (e.g., on the Moos Menstrual Distress Questionnaire) tend to report such symptoms in other situations as well (Paige, 1973). Fluctuation in mood seems to be associated with other situations rather than the menstrual cycle. For example, Rossi and Rossi (1977) found that negative mood varies according to the day of the week, with more negative moods occurring when the premenstrual phase of the cycle falls at midweek. The mood variation of married couples seems to be comparable over a given period of time regardless of menstrual cycle (Dan, 1976). These data raise the possibility that psychiatric disturbance in some women during the premenstrual and menstrual phases of the cycle reflects a general vulnerability instead of a disturbance specific to these periods. Also, stress associated with hormonal changes may affect those women who are vulnerable to psychiatric disturbance through personality predisposition or other factors.

Cognitive factors such as attitudes and expectations have been suggested as explanations of behavioral changes during the menstrual cycle. Koeske (1980) demonstrated that when negative mood and behavior occur premenstrually, they tend to be attributed to the influence of biology with no consideration of the situational factors that are simultaneously influencing them. However, identical behavior that is displayed by either a nonmenstrual female or a male is not attributed to biological factors. Koeske also found that among many women there is a tendency for an increased premenstrual arousability and, in particular, an enhanced general sensitivity to strong stimuli. Consistent with the theory of Schachter and Singer (1962), she found that situational cues present at the time, rather than the pattern of physiological response, determine whether positive or negative emotions are experienced.

Cognitive theory would also suggest that since the connotative meaning of *menstruation* is almost universally perceived in negative terms, it could be seen as resulting in negative rather than positive symptoms. Brooks, Ruble, and Clark (1977) found that women who believed that menstruation is debilitating reported significantly higher symptoms for the premenstrual (a day or two before the period) than the intermenstrual phase (7-10 days before the period). In another study, Ruble (1977) found that women who thought they were premenstrual reported a higher degree of symptoms than women who thought they were intermenstrual, even though the actual cycle phase of the two groups of women was the same (6-7 days before the next period was to begin). Parlee (1974) asked both men and women to fill the Moos Menstrual Distress Questionnaire according to what they think women experience. She found that men and women reported similar symptom patterns that are not different from those reported by women who described their actual menstrual experiences. Parlee concluded that self-report of symptoms during the menstrual cycle may reflect social expectations of what is considered the normal menstrual experience.

Paige (1973) found that Jewish women who found coitus embarrassing or were overconcerned about hygiene during menstruation were most likely to experience distress. Similarly, Catholic women, who held the most traditional views of femininity (women's place is in the home), also had the most menstrual problems. It seems that religious affiliation and general attitudes rather than physiological changes during menstruation are influencing the report of symptoms.

Relevant to emotional changes during the menstrual cycle in the human female is animal research relating sex differences in emotionality to female hormones (Archer, 1975; Gray, 1971). Results indicating that female rats are less emotional than male rats in the open field test, in emergence tests, and in both active and passive avoidance tests were explained on an endocrine basis (Archer, 1975; Gray, 1971). In particular, evidence indicating that female rats are less emotional following estrogen injections or at estrus than diestrus (Burke & Broadhurst, 1966; Gray & Levine, 1964) bears striking similarity to mood changes during the human menstrual cycle. However, the use of activity level and defecation as indexes of emotionality has been questioned (Archer, 1975). Archer suggested that sex differences in defecation may be only secondary to the effects of estrogen on food intake. Because of reduced food intake during estrus, female rats defecate less than male rats in both the test situation and in the home environment. Similarly, estrogen increases the general level of activity of female rats and sex differences in the test situation may also be secondary to the general effect of estrogen. The main objection to animal work is that the definition of animal emotionality is hardly comparable with the human subjective experience of depression or fear. However, the parallel between human and animal studies of the effects of female hormonal levels on emotionality is quite hard to ignore.

It is believed that the menopause is linked with psychological and somatic complaints. However, reliable studies that are not based on clinical impressions of selected cases indicate that many of these complaints are not reported more frequently by menopausal women (McKinlay & McKinlay, 1973). Symptoms such as insomnia, irritability, depression, reduced sexual drive, headache, dizzy spells, and palpitation do not occur consistently during the menopause (Notman, 1980). When they occur, however, they are mostly related to depression or general anxiety (Barnett & Baruch, 1978; Perlmutter, 1978). The only symptoms that are consistently reported during the menopause are those associated with vasomotor instability (hot flashes, flushes, episodes of perspiration) (Notman, 1980). Yet, the biological etiology of these symptoms is not very clear since other disease processes in which estrogen levels are low are not characterized by vasomotor instability (Perlmutter, 1978).

Community studies of premenopausal, menopausal, and postmenopausal women indicate no difference between these groups in the rate of depression (Hallstrom, 1973; McKinlay & Jeffreys, 1974). Thus, contrary to common expectation, a high rate of depression does not coincide with the menopause. However, those women who become depressed during the menopause tend to report more symptoms prior to the menopause than do nondepressed women (Ballinger, 1976). Women of lower socioeconomic status also report more symptoms than those of higher status (van Keep & Kellerhals, 1975), which may reflect a higher rate of depression in the former group not only during the menopause but in other life stages (Brown & Harris, 1978). Notman (1980) reported that women who are generally low on self-esteem or life satisfaction are more likely to have difficulties during the menopause. She suggested that the menopause should be considered in the context of other life stages and that women's reaction to it may be consistent with their reaction to other reproductive events (menstruation, pregnancy, and childbirth).

It has been suggested that depression during middle-age is not related to the menopause but to the departure of children from the home (i.e., the empty nest syndrome). However, the validity of this hypothesis has been questioned. Radloff (1975) found that for both males and females, those who had had children but who were no longer living with them were less depressed than women in other life stages. In contrast, Brown, Bhrolchain, and Harris (1975) found that young women with children have the highest rate of depression. Overall, childless couples (Houseknecht, 1979) and women whose children have left home (Lowenthal, Thurnher, Chiriboga, & Associates, 1975) report that they are more satisfied and happier than those with children. Bart (1971) suggested that after the departure of children, middle-aged Jewish women are more likely to be depressed than non-Jewish women because of their overprotective relationship with their children. This interpretation is, however, weakened by the finding that maternal overprotection is almost equally common among Jews and Protestants, both in depressed groups and normals (Fernando, 1975).

In conclusion, the evidence suggests that psychiatric disturbance is not more common among middle-aged women when there is a hormonal depletion during the menopause. Psychiatric disturbance during middle-age cannot be viewed separately from other life stages of the female, particularly her past experience with other reproductive functions. There seems to be no overall increase in stress during the menopause that might result in excessive depression (Greene & Cooke, 1980).

The rapid fall in hormonal levels postpartum seems to increase the risk of psychiatric disturbance (Pugh, Jerath, Schmidt, & Reed, 1963; Uddenberg & Nilsson, 1975; Weissman & Klerman, 1977). The "baby blues," which involve mood swings and crying episodes, are experienced during the first 10 days after childbirth by 50-80% of women (Pitt, 1973; Yalom, Lunde, Moos, & Hamburg, 1968). Psychotic states and more severe depression occur in only 1-2 cases per 1000 deliveries.

The duration of the baby blues is so brief and their incidence so common that they could be the result of massive hormonal changes rather than social factors (Yalom *et al.*, 1968). However, hormonal imbalance not only postpartum but also during pregnancy may impair the female's ability to deal with conflicts that could result in long-term psychiatric illness (Uddenberg, 1974). For example, it was found that only pregnancies and childbirth associated with severe problems such as bad marriages or inadequate living conditions increase the risk for depression (Brown & Harris, 1978; Melges, 1968; Uddenberg & Nilsson, 1975). Sources of stress that might precipitate psychiatric disturbance after childbirth may include lack of assistance and support for caretaking, unplanned and unwanted pregnancies, attitudes toward mothering, worries about responsibilities, and exhaustion (Magnus, 1980).

Some women taking oral contraceptives may report psychiatric symptoms, but the pharmacological basis of their complaints has not been established. It is still uncertain whether the reaction of these women is the result of suggestibility and psychological reaction to the pill (conflict and guilt over sexual freedom or desire for more children) or due to the pharmacological agent. Weissman and Slaby (1973) have observed that women with prior psychiatric disturbance as well as those with the expectation of negative effects tend to develop more symptoms while taking the pill. Hormonal changes may precipitate psychiatric disturbance in women who are already vulnerable or who are exposed to another life-stress.

Male versus Female Hormonal Cyclicity

Males seem to have a biological rhythm of sex hormone secretion similar to that of females. Contrary to the general belief in the acyclic nature of male hormones, Doering, Kraemer, Brody, and Hamburg (1975) found that the concentration of testosterone in the blood reveals a cyclic trend, with cycle lengths ranging from 8 to 30 days and the majority averaging 20-22 days.

There is also a synchrony of physiological reactions between married couples. Persky, Lief, O'Brien, Strauss, and Miller (1977) found that the level of the husband's blood testosterone tends to reach its maximum value at around 7 days after his wife's ovulation, which is the same time the wife's testosterone level reaches its postovulatory peak during the cycle. Henderson (1976) found a synchrony of body temperature between married couples during the menstrual cycle, with the female's midcycle temperature at a low point and subsequent postovulatory rise. Henderson also found that the basal body temperature of a homosexual male couple fluctuates synchronically. Women living in the same dormitory show menstrual synchronization, which seems to result from axillary odors (McClintock, 1971).

The behavioral implication of and the underlying factors in couple synchrony still requires further investigation. In the area of erotic synchrony, Money (1980) suggested that it could be mediated through the sense of smell by way of pheromones or odors. In subhuman primates and other mammals, the female at the ovulatory period emits a vaginal odor or pheromone that attracts the male. The human female emits the same ovulatory pheromone, but its effects on human male sexuality are not clearly established. One study has revealed that these pheromones have no effect on the frequency of intercourse of young couples (Udry & Morris, 1968).

Summary and Conclusion

Animal research indicates that the presence or absence of androgen prenatally or neonatally affects the differentiation of the genitalia as well as sexually dimorphic behavior such as aggression and sexual orientation or sexual inversion. During a critical period of development, hormones also affect the differentiation of the brain and thus sensitize the animal to the effect of hormones in maturity. Animal work has been extrapolated to human beings, but due to ethical considerations, the manipulation of the biological environment of animals perinatally has no parallel on the human level. However, studies of clinical cases in which there is either a prenatal excess of hormones (the androgenital syndrome, progestin treatment) or a prenatal deficiency in the amount of, or reaction to, sex-appropriate hormones (Turner's syndrome, androgen insensitivity syndrome) support animal work. Evidence for the relationship between circulating hormones in adulthood and aggression seems to be inconsistent. Androgen seems to be the libido hormone for both sexes. When given to a genetic and hormonal female, it has a libido-enhancing effect. Estrogen seems to have a castrating and antiandrogenizing effect on the male. However, there is no direct relationship between levels of androgen circulating in the blood and libido (exceptions are cases with extreme deficiency of androgen). Adult levels of hormones are not associated with homosexuality, but animal work would suggest that sexual orientation may be determined during the fetal period of brain differentiation.

Hormones may have indirect influence on the assignment of gender identity. Genital differentiation as a result of the presence or absence of androgen influences those who assign sex and rear the child as a boy or a girl. Later, the child develops a gender identity that is consistent with his or her anatomy. However, studies of hermaphrodites who are chromosomally, gonadally, and diagnostically the same but have the opposite sex assignment and gender of rearing, tend to develop opposite gender identity. Their erotic-stimulus arousal (love affairs, erotic responsiveness) is also concordant with the gender of rearing. Studies of hermaphrodites demonstrate that gender identity and the choice of erotic stimulus are influenced by the gender of rearing. In contrast, there are children and adults with normal anatomy (i.e., whose genitalia are compatible with their assigned sex) who express behavior and identity appropriate to the opposite sex. Research on the influence of fetal hormones raises the possibility that a prenatally determined predisposition may make these individuals more vulnerable to gender identity disorders. Thus, there may be many genetic females born with normal female genitalia who have been exposed to prenatal androgen not quite enough to have noticeable influence on external anatomy, but enough to influence the brain. The same may happen to a genetic male with normal genitalia with a history of prenatal androgen deficit. These prenatal influences may provide an explanation not only to gender identity disorders but also to the findings of overlap in gender roles and sexual attitudes of males and females in the general population.

Studies of the menstrual cycle, menopause, pregnancy, and childbirth, and the ingestion of oral contraceptives reveal that hormonal changes may precipitate psychiatric disturbance and influence other behavior in females who are already vulnerable. Attitudes and expectations seem to affect the behavioral and emotional reactions to hormonal fluctuations. Male hormonal cyclicity and couple physiological synchrony have been given some attention in recent years, but the behavioral implication of these phenomena requires further research.

References

Archer, J. Rodent sex differences in emotional and related behavior. *Behavioral Biology*, 1975, *14*, 450-479.

Ballinger, C. B. Psychiatric morbidity and the menopause: Clinical features. *British Medical Journal*, 1976, *1*, 1183-1185.

Bandura, A. *Principles of behavior modification*. New York: Holt, 1969.

Barnett, R., & Baruch, G. Women in the middle years: A critique of research and theory. *Psychology of Women Quarterly*, 1978, *3*, 187-197.

Bart, P. B. Depression in middle-aged women. I. V. Gornick & K. Moran (Eds.), *Woman in sexist society*. New York: Basic Books, 1971.

Beach, F. A. *Sex and behavior*. New York: Wiley, 1965.

Beach, F. A. Behavioral endocrinology and the study of reproduction. *Biology of Reproduction*, 1974, *10*, 12-18.

Beeman, E. A. The effect of male hormone on aggressive behavior in mice. *Physiological Zoology*, 1947, *20*, 373-405.

Bremer, J. Asexualization: A follow-up study of 244 cases. Oslo, Norway: Oslo University Press, 1958.

Brodie, H. K. H., Gartrell, N., Doering, C., & Rhue, T. Plasma testosterone levels in heterosexual and homosexual men. *American Journal of Psychiatry*, 1974, *131*, 82-83.

Brooks, J., Ruble, D., & Clark, A. College women's attitudes and expectations concerning menstrual-related changes. *Psychosomatic Medicine*, 1977, *39*, 288-298.

Brown, G. W., Bhrolchain, M. N., & Harris, T. Social class and psychiatric disturbance among women in an urban population. *Sociology*, 1975, *9*, 225-254.

Brown, G. W., & Harris, T. *Social origins of depression: A study of psychiatric disorders in women*. London, England: Tavistock Publications, 1978.

Buckle, R. C., Linnane, J., & McConacky, N. Attempted suicide presenting at the Alfred Hospital, Melbourne. *Medical Journal of Australia*, 1965, *1*, 754-761.

Burke, A. W., & Broadhurst, P. L. Behavioral correlates of oestrous cycle in the rat. *Nature*, 1966, *209*, 223-224.

Coppen, A. J. Body-build of male homosexuals. *British Medical Journal II*, 1959, *5164*, 1443-1445.

Coppen, A., & Kessel, N. Menstruation and personality. *British Journal of Psychiatry*, 1963, *109*, 711-721.

Cornu, F. *Katamnesen be: Kastrierten sittlichkeitsdelinquenten aus forensisch—Psychiatrischer sicht*. Basel, Switzerland: Kanger, 1973.

Dalton, K. Menstruation and acute psychiatric illness. *British Medical Journal*, 1959, *1*, 326-328.

Dalton, K. Menstruation and accidents. *British Medical Journal*, 1960, *2*, 1425-1426.

Dalton, K. Menstruation and crime. *British Medical Journal*, 1961, *2*, 1752-1753.

Dan, A. J. *Behavioral variability and the menstrual cycle*. Paper presented at the annual meeting of the American Psychological Association, Washington, D.C., September 1976.

Diamond, M., & Young, W. C. Differential responsiveness of pregnant and non-pregnant guinea pigs to the masculinizing action of testosterone propionate, *Endocrinology*, 1963, *72*, 429-438.

Doering, C. H., Kraemer, H. C., Brody, K., & Hamburg, D. A. A cycle of plasma testosterone in the human male, *Journal of Clinical Endocrinology and Metabolism*, 1975, *40*, 492-500.

Doerr, P., Kockott, G., Vogt, H. J., Pirke, K. M., & Dittmar, F. Plasma testosterone, estradiol, and semen analysis in male homosexuals. *Archives of General Psychiatry*, 1973, *29*, 829-833.

Dörner, G. *Hormones and brain differentiation*. Amsterdam, The Netherlands: Elsevier, 1976.

Edwards, D. A. Early androgen stimulation and aggressive behavior in male and female mice. *Physiology and Behavior*, 1969, *4*, 333-338.

Edwards, D. A., & Herndon, J. Neonatal estrogen stimulation and aggressive behavior in female mice. *Physiology and Behavior*, 1970, *5*, 993-995.

Ehrhardt, A. A. Maternalism in fetal hormonal and related syndromes. In J. Zubin & J. Money (Eds.), *Contemporary sexual behavior: Critical issues in the 1970's*. Baltimore, Maryland: Johns Hopkins University Press, 1973.

Ehrhardt, A. A., Epstein, R., & Money, J. Fetal androgens and female gender identity in the early-treated androgenital syndrome. *Johns Hopkins Medical Journal*, 1968, *122*, 160-167.

Ehrhardt, A. A., Evers, K., & Money, J. Influence of androgen and some aspects of sexually dimorphic behavior in women with the late-treated androgenital syndrome. *Johns Hopkins Medical Journal*, 1968, *123*, 115-122.

Ehrhardt, A. A., Greenberg, N., & Money, J. Female gender identity and absence of fetal gonadal hormones: Turner's Syndrome. *Johns Hopkins Medical Journal*, 1970, *126*, 237-248.

Ehrhardt, A. A., & Money, J. Progestin-induced hermaphroditism: I.Q. and psychosexual identity in a study of ten girls. *Journal of Sex Research*, 1967, *3*, 83-100.

Evans, R. B. Physical and biochemical characteristics of homosexual men. *Journal of Consulting and Clinical Psychology*, 1972, *39*, 140-147.

Eysenck, H. J. *Sex and personality*. London, England: Open Books, 1976.

Fernando, S. J. M. A cross-cultural study of some familial and social factors in depressive illness. *British Journal of Psychiatry*, 1975, *127*, 40-53.

Friedman, R. C., Wollesen, F., & Tendler, R. Psychological development and blood levels of sex steroids in male identical twins of divergent sexual orientation. *Journal of Nervous and Mental Diseases*, 1976, *163*, 282-288.

Goldberg, S. *The inevitability of patriarchy*. New York: William Morrow, 1973.

Goy, R. W. Early hormonal influence on the development of sexual and sex-related behavior. In G. C. Quarton, T. Melanchuk, & F. O. Schmitt (Eds.), *Neuro-sciences: A study program*. New York: Rockefeller Univ. Press, 1970.

Goy, R. W., & Goldfoot, D. A. Experiential and hormonal factors influencing development of sexual behavior in the male rhesus monkey. In F. O. Schmitt & F. G. Worden (Eds.), *The neurosciences: Third study program*. Cambridge, Massachusetts: MIT Press, 1974.

Gray, J. A., & Levine, S. Effect of induced oestrus on emotional behavior in selected strains of rats. *Nature*, 1964, *201*, 1198-1200.

Gray, J. A. Sex differences in emotional behavior in mammals including man: Endocrine base. *Acta Psychologica*, 1971, *35*, 29-46.

Greene, J. G., & Cooke, D. J. Life stress and symptoms at the climacterium. *British Journal of Psychiatry*, 1980, *136*, 486-491.

Griffiths, P. D., Merry, J., Browning, M. C. K., Eisinger, A. J., Huntsman, R. G., Lord, E. J. A., Polani, P. E., Tanner, J. M., & Whitehouse, R. H. Homosexual women: An endocrine and psychological study. *Journal of Endocrinology*, 1974, *63*, 549-556.

Gruendel, A. D., & Arnold, W. J. Influence of preadolescent experiential factors on the development of sexual behavior in albino rats. *Journal of Comparative and Physiological Psychology*, 1974, *86*, 172-178.

Guttman, D. Parenthood: A key to the comparative study of the life cycle. In N. Datan & L. H. Ginsburg (Eds.), *Life-span Developmental Psychology*. New York: Academic Press, 1975.

Hallstrom, T. *Mental disorder and sexuality in the climacteric*. Goteborg, Sweden: Orstadius Biktryckeri, 1973.

Harris, G. W. Sex hormones, brain development and brain function. *Endrocrinology* 1964, *75*, 627-648.

Harris, G. W., & Levine, S. Sexual differentiation of the brain and its experimental control. *Journal of Physiology*, 1965, *181*, 379-400.

Henderson, M. E. Evidence for a male menstrual temperature cycle and synchrony with the female menstrual cycle. *Australian and New Zealand Journal of Medicine*, 1976, *84*, 164.

Holding, T. A., & Minkoff, K. Parasuicide and the menstrual cycle. *Journal of Psychosomatic Research*, 1973, *17*, 365-368.

Houseknecht, S. K. Childlessness and marital adjustment. *Journal of Marriage and the Family*, 979, *41*, 259-265.

Janowsky, D. S., Gomey, R., Castelnuovo-Tedesco, P., & Stone, C. B. Premenstrual-menstrual increase in psychiatric hospital admission rates. *American Journal of Obstetrics and Gynecology*, 1969, *103*, 189-191.

Kaplan, A. G. Human sex-hormone abnormalities viewed from an androgynous perspective: A reconsideration of the work of John Money. In S. E. Parsons (Ed.), *The psychobiology of sex roles and sex differences*. New York: Hemisphere, 1980.

Kashiwagi, T., McClure, J. N., & Wetzel, R. D. Premenstrual affective syndrome and psychiatric disorder. *Diseases of the Nervous System*, 1976, *37*, 116-119.

Kenyon, F. E. Studies in female homosexuality, VI. The exclusively homosexual group. *Acta Psychiatrica Scandinavica*, 1968, *44*, 224-237.

Kester, P., Green, R., Finch, S. J., & Williams, K. Prenatal "female hormone" administration and psychosexual development in human males. *Psychoneuroendocrinology*, 1980, *5*, 269-285.

Kinel, F. A., & Maqueo, M. Prevention by progesterone of steroid-induced sterility in neonatal male and female rats. *Endocrinology*, 1965, *77*, 859.

Koeske, R. K. D. Theoretical-conceptual implications of study design and statistical analysis: Research on the menstrual cycle. In C. Stark-Adamec (Ed.), *Sex roles: Origins, influences, and implications for women*. Montreal, Canada: Eden, 1980.

Kolodny, R. C., Jacobs, L. S., Masters, W. H., Toro, G., & Daughaday, W. H. Plasma gonadotrophins and prolactin in male homosexuals. *Lancet*, 1972, *2* (7766), 18-20.

Kreuz, L. E., Rose, R. M., & Jennings, J. R. Suppression of plasma testosterone levels and psychological stress. *Archives of General Psychiatry*, 1972, *26*, 479-482.

Ledwitz-Rigby, F. Biochemical and neurophysiological influences on human sexual behavior. In J. E. Parsons (Ed.), *The psychobiology of sex roles and sex differences*. New York: Hemisphere, 1980.

Loraine, J. A., Adamopoulos, D. A., Kirkham, K. E., Ismail, A. A. A., & Dove, G. A. Patterns of hormone excretion in male and female homosexuals. *Nature*, 1971, *234*, 552-555.

Lowenthal, M. F., Thurnher, M., Chiriboga, D., & Associates. *Four stages of life: A comparative study of women and men facing transitions*. San Francisco, California: Jossey-Bass, 1975.

McClintock, M. K. Menstrual synchrony and suppression. *Nature*, 1971, *229*, 244-245.

Maccoby, E. E., & Jacklin, N. J. *The psychology of sex differences*. Stanford, California: Stanford Univ. Press, 1974.

McEwen, B. S. Interaction between hormones and nerve tissue. *Scientific American*, 1976, *235*(1), 48-58.

McKinlay, S., & Jeffreys, M. The menopausal syndrome. *British Journal of Preventive Social Medicine*, 1974, *28*, 108-115.

McKinlay, S., & McKinlay, J. Selected studies on the menopause. *Journal of Biosocial Science*, 1973, *5*, 533-555. (Annotated bibliography)

MacKinnon, I. L., MacKinnon, P. C. B., & Thompson, A. D. Lethal hazards and the luteal phase of the menstrual cycle. *British Medical Journal*, 1959, *1*, 1015-1017.

Magnus, E. M. Sources of maternal stress in the postpartum period: A review of the literature and an alternative view. In J. E. Parsons (Ed.), *The psychobiology of sex differences and sex roles*. New York: Hemisphere, 1980.

Marcus, R., & Korenman, S. G. Estrogens and the human male. *Annual Review of Medicine*, 1976, *27*, 357-370.

Mead, M. Sex and temperament in three primitive societies. New York: Morrow, 1935.

Melges, F. T. Postpartum psychiatric syndromes. *Psychosomatic Medicine*, 1968, *30*(1), 95-107.

Meyer-Bahlburg, H. F. L. Sex hormones and male homosexuality in comparative perspective. *Archives of Sexual Behavior*, 1977, *6*, 297-325.

Meyer-Bahlburg, H. F. L. Homosexual orientation in women and men: A hormonal basis? In J. E. Parsons (Ed.), *The psychobiology of sex differences and sex roles*. New York: Hemisphere, 1980.

Money, J. Use of an androgen-depleting hormone in the treatment of male sex offenders. *Journal of Sex Research*, 1970, *6*, 165-172.

Money, J. Endocrine influences on psychosexual status spanning the life cycle. In H. M. van Praag (Ed.), *Handbook of biological psychiatry. Part III. Brain mechanisms and abnormal behavior—genetics and neuroendocrinology*. New York: Marcel Dekker, 1980.

Money, J., & Ehrhardt, A. A. *Man and woman, boy and girl*. Baltimore, Maryland: Johns Hopkins Univ. Press, 1972.

Money, J., Ehrhardt, A. A.,& Masica, D. N. Fetal feminization induced by androgen insensitivity in the testicular feminization syndrome: Effects on marriage and maternalism. *Johns Hopkins Medical Journal*, 1968, *123*, 105-114.

Money, J., & Schwartz, M. Fetal androgen in the early treated androgenital syndrome of 46, XX hermaphroditism: Influence on assertive and aggressive types of behavior. *Aggressive Behavior*, 1976, *2*, 19-30.

Moos, R. H. A typology of menstrual cycle symptoms. *American Obstetrics and Gynecology*, 1969, *103*, 390-402.

Moos, R. H., Kopell, B. S., Melges, F. T., Yalom, I. D., Lunde, D. T., Clayton, R. B., & Hamburg, D. A. Fluctuations in symptoms and moods during the menstrual cycle. *Journal of Psychosomatic Research*, 1969, *13*, 37-44.

Morton, J. H., Addition, H., Addison, R. G., Hunt, L., & Sullivan, J. J. A clinical study of premenstrual tension. *American Journal of Obstetrics and Gynecology*, 1953, *65*, 1182-1191.

Moyer, K. E. Sex differences in aggression. In R. C. Friedman, R. M. Richart, & R. L. Vande Wiele (Eds.), *Sex differences in behavior*. New York: Wiley, 1974.

Murray, M. A. F., Bancroft, J. H. J., Anderson, D. C., Tennent, T. G., & Carr, P. J. Endocrine changes in male sexual deviants after treatment with anti-androgens, oestrogens, or tranquilizers. *Journal of Endocrinology*, 1975, *67*, 179-188.

Notman, M. Adult life cycles: Changing roles and changing hormones. In J. E. Parsons (Ed.), *The psychobiology of sex differences and sex roles*. New York: Hemisphere, 1980.

Paige, K. E. Women learn to sing the menstrual blues. *Psychology Today*, 1973, *7*, 41-46.

Parks, G. A., Korth-Schütz, S., Penny, R., Hilding, R. F., Dumars, K. W., Frasier, S. D., & New, M. I. Variation in pituitary-gonadal function in adolescent male homosexuals and heterosexuals. *Journal of Clinical Endocrinology and Metabolism*, 1974, *39*, 796-801.

Parlee, M. B. The premenstrual syndrome. *Psychological Bulletin*, 1973, *80*, 454-465.
Parlee, M. B. Stereotypic beliefs about menstruation: A methodological note on the Moos Menstrual Distress Questionnaire and some new data. *Psychosomatic Medicine*, 1974, *36*, 229-240.
Paulson, M. J. Psychological concomitants of premenstrual tension. *American Journal of Obstetrics and Gynecology*, 1961, *81*, 733-738.
Perlmutter, J. The menopause: A gynecologist's view. In M. Notman & C. Nadelson (Eds.), *The woman as a patient*. New York: Plenum, 1978.
Persky, H. Reproductive hormones, moods and the menstrual cycle. In R. C. Friedman, R. M. Richart, & R. L. Vande Wiele (Eds.), *Sex differences in behavior*. New York: Wiley, 1974.
Persky, H., Lief, H. I., O'Brien, C. P., Strauss, D., & Miller, W. Reproductive hormone levels and sexual behavior of young couples during the menstrual cycle. In R. Gemme & C. C. Wheeler (Eds.), *Progress in sexology*. New York: Plenum, 1977.
Persky, H., Smith, K. D., & Basu, G. K. Relation of psychologic measures of aggression and hostility to testosterone production in man. *Psychosomatic Medicine*, 1971, *33*, 265-277.
Pfaff, D. W., & Zigmond, R. E. Neonatal androgen effects on sexual and non-sexual behavior of adult rats tested under various hormone regimes. *Neuroendocrinology*, 1971, *7*, 129-145.
Phoenix, C. H., Goy, R. W., Gerall, A. A., & Young, W. C. Organizing action of prenatally administered testosterone propionate on the tissues mediating mating behavior in the female guinea pig. *Endocrinology*, 1959, *65*, 369-382.
Phoenix, C. H., Goy, R. W., & Resko, J. A. Sexual differentiation as a function of androgenic stimulation. In M. Diamond (Ed.), *Perspectives in reproduction and sexual behavior*. Bloomington, Indiana: Indiana Univ. Press, 1968.
Pillard, R. C., Rose, R. M., & Sherwood, M. Plasma testosterone levels in homosexual men. *Archives of Sexual Behavior*, 1974, *3*, 453-458.
Pitt, B. Maternity blues. *British Journal of Psychiatry*, 1973, *122*, 431-433.
Pugh, T. F., Jerath, B. K., Schmidt, W. M., & Reed, R. B. Rates of mental disease related to childbearing. *New England Journal of Medicine*, 1963, *268*, 1224-1228.
Rada, R. T., Laws, D. R., & Kellner, R. Plasma testosterone levels in the rapist. *Psychosomatic Medicine*, 1976, *38*, 257-268.
Radloff, L. S. Sex differences in depression. *Sex Roles*, 1975, *1*, 249-265.
Rees, L. Psychosomatic aspects of the premenstrual tension syndrome. *Journal of Mental Science*, 1953, *99*, 62-93.
Reinisch, J. M. Fetal hormones, the brain and human sex differences: A heuristic, integrative review of the recent literature. *Archives of Sexual Behavior*, 1974, *3*, 51-90.
Reinisch, J. M. Prenatal exposure to synthetic progestins increases the potential for aggression in humans. *Science*, 1981, *211*, 1171-1173.
Reinisch, J. M., & Karow, W. G. Parental exposure to synthetic progestins and estrogens: Effects on human development. *Archives of Sexual Behavior*, 1977, *6*, 257-288.
Rohner, R. P. Sex differences in aggression: Phylogenetic and enculturation perspectives. *Ethos*, 1976, *4*, 57-72.
Rossi, A. S., & Rossi, P. E. Body time and social time: Mood patterns are affected by menstrual cycle phase and day of week. *Social Science Research*, 1977, *6*, 273-308.
Ruble, D. N. Premenstrual symptoms: A reinterpretation. *Scence*, 1977, *197*, 291-292.
Ruble, D. N., & Brooks-Gunn, J. Menstrual symptoms: A social cognition analysis. *Journal of Behavioral Medicine*, 1979, *2*, 171-194.
Schachter, S., & Singer, J. E. Cognitive, social and physiological determinants of emotional states. *Psychological Review*, 1962, *69*, 379-399.
Schlegel, W. S. Die Konstitutionsbiologischen Grundlagen der Homosexualität. *Zeitschrift für menschlische Vererbungs und Konstitutionslehre*, 1962, *36*, 341-364.

Schlegel, W. S. *Die Sexualinstinkte des Menschen*. Munich, W. Germany: Rutten Verlag, 1966.
Schuckit, M. A., Daly, V., Herrman, G., & Hineman, S. Premenstrual symptoms and depression in a university population. *Diseases of the Nervous System*, 1975, *36*, 516-517.
Silbergeld, S., Brast, N., & Noble, E. P. The premenstrual cycle: A double blind study of symptoms, mood and behavior, and biochemical variables using Enovid and placebo. *Psychosomatic Medicine*, 1971, *33*, 411-428.
Smith, S. L., & Sauder, C. Food cravings, depression and menstrual problems. *Psychosomatic Medicine*, 1969, *31*, 281-287.
Sommer, B. The effect of menstruation on cognitive and perceptual-motor behavior: A review. *Psychosomatic Medicine*, 1973, *35*, 515-534.
Swanson, H. H. Alteration of sex-typical behavior of hamsters in open field and emergence tests by neo-natal administration of androgen or oestrogen. *Animal Behavior*, 1967, *115*, 209-216.
Tonks, C. M., Rack, P. H., & Rose, M. J. Attempted suicide and the menstrual cycle. *Journal of Psychosomatic Research*, 1968, *11*, 319-323.
Uddenberg, N. Reproduction adaptation in mother and daughter: A study of personality development and adaptation to motherhood. *Acta Psychiatrica Scandinavica*, 1974, 1-115. (Suppl. 254)
Uddenberg, N., & Nilsson, L. The longitudinal course of para-natal emotional disturbance. *Acta Psychiatrica Scandinavica*, 1975, *52*, 160-169.
Udry, J. R., & Morris, N. M. Distribution of coitus in the menstrual cycle. *Nature*, 1968, *220*, 593-596.
Valenstein, E. S. *Brain control*. New York: Wiley, 1973.
van Keep, P. A., & Kellerhals, J. M. The aging woman: About the influence of some social and cultural factors on the changes in attitudes and behaviour that occur during and after the menopause. *Acta Obstetrica and Gynecologica Scandinavica Supplement*, 1975, *51*, 17-27.
Von Saal, F. S., Svare, B., & Gandelman, R. Time of neonatal androgen exposure influences length of testosterone treatment required to induce aggression in adult male and female mice. *Behavioral Biology*, 1976, *17*, 391-397.
Walker, P. Medroxyprogesterone acetate as an antiandrogen for the rehabilitation of sex offenders. In R. Gemme & C. Wheeler (Eds.), *Progress in sexology*. New York: Plenum, 1977.
Weissman, M. M., & Klerman, G. L. Sex differences and the epidemiology of depression. *Archives of General Psychiatry*, 1977, *34*, 98-111.
Weissman, M. M., & Slaby, A. E. Oral contraceptives and psychiatric disturbance: Evidence from research. *British Journal of Psychiatry*, 1973, *123*, 513-518.
Yalom, I. D., Lunde, D. T., Moos, R. H., & Hamburg, D. A. "Postpartum blues" syndrome: A description and related variables. *Archives of General Psychiatry*, 1968, *18*, 16-27.
Young, W. C., Goy, R. W., & Phoenix, C. H. Hormones and sexual behavior. *Science*, 1964, *143*, 212-218.

14

JULIA R. HEIMAN
JOHAN VERHULST

Gender and Sexual Functioning

Gender has often been used to descriptively separate the physiological, psychological, and sociocultural factors involved in sexual functioning. However, the meaning of gender, particularly in the development of sexual dysfunctions, has been given only passing attention. The purposes of the present chapter are: (*a*) to underscore several differences in male and female sexual functioning; (*b*) to outline the extent to which gender issues may be imbedded in the expression of sexual dysfunctions; and (*c*) to introduce several examples where clinical and research assumptions about sexuality are gender-biased. These remarks are limited to heterosexuals, with the acknowledgment that homosexual dysfunctions may not differ in structure but may raise different issues in terms of gender-related interaction patterns.

Physiological Patterns of Sexual Response

The Sexual Response Cycles

As with many aspects of gender research and theory, the degree to which one sees differences in physiological patterns of sexual response depends on the importance one places on similarities versus differences.

For example, when Masters and Johnson (1966) observed and researched over 10,000 sexual response cycles (defined by them as *excitement, plateau,*

ISBN: 0-12-050350-6

orgasm, resolution), they emphasized the *similarities* in the patterns of response for both sexes. Male and female sexual responses involved similar increases in heart rate, blood pressure, vasocongestion, and myotonia throughout the cycle, as well as genital, urethral, and anal contractions during orgasm. Men and women were also able to reach orgasm during masturbation in approximately the same amount of time. The differences in the sexual response cycles, according to Masters and Johnson (1966), were that men ejaculated and women were capable of multiple orgasms.

If we shift our emphasis for a moment to examine instead the *dissimilarities* between male and female responding, perhaps we can shed light on a few aspects of sexual dysfunction. Starting with Masters and Johnson's (1966) data, it is interesting that 7000 of the 10,000 sexual response cycles were those of women. These numbers are not proportional to the sex differences of the sample (382 women, 312 men). The difference is, in part, due to the multiorgasmic ability of the women participating and, in part, is assumed by Masters and Johnson to be due to women feeling more comfortable in the laboratory setting. The possibility that men's sexual response may be the more sensitive to a particular environmental situation is an interesting contradiction to typical assumptions that women are relatively inhibited sexually and are dependent on a great deal of special attention in order to reach orgasm. However, it may be that these assumptions about women, along with a performance expectancy on men, combine to decrease the ease of response in a laboratory or, for that matter, in any setting in which men feel evaluated or observed.

In the overall pattern of physical components of the sexual response cycle, women have been reported to be more variable than men (Masters & Johnson, 1966). Although these data await replication, perhaps it can be said that in terms of the presence of orgasm(s) and the time to reach orgasm, women *can* be far more variable *during intercourse*. Depending on the level of arousal before intercourse, the presence of concurrent clitoral stimulation, and the degree to which both partners attempt to control their own response progression, the woman's arousal pattern will be variously affected. A predetermined feature of intercourse is that it is usually a mode of more direct stimulation for the male, since penile thrusting results in direct vaginal, but indirect clitoral, stimulation for the female.

Although there are many homologous structures (Money & Erhardt, 1972) when comparing male and female genitalia, there are several essential differences. Of importance to sexual response are the vasocongestive systems. In the genital area, men have three and women have five erectile bodies. The blood capacity of the clitoris and crura are negligible when compared to the penis. However, with the addition of the female erectile bodies, women have a greater generalized vasocongestive capacity (Sherfey, 1973). This is particularly true if they have borne children.

Orgasm is also different for the two sexes. Masters and Johnson (1966) noted that men usually show 3-4 strong and regular contractions followed by numerous irregular contractions. Women may show 3-5 to 10-15, with the first 5 or 6 usually the strongest. Also, it is estimated that between 25% and 100% of women are capable of multiple orgasms, that is, several orgasms in succession without loss of high arousal and vasocongestion. All of the women in Masters and Johnson's (1966) sample were multiply orgasmic, an unusually orgasmic group compared to reports of other researchers (Kinsey, Pomeroy, Martin, & Gebhard, 1953). Sherfey (1973) has argued that the capacity for multiple orgasms is a universal phenomenon in women, noting that a woman's greater vasocongestive capacity requires more orgasmic release for sexual satisfaction. Sherfey also claims that more orgasmic experience physiologically increases a woman's ability to have and need more orgasms for full satisfaction. This proposal is based on the view that women show continuous labial congestion and edema, especially in the luteal phase of their menstrual cycle or after bearing children. The picture painted by Sherfey is one of women being physiologically insatiable. Sherfey's theory allows us to consider the difference between physiological satiation and psychological satisfaction. Satisfaction with one orgasm may be due to lesser vasocongestive capacity related to degree of sexual experience or to the psychological meaning that one orgasm has for women.

There is some evidence for multiple orgasms and multiple ejaculation in men (Kinsey *et al.*, 1953; Masters & Johnson, 1966; Robbins & Jensen, 1978). The infrequency of this phenomenon may be a result of the expectation, and the physiological fact, that orgasm and ejaculation usually occur together.

What the physiological information suggests is that, at least in terms of capacity for arousal and orgasm, women are highly sexual. Why, then, do more women than men report sexual dissatisfaction or dysfunction (e.g., Frank, Anderson & Rubenstein, 1978)? Although a pure physiological explanation is possible—needing more stimulation than the male to achieve more complete sexual release—it is unsatisfying. Social and psychological factors do have an impact, as we shall discuss in a moment, but, in fact, the question remains one open to speculation.

Life-span Physiological Factors

Although menstruation is an obvious difference in male and female physiology, and one that clearly affects general vasocongestion (Hoon, Wincze, & Hoon, 1976; Masters & Johnson, 1966; Schreiner-Engle, Schiavi,

Smith, & White, 1981), its effect on sexual functioning is not clear (cf. Luschen & Pierce, 1972; Masters & Johnson, 1966; Rossi & Rossi, 1980; Udry & Morris, 1968).

Similarly, the physiological effects of pregnancy are quite dramatic, with hormonal surges and increased levels of genital vasocongestion. The typical pattern noticed by Masters and Johnson (1966) was one of: (*a*) decreased arousal during the first trimester; (*b*) increased vasocongestion of the orgasmic platform (the distal third of the vagina) and increased resolution time following orgasm, accompanied by increased sexual interest in the second trimester; and (*c*) decreased sexual interest in the third trimester. During the second trimester, a woman is likely to continue to feel arousal after orgasm, and orgasm does not seem to reduce sexual tension for very long. More important is the relationship between pregnancy, delivery, and sexual response. Postpartum disturbances are common in women, ranging from mild hyperemotionality, thought to affect up to 80% of women, to more serious psychiatric symptoms, reported to affect between 15% and 25% of women (see Magnus, 1980). We have very limited information about the relationship between sexual functioning and postdelivery adjustment. However, Fisher (1973) found that greater orgasm consistency, greater happiness and satisfaction after orgasm, and greater interest in sex during pregnancy all were related to less postdelivery disturbance.

The fact that men do not experience the hormonal and physiological shifts that women do (although they pass through diurnal and possibly seasonal hormonal fluctuations) may be an important ingredient in the relative variability of female sexual interest and even her arousability. Most likely, the difference depends less on the actual physiological changes than on the awareness of such changes (Rossi & Rossi, 1980). Being continuously aware of physical changes related to genital functioning is also being reminded that one's body is not totally under one's own control. This is a subtle message, one of many that women are given, that may contribute to the classical expectancy that female sexuality is more a responsive than an active phenomenon.

Age-related physiological changes occur in both men and women. Sociological and physiological data have shown that men's ejaculatory capacity and orgasmic frequency is age-limited, peaking in the middle to late teens and gradually declining thereafter (e.g., Kinsey, 1948; Masters & Johnson, 1966). Women tend to increase their orgasmic ease and frequency up to their late thirties and then gradually decline (e.g., Kinsey *et al.*, 1953; Sherfey, 1973). Over the years, age seems to slow down the sexual response cycle. For men, this involves a longer period from arousal to orgasm and decreased firmness of erections. For women, menopause results in decreased levels of circulating estrogen and thus a thinning of the vaginal mucosa and decreased lubrication (Masters & Johnson, 1966). Regular access to coital contact, not always possible in older couples, seems to be a good preventive strategy for genital functioning. What one sees in dysfunctional older men and women are two typical patterns: One is concern about decreased "potency," particularly for men who make comparisons to their younger days; the other is the psychological impact of aging including the antisexual norms, decreased sense of sexual attractiveness, and general adjustment to growing further from one's youth. It should be kept in mind that desire and frequency of activity do not decrease as much as was once believed. Barring critical events such as severe illness, severe social stress, or loss of a partner (more true for women), when one follows people developmentally across their life span, there is a consistency of sexual frequency and interest in most individuals (George & Weiler, 1981).

Psychological Patterns and Sexual Function

The sex role stereotypical sexual interaction assumes the male to be the initiator, the director, and the aggressive actor and the female to be the receptive, reacting, relatively passive participant. In the past two decades, this complementary style has been challenged to the point of labeling traditional sex role stereotypes, whether social or sexual, as bordering on the pathological. Indeed, the most extreme form of the active-passive role may be seen or experienced as a form of rape. Beyond the extreme form, however, it is of value to examine the relationship between sex roles and dysfunctional versus functional sexual response patterns. It also is worthwhile to examine the variety of psychological factors that appear to interfere with sexual response.

Such information comes from three basic sources: clinical theory, psychological assessment, and laboratory studies of sexual arousal. Clinical theory generally supports the notion that *rigid* adherence to sex roles is characteristic of dysfunctional couples (Kaplan, 1974; LoPiccolo, 1978; Zilbergeld & Rinkleib, 1980), although the problem may be more in the inflexibility than in the sex role structure itself. Nevertheless, for the two most commonly mentioned inhibitors of good sexual functioning, anxiety and depression (Kaplan, 1974), no gender differentiation has been proposed.

Research on psychological characteristics has revealed distinct profiles for males and females and characteristic patterns for dysfunctional patients. For example, Derogatis and Meyer (1979) compared 47 male and 40 female dysfunctional patients with 200 sexually functional subjects on a variety of inventories. Contrary to expectation, functional males scored significantly higher on the Masculinity Scale and showed a tendency for more polarized Gender Role scores than dysfunctional males. Functional females had significantly higher Femininity Scale and Masculinity Scale scores than the dysfunctional group, although their Gender Role Scales did not differ. One interpretation of these results is that masculine role identity is more closely connected to sexual functioning in males than in females, and that functional female sexuality requires both traditional masculine and feminine characteristics. However, the fact that dysfunctional individuals showed anxious and depressive symptoms as well as feelings of inferiority and self-depreciation suggests that these factors may also be differentially influencing gender self-concept, especially for men and women who are experiencing sexual problems. Derogatis and Meyer (1979) have offered a more comprehensive hypothesis, proposing that the distinction in psychological profiles for dysfunctional males and females was "related to fundamental differences in the nature of dysfunctions across the sexes, i.e., that male disorders are related to performance decrements while females are faced primarily with disorders of satisfaction [pp. 221-222]."

The connection between a broad number of psychological factors and sexual dysfunction is reflected by a German study of 92 seriously dysfunctional couples (Clement & Pfafflin, 1980). One year after therapy, women treated for orgasmic or vaginismus problems were found to be less nervous and depressed, less irritable, less psychosomatic, and more self-confident than they were prior to therapy. Male patients treated for erectile disturbances or premature ejaculation were found to be less depressed, less dominant, and less masculine at the 1-year follow-up as compared to pretherapy measures. Interestingly, the partners of the dysfunctional individuals showed parallel changes with some interesting additions: The female partners of dysfunctional males also became less inhibited and less emotionally labile, whereas the male partners of dysfunctional females became less sociable and less extroverted. Furthermore, both sexes in the dysfunctional group became less sex role stereotyped, as did the female partners of men with a dysfunction.

To summarize the psychological factors: As females became sexually functional, they also showed increasingly permissive, egalitarian, and realistic (less romantic) attitudes toward sex; as males became functional they became less reactive-aggressive, less extroverted, and less masculine stereotyped in their behavior. The fact that one study found normal males to be more polarized in a masculine direction (Derogatis & Meyer, 1979), though disputed in earlier work by the same authors (Derogatis, Meyer, & Gallant, 1977), may be an important clue to understanding the process of sexual improvement for males. That is, whereas sexually functional males are more typically masculine, men and their partners who are vulnerable to sexual dysfunctions may have to accommodate a less sex role stereotyped perspective in order to become functional. Like other traditional stereotypes, those surrounding sexuality may work quite well for some individuals and be a disruptive pressure for others.

Recently, laboratory research on sexual response has attempted to differentiate sexual dysfunction patterns. Of particular interest are studies bridging the physiological-psychological connection by including measures of genital vasocongestion, self-reported sexual arousal, and affective reactions to erotic stimuli. The striking aspect of such studies on sexually functional individuals is the paucity of sex differences on most measures. For example, sexually functional men and women are both physiologically (genitally) and psychologically aroused by sexually explicit stimuli and fantasy, regardless of the extent of romantic elements in the taped script (Heiman, 1977). Similarly, sexually functional men and women both become more physiologically sexually aroused to an erotic videotape if it is preceded by a videotape that is anxiety- and anger-inducing (Hoon, Wincze, & Hoon, 1977; Wolchik, Beggs, Wincze, Sakheim, Barlow, & Mavissakalian, 1980).

Laboratory studies with sexually dysfunctional individuals have resulted in a more complex picture. Women with orgasmic and arousal problems have been found to show less genital vasocongestion to erotic materials than do functional women (Heiman, 1978; Wincze, Hoon, & Hoon, 1976). Dysfunctional women have also been found to have equal levels of genital response but lower levels of self-reported arousal (Morokoff & Heiman, 1980). Men with erectile problems respond to erotic tapes. However, if the diagnosis is secondary erectile failure, penile response is significantly less than for sexually functional men (Kockott, Feil, Ferstl, Aldenhoff, & Besinger, 1980).

Clinically, the more interesting features of arousal to erotica are the degree to which genital and self-reported levels of arousal are in agreement. These findings are conflicted, but there is some indication that sexually dysfunctional women show poor subjective-physiological correlations and, in fact, may report anxiety rather than sexual arousal during higher levels of physiological arousal (Morokoff & Heiman, 1980). Sexually dysfunctional men show inconsistent but positive correlations (Kockott *et al.*, 1980), and sexually functional males and females may show positive or no correlations between the two measures (Geer, Morokoff, & Greenwood, 1974; Heiman, 1977; Heiman & Hatch, 1981; Hoon *et al.*, 1976; Kockott *et al.*, 1980). The degree of agreement between psychological and physical arousal seems to be heavily influenced by the level of physiological arousal, the rate of arousal increase, general expectation for becoming aroused, and the overriding affective constellation of feelings surrounding the erotic content. With respect to the latter point, both positive and negative affects have been reported to correlate with sexual response in the laboratory. Yet, for both men and women, lower arousal levels have been found to be associated with negative affect, higher levels with positive affect (Heiman, 1980; Heiman & Hatch, 1981a).

Sociocultural Influences

The variability of individual sexual expression is not only determined by biological potentialities and limitations but also by the structure of the social groups and the culture to which this person belongs (Davenport, 1977). In order to remain a member of a particular society, each individual has to assimilate the sexual ideology of the group. Furthermore, sexual interactions also reflect the general characteristics of the relationships in one's social group and culture.

Sexual behavior patterns vary considerably among different cultures. For instance, pre- and extramarital sex, homosexuality, and certain specific intercourse positions are, depending on the culture, encouraged, tolerated, or severely punished (Ford & Beach, 1951). These rules often influence the sexual behavior of men and women differently. It seems, however, that one can make the generalization that rules for sexual repression affect women more often than men. Indeed, most cultures are more interested in monitoring and controlling female than male sexuality. The double standard for sexual expression is based on the almost universal belief that, by nature, men have stronger sexual needs than women. Consequently, more opportunities are created for male sexual outlet. In cultures that are extremely repressive sexually, women are considered to have no sexual needs, and female orgasm can be an almost unknown phenomenon (Mead, 1949; Messenger, 1971). In contrast, in the few cultures with a high degree of sexual freedom, most women are sexually assertive and almost all of them experience multiple orgasms (Marshall & Suggs, 1971). That sexual repression is more often directed at women can be explained, on the one hand, by the fact that most cultures are male dominated, and, on the other, by the fact that excessive repression of male sexuality could interfere with procreation.

In Western society, there also seems to be a correlation between the degree of sexual repression and the acceptance of a double standard for sexual expression between men and women. Although only a few variables of sexual activity (i.e., premarital sex, intercourse and frequency of orgasm, sexual preference, contraception, etc.) have been consistently studied and correlated with demographic characteristics, it has been shown that population groups with more conservative sexual standards are also less active sexually, and that this relationship is much stronger for women than for men.

People living in isolated rural areas, for instance, are found to adhere to more conservative sexual standards and to support a double-standard philosophy (Harrison, Bennett, & Alsikafi, 1974). Certain religious groups such as Orthodox Jews, Catholics, and practicing Protestants traditionally have expressed conservative sexual standards. In 1953, Kinsey *et al.* reported that religious women had the lowest rates of masturbation, petting, intercourse, and orgasmic response. In the meantime, a number of church leaders have adopted a more sex-positive attitude, at least toward marital sex and, in his 1974 survey, Hunt reported that the new generation of young married women who are religious actually had more frequent orgasms than the non-religious women.

However, the correlation between sexual repression and a double standard cannot account for all the gender differences in sexual behavior among the various social groups. A second approach seems to be to observe how sexual gender differences are a reflection of the structure of male-female relationships in a particular social group and how this structure is influenced by socioeconomic factors.

For instance, Stephens (1976) studied single-room occupancy slum hotels in a deteriorating neighborhood of a central city. The hotel tenants lived in poverty, in a dangerous, high-crime neighborhood. Human relationships were characterized by abuse, exploitation, distrust, and avoidance. Other people could not be trusted since they always represented a potential threat and never a potential source of genuine friendship and support. The sexual relationships of the hotel tenants reflected these general relationship characteristics and were also determined by the structure of this particular socioeconomic milieu. The women and men living in the hotel tended not to become involved with one another. Romances were rare and short-lived. They tended to end in conflicts over trivia. The men perceived the women as just trying to get something out of them. The women felt bitter and resentful toward the men and accused them of only being interested in sex. The men spent a lot of time in the hotel bar, talking about sex. Each month, when the welfare checks arrived, the hotel was "worked" by prostitutes. On this occasion the men spent more money than they could afford, or, even worse, were assaulted and robbed. The women were much more isolated and helpless. Their only sexual outlet was masturbation (Stephens, 1976).

Results from surveys of sexual behavior in different social classes should also be interpreted in the context of the socioeconomic and relationship structure of each group. In order to account for social class differences in marital sex, Rainwater (1971), for instance, also described the prevalent role-relationship structure. Sex in the lower classes was found to be oriented more toward male genital performance and tension release. In the middle and upper classes, the partners valued more foreplay and variation and put more emphasis on mutual satisfaction. Consequently, the women in the lower classes saw marital sex as a duty or a favor, intended primarily to gratify the male partner. Rainwater related this to the observation that the relationship between the marital partners was, in the lower classes, more segregated; that is, marriage had more clearly defined sex roles and separate responsibilities and interests. In the middle and upper classes, on the other hand, the marital partners were more interested in joint activities, in role diffusion, in "tuning in" to one another. In our opinion, it is important to take this idea one step further and to study, as Stephens (1976) did, the characteristics of the socioeconomic situation in each social class as potential determinants of the marital relationship. Furthermore, social, economic, and cultural situations change continuously. Consequently, gender differences in sexual behavior change over time (Hunt, 1974; Reiss, 1963). In order to determine the underlying basic patterns, more sophisticated and broadly conceptualized research is clearly needed.

Sexual Dysfunctions and Gender

The term *sexual dysfunction* refers to an impairment of the ability to engage in and/or enjoy sexual activities. This excludes deviant sexual variations, such as unconventional sexual behavior or unusual object choice (i.e., paraphilias).

There is no universally recognized classification system for the sexual dysfunctions. Currently, the most favored system is based on a physiological-biological definition of adequate sex, which has been adopted by the American Psychiatric Association for the *Diagnostic and Statistical Manual of Mental Disorders (DSM-III)* (Spitzer, Sheeny, & Endicott, 1977). Sexual function is divided into three phases: desire, excitement-arousal, and orgasm (Kaplan, 1974, 1979). The first phase, sexual desire, includes problems with too little and too much desire. Phase two, excitement-arousal, consists of female general sexual dysfunction (lack of arousal and vasocongestion) and male erectile dysfunction (erection insufficient to achieve completed intercourse). The orgasm phase includes, for males, premature ejaculation (lack of ejaculatory control, with ejaculation prior to, or soon after, intromission), and retarded ejaculation (inhibition of the ejaculatory reflex) and, for females, orgasmic dysfunction (inability to experience orgasm). All dysfunctions are divided along a temporal dimension (*primary*, i.e., having always existed, versus *secondary*) and a situational dimension (absolute versus situation-bound). Vaginismus (involuntary contractions of the vaginal introitus muscles) and dyspareunia (painful intercourse) can be considered special cases of excitement problems (Heiman & Hatch, 1981b).

In spite of extensive research efforts in the area of human sexuality during the last decennia, little is known about the incidence and prevalence of sexual problems in the population (Heiman & Hatch, 1981b). However, there is considerable evidence of gender differences, with women reporting a higher incidence of sexual dysfunction than men. In their study of 100 nonclinical couples Frank, Anderson, and Rubenstein (1978) found that 63% of the women and 40% of the men reported specific sexual dysfunctions. In addition, 77% of the women and 50% of the men reported general dissatisfactions such as loss of sexual interest and inability to relax. In Europe, Frenken (1976) studied a stratified sample of 250 middle-class, married Dutch men and women, below the age of 50. He found that 52% of the women and 26% of the men experienced difficulties related to the ability to be sexually aroused, whereas 38% of the women and 12% of the men experienced difficulties related to the ability to have satisfactory orgasms.

At the same time, it seems that men may be more likely to seek help for sexual problems than women. Although this may be biased by the research design, one notices in the Masters and Johnson (1970) sample of 790 patients, for instance, that 448 (56.7%) were men and 342 (43.3%) were women (Masters & Johnson, 1970). In the previously mentioned Frank *et al.* (1978) sample, 33% of the men had a specific complaint about sex in their marriage, versus only 21% of the women.

Little can be said with an acceptable degree of certainty about the effectiveness of the new sex therapies. Indeed, several recent literature review articles point to the methodological shortcomings in sex therapy research: no unified diagnostic system, unspecified selection criteria, broad-spectrum, eclectic treatment procedures, lack of clear success criteria, lack of follow-up data, lack of controlled studies (Heiman, LoPiccolo, & LoPiccolo, 1981; Hogan, 1978; Wright, Perreault, & Mathieu, 1977). Success rates are mostly reported by diagnostic category, and it has not been established whether there is an overall gender difference in response to the new sex therapy approach. Using the summary presented by Heiman *et al.* (1981), the range of success rates reported in the literature for the diagnostic categories of *male* dysfunctions is as follows: premature ejaculation, 90-95% success rate; retarded ejaculation or ejaculatory incompetence, 50-82%; secondary erectile failure, 60-80%; primary erectile failure, 40-60%. The outcome data for *female* dysfunctions are more complex, which, as will be discussed at the end of this chapter, may be related to the fact that female sexual experience cannot as easily be reduced to objective performance variables. The success rate for primary orgasmic dysfunction averages 85-95%, if success is defined as being able to reach orgasm in either solo or partner sex. In terms of reaching orgasm during coitus, the rates are lower (30-50%). Similarly, the success rates for secondary orgasmic dysfunction are quite high (70-80%) if one accepts a definition of success as involving the ability to regularly reach orgasm during some form of heterosexual contact. If one requires regular *coital* orgasm, the success rates are between 30 and 50%. In the case of vaginismus, 90 to 95% of the women gain control over the involuntary vaginal muscle contractions, using a physical dilation program. No reliable outcome statistics are available with regard to the treatment of male and female low sexual desire problems.

Special Medical Issues

Sexual dysfunctions can be associated with a number of *medical conditions*. Patients with diabetes mellitus, for instance, often report sexual problems. About one-half of the men having diabetes for over 6 years report erectile dysfunction, which can be caused directly by organic factors (i.e., diabetic neuropathy and/or angiopathy) as well as by psychological factors (i.e., anxiety and depression secondary to the chronic illness, and iatrogenic factors) (Ellenberg, 1978; Renshaw, 1978, 1979). Interestingly, the sexual functioning of diabetic women has hardly been considered at all (Kolodny, 1971).

Looking at other medical illnesses with a high frequency of associated sexual dysfunction—for instance, chronic renal failure, multiple sclerosis, spinal cord injury, and myocardial infarction—one observes the same phenomenon: Studies report primarily on male patients and few data are available on the sexual dysfunctions of the female patients. Yet the physiological impairment and its relationship to sexual functioning is basically the same in both sexes.

Dysfunctions can also occur as a side-effect of drug treatment or of alcohol and substance abuse. Antihypertensive drugs, neuroleptics, antidepressant drugs, lithium, and anticholinergic drugs are especially known to induce sexual dysfunctions. Most reports are anecdotal and not based on controlled studies. The vast majority of the reports describe male dysfunction, especially erectile and ejaculatory problems. In an excellent review of the literature on pharmacological agents causing sexual dysfunction, Segraves (1977) also notes that there have been very few investigations of drug effects on the female sexual response. He was able to locate only three articles specifically addressing this question (Segraves, 1977, p. 172).

Alcohol is perhaps the most common cause of erectile and ejaculatory dysfunction. Although alcohol is reported to reduce arousal and to inhibit orgasm in females, the literature clearly focuses on the male problems (Renshaw, 1975, 1978). There is also a series of articles reporting erectile failure as a side-effect of minor tranquilizers, of cannabis, and of heroin (Segraves, 1977).

It is unclear what accounts for the lack of attention to female sexuality in conjunction with medical problems. Since most physicians are male, it may represent a tendency for male physicians to be uninterested in female sexual experience (Sherfey, 1973). It may represent a tendency for researchers to focus on the more objective phenomena such as erection and ejaculation rather than on reports of experienced arousal and orgasm. It may represent a tendency for male patients to report sexual difficulties more frequently than females. Finally, one should also consider the possibility that the male sexual response may be more vulnerable to noxious agents.

Some support for the latter hypothesis can be found in looking at the association between sexual dysfunction and *psychiatric* illness. Depression is known to cause low sexual desire in males and females. Sexual hyperactivity is a classical symptom of mania in both sexes. Personality disorders and organic brain syndromes often result in poor sexual impulse control (Freedman, Kaplan, & Sadock, 1977). Psychodynamic theories describe neurotic partner choice and neurotic sexual courting behavior for both sexes, although hysteria is more frequently linked with female frigidity (Freud, 1905/1962). Schizophrenic patients develop major sexual relationship problems without direct impairment of sexual functioning, which seems to be mainly due to (*a*) the deficit in social skills characteristic of schizophrenia and (*b*) a progressive deterioration in social functioning (Verhulst & Schneidman, 1981). Male schizophrenics are relatively isolated beginning with the onset of the illness, as they lack the skills for approaching and courting potential partners. Their major sexual outlet is masturbation. Females respond to partners but are unable to maintain a stable relationship. They seem to often go through a period of promiscuity, with less and less desirable partners, and become gradually more isolated (Verhulst & Schneidman, 1981). Schizophrenic patients seem to gyrate gradually toward socially deprived milieus, where relationships in general are repressive and exploitative. As has been pointed out earlier, this also entails a deterioration of the quality of their sexual relationships.

Conclusion and Comments

Looking at the literature on gender differences and sexual dysfunctions, it seems, at first view, that sex therapists and researchers are biased toward the traditional sex role stereotypes. Clinical reports on the sexual effects of medical illness and drugs focus almost exclusively on the male patients. More convincingly, the classification system of the sexual dysfunctions and the descriptive labels used, are cast, for males, in terms of *performance* and, for females, in terms of *experience*. This is not only the case for traditional labels such as *impotence* versus *frigidity* but also for modern labels such as *erectile failure* and *ejaculatory incompetence* versus *general sexual dysfunction* and *orgasmic dysfunction*. These descriptions seem to reflect cultural attitudes and values. In view of the physiological similarities between the male and female sexual response cycles, one could, for instance, stress the parallel between male and female dysfunctions by describing the latter with labels such as *lubrication failure, orgasmic incompetence,* or even *premature c.q. retarded orgasm*. It is likely that such a classification would have a profound influence on research and clinical approaches. Indeed, the influence of labels on behavior has been convincingly demonstrated.

However, in addition to trying to correct potentially sexist labeling, scientists may find it of more fundamental interest to investigate whether male sexuality is indeed more performance-oriented, whereas female sexuality could be, by nature, more experience-centered. Is the male more inescapably aware of the aspect of "doing something to the partner," and the female of the aspect of "receiving stimulation"? It seems to us that further research could benefit from a truly complementary effort between experimentalists and clinical phenomenologists.

Another striking factor is that although sex therapists and researchers often acknowledge the interpersonal nature of human sexuality, their epistemology reflects a medical, biological, individual-centered bias. Maybe this accounts for the fact that those dysfunctions that seem to depend most on the interaction between the sexual partners (i.e., secondary dysfunction, low sex drive) have also the lowest success rates. Models for an interactional approach to sexual dysfunction have been proposed (Verhulst & Heiman, 1979). Additional research using an interactional framework could provide clinicians and researchers with conceptual power in seeing the extent to which gender-related issues have as much power over interactions as they do over individuals.

References

Clement, U., & Pfafflin, F. Changes in personality scores among couples subsequent to sex therapy. *Archives of Sexual Behavior,* 1980, *9,* 235-244.

Davenport, W. Sex in cross-cultural perspective. In F. Beach (Ed.), *Human sexuality in four perspectives.* Baltimore, Maryland: Johns Hopkins Univ. Press, 1977.

Derogatis, L. R., & Meyer, J. K. A psychological profile of the sexual dysfunctions. *Archives of Sexual Behavior,* 1979, *8,* 201-224.

Derogatis, L. R., Meyer, J. K., & Gallant, B. W. Distinctions between male and female invested partners in sexual disorders. *American Journal of Psychiatry,* 1977, *134,* 385-390.

Ellenberg, M. Impotence in diabetes: The neurologic factor. In J. LoPiccolo & L. LoPiccolo (Eds.), *Handbook of sex therapy.* New York: Plenum, 1978.

Fisher, S. *The female orgasm.* New York: Basic Books, 1973.

Ford, C., & Beach, F. *Patterns of sexual behavior.* New York: Harper & Row, 1951.

Frank, E., Anderson, A., & Rubenstein, D. Frequency of sexual dysfunction in "normal" couples. *New England Journal of Medicine,* 1978, *299,* 111-115.

Freedman, A. M., Kaplan, H. S., & Sadock, B. J. *Comprehensive textbook of psychiatry II* (2nd ed.). Baltimore, Maryland: Williams and Wilkins, 1977.

Frenken, J. *Afkeer van de seksualiteit.* Deventer, The Netherlands: Van Loghum Slaterus, 1976.

Freud, S. *Three essays on the theory of sexuality.* (Standard ed., Vol. 7). London, England: Hogarth, 1962. (Originally published, 1905)

George, L. K., & Weiler, S. J. Sexuality in middle and later life. *Archives of General Psychiatry,* 1981, *38,* 919-923.

Geer, J. H., Morokoff, P. J., & Greenwood, P. Sexual arousal in women: The development of a measurement device for vaginal blood volume. *Archives of Sexual Behavior,* 1974, *3,* 559-564.

Harrison, D., Bennett, W., & Alsikafi, M. Premarital sexual standards of rural youth. *Journal of Sex Research*, 1974, *10*, 266-277.

Heiman, J. A psychophysiological exploration of sexual arousal patterns in females and males. *Psychophysiology*, 1977, *14*, 266-274.

Heiman, J. Uses of psychophysiology in the assessment and treatment of sexual dysfunction. In J. LoPiccolo & L. LoPiccolo (Eds.), *Handbook of sex therapy*. New York: Plenum, 1978.

Heiman, J. Female sexual response patterns: Interactions of physiological, affective, and contextual cues. *Archives of General Psychiatry*, 1980, *37*, 1311-1316.

Heiman, J., & Hatch, J. Affective and physiological dimensions of male sexual response to erotica. *Basic and Applied Social Psychology*, 1981, *1*, 315-327. (a)

Heiman, J., & Hatch, J. Conceptual and therapeutic contributions of psychophysiology to sexual dysfunction. In S. Haynes & L. Gannon (Eds.), *Psychosomatic disorders: A psychophysiological approach to etiology and treatment*. New York: Praeger, 1981. (b)

Heiman, J., LoPiccolo, L., & LoPiccolo, J. The treatment of sexual dysfunction. In A. S. Gurman & D. P. Kniskern (Eds.), *Handbook of family therapy*. New York: Brunner/Mazel, 1981.

Hogan, D. The effectiveness of sex therapy: A review of the literature. In J. LoPiccolo & L. LoPiccolo (Eds.), *Handbook of sex therapy*. New York: Plenum, 1978.

Hoon, P. W., Wincze, J. P., & Hoon, E. F. Physiological assessment of sexual arousal in women. *Psychophysiology*, 1976, *13*, 196-204.

Hoon, P. W., Wincze, J. P., & Hoon, E. F. A test of reciprocal inhibition: Are anxiety and sexual arousal mutually inhibitory? *Journal of Abnormal Psychology*, 1977, *86*, 65-74.

Hunt, M. *Sexual behavior in the 70's*. Chicago, Illinois: Playboy Press, 1974.

Kaplan, H. S. *The new sex therapy*. New York: Brunner/Mazel, 1974.

Kaplan, H. S. *Disorders of sexual desire*. New York: Brunner/Mazel, 1979.

Kinsey, A. C., Pomeroy, W. B., & Martin, C. E. *Sexual behavior in the human male*. Philadelphia, Pennsylvania: Saunders, 1948.

Kinsey, A. C., Pomeroy, W., Martin, C., & Gebhard, P. *Sexual behavior in the human female*. Philadelphia, Pennsylvania: Saunders, 1953.

Kockott, G., Feil, W., Ferstl, R., Aldenhoff, J., & Besinger, V. Psychophysiological aspects of male sexual inadequacy: Results of an experimental study. *Archives of Sexual Behavior*, 1980, *9*, 477-494.

Kolodny, R. D. Sexual dysfunction in diabetic females. *Diabetes*, 1971, *20*, 557-559.

LoPiccolo, J. Direct treatment of sexual dysfunction. In J. LoPiccolo & L. LoPiccolo (Eds.), *Handbook of sex therapy*. New York: Plenum, 1978.

Luschen, M. E., & Pierce, D. M. Effect of the menstrual cycle on mood and sexual arousability. *Journal of Sex Research*, 1972, *8*, 41-47.

Magnus, E. M. Sources of maternal stress in the post-partum period: A review of the literature and an alternative view. In J. E. Parsons (Ed.), *The psychobiology of sex differences and sex roles*. New York: McGraw-Hill, 1980.

Marshall, D., & Suggs, R. (Eds.). *Human sexual behavior: Variations in the ethnographic spectrum*. New York: Basic Books, 1971.

Masters, W., & Johnson, V. *Human sexual response*. Boston, Massachusetts: Little, Brown, 1966.

Masters, W., & Johnson, V. *Human sexual inadequacy*. Boston, Massachusetts: Little, Brown, 1970.

Mead, M. *Male and female*. New York: William Morrow, 1949.

Messenger, J. C. Sex and repression in an Irish folk community. In D. S. Marshall & R. C. Suggs (Eds.), *Human sexual behavior: Variations in the ethnographic spectrum*. New York: Basic Books, 1971.

Money, J., & Erhardt, A. A. *Man and woman/boy and girl.* Baltimore, Maryland: Johns Hopkins Univ. Press, 1972.

Morokoff, P., & Heiman, J. R. Effects of erotic stimuli on sexually functional and dysfunctional women: Multiple measures before and after sex therapy. *Behavior Research and Therapy,* 1980, *18,* 127-137.

Rainwater, L. *Sexuality and class struggle.* New York: Praeger, 1971.

Reiss, I. Sociological studies of sexual behavior. In G. Winokur (Ed.), *Determinants.* Springfield, Illinois: Thomas, 1963.

Renshaw, D. Sex problems of alcoholics. *Chicago Medicine,* 1975, *78,* 433-435.

Renshaw, D. Impotence in diabetics. In J. LoPiccolo & L. LoPiccolo (Eds.), *Handbook of sex therapy.* New York: Plenum, 1978.

Renshaw, D. Sexual function and diabetes. *Psychosomatics,* 1979, *20,* 54-60.

Robbins, M., & Jensen, G. Multiple orgasm in males. *The Journal of Sex Research,* 1978, *14,* 21-26.

Rossi, A. S., & Rossi, P. E. Body time and social time: Mood patterns by menstrual cycle phase and day of the week. In J. E. Parsons (Ed.), *The psychobiology of sex differences and sex roles.* New York: McGraw-Hill, 1980.

Schriener-Engel, P., Schiavi, R. C., Smith, H., & White, D. Sexual arousability and the menstrual cycle in submission. *Psychosomatic Medicine,* 1981, *43*(3), 199-214.

Segraves, R. T. Pharmacological agents causing sexual dysfunctions. *Journal of Sex and Marital Therapy,* 1977, *3,* 157-176.

Sherfey, M. J. *The nature and evolution of female sexuality.* New York: Vintage, 1973.

Spitzer, R. L., Sheeny, M., & Endicott, J. DSM-III: Guiding principles. In V. M. Rakoff, H. C. Stancer, & H. B. Kedward (Eds.), *Psychiatric diagnosis.* New York: Brunner/Mazel, 1977.

Stephens, J. *Loners, losers, and lovers: Elderly tenants in a slum hotel.* Seattle: Univ. of Washington Press, 1976.

Udry, J. R., & Morris, N. M. Distribution of coitus in the menstrual cycle. *Nature,* 1968, *220,* 593-596.

Verhulst, J., & Heiman, J. An interactional approach to sexual dysfunction. *American Journal of Family Therapy,* 1979, *7,* 19-36.

Verhulst, J., & Schneidman, B. Schizophrenia and sexual functioning. *Hospital and Community Psychiatry,* 1981, *32,* 259-262.

Wincze, J., Hoon, E., & Hoon, P. Physiological responsivity of normal and sexually dysfunctional women during erotic stimulus exposure. *Journal of Psychosomatic Research,* 1976, *20,* 445-451.

Wolchik, S. A., Beggs, V. E., Wincze, J. P., Sakheim, D. K., Barlow, D. H., & Mavissakalian, M. The effect of emotional arousal on subsequent sexual arousal in men. *Journal of Abnormal Psychology,* 1980, *89,* 595-598.

Wright, J., Perreault, R., & Mathieu, M. The treatment of sexual dysfunction. *Archives of General Psychiatry,* 1977, *34,* 881-890.

Zilbergeld, B., & Rinkleib, C. E. Desire discrepancies and arousal problems in sex therapy. In S. Leiblum & L. Pervin (Eds.), *Casebook of sex therapy.* New York: Guilford, 1980.

15

INGRID WALDRON

Gender, Psychophysiological Disorders, and Mortality

In this brief review of sex differences in psychophysiological disorders and mortality, attention is focused on two major topics. One topic is the extent of historical and cross-cultural variability or uniformity in sex differences. Variability in sex differences suggests that environmental factors have an important influence, whereas uniformity of sex differences suggests that genetically determined differences between the sexes play a role. In most cases, detailed examination of the evidence actually reveals an interplay of environmental and genetic factors, as discussed in the following sections.

The other major topic considered is the nature of the specific factors that contribute to sex differences for specific psychophysiological disorders or specific causes of death. Although many questions remain unanswered, current evidence is sufficient to indicate that these sex differences are influenced by an enormous diversity of factors, including anatomical, physiological, psychological, and behavioral differences between the sexes.

Psychophysiological Disorders

The term *psychophysiological disorders* refers to diseases to which psychological factors are believed to make a significant contribution. It should be understood that for several reasons this is not a clear-cut category. It appears that there is no sharp distinction between disorders in which psy-

ISBN: 0-12-050350-6

chological factors make little or no contribution and disorders in which psychological factors make a substantial contribution, but rather there appears to be a continuum between these extremes. For some diseases, the importance of psychological factors is in dispute. The contribution of psychological factors may vary for different individuals with the same disease. Thus, *psychophysiological disorders* is not a precise term, but rather is used here in a loose, general sense.

The patterns of sex differences for specific psychophysiological disorders are extremely diverse. Asthma is more common among women than among men, but, in children, asthma is more common among boys than among girls (Derrick, 1971; Speizer, 1976). More women than men report having headaches (Newland, Illis, Robinson, Batchelor & Waters, 1978), but this sex difference is not observed for school children aged 6-10 (Øster, 1972). Peptic ulcer rates are higher for men than for women in most contemporary studies (Pflanz, 1978). However, sex differences in peptic ulcer mortality have shown considerable historical variation, with higher rates for women than for men before 1900 in several European countries, then substantially higher rates for men from about 1920 to 1950, and finally, decreasing sex differences since 1950 in many industrial countries (Pflanz, 1978). Sex differences also differ for the two types of peptic ulcer, with a greater male excess for duodenal than for gastric ulcers in contemporary data (Sturdevant, 1976). Additional examples of variation in sex differences in psychophysiological disorders are given in the following sections, which present brief analyses of sex differences in coronary heart disease, hypertension, and rheumatoid arthritis.

Coronary Heart Disease

Death rates for coronary heart disease are approximately twice as high for men as for women in the contemporary United States (Waldron, 1982a). Sex differences for coronary heart disease mortality have been smaller in the United States in the past, and smaller sex differences have also been observed in historical or contemporary data for many other countries (Segi, Kurihara, & Tsukahara, 1966; Waldron, 1982a). Although there has been considerable variation in the magnitude of sex differences in mortality, there does not appear to be any country in which there has been a reversal, with higher coronary heart disease mortality for women. These observations suggest that sex differences in coronary heart disease in the contemporary United States reflect both factors that vary cross-culturally and historically (such as cigarette smoking) and factors that are consistent cross-culturally (such as a possible protective effect of female sex hormones).

Sex differences in cigarette smoking make a major contribution to sex differences in coronary heart disease in the contemporary United States (U.S. Department of Health and Human Services, 1980; Waldron, 1976, 1982a). In the United States, more men than women smoke and, among smokers, men inhale more, smoke more cigarettes per day, and are less likely to use low tar or filter cigarettes. Sex differences in cigarette smoking vary with age, with the largest differences at older ages, smaller differences for middle-aged adults, and no consistent sex differences for teenagers. Since most cigarette smokers begin smoking before age 25, the smoking habits of older people continue to be influenced by the social mores of the early twentieth century. Thus, one reason why relatively few older women are cigarette smokers is that social pressures against smoking by women were strong during the early twentieth century, when these women were young. Other factors may also have contributed to the sex differences in cigarette smoking. For example, girls may be more susceptible to nicotine overdose reactions than boys, and consequently girls may more often feel sick as a result of smoking their first cigarette. This difference may have contributed to lower rates of cigarette smoking for females in the period before low-nicotine cigarettes were in widespread use (Silverstein, Feld, & Kozlowski, 1980).

Another factor that appears to contribute to sex differences in coronary heart disease in the United States is the Type A or coronary-prone behavior pattern (Waldron, 1978, 1982a). This is a hard-driving style of life that is characterized by aggressiveness, competitiveness, hostility, impatience, a chronic sense of time urgency, and a strong drive to achieve. The Type A behavior pattern is associated with a substantially increased risk of developing or dying of coronary heart disease. As might be expected, this behavior pattern is more common among men than among women in the United States. The high levels of Type A behavior among men in the United States appear to be due in large part to cultural influences. Type A behavior may be encouraged more in males than in females in the United States because this hard-driving style of life appears to contribute more to success in traditional male roles than in traditional female roles.

There has been considerable interest in the possibility that female sex hormones may reduce women's risk of coronary heart disease (McGill & Stern, 1979; Waldron, 1976, 1982b). Women who have had their ovaries removed or had early natural menopause appear to have an increased risk of coronary heart disease. This suggests that the sex hormones secreted by women's ovaries reduce the risk of coronary heart disease, although this conclusion is controversial at present. Therapy with female sex hormones generally does not reduce the risk of coronary heart disease, which suggests that there may be something about the particular pattern of hormones secreted by women's ovaries that contributes to the protective effect. Male sex hormones do not appear to increase the risk of coronary heart disease.

Two major forms of coronary heart disease are myocardial infarctions, which are commonly known as heart attacks, and angina pectoris. Rates of myocardial infarction in the United States have been over twice as high for men as for women, but sex differences for angina pectoris have been much smaller (Waldron, 1982a). The mortality risk associated with a myocardial infarction is similar for men and women, but the mortality associated with angina is lower for women than for men. This suggests that the angina identified in women is less serious than the angina identified in men. In addition, angina is more likely to be first diagnosed as a sequel of myocardial infarction for men, whereas angina is more often the presenting complaint for women. These observations suggest that women may be more likely than men to perceive and to report symptoms that lead to a diagnosis of angina, and this may be one reason why sex differences are smaller for angina than for myocardial infarctions.

In summary, sex differences in the risk of coronary heart disease in the contemporary United States are caused by sex differences in cigarette smoking and probably also by sex differences in Type A behavior pattern and protective effects of the sex hormones secreted by women's ovaries. Sex differences for angina are smaller than for myocardial infarctions, and this may reflect sex differences in the predisposition to report the symptoms that lead to a diagnosis of angina.

Hypertension

In the contemporary United States, hypertension is more common among men than among women for adults under age 50 (U.S. National Center for Health Statistics, 1973*a*, 1977). At older ages, hypertension is more common among women. These findings reflect higher blood pressures for men than for women at young adult ages, but a steeper gradient of blood pressure with age for women. These statements are based on national cross-sectional data. Longitudinal data from the Framingham study indicate that the differences at older ages are probably due in part to high mortality of men with high blood pressures, so that men with hypertension are less likely to survive to older ages (Gordon & Shurtleff, 1973). In addition to this factor of selective survival, the longitudinal data indicate that, up to age 50, women's blood pressures tend to increase more rapidly with age, especially for systolic blood pressure.

Cross-cultural evidence indicates that a similar pattern is observed in many groups, with systolic blood pressures higher for women than for men at older ages, but not at young adult ages (Henry & Cassel, 1969; Maddocks, 1967; Waldron *et al.*, 1982). This pattern is observed even in groups in which blood pressures are relatively low throughout life, and hypertension and associated mortality risks are rare for both men and women at all ages. These observations suggest that there may be an inherent biological tendency for women's blood pressures to rise more rapidly than men's with age.

It is at present unclear what biological factors might contribute to a greater increase of blood pressure with age for women. For some women, pregnancy is associated with increased blood pressures, but women who have had many children do not appear to have more hypertension than women who have had few or no children (Lee-Feldstein, Harburg, & Hauenstein, 1980; U.S. National Center for Health Statistics, 1973b). Menopause does not appear to be associated with a significant increase in blood pressure (Hjortland, McNamara, & Kannel, 1976; Waldron 1976). Thus, the causes of sex differences in change in blood pressure with age are not known at the present time.

The magnitude of the sex differences in blood pressure varies considerably in different societies. For ages 20–30, the excess of male relative to female blood pressures has been found to be greater in societies with more economic competition, more contact with people who are substantially poorer, and more contact with people of different culture or beliefs (Waldron *et al.*, 1982 and unpublished analyses). It appears that stresses associated with economic competition and insecurity and with contact with another culture may be experienced more by men than by women, and these factors may contribute to a greater excess of hypertension for young men relative to young women in some societies.

In summary, in societies such as the United States, in which hypertension is relatively common, young men have hypertension more often than young women, but at older ages women have hypertension more often than men. This reversal of sex differences at older ages appears to be due in part to the higher mortality of men with hypertension, and perhaps also to biological factors that contribute to a more rapid increase of blood pressure with age for women. For young adults, the excess of hypertension among males varies cross-culturally and may be influenced by social factors such as the amount of economic competition.

Rheumatoid Arthritis

Women have been found to have higher rates of rheumatoid arthritis than men in epidemiological surveys of several racial groups and quite a few different regions of the world (Cobb, 1971; Kato *et al.*, 1971). Although there is widespread agreement that rheumatoid arthritis is more common in women, sex differences in the individual indicators of rheumatoid arthritis are quite variable. Joint swelling and reports of joint pain or morning stiffness are more common for women, but no consistent sex differences have been observed for x-ray evidence of erosive arthritis or for rheumatoid factors (immune factors in the blood) (Cathcart & O'Sullivan, 1970; Mikkelsen, 1972; U.S. National

Center for Health Statistics, 1966; Wood, 1968). In evaluating these findings, it is important to realize that no single indicator is entirely specific for rheumatoid arthritis. Although positive tests for rheumatoid factors or x-ray evidence of erosive arthritis are more common in people with rheumatoid arthritis, both of these indicators are also observed in other individuals. In fact, since only a small proportion of the population has rheumatoid arthritis, the majority of individuals with either one of these indicators does not have rheumatoid arthritis (Kato *et al.*, 1971; Kellgren, 1968; Mikkelsen, 1972; Wood, 1972). In summary, no single indicator is adequate to identify individuals with rheumatoid arthritis. Sex differences are observed primarily for joint swelling and for reports of joint pain and morning stiffness.

These observations suggest that one reason why rheumatoid arthritis is detected in more women than men may be that women may have a greater sensitivity to or willingness to report the symptoms that contribute to a diagnosis of rheumatoid arthritis. If sex differences in symptom-reporting were a major cause of women's higher rates of rheumatoid arthritis, then it would be expected that women would have less serious disease than men. Contrary to this expectation, the prognosis in rheumatoid arthritis is generally found to be worse for women; deterioration of the joints, as assessed medically, is more frequent for women than for men in follow-up studies of rheumatoid arthritis patients (Masi, Maldonado-Cocco, Kaplan, Feigenbaum, & Chandler, 1976). This suggests that sex differences in rheumatoid arthritis rates are probably not due primarily to sex differences in the predisposition to report symptoms.

It may be that women are more vulnerable to rheumatoid arthritis because more women than men have psychological characteristics that may predispose an individual to develop rheumatoid arthritis. A variety of evidence indicates that rheumatoid arthritis patients tend to be self-sacrificing, depressed, and inclined to deny anger (Weiner, 1977). These data should be interpreted with caution, because almost all studies were retrospective, so it is possible that these psychological characteristics may have developed as a consequence of the disease.

One particularly interesting study (Crown & Crown, 1973) found that scores for neurotic symptoms were higher in rheumatoid arthritis patients with a negative test for rheumatoid factor than in those with a positive test for rheumatoid factor. This suggests that neuroticism may contribute particularly to the development of arthritis when levels of rheumatoid factors are low. Thus the greater neuroticism of women (Dohrenwend & Dohrenwend, 1976) could be one reason why women develop rheumatoid arthritis more often than men even though women do not have higher levels of rheumatoid factors than men.

Female sex hormones do not appear to contribute to women's higher rates of rheumatoid arthritis. In fact, female sex hormones may decrease the risk of rheumatoid arthritis, since pregnancy is generally associated with a reduction of symptoms in rheumatoid arthritis patients (McCarty, 1979) and use of oral contraceptives appears to be associated with a decreased incidence of rheumatoid arthritis (Wingrave, 1978). No evidence was found concerning the relationship of male sex hormones to rheumatoid arthritis, but one study of an experimental analogue of rheumatoid arthritis in rats found no effect of testosterone and a strong protective effect of estrogens (Mueller & Kappas, 1964). These data suggest that sex hormones are not responsible for the sex difference in rheumatoid arthritis rates.

An inherent difference between the sexes that could contribute to women's higher rates of rheumatoid arthritis is the enhanced immune activity associated with the pair of X chromosomes in females, as contrasted with the single X chromosome in males (Waldron, 1976, 1982b). However, the observation that there are no consistent sex differences in rheumatoid factors suggests that, if inherent sex differences in immune responsiveness play a role, these differences are not evident in the general immune responses indexed by rheumatoid factors. A final hypothesis is that there may be inherent sex differences in vulnerability to inflammatory processes locally in the joints, possibly due to inherent sex differences in immune responsiveness and/or to specific vulnerability of women's joint tissues (Kellgren, 1968; Masi *et al.*, 1976).

In summary, current evidence concerning the causes of sex differences in rheumatoid arthritis is inconclusive. It appears that women's higher rates of diagnosed rheumatoid arthritis may be due to both psychological factors, including possibly greater neuroticism for women, and biological factors, including possibly inherently greater vulnerability to inflammatory processes in the joints for women.

Mortality

The Contemporary United States

In the contemporary United States, total mortality is substantially higher for males than for females (Table 15.1). Male death rates are over twice as high as female death rates for eight causes of death with major behavioral components. These are homicide, suicide, motor vehicle accidents, other accidents, cirrhosis of the liver, malignant neoplasms of the respiratory system, emphysema/bronchitis/asthma, and coronary heart disease (Table 15.1). Taken together, these causes account for 74% of the excess of male over female death rates. The following paragraphs briefly review evidence that, for each of these causes of death, behaviors that have been expected of males or

TABLE 15.1
Major Causes of Higher Mortality for Males, United States, 1978[a]

Cause of death	Sex mortality ratio	Male death rate[b]	Female death rate[b]
Homicide	3.64	15.3	4.2
Malignant neoplasms of respiratory system	3.53	59.0	16.7
Suicide	2.98	18.5	6.2
Emphysema, bronchitis, and asthma	2.92	11.1	3.8
Motor vehicle accidents	2.85	35.1	12.3
All other accidents	2.85	31.4	11.0
Cirrhosis of liver	2.17	17.6	8.1
Coronary heart disease[c]	2.13	256.3	120.6
All causes	1.80	802.8	447.0

Data from U.S. National Center for Health Statistics, 1980.

[a] This table lists all causes of death that were responsible for at least 1% of all deaths in the United States in 1978 and had a sex mortality ratio greater than 2.0. The sex mortality ratio is the ratio of male to female death rates.

[b] Death rates are deaths per 100,000 population. These death rates have been age-adjusted, so male and female death rates are directly comparable and are not affected by the higher proportion of females at older ages.

[c] This category is officially designated *ischemic heart disease*, but the more familiar term *coronary heart disease* is used throughout this paper.

have been more socially acceptable for males make a major contribution to their higher mortality.

Coronary heart disease is responsible for 33% of all deaths and 38% of the sex difference in death rates in the United States (Table 15.1). As discussed previously, one behavior that makes a major contribution to men's higher rates of coronary heart disease is cigarette smoking, and a major cause of the sex differences in cigarette smoking has been the social pressure against cigarette smoking by women during the early twentieth century. Another behavior that appears to contribute to the sex difference in coronary heart disease is the hard-driving Type A behavior pattern, which may be encouraged more among males than females because Type A behavior appears to contribute to success in traditional male roles but not in traditional female roles.

Sex differences in cigarette smoking are a major cause of the sex differences in malignant neoplasms of the respiratory system (which are primarily lung cancer) and emphysema, bronchitis, and asthma (which is primarily emphysema). Greater exposure to occupational hazards, such as asbestos, also contributes to men's higher rates of lung cancer and other lung diseases (Waldron, 1982a).

Men's higher death rates for motor vehicle accidents appear to be due in part to less safe driving habits for men (Waldron, 1976, 1982a). Sex differences in alcohol consumption also appear to play a major role (Ferrence, 1980; Waldron, 1982a). For drivers involved in fatal motor vehicle accidents, men more often than women were under the influence of alcohol. Surveys of alcohol levels in drivers have found that a higher proportion of men than women drivers have high alcohol levels. These sex differences in alcohol levels while driving reflect general sex differences in alcohol consumption.

A variety of evidence supports the conclusion that substantially more men than women are heavy drinkers (Ferrence, 1980). It appears that one important reason why more men than women become heavy drinkers is that heavy drinking is more socially acceptable for men (Ferrence, 1980; Waldron, 1982a). This sex difference in the prevalence of heavy drinking contributes not only to sex differences in motor vehicle accident fatalities but also to sex differences in other accidents, homicide, suicide, and cirrhosis of the liver (Galambos, 1979; Waldron, 1976, 1982a).

For accidents other than motor vehicle accidents, about 30% of the sex difference in death rates is due to accidents at work (Waldron, 1982a). Fatal work accidents are more frequent for men because more men are employed and because the jobs men hold are more physically hazardous, on the average. An additional 40% of the sex difference in death rates for non-motor vehicle accidents is accounted for by gun accidents, accidental drownings, and water and air transport accidents, which are each over five times more common for males. Thus, the higher accident death rates for males are due in large part to behaviors that are more expected or accepted for men and boys, such as using guns, being adventurous, working at sometimes hazardous jobs, and heavy drinking.

Suicide rates are three times as high for men as for women, but women make twice as many suicide attempts (Jarvis, Ferrence, Johnson, & Whitehead, 1976; Waldron, 1976, 1982a). One reason for this difference is that suicidal men are particularly likely to use guns, with consequences that are often irreversible and fatal, whereas women are more likely to use poisons, which are less often fatal and can be treated by the use of stomach pumps and antidotes. In addition, it appears that women are more able than men to use a suicide attempt as a desperate plea for help, whereas men may be less able to use a suicide attempt in this way and thus may be more likely to carry a suicidal act through to a fatal conclusion.

In summary, three-quarters of the sex difference in mortality in the contemporary United States can be accounted for by eight causes of death that have major behavioral components. In each case, behaviors that have been more expected or acceptable for males contribute to men's higher death rates. The behaviors that contribute to sex differences in mortality include cigarette smoking, heavy alcohol consumption, use of guns, working at jobs with exposures to occupational hazards, and probably the hard-driving Type A behavior pattern.

Historical and Cross-Cultural Variation

There has been considerable historical and cross-cultural variation in sex differences in death rates. For the United States, the ratios of male to female death rates (called the sex mortality ratios) increased substantially during the twentieth century (Figure 15.1). The most dramatic increases in sex mortality ratios and the highest contemporary sex mortality ratios are observed for the 15-24-year-old age group. For whites in this age range, the increase in sex mortality ratios between 1930 and 1958 was due in large part to decreases in deaths due to two causes for which young women had substantially higher mortality than young men in the early period, namely, tuberculosis and maternal mortality (Enterline, 1961). Since 1960, the continuing increase in sex mortality ratios for this age group has been due in large part to an increase in the proportion of deaths due to two causes with a large male excess, namely suicide and homicide (Waldron, 1982a).

In the United States before 1950, the increase in sex mortality ratios at older ages was due in large part to increases in men's death rates for coronary heart disease and lung cancer (Enterline, 1961; Waldron, 1982a). One major cause of these trends was the rise in cigarette smoking among men several decades before cigarette smoking became common among women (U.S. Department of Health and Human Services, 1980). In the United States since 1960, there has been a continued increase in sex mortality ratios for most age groups, but not for 45-64-year-olds (Waldron, 1982a). Trends for specific causes of death have been varied. Sex mortality ratios for coronary heart disease have been relatively stable, with parallel declines in coronary heart disease mortality for both sexes since the mid-sixties. The causes of these trends are not clearly understood at present. For lung cancer, sex mortality ratios have decreased substantially due to rapid increases in women's lung cancer death rates as a consequence of increased cigarette smoking among women.

In western European countries, the excess of male relative to female death rates has also increased during the twentieth century (Tabutin, 1978; Waldron, 1982a). During earlier periods there were even reversals of the contemporary sex differences in mortality, with higher death rates for girls and young women than for boys and young men in many European countries.

In contemporary data, death rates are higher for females than for males for ages 1-40 in India and several other regions in South Asia (Figure 15.1; Miller, 1981; Waldron, 1982a; Wyon & Gordon, 1971). The available evidence indicates that in northern India and Bangladesh boys are better fed than girls, and less adequate nutrition for girls is probably a major cause of their greater vulnerability to infectious diseases. There is also evidence that in these

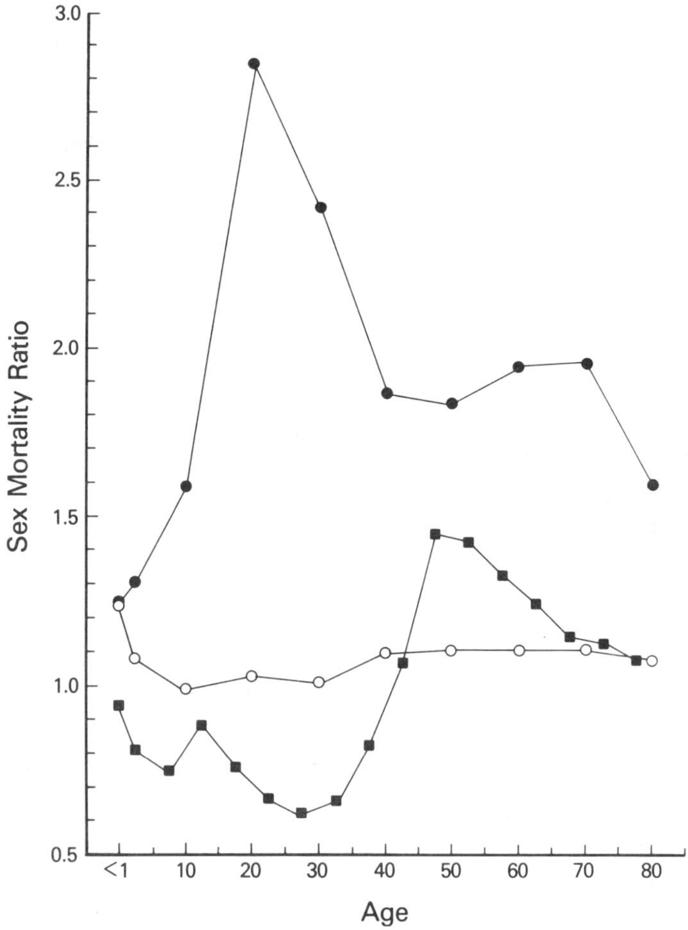

FIGURE 15.1. ***Sex mortality ratios for the United States and India. A sex mortality ratio greater than 1 indicates higher male death rates, whereas a ratio less than 1 indicates higher female death rates. The filled-in circles indicate sex mortality ratios for the United States in 1978; the empty circles indicate sex mortality ratios for death registration states in the United States in 1900; the filled-in squares indicate sex mortality ratios for India in 1969, based on estimated life table values. (Data from Metropolitan Life, 1974; U.S. Bureau of the Census, 1978; U.S. National Center for Health Statistics, 1980.)***

regions males receive more medical care than females. In addition, physiological strains due to repeated pregnancies and lactation, as well as mortality directly due to pregnancy and childbirth, contribute to higher mortality for women in these regions where nutrition and health care are frequently inadequate.

Although sex differences in mortality have shown considerable variation historically and cross-culturally, certain relatively consistent patterns have been observed. Mortality during the first year of life has been higher for males than for females in almost all available data, although exceptions have been observed in some cases, for example, in contemporary data for South Asia (Waldron, 1982a). For ages above 50, men's mortality is also higher than women's mortality in almost all available data. For coronary heart disease, accidents, suicide, and homicide, it appears that male death rates have been quite consistently higher than female death rates, although the magnitude of the sex differences have varied considerably (Preston, 1976; Segi *et al.*, 1966; Waldron, 1982a).

The rather consistent sex differences in accident, suicide, and homicide rates reflect widespread sex differences in behavior (Waldron, 1982b). These sex differences in behavior appear to be due in part to hormonal influences and in part to widespread cultural influences. There appear to be pervasive differences in cultural expectations for male and female behavior that may have developed nearly universally as a consequence of the sex differences in reproductive functions. Specifically, it appears that, because only women can bear and nurse children, women have been assigned the primary responsibility for care of young children in almost all cultures and, probably as a consequence, tasks that are incompatible with child care have been assigned primarily to men (Brown, 1970). Since dangerous tasks are typically incompatible with care of young children, this argument leads to the expectation that the most dangerous tasks and related behaviors and associated risks would in almost all cultures be assigned primarily to men.

In summary, historical and cross-cultural data show considerable variation in sex differences in mortality. For example, death rates are higher for males at all ages in modern industrial countries, but death rates are higher for females among children and young adults in contemporary data for some South Asian countries and in historical data for many European countries. On the other hand, for some age groups and for certain causes of death, male death rates have been quite consistently higher than female death rates. These observations suggest that sex differences in mortality are influenced both by factors that vary historically and cross-culturally, such as cigarette smoking and nutrition, and by factors that are relatively invariant, including inherent sex differences in vulnerability to certain specific types of mortality.

Conclusion

It is clear that sex differences in psychophysiological disorders and mortality are influenced by an enormous diversity of factors. Despite the complexities, several general conclusions emerge. The evidence presented indicates that both environmental and genetic factors have an important influence on sex differences in psychophysiological disorders and mortality. Another conclusion is that behaviors that have been expected or more acceptable for males are major contributors to men's higher death rates in the contemporary United States. Behaviors that contribute to men's higher death rates include cigarette smoking, heavy alcohol consumption, use of guns, working at sometimes hazardous jobs, and probably the hard-driving Type A behavior pattern. Variation in these behaviors has been one major cause of the substantial historical and cross-cultural variation in sex differences in mortality.

References

Brown, J. K. A note on the division of labor by sex. *American Anthropologist*, 1970, *72*, 1073-1078.

Cathcart, E. S., & O'Sullivan, J. B. Rheumatoid arthritis in a New England town. *New England Journal of Medicine*, 1970, *282*, 421-424.

Cobb, S. *The frequency of rheumatic diseases*. Cambridge, Massachusetts: Harvard Univ. Press, 1971.

Crown, J. M., & Crown, S. The relationship between personality and the presence of rheumatoid factor in early rheumatoid disease. *Scandinavian Journal of Rheumatology*, 1973, *2*, 123-126.

Derrick, E. H. The significance of the age of onset of asthma. *Medical Journal of Australia*, 1971, *1*, 1317-1319.

Dohrenwend, B. P., & Dohrenwend, B. S. Sex differences and psychiatric disorder. *American Journal of Sociology*, 1976, *81*, 1447-1454.

Enterline, P. E. Causes of death responsible for recent increases in sex mortality differentials in the U.S. *Milbank Memorial Fund Quarterly*, 1961, *39*, 312-338.

Ferrence, R. G. Sex differences in the prevalence of problem drinking. *Research Advances in Alcohol and Drug Problems*, 1980, *5*, 69-124.

Galambos, J. T. Cirrhosis. *Major Problems in Internal Medicine*, 1979, *17*, 1-376.

Gordon, T., & Shurtleff, D. Means at each examination and inter-examination variation of specified characteristics. *The Framingham Study, Section 29* (DHEW Publication No. [NIH] 74-478). Washington, D.C.: Department of Health, Education and Welfare, 1973.

Henry, J. P., & Cassel, J. C. Psychosocial factors in essential hypertension: Recent epidemiologic and animal experimental evidence. *American Journal of Epidemiology*, 1969, *90*, 171-200.

Hjortland, M. S., McNamara, P. M., & Kannel, W. B. Some atherogenic concomitants of menopause: The Framingham Study. *American Journal of Epidemiology*, 1976, *103*, 304-311.

Jarvis, G. K., Ferrence, R. G., Johnson, F. G., & Whitehead, P. C. Sex and age patterns in self-injury. *Journal of Health and Social Behavior*, 1976, *17*, 145-154.

Kato, H., Duff, I. F., Russell, W. J., Uda, Y., Hamilton, H. B., Kawamoto, S., & Johnson, K. G. Rheumatoid arthritis and gout in Hiroshima and Nagasaki, Japan. *Journal of Chronic Diseases*, 1971, *23*, 659-679.

Kellgren, J. H. Epidemiology of rheumatoid arthritis. In J. J. R. Duthie & W. R. M. Alexander (Eds.), *Rheumatic diseases*. Baltimore, Maryland: Williams and Wilkins, 1968.

Lee-Feldstein, A., Harburg, E., & Hauenstein, L. Parity and blood pressure among four race-stress groups of females in Detroit *American Journal of Epidemiology*, 1980, *111*, 356-366.

McCarty, J. D. J. (Ed.). *Arthritis and allied conditions* (9th ed.). Philadelphia, Pennsylvania: Lea & Febiger, 1979.

McGill, H. C., & Stern, M. P. Sex and atherosclerosis. *Atherosclerosis Review*, 1979, *4*, 157-242.

Maddocks, I. Blood pressures in Melanesians. *Medical Journal of Australia*, 1967, 1123-1126.

Masi, A. T., Maldonado-Cocco, J. A., Kaplan, S. B., Feigenbaum, S. L., & Chandler, R. W. Prospective study of the early course of rheumatoid arthritis in young adults. *Seminars in Arthritis and Rheumatism*, 1976, *5*, 299-326.

Metropolitan Life. Sex differentials in mortality. *Statistical Bulletin*, 1974, *55*, 2-5.

Mikkelsen, W. M. The epidemiology of rheumatic diseases. In J. L. Hollander & D. J. McCarty (Eds.), *Arthritis and allied conditions* (8th ed.). Philadelphia, Pennsylvania: Lea & Febiger, 1972.

Miller, B. D. *The endangered sex: Neglect of female children in rural North India*. Ithaca, New York: Cornell Univ. Press, 1981.

Mueller, M. N., & Kappas, A. Estrogen pharmacology. II. Suppression of experimental immune polyarthritis. *Proceedings of the Society for Experimental Biology and Medicine*, 1964, *117*, 845-847.

Newland, C. A., Illis, L. S., Robinson, P. K., Batchelor, B. G., & Waters, W. E. A survey of headache in an English city. *Research and Clinical Studies of Headache*, 1978, *5*, 1-20.

Øster, J. Recurrent abdominal pain, headache and limb pains in children and adolescents. *Pediatrics*, 1972, *50*, 429-436.

Pflanz, M. Sex differences in abdominal illness. *Social Science and Medicine*, 1978, *12B*, 171-176.

Preston, S. H. *Mortality patterns in national populations*. New York: Academic Press, 1976.

Segi, M., Kurihara, M., & Tsukahara, Y. *Mortality for selected causes in 30 countries (1950-1961)*. Tokyo, Japan: Kosei Tokei Kyokai, 1966.

Silverstein, B., Feld, S., & Kozlowski, L. T. The availability of low-nicotine cigarettes as a cause of cigarette smoking among teenage females. *Journal of Health and Social Behavior*, 1980, *21*, 383-388.

Speizer, F. B. Epidemiology, prevalence and mortality in asthma. In E. B. Weiss & M. S. Segal (Eds.), *Bronchial asthma*. Boston, Massachusetts: Little, Brown, 1976.

Sturdevant, R. A. Epidemiology of peptic ulcer. *American Journal of Epidemiology*, 1976, *104*, 9-14.

Tabutin, D. La surmortalité féminine en Europe avant 1940. *Population*, 1978 (No. 1), 121-148.

U.S. Bureau of the Census. *Country demographic profiles: India*. Washington, D.C.: US Govt. Printing Office, 1978.

U.S. Department of Health and Human Services. *The health consequences of smoking for women: A report of the surgeon general*. Washington, D.C.: U.S. Department of Health and Human Services, Public Health Service, 1980.

U.S. National Center for Health Statistics. Rheumatoid arthritis in adults, 1960-2. *Vital and Health Statistics* (Series 11, No. 17). Rockville, Maryland: U.S. Department of Health, Education and Welfare, 1966.

U.S. National Center for Health Statistics. Hypertension and hypertensive heart disease in adults. *Vital and Health Statistics* (Series 11, No. 13). Rockville, Maryland: U.S. Department of Health, Education and Welfare, 1973. (a)

U.S. National Center for Health Statistics. Parity and hypertension. *Vital and Health Statistics* (Series 11, No. 38). Rockville, Maryland: U.S. Department of Health, Education and Welfare, 1973. (b)

U.S. National Center for Health Statistics. Blood pressure levels of persons 6-74 years, U.S., 1971-1974. *Vital and Health Statistics* (Series 11, No. 203). Hyattsville, Maryland: U.S. Department of Health, Education and Welfare, 1977.

U.S. National Center for Health Statistics. Advance report: Final mortality statistics, 1978. *Monthly Vital Statistics Report*, 1980, *29*(6), (Suppl. 2).

Waldron, I. Why do women live longer than men? *Social Science and Medicine*, 1976, *10*, 349-362.

Waldron, I. Sex differences in the coronary-prone behavior pattern. In T. M. Dembroski, S. M. Weiss, J. L. Shields, S. G. Haynes, & M. Feinleib (Eds.), *Coronary-prone behavior*. New York: Springer, 1978.

Waldron, I. An analysis of causes of sex differences in mortality and morbidity. In W. Gove & G. R. Carpenter (Eds.), *The fundamental connection between nature and nurture*. Lexington, Massachusetts: Lexington Books, 1982a, pp. 69-116.

Waldron, I. The role of genetic and biological factors in sex differences in mortality. In A. Lopez & L. T. Ruzicka (Eds.), *Sex differentials in mortality: Trends, determinants and consequences, proceedings of a World Health Organization-sponsored conference*. Canberra, Australia: Australian National Univ. Press, 1982b. (In Press).

Waldron, I., Nowotarski, M., Freimer, M., Henry, J. P., Post, N., & Witten, C. Cross-cultural variation in blood pressure: A quantitative analysis of the relationships of blood pressure to cultural characteristics, salt consumption and body weight. *Social Science and Medicine*, 1982, *16*, 419-430.

Weiner, H. *Psychobiology and human disease*. New York: Elsevier, 1977.

Wingrave, S. J. Reduction in incidence of rheumatoid arthritis associated with oral contraceptives. *Lancet*, 1978, *1*, 569-571.

Wood, P. H. N. Age and the rheumatic diseases. In P. H. Bennett & P. H. N. Wood (Eds.), *Population studies of the rheumatic diseases*. Amsterdam, The Netherlands: Excerpta Medica Foundation, 1968.

Wood, P. H. N. Radiology in the diagnosis of arthritis and rheumatism. *Transactions of the Society of Occupational Medicine*, 1972, *22*, 69-73.

Wyon, J. B., & Gordon, J. E. *The Khanna study*. Cambridge, Massachusetts: Harvard Univ. Press, 1971.

16

JOHN P. FOREYT
G. KEN GOODRICK

Gender and Obesity[1]

In the seventeenth century, the ideal of feminine beauty as represented by Rubens clearly showed a percentage of body fat well in excess of that now recommended by life insurance companies. This early ideal represented an upper-class female, protected from physical labor and food scarcity; her fat was a status symbol. Today, in industrialized societies, some women achieve a similar state of obesity through the wonders of labor-saving devices, along with our plentiful food supply. However, in modern society a different set of norms has developed regarding preferred physical characteristics, particularly of females. Among the millions of obese women in the United States, virtually all are aware that their bodies deviate from today's ideal. Most who try to lose weight fail to achieve lasting success. In this age of hedonism and narcissism, many of these obese women are depressed and have poor self-esteem.

In exploring gender differences in the psychology of obesity one is struck by the fact that the preponderance of psychological disturbance and research involves women. This chapter therefore focuses mainly on the problems of obese females in an unaccepting society. In the first section, the incidence of obesity by sex, social class, and race is given. In the second section, the social-psychological context in which the obese person exists is discussed since, without this context, female obesity might not be a major concern. The

[1] This research is supported by Grants No. HL17269 and No. 1 T32 HL07258-01A1 from the National Heart, Lung, and Blood Institute, National Institutes of Health, Bethesda, Maryland.

ISBN: 0-12-050350-6

third section examines the possible etiologies of obesity. How do people allow themselves gradually to attain a state that is so negatively regarded both by themselves and by society? The psychological burden of obesity is discussed in the fourth section. More damaging than being obese may be the repetition of ineffective weight-loss techniques. The physical and psychological self-destruction involved in trying to reach and maintain a social ideal is outlined in the fifth section. The final section makes suggestions for therapy that run counter to the prevailing public and scientific moods. Until treatments are effective and without deleterious side effects, acceptance rather than intervention may be indicated in many cases.

Incidence of Obesity

Obesity refers to excess body fat. *Excess* requires some judgment for the population being studied. Obesity is most easily defined as a deviation from a norm, using arbitrary cutoff points. Ten percent (Lauer, Connor, Leaverton, Reiter, & Clarke, 1975) and 20% (Weil, 1977) over ideal body weight at different ages and heights have been used in research studies for years to define *overweight* and *obesity*, respectively. The ideal body weights are usually those listed in the popular height-weight tables of desirable weights for males and females according to height and frame from the 1959 Build and Blood Pressure Study of the Society of Actuaries (Society of Actuaries, 1959). According to these tables, which were derived from over 5 million insured males and females, 60% of males and 59% of females aged 40-49 years, and 63% of males and 67% of females aged 50-59 years exceed their ideal weight by 10% or more.

Recently, it has been suggested that these tables of ideal weights are at least 15 pounds *too low* (Keys, 1980). The tables were based on biased and perhaps faulty data. They were originally produced for actuarial purposes by the Metropolitan Life Insurance Company and were developed from data supplied to them by their potential customers. Apparently, some of these customers may have underreported their weights since they were aware that high weights carried penalties. Also, the final tables reflected only those people who were accepted by the Life Insurance Company, which probably skewed the database (Andres, 1980).

Even though we may not need to be as thin as the tables suggest, obesity is undoubtedly still a major problem in our society, with about 50% of all adults considered to have a significant weight problem. In fact, males are heavier today than their counterparts of the same height 25 years ago; females are lighter (Dawber, 1980; Montegriffo, 1971).

Height-weight tables are obviously not the best measure of obesity; body fat (i.e., the quantity of triglyceride and other fats that form the major component of adipose tissue) is a much better index. The density of fat is about .90 (90% as dense as water), compared to lean body mass (everything else), which has a density of about 1.10 (Bray, 1976). When a person is totally immersed in water, the amount of water displaced equals the person's volume. Weight divided by volume equals density. From this measure, an approximation of a person's percentage fat can be made. Unfortunately, because of the difficulty involved in making this measure, most physicians rely on either skinfold calipers for approximating body fat or body weight measured on a scale. Prevalence of obesity then depends on what operational definition and what cutoff points are used.

Obesity also varies depending on gender, age, race, social class, and other parameters. Prior to puberty, males and females do not differ much in body composition (Forbes, 1972) except for the greater skinfold thickness around the hips in females (Huenemann, 1974). At the onset of puberty, however, skinfold thickness increases significantly in females along with a decrease in potassium content (Seltzer & Mayer, 1965). By the time adolescents reach adulthood, the female body is composed of about 21% fat, compared to about 15% fat in the male body (Cheek, Schultz, Parra, & Reba, 1970). This higher level of fat may be an adaptation of mammals to increase the survivability of pregnant females and their babies in times of food scarcity. Adult women have a greater number of fat cells than men, and thus have a greater capacity proportionally to store fat through fat cell hypertrophy. Thus, women have a greater biological predisposition to become obese than men, and their relatively greater number of fat cells when they are obese may make success at weight loss more difficult. In studies with obese women, Björntorp, Carlgren, and Isaksson (1975) found that women with a relatively greater number of fat cells were less likely to respond to weight reduction treatment, since there appeared to be a lower limit to fat cell size.

In adults, there is an increase in the percentage of body fat and a decrease in lean body mass (Forbes & Reina, 1970). This increase in body fat is accompanied by a decrease in body water and body density, which drops from 1.040 to 1.016 gm per cm^3 in females and 1.072 to 1.041 in males.

Exercise makes a difference in these figures. For example, in an interesting report studying females training for the Olympics, Parizkova (1963) found that the athletes increased their body density from 1.054 to 1.058 gm per cm^3 and decreased their total skinfold thickness from 100 to 85 mm without changing their weight. After training, body density was less than 1.050 and skinfold thickness and weight increased.

Race is another factor (U.S. Department of Health, Education and Welfare, 1972). White males are heavier than black males but black females weigh more than white females. For both black and white males, obesity correlates directly with income level: the higher the income, the greater the prevalence of obesity. For females, the results are not quite so clear. In older women, the same trend holds for both blacks and whites: the higher the income level, the greater the prevalence of obesity. However, for younger women, there is more obesity in the lower-income groups for both races. Women of lower-income groups have an incidence of overweight of 30% compared to 5% of women in higher socioeconomic groups (Goldblatt, Moore, & Stunkard, 1965). The highest prevalence of obesity exists in middle-aged males and females (U.S. DHEW, 1972).

Women who recently immigrated to the United States have a higher prevalence of obesity (24%) compared with fourth generation women (5%) of the same ethnic and socioeconomic status. About 41% of females of Czechoslovakian ancestry are overweight, compared with 27% of Italian and 10% of British ancestry. As social mobility increases, overweight decreases (Goldblatt *et al.*, 1965).

Social factors are clearly more important for females than males in determining overweight. In one large study of 563 persons, 37% of males and 49% of females were found to be overweight. However, in the lower income females, 72% were overweight, compared to 39% in the highest-income group. In the males, the differences were much less marked (Silverstone, Gordon, & Stunkard, 1969).

To summarize, obesity, no matter what definition is used, is clearly a major problem for both males and females in our society. It is more prevalent in females than males and its development is strongly influenced by a large number of sociocultural factors.

Social-Psychological Context

It is clear that obesity is one of the physical conditions that Western industrialized societies regard as unattractive. Along with negative evaluation of appearance, negative personality attributions also exist. The formation of attitudes and prejudices against the obese are part of our socialization process. O. Wooley, Wooley, and Dyrenforth (1979) reviewed the literature, which documents the hatred of obese children by other children. Typically, obese children are seen as more lazy, ugly, dishonest, sloppy, mean, and dirty than normal-weight or thin children. These prejudices continue into adulthood. Waldroop (1980) found that young adults attributed negative adjectives such as self-pitying, obnoxious, and anxious far more frequently to obese than to normal-weight persons. Positive attributes such as alertness, capability, responsibility, and wisdom were more frequently given to normal-weight persons.

Behavioral evidence of discrimination against obese women has also been reviewed (O. Wooley *et al.*, 1979). Social mobility for obese women tends to be downward in terms of socioeconomic status attainment relative to that of parents. Obese adolescent females are less likely to be admitted to college than are normal-weight women, academic promise held equal.

Media representation of the female ideal clearly favors slimness. Advertisers know that attractive models sell more; actresses in television ads are selected on the basis of much research. Although the female ideal qua sex-object for males allows for more fat than advertising models, the female ideal for women themselves, as represented in the world of fashion, borders on the anorectic.

This general negativism toward deviations from ideal body fat is a specific case of the general problem of unattractiveness. People can reliably agree on judgments of attractiveness, although the criteria for judgment are not well delineated. Attractive people are judged more positively across a wide range of personality attributes and are seen to hold higher social and occupational status (Al-Issa, 1980).

To understand why obesity is thought to be unattractive, it may be of help to consider why physical attributes are considered positive or negative. In the case of ugliness, the parts of the body do not conform to acceptable standards. Our socialization process involves the depiction of evil persons as ugly and heroes as handsome. Standards of beauty may have originated from styles set by those in control of society, or there may be instinctive predispositions to select mates, and thus friends and heroes, from those who "fit" the ideal. Style of body and physiognomy have become as important as style of dress and demeanor. In some primitive cultures, the concept of differences in physical attractiveness does not exist; in others, marriages are arranged without concern for appearance. Some cultures value excess fat and consider it a positive sexual attribute in women (Al-Issa, 1980).

If evil is associated with unattractiveness in the socialization process, and if the opinion leaders, politicians, and entertainment personalities are perceived as attractive, then the social context exists for the development of prejudices that can become self-fulfilling. Whatever potential personal or social value an obese person may have is quashed by the rejection of society. The obese person is less likely to succeed and is more likely to have psychological problems, thus affirming the prejudices.

Although there are examples of highly successful and socially prominent obese men and women, the stereotypic obese person is perceived negatively. There are several possible explanations for the maintenance of this stereotype in addition to the socialization process and self-fulfilling prophecies just discussed. For one, the state of obesity is regarded as a voluntary condition (Wooley & Wooley, 1980). Although some evidence suggests that many obese persons eat no more than their normal-weight peers (Garrow, 1978), they are viewed by the public as gluttonous, lazy, and lacking in self-control. Although some persons feel that inactivity is not causal in maintaining obesity (Garrow, 1978), there is a strong negative correlation between amount of body fat and aerobic fitness (Rogers, Mahoney, Mahoney, Straw, & Kenigsberg, 1980) (see p. 350).

Some commercial weight-loss clinics advertise in such a way as to imply that obesity could be cured if only a person had enough willpower. Women's magazines, which tend to be filled with diet and recipe suggestions, are replete with advertisements and articles depicting before and after photographs of successful weight losers. These advertisements and articles support the belief that those who remain obese are not trying hard enough to lose; in reality, fewer than one-fourth of all obese people who try to reduce and to maintain a lower weight ever succeed, and many who do succeed pay a high price in terms of the stress of dieting and inadequate nutrition.

The stereotype is also supported by the observation that women of the lower social strata are generally fatter than those of the upper strata, with the degree of obesity greater for the racial minorities. Hence prejudices against poor and nonwhite people are reinforced, since obesity is frequently a characteristic of these groups. Also, thinness is characteristic of females in the upper classes; social pressures are oftentimes powerful enough to keep many of these women on starvation diets.

Over the last half-century, the public has come to believe that obesity is an unhealthy condition. Although obesity is related to increased mortality in men, there is evidence that moderate levels of obesity are not a significant health risk for women (Gubner, 1974). However, the stereotype for obese women includes attributions of poor health.

Another very important aspect of the prejudices against obese women involves their desirability as sexual partners. A few centuries ago, plumpness was prized in Europe, and some cultures still consider obesity a sexual plus (Al-Issa, 1980). Many men find adiposity of breasts and buttocks stimulating, whereas fat in other areas of the body is considered undesirable. Perhaps thinness of legs and waist serves to accentuate breasts and buttocks. Also, obesity in women may be associated with older age. Given the negative attitudes toward female obesity, it is unlikely that many men even consider obese females as potential sexual partners.

Obesity stigmatizes women more than men in our society. Most women will be unable to rid themselves of significant excess fat. Nor is fat something that can be hidden. It is more visible on women than on men. Biologically, women have almost twice the percentage of body fat as men, and this fat is conspicuously deposited on the extremities, hips and chest. Men's fat tends to accumulate on the torso, where it can be partially hidden by a suit jacket (Stuart & Jacobson, 1979). The problem of differential visibility of fat is compounded by the fact that women oftentimes are expected to dress in a way that reveals and accentuates their bodies to a greater degree than are men.

Factors in the Etiology and Maintenance of Obesity in Women

Females learn at an early age that obesity is to be avoided. Since heredity accounts for only about 10% of the variance in obesity (Hartz, Giefer, & Rimm, 1977), environmental, psychological, and behavioral processes must play a significant role in the development of obesity. In attempting to offer theories to explain the development of obesity in women, two distinctions should be made. First, processes leading to fat gain may be different from those involved in fat maintenance or loss. Second, juvenile- and adult-onset obesity may have unique etiologies.

Dieting and exercise programs have not been successful in helping most of those treated to lose significant fat. Physiological mechanisms seem to work against fat loss once a state of obesity has been established (see pp. 339, 348). However, it is impossible to become fat unless caloric intake exceeds energy and metabolic expenditure over an extended period. Therefore, fat gain can be said to be the result of voluntary behaviors.

For young women especially, there are several conditions that may foster fat storage. When a girl reaches puberty, her activity level from play diminishes. In the last decade, there has been an increasing emphasis on vigorous exercise for women. However, the aerobic fitness level for most females reaches a peak at about 12 years of age and then drops to a low level (Bailey, 1973), presumably because it is less fashionable among teenage females to involve themselves in aerobic activities. Although female adolescents may be involved in sports during physical education classes, they are less likely to engage in afterschool activities such as touch football or basketball than are males. Mothers and older peers emphasize the importance of lady-like behavior. There is much preoccupation with preparing the young girl for womanhood, with an emphasis on personal appearance. Activity becomes less important at the same time that food becomes more salient. Part of the role modeling provided by mothers involves the learning of food preparation and cooking skills.

Mothers influence the eating habits of their children more than fathers, presumably because mothers are generally responsible for food buying and preparation (Stuart & Davis, 1972). The mother-daughter bond may become stronger at the beginning of adolescence when the daughter's weight consciousness and dieting begin. The fact that 60% of obese persons have at least one obese parent (Rodin, 1977) shows that such family influences can be stronger than genetic inheritance in producing obesity.

At one time, it was thought by some that persons became obese because they were more sensitive to external food cues than normal weight persons (Schachter, 1971). Their response to these food cues was overeating, regardless of internal hunger cues. The current view (Rodin, 1981) is that hypersensitivity to food cues is a characteristic that is distributed equally among persons of all weight categories. Thus the externality theory is not sufficient to explain obesity. However, according to Rodin (1981), in persons who are more externally responsive, there is an increased insulin response related to perceived palatability of foods presented even without eating. Since women are frequently exposed to such food cues in their role as housewife/cook, they may oversecrete insulin, causing them to eat more calories and to store more of the excess calories as fat.

These influences on caloric output and intake occur when sensitivity to personal appearance becomes heightened. Stuart and Jacobson (1979) reviewed studies showing that adolescent females are highly sensitive to their weight and appearance. Most of these females attempt to control their weight through dieting. The dieting may actually lead to an increased propensity to put on fat and it can exacerbate psychological stress levels (see pp. 347-348). Dieting may also result in feeling less energetic, thus reducing desirable physical exercise. Puberty also brings menstruation, which is still considered unclean by some in our society, and the weight fluctuation associated with fluid retention.

All of these conditions create a great amount of distress regarding fat. The self-control needed for dietary restraint is difficult to maintain under such stress (Foreyt, Goodrick, & Gotto, 1981). When willpower breaks down and inappropriate eating occurs, a sense of failure and lack of self-control can develop. Although no association between emotional disturbance and overeating has been found in adults (Rodin, 1977), Funabiki, Bologna, Pepping, and Fitz-Gerald (1980) reported that college-aged females were more likely than their male peers to increase their food intake in response to depression.

The pressure to attain or maintain an ideal figure in order to be competitive sexually, to be attractive to males, or to feel superior to other females may be so high as to provoke an opposite reaction (Brehm, 1966; Wardle, 1980). This opposite reaction might take the form of total rejection of food, as in the case of anorexia; rejection of dieting, as expressed in overeating; or alternation between these extremes.

The condition of chronic dieting appears to be unstable since moderate caloric restriction may increase food cravings (cf. S. Wooley, Wooley, & Dyrenforth, 1979b). Anorexia produces less hunger stress since severe fasting is oftentimes associated with minimal hunger pangs. On the other hand, overeating may tend to reduce stress because it represents an end to the struggle against fat, or giving up. However, for many, the pressure to be thin is so strong that they react to their overeating by self-induced vomiting and/or anorexia. Wooley and Wooley (1980) discuss the bulimarexia syndrome in which binging and vomiting are used to maintain normal weight. Clearly, the stress of adolescence and the stress of maladaptive weight control behaviors and reactions to them are part of a vicious cycle that can frequently lead to end states of obesity, anorexia, bulimarexia, or normal weight associated with constant stress from hunger due to chronic self-imposed dieting and the constant threat of losing control.

This threat of loss of self-control is related to the amount of willpower or self-restraint that one perceives as necessary to eat appropriately. Given the greater stress on women concerning figure control, it is no wonder that they score higher on a scale of eating restraint (Herman & Polivy, 1975) than do men, and that men and women who score higher are more likely to experience food cravings and to have more eating binges (Wardle, 1980).

The processes leading to obesity may be distinct from those that maintain it. Although virtually all young women who feel that they have too much fat make some attempt to lose it, there are contingencies for obesity that may serve to reinforce its continuance. The struggle to appear sexually attractive produces much stress. The adolescent who finds herself overweight may withdraw from heterosexual interactions until she has made herself more attractive. This withdrawal will remove her from the stresses of dating, and this reduction of stress can be rewarding. A slightly overweight female may fear rejection because of chubbiness. A grossly overweight female may feel that there is no chance for interaction. Hope with fear may be more stressful than hopelessness.

As the female enters adulthood, additional influences may work to maintain or produce obesity. As a homemaker, a woman may be surrounded by food and food preparations and less likely to engage in physical activity. Childbearing is often associated with fat increases that are difficult to lose. Some married women may feel little need to continue dieting after they marry. Some husbands may not disapprove strongly of their wives' obesity, for it makes them less attractive and less likely to be lost to other males, thus increasing their dependence on the husbands.

In the traditional household, the husband is the dominant provider and the wife's role is limited to a supportive, rather than a self-actualizing role. The female sex role and subordinate status preclude the use of direct power to satisfy emotional and intellectual needs. Obesity may be one of a variety of psychophysiological symptoms that represent an indirect way of exerting power or expressing resentment or hostility (Sturdivant, 1980). Becoming sexually unattractive may serve the same purpose as a chronic headache when a woman is unable otherwise to communicate to her mate problems in their relationship.

Psychological Correlates of Obesity

The psychological problems associated with obesity can be compared to those related to unattractiveness. Mathes and Kahn (1975), for example, found that attractive women tended to be happier, more satisfied with themselves, and more emotionally stable than unattractive women. This relationship between appearance and emotional adjustment was not found among men. The prejudice against unattractive people results in social disadvantages and discrimination. This may be the reason that persons rated as less attractive are more likely to have mental illness (Napoleon, Chassin, & Young, 1980). Al-Issa (1980) has recently reviewed the literature with respect to the link between physical appearance and mental health in women, covering not only obesity and anorexia but also the motivation for cosmetic plastic surgery.

Although obese people generally consider themselves to be unattractive because of excess fat, no profile of the obese personality has been found (Stuart, 1978). Holland, Masling, and Copley (1970) reported that obese individuals are no more often psychologically disturbed than normal-weight individuals, and Louderback (1970) concludes that the majority of obese persons are psychologically unimpaired. In lower socioeconomic groups where obesity is more accepted, there is little relation between obesity and mental illness. However, in the upper classes, where social pressures to be thin are greater, problems exist with respect to a frequent obsession with weight. This obsession appears to bear little relationship to actual body weight. Among women seeking treatment, the intensity of this obsession may be greatest in women who are only minimally overweight, since they tend to feel that they can achieve success, whereas the very obese may be less obsessive or better able to accept the futility of trying to achieve an ideal figure (Wooley & Wooley, 1980).

Obsessiveness with an ideal body weight is a preoccupation that many women in our society have about their physical appearance. During the socialization process, some women are taught that their bodies are weak, sick, and unclean, especially in relation to menstruation. Society also puts a greater emphasis on female than on male appearance (Sturdivant, 1980). This conflict between striving to be beautiful while harboring strong doubts about one's body can lead to problems with body image, especially when obesity is involved. Waldroop (1980) recently reviewed the research bearing on body image and obesity. He cites evidence suggesting that the obese have negative feelings regarding body size and shape. Such body image disturbance appears to be unrelated to gender, extent of obesity, or intelligence. Those who were obese as adolescents are more likely to suffer such self-perceptions, including guilt, shame, and feelings of inadequacy. Waldroop (1980) found that college women were more likely to describe themselves as overweight than were college men, the actual incidence of obesity being equal, suggesting that women are more weight conscious than men. In general, women with body image disturbances have internalized the cultural norms discussed on p. 340.

This increased weight consciousness results in women weighing themselves more frequently than men and concluding more often that reducing is necessary, even though their weight may be within normal range (Stuart & Jacobson, 1979). Some young females feel a need to be smaller than other females in all dimensions except bust (Jourard & Secord, 1955). This need increases stress even though the goal is in most cases unrealistic.

Stress of Dieting

The most serious psychological and physiological problems for the moderately obese are not with the obesity per se, but with the effects of attempts to reduce through dietary restriction. To the extent that women are under greater pressure to be thin, and since they are far more likely to diet than are men, psychological problems associated with dieting are found mainly in women. It stands to reason that women dieters would experience more psychological stress than men dieters; as discussed earlier, some reports suggest that women perceive themselves as requiring a greater degree of dietary self-discipline (restraint) than do men.

The process of dieting is a negative and intrapunitive experience for most. Although it is not clear that all obese women eat more than their normal-weight peers, it is true that many enjoy eating. A history of chronic dieting can make food a very salient and prominent feature of one's lifestyle. Dietary restriction can increase cravings, especially for inappropriate foods such as those loaded with sugar (S. Wooley *et al.*, 1979b). Some obese females come to the realization that the self-deprivation of dieting will be with them for the rest of their lives, and that the conflict between self-control and indulgence will be in their thoughts on a daily basis. This food deprivation may be experienced along with a perceived deprivation in social contact and heterosexual interaction due to obesity.

One tragic aspect of dieting is that many dieters seem to share a belief that dieting can work if only enough willpower is applied. The massive proliferation of diets by those who claim efficacy is incongruous, given that only about 5%

of dieters ever achieve and maintain a goal weight, and many who do succeed no doubt maintain their weight at the cost of their psychological and physical ill-health. Nevertheless, the decision to diet is often followed by elation (Stunkard, 1957); every new diet strategy brings with it new hope.

The psychological reactions to dieting have been studied by Stunkard (1957; Stunkard & Rush, 1974). The first few weeks of dieting may be marked by intense anxiety, possibly due to the fear of failure. This period of anxiety may be followed by months of depression, with feelings of weakness, nervousness, and irritability. Patterns of nocturnal eating, insomnia, and morning anorexia may develop with chronic dieting.

Behavior therapy for obesity has been notable for the apparent lack of negative emotional side-effects (Wilson & Brownell, 1980). However, some investigators have reported that emotional stress and associated distorted reasoning due to dieting may lead to a failure to use self-management techniques (Sjöberg & Persson, 1977). This may be one of the reasons for the modest success rate of behavior therapy to date in treating obese individuals. Stress management may increase behavior therapy's success with this population.

Regardless of psychological side-effects, both dieting alone and behavior therapy along with dieting rely essentially on caloric restriction to achieve a calorie deficit for fat loss. S. Wooley *et al.* (1979) suggest that the long-term effect of caloric restriction for most persons is an obese state maintained with a low-calorie diet. Dieting slows the metabolic rate as much as 30%. When weight is regained, a higher percentage of it is fat than when it was lost. These changes, which are thought to be a mammalian adaptation to interruptions in the food supply, may become more pronounced with each successive diet. Furthermore, calorie restriction is likely to inhibit caloric expenditure through exercise. Thus, individuals, after a history of many attempts to lose weight through dieting, may end up being obese and maintaining their weight on a diet that would be considered restrictive for persons of normal weight.

Because of these psychological and physiological effects of dieting, failure is the most common outcome. Repeated failure adds to the psychological misery of the obese. This sense of failure in weight loss is probably more damaging to women since the control of food intake and body fat may become a symbol or index of their ability to control life in general (Wooley & Wooley, 1980). The feeling of failure may pervade other areas of life; since failure is viewed by women and society as the result of personal weakness, the effect on self-esteem is severe. The small, temporary weight losses experienced during past dietary attempts carry such hope of future achievement and such a boost to self-esteem that dieting behavior is reinforced despite continued long-term failure.

The stress of dietary restriction may cause physiological harm. The continuing loss-regain cycle puts stress on the cardiovascular system and can increase the atherogenic action of cholesterol (Bray, 1976). The higher levels of cholesterol seen in the obese may also be evidence of dietary stress rather than of obesity per se (Herman, 1978). This stress of obesity oftentimes leads to apparent and real physiological disorders. If the obese individuals are denied attention because of the unattractiveness of obesity, any attention given them when symptoms are expressed may be especially reinforcing and lead to the psychosomatic maintenance of a disorder. This in turn can reinforce the popular notion that obesity is unhealthy.

Treatment Considerations

There is no treatment for obesity that results in lasting, significant weight losses for most of those treated. Most people who try to lose weight resort to some form of dieting or behavioral self-management. Most of these fail to lose fat, and, as a consequence many suffer lowered self-esteem, poor body image, and discrimination. The question arises, Should therapies be offered that will result in failure for the great majority of those treated? There is always the chance that the obese person will be among the small number of those who do achieve significant fat loss. However, there is a need to communicate to patients that long-term success is very difficult to achieve and to explain the reasons for this so that self-attribution for failure will be minimized. Of course, a realistic assessment of the probability of success may dampen the obese person's enthusiasm for beginning or maintaining therapeutic recommendations. Until successful treatments are found, these issues will remain problematic (Hall & Havassy, 1981). Until then, therapists treating obese women should consider several approaches including:

1. Careful assessment to determine if dieting is indicated
2. An emphasis on aerobic exercise
3. Feminist approaches to therapy
4. Social support

Is Dieting Indicated?

Given the limitations of dieting previously discussed, it may be contraindicated for many patients. Patients should first establish a dietary pattern that maintains a stable weight. For women, a caloric intake of about 11 times the weight in pounds will generally maintain that weight. To this should be added the calories expended during routine daily exercise. This total should be about the same as caloric intake, as assessed through careful food records. If calorie intake equals the estimated need, calorie reduction through switching to lower-fat food alternatives may be indicated. If the intake is low compared to the estimated need, it is likely that the metabolic rate is also low. A stalemate of diet versus fat may have been achieved, resulting in chronic obesity with hunger.

Rather than attempt further caloric restriction, which results only rarely in long-term success without the stress of dieting, some writers have suggested counseling that will help these patients adapt to their obesity (S. Wooley, Wooley, & Dyrenforth, 1979a). An alternative is to allow the patients to relieve hunger by increasing their caloric intake while increasing exercise.

Exercise

Exercise is now becoming recognized as possibly more important and beneficial than dieting for many obese individuals (e.g., Brownell & Stunkard, 1980). There is a strong negative correlation between percentage of body fat and aerobic fitness (Rogers *et al.*, 1980) indicating that many obese individuals need physical fitness training. The physiological benefits of aerobic exercise for the obese include, in addition to conditioning the cardiovascular system, reduction of fat tissue and an increase in lean tissue, which can result in "firming." This reduction of the jello-like quality of the obese body may help improve body image. Also, the metabolic rate may be increased, thus helping to reduce fat beyond the effect of the exercise itself (Brownell & Stunkard, 1980). There has yet to be a clear demonstration for the efficacy of aerobic exercise in producing significant weight loss in the majority of those entering exercise treatment (Epstein & Wing, 1980). This may be due to the large nonadherence rate, which might be improved with behavioral techniques designed specifically to help the obese maintain an aerobic lifestyle (Foreyt & Goodrick, 1981). Also, many of the studies that failed to show significant fat loss from exercise involved exercise periods equal to or less than 30 min in duration. Gwinup (1975) found that obese women experienced no weight reduction until their exercise periods exceeded 30 min daily. The human body does not begin to rely on its fat stores for energy until after this period of exercise (Christensen & Hansen, cited in Franklin & Rubenfire, 1980). Thus, it would seem that exercise periods should last for about 1 hour.

Even if aerobic exercise fails to have an appreciable cosmetic effect on the obese person's body, it should prove to be a valuable adjunct to any therapy program. This is because the psychology of aerobic fitness behavior contrasts so markedly with that of dietary restriction. For example, the subjects in Gwinup's (1975) study reported a history of weakness, nervousness, and failure associated with dieting, but felt stronger and more relaxed, with enhanced feelings of well-being, as a result of regular exercise.

As a therapy for obese women, exercise can be presented as a positive activity that the body needs for proper functioning, in contrast to dieting, which is oftentimes a negative, intrapunitive behavior with no direct health benefits and poor psychological effects. The obese woman frequently regards herself as deviating from health norms. Physiological considerations indicate that dieting may trigger mechanisms that work against fat loss unless the patient is willing to starve herself. But an appropriate level of exercise results in increased cardiovascular endurance. Thus, an aerobic exercise regimen can allow a formerly obese individual to achieve a level of fitness well above that of the average, normal-weight person. This achievement can raise self-esteem, helping the patient to feel healthy and to have a more positive regard for her body (Goodrick, 1978).

Along with enhanced self-concept, aerobic fitness can result in other benefits (cf. Morgan, 1979) such as less disturbed sleep, anxiety reduction, reduced stress reactivity, as well as reduced depression (Greist, Eischens, Klein, & Faris, 1979). These benefits are needed by many obese women. It remains to be seen, however, if, at the same time social and spousal pressure to be thin is being felt by the obese female, similar pressures prevent the lifestyle changes needed to include 4-5 hours a week of exercise. Another problem may be that some women believe that exercise is another form of punishment, like dieting, for being fat. Careful counseling showing how exercise can be enjoyable will be needed (Foreyt & Goodrick, 1981).

Feminist Approaches

The feminist approach recognizes that psychological disturbances and maladaptive behaviors are the result of being obese in a society that places undue importance on meeting standards of physical beauty for women (Wooley & Wooley, 1980; S. Wooley *et al.*, 1979a). In feminist therapy, patients come to realize that their sense of self-worth need not be based on the judgments of men or other women. Patients learn that the value of a human being should not be based on a physical condition that is so resistant to treatment. The punitive nature of dieting is made clear. Improving fitness through exercise would be congruent with the feminist paradigm, which tries to overcome feelings of shame and weakness regarding the female body.

Because of their socialization, many obese women devote considerable time and energy to finding a man or to pleasing the one they have. Since these efforts may prove futile and self-damaging, feminist therapists encourage women to develop interests and activities independent of men and to be assertive in taking such new directions (Boskind-Lodahl & Sirlin, 1977).

Poor body image represents the sensitization to physical appearance caused by social pressures. The feminist approach thus might make use of desensitization procedures regarding body image. Patients could be asked to explore their emotional reactions to photographs of themselves in bathing suits, focusing on each body part. The development of aesthetic values that equate fat with ugliness could be discussed and compared with those of other cultures and historical periods that had different norms.

Social Support

During the last few years, use of structured social support from spouses and friends has been attempted in obesity treatment programs with mixed results (Wilson & Brownell, 1980). To the extent that a wife's obesity and her attempts to lose fat may have a significant impact on marital adjustment, the participation of a husband in therapy may help their relationship, and the husband's support may ease the wife's depression (Weisz & Bucher, 1980). However, the spouse may be motivated to work against his wife's weight loss. His fear that his wife will become more sexually attractive to other men; his need to sabotage her efforts to retaliate for some unresolved marital conflict; or his sexual preference for obese women may affect his level of support (Title, 1973). Also, care should be taken when including significant others in the therapy for obesity. Since most individuals fail to lose or maintain significant losses, the increased social attention may only increase shame, unless these others fully understand the refractory nature of the disorder and are willing to give the support needed to help the person with her psychological reactions to failure (S. Wooley *et al.*, 1979a). Training in assertiveness to cope with discrimination and joining the National Association to Aid Fat Americans are two other ways to help individuals with the social alienation of obesity.

Conclusion

For most obese individuals, the weight lost during any treatment program is only a portion of what had been desired. Following intensive treatment, little additional weight loss is seen in most individuals (Foreyt *et al.*, 1981). Unless individuals are only mildly overweight, it is questionable, given the current modest results of all obesity treatment programs, whether they should be referred to treatment programs. This is especially true since major population studies of obesity and mortality have failed to show that overall obesity leads to greater risk and there may be possible associated benefits of moderate obesity (Andres, 1980). In the absence of hypertension, overweight is not a risk factor of future ill health at all (Keys, 1980). For many, therefore, the reason for trying to lose weight is cosmetic, the result of intense social pressure, primarily on females. Future intervention for many obese females, where poor health is not a problem, might more importantly focus on attempts to combat these social pressures rather than on weight loss per se.

References

Al-Issa, I. *The psychopathology of women*. Englewood Cliffs, New Jersey: Prentice-Hall, 1980.

Andres, R. Effect of obesity on total mortality. *International Journal of Obesity*, 1980, *4*, 381-386.

Bailey, D. A. Exercise, fitness and physical education for the growing child—A concern. *Canadian Journal of Public Health*, 1973, *64*, 421-430.

Björntorp, P., Carlgren, G., & Isaksson, B. Effect of an energy-reduced dietary regimen in relation to adipose tissue cellularity in obese women. *American Journal of Clinical Nutrition*, 1975, *28*, 445-452.

Boskind-Lodahl, M., & Sirlin, J. The gorging-purging syndrome. *Psychology Today*, 1977, *10*, 50.

Bray, G. A. *The obese patient*. Philadelphia, Pennsylvania: Saunders, 1976.

Brehm, J. W. *A theory of psychological reactance*. New York: Academic Press, 1966.

Brownell, K. D., & Stunkard, A. J. Physical activity in the development and control of obesity. In A. J. Stunkard (Ed.), *Obesity*. Philadelphia, Pennsylvania: Saunders, 1980.

Cheek, D. B., Schultz, R. B., Parra, A., & Reba, R. C. Overgrowth of lean and adipose tissues in adolescent obesity. *Pediatric Research*, 1970, *4*, 268-279.

Dawber, T. R. *The Framingham Study: The epidemiology of atherosclerotic disease*. Cambridge, Massachusetts: Harvard Univ. Press, 1980.

Epstein, L. H., & Wing, R. R. Aerobic exercise and weight. *Addictive Behaviors*, 1980, *5*, 371-388.

Forbes, G. B. Relation of lean body mass to height in children and adolescents. *Pediatric Research*, 1972, *6*, 32-37.

Forbes, G. B., & Reina, J. C. Adult lean body mass declines with age: Some longitudinal observations. *Metabolism*, 1970, *19*, 653-663.

Foreyt, J. P., & Goodrick, G. K. Weight disorders. In C. J. Golden, S. S. Alcaparras, F. D. Strider, & B. Graber (Eds.), *Applied techniques in behavioral medicine*. New York: Grune & Stratton, 1981.

Foreyt, J. P., Goodrick, G. K., & Gotto, A. M. Limitations of behavioral treatment of obesity: Review and analysis. *Journal of Behavioral Medicine*, 1981, *4*, 159-174.

Franklin, B. A., & Rubenfire, M. Losing weight through exercise. *Journal of the American Medical Association*, 1980, *244*, 377-379.

Funabiki, D., Bologna, N. C., Pepping, M., & FitzGerald, K. C. Revisiting sex differences in the expression of depression. *Journal of Abnormal Psychology*, 1980, *89*, 194-202.

Garrow, J. *Energy balance and obesity in man* (2nd ed.). New York: Elsevier, 1978.

Goldblatt, P. E., Moore, M. E., & Stunkard, A. J. Social factors in obesity. *Journal of the American Medical Association*, 1965, *192*, 1039-1044.

Goodrick, G. K. An alternative approach to risk reduction. *Health Values*, 1978, *2*, 297-300.

Greist, J. H., Eischens, R. R., Klein, M. H., & Faris, J. W. Antidepressant running. *Psychiatric Annals*, 1979, *9*, 134-140.

Gubner, R. Overweight and health: Prognostic realities and therapeutic possibilities. In L. Lasagna (Ed.), *Obesity: Causes, consequences, and treatment*. New York: Medcom, 1974.

Gwinup, G. Effect of exercise alone on the weight of obese women. *Archives of Internal Medicine*, 1975, *135*, 676-680.

Hall, S. M., & Havassy, B. The obese woman: Causes, correlates, and treatment. *Professional Psychology*, 1981, *12*, 163-170.

Hartz, A., Giefer, E., & Rimm, A. A. Relative importance of the effect of family environment and heredity on obesity. *Annals of Human Genetics*, 1977, *41*, 185-193.

Herman, C. P. Restrained eating. *Psychiatric Clinics of North America*, 1978, *1*, 593-607.

Herman, C. B., & Polivy, J. Anxiety, restraint, and eating behavior. *Journal of Abnormal Psychology*, 1975, *84*, 666-672.

Holland, J., Masling, J., & Copley, D. Mental illness in lower class normal, obese and hyperobese women. *Psychosomatic Medicine*, 1970, *32*, 351-357.

Huenemann, R. L. 1. Obesity in six-month-old children. Environmental factors associated with preschool obesity. *Journal of the American Dietetic Association*, 1974, *64*, 480-487.

Jourard, S. M., & Secord, P. R. Body-cathexis and the ideal female figure. *Journal of Abnormal and Social Psychology*, 1955, *50*, 243-246.

Keys, A. Overweight, obesity, coronary heart disease and mortality. *Nutrition Reviews*, 1980, *38*, 297-307.

Lauer, R. M., Connor, W. E., Leaverton, P. E., Reiter, M. A., & Clarke, W. R. Coronary heart disease risk factors in school children: The Muscatine study. *Journal of Pediatrics*, 1975, *86*, 697-706.

Louderback, L. *Fat power: Whatever you weigh is right*. New York: Hawthorne, 1970.

Mathes, E. W., & Kahn, A. Physical attractiveness, happiness, neuroticism and self-esteem. *Journal of Psychology*, 1975, *90*, 27-30.

Montegriffo, V. M. E. A survey of the incidence of obesity in the United Kingdom. *Postgraduate Medicine*, 1971, *47*, 418-422.

Morgan, W. P. Psychological effects of physical activity. In F. J. Nagle & H. J. Montoye (Eds.), *Exercise, health and disease*. Springfield, Illinois: Thomas, 1979.

Napoleon, T., Chassin, L., & Young, R. D. A replication and extension of "Physical attractiveness and mental illness." *Journal of Abnormal Psychology*, 1980, *89*, 250-253.

Parizkova, J. Impact of age, diet, and exercise on man's body composition. *Annals of the New York Academy of Science*, 1963, *110*, 661-674.

Rodin, J. Bidirectional influences in emotionality, stimulus responsivity, and metabolic events in obesity. In J. D. Masek & M. E. P. Seligman (Eds.), *Psychopathology: Experimental models*. San Francisco, California: Freeman, 1977.

Rodin, J. Current status of the internal-external hypothesis for obesity: What went wrong? *American Psychologist*, 1981, *36*, 361-372.

Rogers, T., Mahoney, M. J., Mahoney, B. K., Straw, M. K., & Kenigsberg, M. I. Clinical assessment of obesity: An empirical evaluation of diverse techniques. *Behavioral Assessment*, 1980, *2*, 161-181.

Schachter, S. Some extraordinary facts about obese humans and rats. *American Psychologist*, 1971, *25*, 120-144.

Seltzer, C. C., & Mayer, J. A simple criterion of obesity. *Postgraduate Medicine*, 1965, *38A*, 101-107.

Silverstone, J. T., Gordon, R. P., & Stunkard, A. J. Social factors in obesity in London. *Practitioner*, 1969, *202*, 682-688.

Sjöberg, L., & Persson, L. A study of attempts by obese patients to regulate eating. *Goteborg Psychological Reports*, 1977, *7*(12), 1-20.

Society of Actuaries. *Build and blood pressure study*. Chicago, Illinois: Author, 1959.

Stuart, R. B. *Act thin, stay thin*. New York: Norton, 1978.

Stuart, R. B., & Davis, B. *Slim chance in a fat world: Behavioral control of obesity*. Champaign, Illinois: Research Press, 1972.

Stuart, R. B., & Jacobson, B. Sex differences in obesity. In E. S. Gomberg & V. Franks (Eds.), *Gender and disordered behavior: Sex differences in psychopathology*. New York: Brunner/Mazel, 1979.

Stunkard, A. J. The dieting depression: Incidence and clinical characteristics of untoward responses to weight reduction regimens. *American Journal of Medicine*, 1957, *23*, 77-86.

Stunkard, A. J., & Rush, J. Dieting and depression reexamined: A critical review of reports of untoward responses during weight reduction for obesity. *Annals of Internal Medicine*, 1974, *81*, 526-533.

Sturdivant, S. *Therapy with women: A feminist philosophy of treatment*. New York: Springer, 1980.

Title, S. H. Comments regarding the sabotaging spouse. *Obesity/Bariatric Medicine*, 1973, *2*, 124-125.

U.S. Department of Health, Education and Welfare. *Ten state nutrition survey, 1968-1970*. (HEW Publication [HSM] 72-8131). Washington, D.C.: Author, 1972.

Waldroop, J. A. *Body image, sexual identity and eating disorders*. Paper presented at a meeting of the American Psychological Association, Montreal, Canada, August, 1980.

Wardle, J. Dietary restraint and binge eating. *Behavior Analysis and Modification*, 1980, *4*, 201-209.

Weil, W. B. Current controversies in childhood obesity. *The Journal of Pediatrics*, 1977, *91*, 175-187.

Weisz, G., & Bucher, B. Involving husbands in treatment of obesity—Effects on weight loss, depression, and marital satisfaction. *Behavior Therapy*, 1980, *11*, 643-650.

Wilson, G. T., & Brownell, K. D. Behavior therapy for obesity: An evaluation of treatment outcome. *Advances in Behavior Research and Therapy*, 1980, *3*, 49-86.

Wooley, O. W., Wooley, S. C., & Dyrenforth, S. R. Obesity and women—II: A neglected feminist topic. *Women's Studies International Quarterly*, 1979, *2*, 81-92.

Wooley, S. C., & Wooley, O. W. Eating disorders: Obesity and anorexia. In A. M. Brodsky & R. T. Hare-Mustin (Eds.), *Women and psychotherapy: An assessment of research and practice*. New York: Guilford, 1980.

Wooley, S. C., Wooley, O. W., & Dyrenforth, S. R. Obesity treatment reexamined: The case for a more tentative and experimental approach. In N. Krasnegor (Ed.), *Behavioral analysis and treatment of substance abuse* (NIDA research monograph No. 25). Washington, D.C.: US Govt. Printing Office, 1979. (a)

Wooley, S. C., Wooley, O. W., & Dyrenforth, S. R. Theoretical, practical and social issues in behavioral treatments of obesity. *Journal of Applied Behavior Analysis*, 1979, *12*, 3-25. (b)

Author Index

B

D

G

L

N

T

Y

Z

Subject Index

A

B

C

D

F

G

O

P

T

PERSONALITY AND PSYCHOPATHOLOGY

25. Prolonged Psychosocial Effects of Disaster: A Study of Buffalo Creek, *Goldine C. Gleser, Bonnie L. Green,* and *Carolyn Winget.*
26. Adult Sexual Interest in Children, *Mark Cook* and *Kevin Howells (Eds.).*
27. Neurosis and the Social Environment, *A. S. Henderson, D. G. Byrne,* and *P. Duncan-Jones.*
28. Suicide and Self-Damaging Behavior: A Sociobiological Perspective, *Denys deCatanzaro.*
29. The Inheritance of Personality and Ability: Research Methods and Findings, *Raymond B. Cattell.*
30. The Abilities and Achievements of Orientals in North America, *Philip E. Vernon.*
31. Symptomatic Affective Disorders: A Study of Depression and Mania Associated with Physical Disease and Medication, *F. A. Whitlock.*
32. Physique and Delinquent Behavior: A Thirty-Year Follow-Up of William H. Sheldon's *Varieties of Delinquent Youth, Emil M. Hartl, Edward P. Monnelly,* and *Roland D. Elderkind.*
33. Gender and Psychopathology, Ihsan Al-Issa (Ed.).